EARLY CHILDHOOD STUDIES

A Multidisciplinary and Holistic Introduction

Edited by
Jayne Taylor, Emma Bond and **Margaret Woods**

HODDER
EDUCATION
AN HACHETTE UK COMPANY

Every effort has been made to trace and acknowledge the ownership of copyright material. The publishers apologise if any inadvertently remain unacknowledged and will be glad to make suitable arrangements to rectify this at the earliest opportunity.

Contains public sector information licensed under the Open Government Licence v1.0.

Photographs © Andrew Callaghan

Although every effort has been made to ensure that website addresses are correct at time of going to press, Hodder Education cannot be held responsible for the content of any website mentioned in this book. It is sometimes possible to find a relocated web page by typing in the address of the home page for a website in the URL window of your browser.

Hachette UK's policy is to use papers that are natural, renewable and recyclable products and made from wood grown in sustainable forests. The logging and manufacturing processes are expected to conform to the environmental regulations of the country of origin.

Orders: please contact Bookpoint Ltd, 130 Milton Park, Abingdon, Oxon OX14 4SB. Telephone: +44 (0)1235 827827. Fax: +44 (0)1235 400401. Lines are open from 9.00 a.m. to 5.00 p.m., Monday to Saturday, with a 24-hour message-answering service. Visit our website at www.hoddereducation.co.uk

© Hodder & Stoughton Limited

First edition published 1998

Second edition published 2005

This edition published 2013 by Hodder Education, an Hachette UK Company, 338 Euston Road, London NW1 3BH

Impression number 10 9 8 7 6 5 4 3 2 1

Year   2018 2017 2016 2015 2014 2013

Cover photo © The Protected Art Archive/Alamy

Typeset in Minion Regular 10/12 by Datapage (India) Pvt. Ltd.

Printed and bound by CPI Group (UK) Ltd., Croydon, CR0 4YY for Hodder Education, an Hachette UK Company, 338 Euston Road, London, NW1 3BH.

A catalogue record for this title is available from the British Library

ISBN: 978 1 4441 7587 5

Contents

List of contributors

Editors

Emma Bond BA (Hons) PGCE FHEA PhD RSA is Senior Lecturer in Applied Social Sciences, University Campus Suffolk and Course Leader MA Childhood and Youth Studies.

Jayne Taylor RN RHV Dip Nursing (London) Cert Ed BSc Nursing (Hons) MBA PhD is Chief Operating Officer for Hertsmere, Herts Valleys Clinical Commissioning Group and formerly the Dean of the School of Health, Suffolk College.

Margaret Woods BA MA Dip Ed is formerly Dean of Quality Enhancement in the Higher Education Sector of Suffolk College.

Contributors

Stuart Agnew BSc (Hons) MSc PGCE is Senior Lecturer in Applied Social Sciences, University Campus Suffolk.

Jessica Clark BA (Hons) MA is Lecturer in Childhood and Youth Studies, University Campus Suffolk and Course leader BA Children, Young People and Policy.

Samantha Chenery-Morris BSc (Hons) RM RGN RSCN MA NMC RTQ is Senior Lecturer in Midwifery, University Campus Suffolk.

Helen Donovan RN, RM, RHV, BSc (Hons), MA in Higher Education is Public Health Advisor for the Royal College of Nursing and Senior Health Protection Nurse in Haringey north London.

Anne Greig MA (Hons) Dip Ed PhD Dip CBT MSc Educational Psychology C Psychol Ax is Chartered Educational Psychologist and Accredited Cognitive Behavioural Psychotherapist and Honorary Lecturer and Tutor at Strathclyde University.

Sue Hollinrake CQSW Advanced Award SW Doctor of Social Work is Senior Lecturer in Social Work, University Campus Suffolk and Programme Leader Social Work.

Beverley Nightingale BA (Hons) MA PGCE is Senior Lecturer, University Campus Suffolk and Course leader, BA (Hons) Dip HE Early Childhood Studies.

Heather Passmore PGCEA MPhil is Senior Lecturer, School of Nursing and Midwifery, Lead Midwife for Education and Course Leader, MA in Clinical Effectiveness, University Campus Suffolk.

Sally Payne BA (Hons) MA PGCE is Lecturer in Early Childhood Studies, University Campus Suffolk and Lead Assessor for the Early Years Professional Status Programme.

Jackie Plenty BSC (Hons) MA DipSW PGCE Dip in Counselling and Psychotherapy is Senior Lecturer in Social Work, University Campus Suffolk.

Sarah Richards BA (Hons) MA PGCE is Senior Lecturer in Childhood and Youth Studies, University Campus Suffolk.

David Rutherford BA MSc MBPS is formerly Senior Lecturer in Social Psychology, University Campus Suffolk.

Preface

This third edition of *Early Childhood Studies: A Multidisciplinary and Holistic Introduction* reflects the continuing success of the BA (Hons) Early Childhood Studies (ECS) which was developed at University College Suffolk in 1992. It was one of the earliest degrees of its kind and had the distinction of producing the country's first Early Childhood Studies graduates. Today, 21 years later in 2013, this subject, at undergraduate and postgraduate level, constitutes a significant programme within the School of Applied Social Sciences at University Campus Suffolk (UCS). Indeed, the current team feel able to claim in the web overview of their courses that this substantial and long-term academic base '*places UCS at the forefront of developments and initiatives within*' what has now become an '*established discipline*'.

Over these 21 years, the various Early Childhood Studies teams have been strongly committed to an holistic view of the young child, and also enthusiastic about providing a degree programme to reflect and promote the essential interdisciplinary approach sustained by the underlying philosophy of holism. This has involved them in bringing together within the ECS degree programmes aspects of their traditional academic disciplines, professional expertise and research interests as they relate to early childhood, e.g. in education, health, psychology, sociology, social policy, child development, linguistics, social work, anthropology and research. The same principles and strategies underpin this text which also retains the original and primary aim to introduce undergraduates and early years' professionals to holism as it applies to early childhood practices and services. It also provides an insight into inter-professional working.

As with the first and second editions, this publication has been written by current and ex members of staff; pleasingly this includes three ECS programme graduates who now teach on the UCS courses. Dr Emma Bond, co-editor, is one of those and, as her personal tutor during her undergraduate studies, I am enormously proud of her subsequent achievements. I am also delighted that my former colleague and friend Dr Jayne Taylor, a talented academic and author as well as a consummate health professional, agreed to undertake the editorial role for a third time.

The elements which readers found most informative and useful in previous editions have been preserved, but the relatively radical update encompasses significant new practices, policies, legislation and research whilst being mindful of the current restrictive economic climate. It is hoped study of the text may contribute to readers being able to meet consequent challenges in working to achieve the highest quality of practice within various early childhood professions and settings.

Readers should find it helpful to delve into single chapters which are complete texts within themselves. It is, however, deemed important and desirable that the book be considered in its entirety; it is only then that an understanding of holism as it applies to early childhood can be fully realised and actively constitute the quintessential *aspect* of the interdisciplinary approach and inter-active professionalism which genuinely supports and enhances the experiences and lives of young children and their families.

Margaret Woods

Retired Dean of Quality Enhancement in the HE sector of University Campus Suffolk. Previously she led development of the initial BA (Hons) in Early Childhood Studies, the MA in Early Childhood Studies and the MA in Special Needs. She was the first Course Leader of the original ECS undergraduate programme and it was Margaret's idea to create the first edition of *Early Childhood Studies: A Multidisciplinary and Holistic Introduction*.

Introduction

Emma Bond

Welcome to the third edition of *Early Childhood Studies: A Multidisciplinary and Holistic Introduction*. This new edition has been updated and benefits not only from the revision of all chapters but also from the addition of four new chapters – Chapter 3 *Embodied childhoods* and Chapter 13 *Children's geographies* by Jessica Clark, and Chapter 8 *Understanding childhood in late modernity* and the concluding Chapter 16 *Children's rights* by Emma Bond and Stuart Agnew. This new edition builds upon the well-established theoretical approaches from the previous edition to consider young children's lives in the context of current policy, recent research and contemporary debate. Early childhood studies (ECS) is an exciting multidisciplinary subject which continues to enjoy increasing popularity at both undergraduate and postgraduate levels and is a rapidly developing area of academic interest, policy and early years professional practice initiatives.

On a personal note, I began my own undergraduate study of early childhood at, what was then Suffolk College, in 1995 under the expert tuition of Margaret Woods – one of the founding editors of this textbook. Margaret inspired my quest for knowledge of childhood which led me on to an academic career in teaching BA Early Childhood Studies, MA Childhood and Youth Studies and to further study with a PhD and then on to further funded childhood and youth-related research projects. The ECS course at University Campus Suffolk (UCS) continues to be extremely popular with students intending to enter a career working with or for children and/or their families. The primary focus of ECS is children from birth to eight years, but it also covers conception through to when a child is approximately 11 years of age. A holistic philosophy permeates this text which takes a multidisciplinary approach and offers a fascinating and stimulating introduction to the academic study of early childhood. This means it includes educational, health, welfare, psychological, sociological, legal, philosophical, political and economic perspectives. It has been a tremendous privilege and honour to edit this third edition, to continue the Taylor and Woods legacy, and I hope that it may motivate and inspire another generation of early childhood scholars to learn and to question and to further their knowledge in this fascinating field.

This introduction outlines the key arguments and debates that are presented in the chapters to follow, including the fundamental importance of understanding children's rights (Chapter 16). This book is not intended to be a prescriptive nor definitive volume, but one which contributes to the ever-growing library of ECS literature and to the learning and understanding of a range of topics related to the academic study of early childhood. To this end, the authors of these chapters do not assume that the readers of this edition are early years practitioners nor perhaps in early years practice (although it is anticipated that many may be so), but that readers have chosen this volume because they are interested in early childhood, in understanding more about it and in learning and thinking about it.

The first chapter – *Early childhood studies: first principles* – considers the academic study of early childhood and how this multidisciplinary subject developed from a range of other related academic disciplines. This chapter, updated from the previous edition, reflects the significant conceptual shift catalysed by the new social studies of childhood (see James *et al.*, 2010), which developed as a critique of developmental psychology and the increasing importance of children's rights. The impact that these developments have had on studying early childhood is discussed and, while the previous edition highlighted observation as a tool for studying early childhood (now considered in Chapter 14, *Perspectives on early childhood research*), this updated chapter places emphasis on adopting a more participatory approach – giving prominence to the importance of listening to children and viewing them as active social agents. To this end, the first chapter critically examines key approaches to studying early childhood and the dominant discourses associated with conceptions of childhood. It examines power relationships alongside an exploration of the key principles of studying early childhood and the importance of viewing children as the experts in their everyday lives. Through an analysis of dominant ideologies in relation to early childhood, including historical perspectives, readers are encouraged to reflect on and critically examine notions of childhood and the diversity of children's lived experiences.

In Chapter 2, Heather Passmore and Samantha Chenery-Morris consider *New beginnings: factors affecting health and well-being in the neonate* and this takes a new approach to focus on the neonate rather than the infant. The neonate is a baby during the first 28 days after birth and this chapter considers the importance of the antenatal and neonatal period to healthy development, which will then be considered further in relation to the other chapters which discuss infant well-being, milestone development and bonding (see Chapters 3, 4 and 5). The importance of pre-conceptual care is considered but, as the authors suggest, although offered to women of child-bearing age with existing health conditions, such as epilepsy and diabetes, it is not the norm in the UK. In reality, the majority of UK conceptions are unplanned, and as such few women access these services. This chapter follows the chronological development from pre-conception, through the antenatal period to 28 days postnatally and reviews the recent changes and developments in both antenatal and newborn screening. Passmore and Chenery-Morris outline the increase in screening tests offered antenatally to women and postnatally to mothers of newborn babies which reflect the earlier timing of antenatal screening, changing demographics of the UK and the altered prevalence of inherited diseases and conditions. It is argued that women are being offered more screening tests for their own well-being, as well as that of their baby, and also conditions which impact upon the health of the whole family, such as antenatal and postnatal maternal mental health.

Following on from this chapter, Chapter 3 *Embodied childhoods* by Jessica Clark focuses on why academic and professionals study child development. Clark undertakes an investigation of the health and growth screening in early childhood and illustrates how various factors influence the growth and development of young children. The chapter critically considers the notion of developmental milestones, in terms of physical growth, and the use of screening and centile charts, but within the wider, updated political context and policy developments in this field. The chapter adopts a deliberately broad focus in order to accommodate a critique of the developmental and physical stages as the dominant ways of assessing the well-being of children in the early years in the UK. Clark pays particular attention to the development of studies into the lives of young children with disabilities that draw on a social model of disability to resist the dominant discourse of atypical development and 'otherness' that uses physical and developmental theory as its evidentiary base. As the title suggests, this chapter introduces readers to the area of 'embodied childhoods' and argues that the physical body mediates young children's everyday experiences. It provides readers with an alternative socio-cultural perspective to the dominant biological and developmental approaches which have traditionally informed both policy and practice. Social inequalities on physical development in early childhood are also examined to acknowledge the role of ethnicity and socio-economic status on the meeting of physical needs in the early years. Finally, the chapter explores the current emphasis on nutrition in preschool and school-age children which reflects the policies and health promotion strategies including the debates surrounding childhood obesity.

Moving from the body in early childhood, Chapter 4 turns its attention to the psychology of early childhood. In *Personal, social and emotional development,* Anne Greig examines seminal ground-breaking psychological research and theory in relation to early childhood. This is important as the last ten years have seen an increase in research into early childhood mental health and well-being, personal risk and resilience factors, with health, education and social policy and practice interventions aimed at improving outcomes for the younger members of society through early intervention. This chapter critically reviews the most recent policy, research and practice in the field and outlines the theoretical approaches to personal, social and emotional (PSE) competence and how emotional intelligence and emotional literacies are defined. Greig demonstrates how we are only just beginning to understand the complex nature of personal, social and emotional development and intelligence. Gaining knowledge and understanding of this aspect of early childhood is vital if we are to effectively work with and provide support for young children.

In Chapter 5, David Rutherford discusses how *Children's relationships* are a fundamental tenet of the emotional, social and cognitive development of children in western societies. He draws on the Good Childhood Report (2012) to examine the importance of the home environment and the relationship between children's well-being and their safety, security, privacy and stability. This chapter outlines parenting styles and examines the complexity of multicultural features, to introduce readers to both societal and community aspects of children's relationships. Current thinking about determinism, politicisation, the Big Society and social capital are explained in order to acquaint students with these concepts and facilitate further understanding of the broader issues that impact on children's lives and their relationships. The chapter also considers notions of vulnerability and resilience in relation to young children and crucially examines the discourse on parenting to raise some thought-provoking and possibly controversial questions about the nature of contemporary parenting (a theme also explored in relation to the risk society in Chapter 8). Sibling relationships, friendships and grandparent relationships are considered and Rutherford here further expands his analysis to explore parent education, poverty, and ethnic and cultural aspects to consider fragile families and resilience, including some recent ideas and research on maternal attachment and on cross-cultural research on fathering, violent men and gay and lesbian parenting.

In *Play, language and learning,* Anne Greig provides readers with a robust exposition of classical theories of child development, primarily from a psychological perspective, with special attention to the interactive and holistic nature of the psychological developments in early childhood. Updated from the previous edition, Chapter 6 interrogates recent and emerging research on the relevant themes, such as the social dynamics of learning in language, literacy and the role of play in early reading. Grieg outlines for readers the theoretical approaches in understanding language development and in play and explores their role in early childhood experiences. These contemporary debates suggest that there is a strong link between attachment and cognitive flexibility in play, language and learning and the chapter examines both the short- and long-term impact of interpersonal experience on neurological development.

Understanding how children learn also underpins the next chapter, *Early childhood education and care* by Beverley Nightingale and Sally Payne, which includes a critical appraisal of the definitions and development of education and care for young children between 0 and 8 years in the UK. To this end, Chapter 7 contextualises early childhood education within an historical, legal and socio-cultural framework, giving both definitions and the underpinning principles and philosophies, and presents readers with a broad overview of education and care provision across the United Kingdom. Nightingale and Payne provide a timely and thorough examination of how children learn and critically consider the roles and responsibilities within early years settings and across early years provision, highlighting curriculum frameworks and the different approaches outlined in Scotland, Wales, Northern Ireland and England. Their chapter promotes reflection related to early childhood education and care (ECEC), including what is understood by high quality, international perspectives and emerging influences.

Moving away from the psychological and developmental perspectives outlined in the preceding chapters, the next chapter, *Understanding childhood in late modernity*, deliberates on the sociological interest in childhood and the attention that studying childhood and children has recently attracted in the social sciences generally. Emma Bond and Stuart Agnew explore key sociological approaches to understanding early childhood and examine some of the dominant themes in the social and cultural constructions of childhood. Building on the themes and debates outlined in Chapter 1, Chapter 8 critically examines sociological developments through theorising key concepts in relation to childhood. The approach adopted encourages readers to understand the complexity of the relationship between social change and children's everyday lives. Their analysis undertakes an examination of late modernity to consider some wider debates in relation to children's everyday lives and the debates presented here require an understanding of modernity, reflexivity and identity. Bond and Agnew develop the ideas of parenting outlined by David Rutherford in Chapter 5 to argue that childhood, understood as a social construct (see Jenks, 1996), illustrates how images of childhood created on notions of innocence, naivety and dependence, have, for example, led to increasing protection and control over children. Furthermore, the concept of the 'child' and 'childhood' in late modernity are considered and how these concepts may shape our understanding of children and contemporary children's social worlds.

This understanding of childhood and contemporary children's worlds also forms the basis for *Children and social policy: an introduction* by Sarah Richards. In Chapter 9, social policy is critically examined in relation to early childhood and Richards offers a detailed explanation concerning the longstanding but varied interest in childhood on the part of the state. How children and childhood(s) fit into diverse ideological and philosophical ideas of what makes a good society is embedded in the historical and current development of social policy. Frequently overlooked in policy discussions is the relationship between sociology and social policy and Chapter 9 argues that understanding how and where children come to be socially constructed through both historical and contemporary values are essential for students to recognise as they begin to explore the academic study of social policy. It is

Early Childhood Studies: A Multidisciplinary and Holistic Introduction

appropriate, therefore, that this chapter addresses some of the key dichotomies of the social construction of childhood and links these ideas about children to actual policy examples which reflect them. As such ideas frequently have an historical legacy in that emerging policies are constructed on previous welfare ideas concerning children's role in society and what children should or should not be, this chapter uses historical examples of policy development which demonstrate this genealogy. Richards's discussion also outlines key areas of significance in recent social policy which reflect the changing shape of childhood as these ideas are moulded to fit current needs of society and the changing political landscape of approaches to welfare delivery.

Chapter 10, *The multidisciplinary child protection system: current policy and practice* by Jackie Plenty is also policy focused but concentrates on the multidisciplinary nature of child protection, particularly as current changes in law and policy support this. This chapter offers an updated and robust analysis of policy that goes beyond the Children Act 1989 and the National Service Framework (2004) to also incorporate the Integrated Children's System, Every Child Matters, the Children Act 2004, Working Together to Safeguard Children (2010), child death inquiries (serious case reviews) and specifically 'Baby P' as well as the recent Eileen Munro report (2011). The current child protection system is presented through discussion of the roles of professionals at child protection case conferences and core groups and the Safeguarding Children's Boards and includes up-to-date statistics on the number of children on child protection plans. Finally, in Chapter 10, Plenty considers inter-agency collaboration and working in partnership which allows readers to link the 'voice of the child' and how an early years child's needs are assessed and represented in cases of risk of harm.

Jayne Taylor and Helen Donovan take the importance of inter-agency collaboration and working in partnership further in Chapter 11, *Child health*. They explore the origins of child health practice from an historical perspective and discuss the current situation and the recent changes to the commissioning of children's health care and public health. Chapter 11 highlights key issues in working with ill children and in particular the need for partnership working as a way of minimising the impact of illness in early childhood. Taylor and Donovan introduce readers to the key historic milestones in health services for children and current policy as it relates to the organisation of health and well-being services for young children. The chapter then explores key issues in child health, including the state of children's health, childhood obesity, physical exercise, immunisation and childhood illness, including acute ill-health and long-term conditions, such as asthma. It emphasises the need for partnership working between different parts of the health services system, schools and social care.

In Chapter 12, *Young children with disabilities*, Sue Hollinrake explores the experiences of disabled children and their families and considers key changes in policy and practice developments in recent years in relation to disabled children and their families. She discusses for readers some of the challenges currently presented to professionals in the field. The chapter carefully considers the lives of young children with disabilities through a detailed consideration of national statistics, contemporary policy and developments in legislation and effective cooperation between local partners for the provision of services for young children and their families. The importance of multi-agency and inter-disciplinary frameworks for addressing the needs of disabled children and promoting shared values and cultures to provide a joined-up service are discussed. Furthermore, poverty, disability and benefits issues are critically considered alongside housing issues, NHS reforms and implications for services for disabled children. Recent social care reforms and the implications they have had for the service delivery for children with disabilities are explored and Hollinrake outlines the importance of early identification and support for families.

Chapter 13 is a new chapter especially written for this edition and in *Children's geographies* Jessica Clark explores children's everyday lives within the various cultures, spaces, places and environments that they inhabit. She argues that this kind of understanding is critical for scholars of ECS to make children's worlds safer, to facilitate their participatory roles in society, and in implementing policies relevant to their geographies. The past few years have witnessed a proliferation in academic work and research into children's lives that examine the diverse experiences of children in numerous spatial locations and these are now finding their place of importance in ECS. These include historical and contemporary constructions of childhood, drawing on sociological, cultural and anthropological theories, discourses and ideologies. Theoretical arguments are interwoven throughout Chapter 13 in relation to specific topic-based discussions which draw on perspectives, such as structuralism, social constructionism and postmodernism, as ways of interpreting cultural experience.

A robust knowledge and understanding of research underpins early childhood studies and, in Jayne Taylor's *Perspectives on early childhood research*, the value of research to the early years professional is explored. She provides readers with an overview of recent advances which emphasise the importance of listening to the voices of children and the participation of children in research. Following on from Chapter 1 (*Early childhood studies: first principles*) and the importance of listening to young children, Chapter 14 discusses the methodological issues in early years research which allow children's voices to be heard and their views and experiences listened to. The chapter explores the current emphasis on the participation of children in research and provides examples of different levels of participation. Central to facilitation participation are ethical considerations and these are critically examined through an interrogation of the historical overview of the development of ethical frameworks in the research process and those involved in undertaking research with young children as participants.

Leading and managing child-centred services forms the penultimate chapter of the third edition of this book, in which Jayne Taylor explores the core principles of leading and managing child-centred services and examines leadership and management principles and how these apply specifically to working with young children. She draws on the National Professional Development Framework to outline the key competencies for leaders of children's services and identifies for readers how leaders and managers can use the collective knowledge base to challenge the status quo and to do things differently to meet the needs of children and families more effectively. ECS is about understanding early childhood and also about thinking about how we can improve young children's lives. As also outlined in Chapter 1 and Chapter 14, the emphasis on how we can listen to young children and their families is again brought into the discussion presented here as one of the key themes for consideration and debate. If we are to work ethically with young children and study early childhood with an integrity based on the principles and values that the chapters of the book put forward, then we need to strive to continually develop the quality of all services offered, ensuring the clear focus is on improving outcomes for young children and their families.

In the final chapter, *Understanding children's rights: examining the rhetoric with reality,* a critical discussion of children's rights and the United Nations Convention on the Rights of the Child (UNCRC) through some of the key themes and debates presented in this volume is set out. It undertakes a critical analysis of the UNCRC and examines the rhetoric of children's rights and notions of protection, provision and participation through the reality of children's lived experiences and through the arguments presented in the preceding chapters. Through recent published research, both qualitative and quantitative in national and international contexts, the chapter encourages a questioning approach to exploring the effectiveness of the UNCRC. This focus on key topics provides a detailed account of the stark divide in the ideology of the rights discourse in relation to the lived experiences of children lives in a globalised context. In this final chapter, Bond and Agnew draw out themes and perspectives from the whole book and critically consider partnership and collaborative working, child-centred services and participation, as well as diversity, inclusivity and holism.

Reference

Jenks, C (1996): *Childhood.* London: Routledge.

1 Early childhood studies: first principles

Emma Bond

This chapter aims to:
- consider a set of globalised rights-based principles that underpin early childhood studies
- present an overview of key developments in early childhood studies as an academic discipline
- provide initial guidance on studying early childhood.

Introduction

The study of childhood is an international and interdisciplinary research field well recognised by the scientific community and as a well-respected and acknowledged voice in public and policy discourse relating to children's lives (Qvortrup, 2005). Early childhood studies (ECS), now well established as an academic discipline in its own right, is an exciting, rapidly developing and increasingly popular interdisciplinary subject at degree level. There are currently (at the time of writing) 222 ECS higher education (HE) courses available through the Universities and Colleges Admissions Service (UCAS). ECS aims to develop a critical and ethical understanding of the ecology of early childhood and young children in an ecological context, drawing on methodologies, perspectives, theories, concepts and debates from academic disciplines, including sociology, anthropology, social policy, psychology, geography, history, social care, education and health (QAA, 2007). In this chapter, we shall consider the ethical underpinnings of early childhood scholarship and the significant conceptual developments catalysed by the new social studies of childhood (see James *et al.*, 2010) which developed as a critique of developmental psychology. This chapter introduces the emphasis given to children's rights throughout the book and discusses the impact that these developments have had on studying early childhood.

The concept of participation is explored in promoting the importance of listening to children and viewing them as active social agents. The chapter critically examines key approaches to studying early childhood and the dominant discourses associated with conceptions of childhood. Power relationships are examined alongside an exploration of the key principles of studying early childhood and the importance of viewing children as experts in their everyday lives. Through an analysis of dominant ideologies in relation to early childhood, readers will be encouraged to reflect on and critically examine notions of childhood and the diversity of children's lived experiences. Furthermore, the concept of 'the child' and 'childhood' in late modernity are considered and how these concepts may shape our understanding of children and contemporary children's social worlds.

As such, we as early childhood scholars, need to carefully question our own beliefs and values in relation to our own understanding of childhood and children.

Value principles for students of early childhood

The introductory chapter to this book considered social and cultural constructions of childhood to illustrate the importance of understanding the complexities of young children's everyday lives. Childhoods differ between cultures and change over time and there is a growing awareness of cultural relativism which influences the dominant discourses of childhood. Thanks to the new social studies of childhood, there is now an increasing awareness of the importance of children's rights and that children are active agents in their own lives. Taylor (2011: 420) observes that 'childhood studies scholars have gone a long way towards retheorizing childhood beyond the "natural" and the "universal" by pointing to its historical and cultural construction'. This conceptual shift has not only challenged the dominance of developmental psychology in studying early childhood, but has also brought about a reflexive turn in *how* we study early childhood. Rather than thinking of children as *becoming* adults, they are now finally beginning to be understood as *beings* in their own right and the notion of the adult as the expert in children's lives has been interrogated (James *et al.*, 2010). Childhood is, however, a complex phenomenon as Archard (2004: 37) notes:

> There are different, indeed contradictory, contemporary views about childhood. Again our conception of the child has been to a considerable degree infused with what are essentially myths, or imaginative projections, deriving from a mixture of cultural and ideological sources. The result is that it is sometimes hard to separate the modern conception proper from what is in fact a symbolic ideal of childhood.

Learning activity

Reflect for a few minutes on your own childhood. Think about it in your mind.
- Where were you?
- Who were the important people in your life?
- What sort of things did you do?
- What influenced what you did?
- What did you enjoy doing?
- What was important to you then?
- How were you treated as a child?
- What about your friends?

- Were their childhoods the same as yours?
- What differences were there?

....

It is well established that ideas about childhood and children's everyday experiences are shaped through dominant ideologies, cultural determinants and the wider political and social environment and there is both continuity and change in constructions of childhood (James and James, 2004a).

From welfare to rights

Children's lives are influenced by wider legislation, theoretical approaches, government policy and the people in their everyday lives. As adults, we often take it for granted that we 'know best' in relation to young children's lives and make assumptions about their lives based on our own (outdated) experiences. Much of current legislation and children's policy developments are based on the notion of 'children's best interests', but this too is problematic. The primacy of the welfare approach to further children's best interests has also been questioned as it places children as passive recipients of adult protection and adults do not always, as repeated child protection inquiries have demonstrated, act in children's best interests (Lansdown, 2009). Lansdown (2005: 125), among others, has been arguing for a rights-based approach for many years but observes how:

> There is a continuing resistance to the concept of rights in this country, particularly when applied to children. It is a resistance shared by many parents, politicians, policy makers and the media. It derives, at least in part, from a fear that children represent a threat to stability and order if they are not kept under control. Furthermore, it reflects the strong cultural tradition that children are 'owned' by their parents and that the state should play as minimal a role as possible in their care.

Hart (1992) defines rights as moral justifications for limiting how others act. In ECS, 'a critical consideration of children's rights and anti-discriminatory practice underpins and permeates the subject' (QAA, 2007: 3). The subject of children's rights has been a contentious issue since the 1990s (Wyness, 2012). (Chapter 16 provides an in-depth critical consideration of children's rights.) The key principles of the United Nations Convention on the Rights of the Child (UNCRC) are pertinent to the discussion here, as rights-based principles should underpin how we study early childhood and how we approach our relationships with young children. Globally applying to all children this specific set of human rights, based on respect for dignity for every individual child no matter what their race, gender, religion, language, ability or wealth, was adopted internationally by all governments (except the United States and Somalia) in 1989 (UNICEF, online). This global initiative provides the most complete statement on children's rights and is the most widely ratified human rights treaty in history. Recent work in the children's rights arena has been and remains highly influential in the domains of both child welfare practice and policy. Children's rights discourses, 'embedded in the evolution of professionalization' have facilitated a better understanding of contemporary social issues concerning children (Reynaert *et al.* 2009: 529). Thus, for scholars of early childhood and for early childhood professionals, a sound understanding of the guiding principles of the UNCRC should underpin both academic study and professional practice.

UNCRC guiding principles

The UNCRC sets out distinct articles in relation to children's rights and they can, broadly speaking, be categorised as rights for survival, rights for development, rights for protection and rights for participation. The guiding principles are set out in Articles 2, 3, 6 and 12.

Article 2	Relates to the principle of non-discrimination and that the rights apply to all children without exception and that children should be treated fairly and protected against discrimination
Article 3	Relates to the best interests of the child and that all actions concerning the child should take account of their best interests and that the state has to provide the child with adequate care when parents, for example, are unable to do so
Article 6	Is about survival and development and that every child has the right to life and that the state has an obligation to ensure every child's survival and development
Article 12	Is about the child's opinion that stresses the importance of the child's rights to express their opinion freely and to have their views listened to in any matter that affects them

The 4Ps approach

Simply put, children's rights as outlined by the UNCRC can be grouped into four areas (Figure 1.1):

Children's rights as granted in recent legislation can be summarized as the '4Ps approach': provision for growth and development; prevention of harm; protection against exploitation; and participation in decisions made on their behalf.

(Burr and Montgomery, 2003)

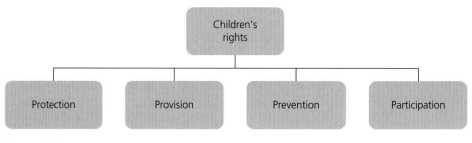

Figure 1.1

How rights are understood will have an impact on how they are supported. According to Franklin (2002: 21), children are often denied rights which adults 'take for granted' – mainly the right to make decisions about matters that concern them – from public policy to the private sphere of the home and family life. The *participation* category can be problematic and controversial; for example, Burr and Montgomery (2003) outline two perspectives on children's rights:

1. **Protectionist.** Philosophies that view children as needing adult protection and help, where adults make decisions on behalf of the child.
2. **Participatory.** Philosophies that view children as needing empowering, where children make decisions on their own behalf.

The controversy between protectionist and participatory perspectives on children's rights centres on the issue of children's competence, but as Alderson (2002: 158–59) observes:

> It is not a question as to whether or not two-year-olds can understand, because they are interpreting and making sense of their experiences all the time. The question is how skilled and respectful are the adults in listening to the child and ensuring that clear relevant information is exchanged with them.

Also, in adopting a rights-based approach, assumptions about childhood and what Prout (2003: 22) describes as the 'unhelpful stereotypes of children that dominate public discussion' can be challenged. Furthermore, adults do not always act in children's best interests and 'have been responsible for decisions, policies and actions that have been inappropriate or even harmful to children, while claiming to be acting to promote their welfare' (Lansdown and Lancaster, 2004: 15). According to Beck (1992), society must become reflexive in order to evolve, and Prout (2003) suggests that hearing the voices of children is a result of such reflexivity and this has been influential in children being viewed as having something valuable to say. Listening to children's views is gaining importance in contemporary social work practice (Holland, 2004), as well as in health and education provision and can have an impact on power relationships, challenging the assumption that adults know best. Empowerment, 'as a mechanism or process through which needs may be met and rights satisfied' (Drake, 2001: 83), is a key principle of legislation ensuring a voice for children, even at national level, and driving the work of the Children's Commissioner in the UK. Thomas (2001: 110) suggests that 'when children have an effective voice, services can be delivered more effectively, and the foundations are being laid for a better, more democratic society in the future'.

Rhetoric versus reality

Twum-Danso (2009: 110) suggests that these four principles are reflected in the treaty and inform both the implementation and the interpretation of children's rights which include the right:

- to life
- to a name and an identity
- to be raised by their own parents within a family or cultural grouping and to have a relationship with both parents even if they are separated
- to express their opinions and to have those opinions heard and acted on when appropriate
- to be protected from abuse or exploitation
- to have their privacy protected.

It is important, however, to bear in mind that any discussion of children's rights would be meaningless without considering the reality of children's lived experiences. While the

UNCRC universally applies to all children, there is considerable diversity in young children's actual lived experiences. As UNICEF (online) point out:

- Worldwide most deaths under age five years are children who die in the first few months of their lives and that young babies are still succumbing to causes directly linked to their mothers' health and well-being.
- Diarrhoea and acute respiratory infections are major causes of child death and improving access to safe water, sanitation and a healthy environment remains a major challenge in many parts of the world.
- Immunisation is not universal and children are still dying of measles and other preventable childhood diseases.
- Malnutrition remains widespread and alarming numbers of young children are anaemic and suffer from other nutrition-related ailments that hinder their development.
- Early childhood development is overlooked and public investment in early childhood development has fallen, while governments increasingly rely on the private sector to provide preschools and day-care centres.

There clearly remains a vast divide between the rhetoric of rights and the reality of being a child. This has yet to be addressed through international initiatives and national legislation. Therefore, an understanding of all aspects of children's rights, including protection, prevention and respect for participation and children's autonomy is fundamental to early childhood studies and should underpin any discussion or debate on young children and childhood. A more child-centred approach can be achieved in striving for empowerment for children through advocacy and research (e.g. the Mosaic approach, see Clark and Moss, 2001) which effectively challenges notions of dependency and listens to children's views and experiences.

Overview of the main theoretical perspectives on early childhood

The globalisation of children's rights has had an impact on all aspects of children's lives, from their relationship with their parents to their participation in school and other social institutions and the paradigm of childhood sociology emphasising children's position as social actors, as creative and inventive users of the world around them, has nurtured a blossoming conceptual and empirical exploration of children's competency and agency in a range of diverse settings (O'Brien *et al.*, 2000). It is diversity rather than commonality that constitutes the main characteristic of childhood (James and James, 2004a). Wells (2009a) argues for the importance of political activism in challenging taken-for-granted assumptions of childhood and children's competency and offers a sound critique of developmental psychology in relation to understanding childhood and children's lives:

The principles of orthodox developmental psychology, which claim that children gradually acquire intellectual and moral capacity throughout their childhood, have become the common sense of our epoch. In particular, Piaget's empirically derived claims that children cannot think logically before the age of seven and are not capable of abstract reasoning before the age of 12 has had an enormous influence on everyday understandings, especially in the West, of children's intellectual and emotional capabilities.

(Wells, 2009a: 24)

The dominance of the Piagetian ideology has resulted in children being educated in 'batches' (see Robinson, 2010) and being viewed as incomplete, inadequate and incompetent. We need to critically consider the reasons and dominant discourses around everyday practice in relation to children's everyday lives. As discussed above, the developmental approach has been extensively criticised elsewhere (see James *et al.*, 2010) and this chapter does not set out to repeat their arguments but draw attention to the debates and to encourage scholars of early childhood to further critically consider the dominant conceptions of childhood in early childhood studies. Part of that critical consideration is based on genuinely trying to understand children's own perspectives. Children generate their own understandings of the world and of culture in response to the structures and images which surround them (James *et al.*, 2010). Much literature explores how children see the world, their values and priorities and the ways in which they themselves feel marginalised (Roche, 1999). However, Scott *et al.* (1998) point out that children's participation in constructing their own everyday world takes place within the constraints set by their subordinate location in relation to adults, as children's understanding of what it means to be a child has been shaped by their interaction with more powerful, adult social actors with pre-existing, albeit negotiable, ideas about childhood and children. As Loreman (2009: 3) observes: 'adults often conceptualise children in very negative ways, viewing their unique characteristics as substandard or in need of improvement'.

Theorising childhood

James *et al.*, (2010) set out the tenets of the new social studies of childhood around four sociological dichotomies, as shown in Figure 1.2:

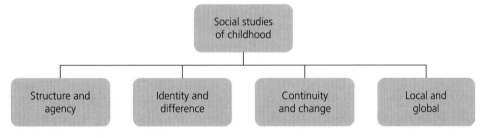

Figure 1.2

In relation to early childhood, it is important to understand how young children's lives are structured by the social processes, policies and social structures and how within these social structures children's agency is controlled, influenced and limited. How children understand their own self-identity, the sense of who they are, and how they view themselves as different to others is usually through interaction with others, usually adults. Debates around continuity and change are often located in understanding cultural reproduction, rather than seeking to gain knowledge of children's contemporary experiences (James, 2011) and different discourses of childhood impact on the way that children are viewed and treated.

Figure 1.3 illustrates the theoretical field for the social study of childhood from James *et al.* (2010: 206):

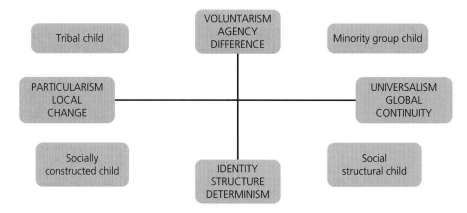

Figure 1.3 James, A, Jenks, C and Prout, A (2010): *Theorizing Childhood.* Cambridge: Polity Press.

In their critique of the socially developing child (the child viewed through the lens of developmental psychology and socialisation theory as incomplete – the becoming adult), James *et al.* (2010) proposed four new ways or discourses of seeing 'the child' – the social structural child, the socially constructed child, the tribal child and the child as a minority group. These are not conceptualised as separate but more as an analytical framework which views the child as being 'a person, a status, a course of action, a set of needs, rights or differences – in sum, as a social actor' (James *et al.*, 2010: 207). Thus, studying childhood today emphasises children as social actors, with rights and with views and opinions to be respected, valued and listened to – it is the study of real children and their everyday experiences of being a child.

Learning activity

Reflect for a few minutes on your values.

● When we are thinking about young children's lives and spending time with young children, our values will be central to how we think about them and how we behave towards them. Spend a few minutes thinking about your everyday life. Your personal values will underpin and influence what you do, what you believe, what you think and what you aim to accomplish. We all make choices in our lives according to our values – perhaps how we choose to spend our time and who we spend our time with, or how we spend our money and how we go about our everyday lives.

● What do you think is important?

● Have a look at the values listed below – which ones are important to you? If you were to put them in order of importance what sort of things would influence your choice?

● Write a list and then think about which are the most important to you. Think about how your own values influence how you think about young children and the way that they are treated. It is important to remember that values are socially and culturally constructed and change over time and in different communities.

Loyalty	Perseverance	Individualism	Modesty
Empathy	Wealth	Conformity	Maturity
Love	Duty	Kindness	Environmentalism
Intelligence	Control	Justice	Creativity
Bravery	Playfulness	Diligence	Accuracy
Success	Originality	Self-control	Honesty
Reputation	Family	Perfection	Self-reliance
Traditionalism	Professionalism	Obedience	Faith
Trust	Integrity	Sympathy	Meekness

Considering values

Lee (2005) outlines the different ways that children are valued – as innocents, as parental investments, as having cultural and familial heritage and as objects of state investment. It is essential as early childhood scholars that we are mindful of ethnocentrism. 'The importance of the child is rising' (Beck, 1992: 118), but childhood remains constructed as a time of innocence, vulnerability and dependence (Jenks, 2005). *The Anthropology of Childhood* (Lancy, 2008: 1) highlights how 'Euroamerican values have come to define all that is good, beautiful and true, including our scientific and pragmatic understanding of the nature of children'. Lancy (2008: 11) illustrates how a child's worth varies across cultures and social classes, generations and families and how for much of human history societies have been dominated by a gerontocracy (attention to the oldest members), but in modern western societies neontocracy (putting the needs and desires of children first) dominates. Thus, it is essential to understand the concepts of time and space in studying childhood.

The history of childhood

Understanding historical perspectives on childhood is an essential element of all ECS programmes. It is important for enabling students to understand how childhood is socially and culturally constructed and that this influences the way that children are viewed and treated and their experience of childhood. Having knowledge and understanding of historical perspectives also encourages us to think critically about contemporary childhoods and some of the current discourses and practices. The influence of past approaches to understanding and studying childhood is still very apparent today.

Studying childhood from a historical perspective requires different approaches to that which we may currently rely upon in contemporary research. Medieval or Elizabethan children are no longer available for us to listen to or to observe, and there are not many documents or photographs from these and other past periods. Understanding historical childhoods relies on material – the stuff left behind – which survives to the present day. We need to be careful about its reliability and the assumptions we make in relation to what we think the evidence may suggest.

How we study childhood in the past

Lebegyev (2009: 29) draws on archeological evidence from burial sites in early Mycenaean Greece, for example, to argue that 'the approximate age thresholds within childhood defined on the basis of different burial treatment indicate that in the earlier periods of Mycenaean culture children were gradually incorporated into society through a series of rites of passage'. Another approach adopted by a study (Crawford, 2009) of toys highlights how the idea of a 'toy' as an object specially designed for children to play with is, in itself, problematic as her evidence suggests that often mundane artefacts are used by children as toys, but that adults may have a different use for the same object. Furthermore, through the identification of archaeological evidence from later medieval countryside in rural England, Lewis (2009) argues that the lack of historical evidence in relation to children's play and children's lives is not necessarily related to a lack of the importance of childhood in those periods in history, but that we may be interpreting what we find from an adult perspective. She argues that, 'we have wiped the sticky fingerprints of children off our views of the past' by not seeing the evidence that is in front of us:

> For too long we approached our study of the past as adult, thinking about adult lives, and too rarely looked down to notice the children who would surely swarm around us if we were able to travel back in time and visit a medieval village. In the future it is imperative that we take more care to check the past for those sticky fingerprints.

(Lewis: 2009: 105)

It was, of course, Philippe Ariès in his publication of *Centuries of Childhood* in 1962 who is most commonly associated with studying the history of childhood. He proposed that in the Middle Ages, childhood did not exist. He was not suggesting that there were no children but that at that time there was no conception of the idea of 'childhood'. Using evidence from artworks, he argued that once children were old enough, around five to seven years, they entered the world of adults, working and experiencing their everyday lives in the same way as the adults did. 'Ariès (1962) interprets medieval art until the 13th century as lacking in child morphology' (O'Brien, 2003: 363) and his work has enjoyed what Heywood (2001: 12) describes as 'mixed fortunes among professional historians'. In other words, Ariès' work and his claim about childhood has been criticised mainly on the grounds of this methodological approach and his analysis of art as historical sources of evidence. It has, however, attracted much attention and debate not only on his work and assumptions about childhood in the past, but on the very nature of childhood itself. Ariès' work, therefore, can without doubt be regarded as highly significant in the study of childhood, not because of what he may have claimed, but that it generated so much interest and further scholarly work which either supported or refuted his argument and the use of art as evidence in studying childhood.

Hendrick (1997: 9) argues that there has been little work on the history of children and that, as a result, it has been difficult for scholars to develop specific methodological approaches but there is, he claims, a general consensus that during the 'late Victorian and Edwardian years new ideas, or in the language of social science, "social constructions" of children and childhood gained currency'. As Cunningham (2005: 58) observes:

> Ariès emphasises the 17th century as the crucial one in the transformation of ideas about childhood, but for most historians the 18th century holds pride of place. Framed by the writings of John Locke at its beginning and of the romantic poets

at the end, and with the strident figure of Rousseau at centre stage, there seems in the 18th century to be a degree of sensitivity to childhood and to children lacking in previous centuries. Some people began to see childhood not as a preparation for something else, whether adulthood or heaven, but as a stage of life to be valued in its own right.

However, not all childhoods experienced the same level of change and the harsh realities of children's lives remained untouched by the romantic ideas that began to influence the middle- and upper-class sectors of society. Inequalities and the idea of the deserving poor did, however, catch the attention of philanthropists, social commentators and influential writers of the time. Thornton (1998) observes how childhood became a preoccupation for literary works around 1840 reflecting a change from the romantically adventurous or crime-based novels to a concern and new interest in domesticity. At the same time, child-rearing practices, previously influenced by religious beliefs and cultural values, were increasingly shaped through nature rather than God and there was a 'shift from a prime focus on the spiritual health of the child to a concern for the development of the individual child' (Cunningham, 2005: 59). Cited as 'the founding father of childhood', it is through the philosophical writing of John Locke, his *Tabula Rasa* metaphor and his 'behaviouristic gaze upon the child' (Stainton Rogers and Stainton Rogers, 1992: 86) and through literature, for example, the writings of Dickens and Thackery, that idealised notions of childhood were not only proposed but also contested. The child becomes what Thornton (1998: 126) describes as 'an emotional vehicle of propaganda', but 'it was Rousseau who shifted the emphasis from decoration to essence and origin, and made the child a symbol of man's potential redemption'. According to Heywood (2001), Jean-Jacques Rousseau was significant in the reconstruction of childhood during the 18th century through his literary writing, for example, in *Emile*. Rousseau challenged Locke's ideas that children could be reasoned with, arguing instead that children, as young innocents, thought differently to adults and should be left to respond to nature accordingly.

The idea of children as innocents gained further influence during the late 18th and early 19th century with the rise in romanticism as depicted in the work of the artists Joshua Reynolds and Thomas Gainsborough (Heywood, 2001). According to Cunningham (2003), childhood as a theme for writing, for poetry and for art provides us with a sound understanding of the ideas about childhood which remain current today. The notion of childhood innocence emerged simultaneously with the development of numerous and now familiar children's charities, including Barnados and the National Society for the Prevention of Cruelty to Children (NSPCC), but England was not the only European country to be concerned about child welfare and the plight of children made more visible through industrialisation. The idea of rescuing children was also apparent both in Europe and across the Atlantic and 'child saving' initiatives across the globe began to shift the importance of discipline and learning from the factory to the school in the later part of the 19th century (Wells, 2009b).

It is, however, important to bear in mind that, although ideas about childhood were beginning to change, social class differences remained very apparent with infant mortality rates (IMR) higher in cities, especially in the working class areas or slums. According to Hendrick (1997), by 1913 the IMR rate was 108 per 1000 live births in England and Wales (in 2010 the infant mortality rate was 4.3 deaths per 1000 live births (Office for National Statistics, 2012)), but this varied between the middle and upper classes at 77, but for the poorer children born to unskilled workers it was 152. Poor children were also far more likely to suffer with morbidity related to chronic illness throughout their childhoods, and children's health status similarly attracted much attention focusing on levels of nutrition and also the frequent outbreak of communicable diseases like smallpox, typhus and scarlet fever. 'The slow gain in life expectancy and the slow drop in a fatal outcome of disease in young people was paralleled by slow progress in understanding disease as more than treatable or untreatable symptoms' (Jordan, 1987: 27). Increasing scientific attention was paid to children and to childhood by hygienists, the medical profession and subsequently psychologists who began to measure and classify children and in consequence a new category of the 'normal child' emerged (Turmel, 2008). Thus, the 19th century was a significant period of reform, and although the welfare of children, especially poor working class children, had been 'ravaged by the factory system', change, starting with the working conditions of chimney sweeps at the end of the 18th century, began to gain momentum and children's living conditions did begin to improve as the standards of living generally began to rise during the latter part of the 19th century (Jordan, 1987: 46). This period is, therefore, significant in the changing construction of childhood, in the separation of childhood and adulthood and in beginning the process of prolonging childhood itself. Stearns (2006: 55) helpfully summarises the three interrelated fundamental changes which underpinned the emergence of the modern childhood in the west during the 18th and 19th centuries as:

- the conversion of childhood from work to schooling
- the decision to limit family size to unprecedentedly low levels (a typical agricultural family of between five and seven children was far too costly when paying for food, clothes and even school fees)
- a drastic reduction in the IMR.

Understanding cultural constructions of childhood

As highlighted in the children's rights section above, children's everyday experiences vary widely according to where they live, family circumstances, national and international policies. A child growing up in sub-Saharan Africa with no access to safe, clean water, an insufficient diet and with no access to education nor health care clearly has a very different childhood to a child growing up in a western society where clean water and food are easily available and compulsory schooling and health surveillance structure their lives. These stark variations in childhood experiences are made increasingly visible through modern media platforms and can form the basis of unquestioned stereotypes and taken-for-granted assumptions about 'other' childhoods. The media is symbolic of wider globalised inequalities and power relationships, and images of children as victims of malnutrition, undereducated, poor and homeless dominate western media as eloquently argued by Holland (2003: 80):

> As with children, so with all those other groups who bear the characteristics of childhood – women, Black people and the whole of the Third World are among those who stand in a childish relation to the exercise of power. The non-white nations are regularly presented as if in themselves they lack potency, and it is among the children of the developing countries – in stark contrast to the well-fed, well-equipped mini-consumers of the domestic image that we find the most frequent pictures of childhood suffering.

Figure 1.4

Bourdieu and Passeron (1990) highlight the importance of cultural capital in defining children's everyday experiences. Tomanovic (2004) suggests that cultural capital for (and by) children constructs different childhood practices and that children's identities are formed on the opportunities, experiences and the abilities to make choices. It is also interesting to note from Katz (2008), however, that dominance of capitalism has led to a commodification of childhood (albeit gendered and classed) where parents compete to invest in their children's future with extra classes, sporting activities and music lessons, and that the shared temporal logics of childhood development and economic development require further interrogation (see Chapter 8 *Understanding childhood in late modernity*, for further discussion).

In everyday life, abstract ideas of the child come up against the actuality of children of different ages and genders, with a range of attributes and capacities (Backett, 1982). Research reflects how contemporary children's everyday social worlds are bound up in differences defined by age, gender, unique personality, culture, family circumstance and personal environment.

Respecting childhood

Understanding and respecting the fact that children, including very young children and babies, are people with rights is essential for early childhood scholars and early years professionals. How we care for young children should be underpinned by a rights-based approach. Although philosophically not everything that we do for young children arises from a consideration of rights, the obligations to provide care emerge from the rights of members of society and the duty of care arises from that relationship we have with them (Ellis, 2012). However, as Loreman

(2009: 99) observes, 'when it comes to children with individual and group differences, there is no shortage of both prejudice and power in society to make discrimination a reality'. It is essential that in our work and in our writing about early childhood that we abandon assumptions and are prepared to challenge discrimination and to confront uncritical stereotypes in order to consider equality of opportunity and how we can develop truly inclusive practice in our work and research with young children (Hohmann, 2010).

Kaufman and Rizzini (2011) set out the powerful relationship between international legal frameworks, as set down by the United Nations Convention on the Rights of the Child (UNCRC), national law and local initiatives which is brought to bear through advocacy. As adults, it is not only our duty to care for children but also to have respect for the dignity of the child. Article 19 of the UNCRC states that 'parties shall take all appropriate legislative, administrative, social and educational measures to protect the child from all forms of physical or mental violence, injury or abuse, neglect or negligent treatment, maltreatment or exploitation', yet currently in the UK there remains controversy in relation to corporal punishment.

Learning activity

Have a look at the debate on corporal punishment on the internet – see www.UNICEF.org and www.childrenareunbeatable.org.

- Consider what they are arguing in relation to corporal punishment for children and whether or not it should be banned.
- Look at some of the debates on websites like the BBC; the Guardian online and the Daily Telegraph and what people have claimed in relation to not changing the law in the UK.
- Summarise the arguments and consider what your feelings are about smacking children.

Listening to young children

Lee (2005) argues 'the child has been understood as someone who belongs to those intimate and minor spaces in which it is deemed safe for them – spaces such as the mother's breast, spaces of play and make-believe, and the family home. This makes 'the child' appear to be, by nature, a stranger to those more public and consequential spaces in which the language of rights and participation is spoken'. Thus, children, despite being social actors, are often rendered silent and invisible by the attitudes and practices of adult society (Roche, 1999). Although the rights of children, as articulated in the UNCRC and the Children Act 1989, would seem to suggest that children's status as citizens is unequivocal, children continue to be marginalised (James and James, 2004b).

Fostering meaningful children's participation and listening to children's voices should underpin all aspects of early childhood study and practice. In this section, initial guidance on listening to young children and involving them as active participants in early childhood research is provided to enable students to gain greater insight into the world of childhood and deepen their knowledge of young children's everyday experiences. As van Beers and Trimmer (2006: 1) argue 'for children's fundamental participation rights to be realized, it is adults, not children, who most urgently need to learn. Children's participation rights demand adults listen to children, understand them and take action based on what children say'.

Stemming from the recent developments in childhood studies outlined above, key methodological questions shape the character and nature of ECS. Methodology refers to philosophies, ideologies and principles (Roberts-Holmes, 2005). Having considered developments in the philosophical and ideological approaches to ECS in the previous section of this chapter, we now turn our attention to *how* we study early childhood. Resonating with the principles of 'emancipatory' science as outlined by Benton and Craib (2001: 8), there is increasing recognition that it is the children themselves who are expert in their own lives and not the adults who have previously dominated the role of the expert. The concept of competence in children's participation that has previously been so dominant has recently been challenged through new approaches (for example, Clark and Moss, 2001 and Lancaster, 2003). The recent developments in childhood studies from being dominated by developmental perspectives to the child-centred participatory approaches are becoming increasingly recognised and used in contemporary research initiatives and early years practice (Kirby, 2002). In exploring ways of working with young children's strengths rather than focusing on what they are unable to do, issues of power and social exclusion can be addressed and facilitate children's active participation and allow their voices to be heard. McLeod (2008) also emphasises that listening to children is not just common sense, or a legal obligation, but one of human rights and that there are differences in *how* we listen – as an attitude of listening or an action of listening.

The concepts of listening as an attitude or listening that leads to action are each grounded in an underlying value. In the case of listening as an ethic of openness, the primary value is respect. In the case of listening as a means of achieving change, the primary value is empowerment. Much that is written about listening to children concerns effective and respectful communication, and much concerns empowering children through promoting their rights and participation (McLeod, 2008: 22).

The concept of knowledge has traditionally excluded children, as adults are viewed as having greater knowledge and understanding than children. Goodenough *et al.* (2003) point out adults' understandings on the best way to work with children and consider issues that may be of importance to children's experiences and needs may well be very different to those of children themselves.

Studying early childhood

Developments in standpoint feminism and the influence of individualisation as 'the tendency for contemporary children to be seen as having a voice in determining their lives and shaping their identity' are important aspects of recent advances in studying early childhood (Christensen and Prout, 2005: 53). MacNaughton *et al.* (2001) outline the values and principles for studying early childhood and high-quality childhood research. They argue that research should be: respectful of children's participatory rights; critical, political and ethical; well-designed, transparent and purposeful and should reflect honesty regarding any assumptions.

Kellett *et al.* (2004) highlight the importance of the impact of Articles 12 and 13 of the UNCRC in encouraging children receiving information on, and being involved and consulted in, all activities affecting their lives. Morgan *et al.* (2002) observe how the increasing acknowledgement of children's rights has encouraged research which aims to understand children's views and experiences and demonstrates the divide between children's and parents' views and concerns. They argue that 'it is neither theoretically nor methodologically appropriate to rely on proxies to represent the views and experiences of children … children's views can and ought to be taken seriously' (Morgan *et al.*, 2002: 146). Interestingly though, it was not until 2008 that legislation in the UK finally placed a duty on all maintained schools to consider children's views.

Barker and Weller (2003: 34) suggest that 'contemporary research undertaken within the new social studies of childhood is very much influenced by and contributes to, the children's rights movement'. Furthermore, an interest in listening to children's views and experiences can 'be allied to a moral perspective on the role and status of children which respects and promotes their entitlement to being considered as persons of value and persons with rights' (Greene and Hogan, 2005: 3).

The recognition of children's social agency and active participation in research has significantly changed children's position within the human and social sciences and led to a weakening of taken-for-granted assumptions found in more conventional approaches to child research. In order to hear the voices of children in the representation of their own lives, it is important to employ research practices such as reflexivity and dialogue (Christensen, 2004: 165).

Greene and Hogan (2005) emphasise the importance of considering children's lives from multiple perspectives and observe that no single theoretical or methodological approach is preferable overall. While young children were traditionally passively positioned in the academic study of childhood, the recent increased emphasis on children's rights and citizenship has led to emphasis now being placed on children's participation (Veale, 2005). Facilitating children's participation emphasises dialogical qualities as beneficial and the need to engage with children's own cultures of communication and as such the power moves between different actors and different social positions – it is produced and negotiated in the social interactions (Christensen, 2004).

Key principles for studying early childhood

Thomas and O'Kane (2000: 832) outline key principles for studying childhood through researching with children and suggest that research with children is improved when it:

- incorporates and builds on children's own definitions of what is interesting or important
- uses methods of communication that children find meaningful and comfortable; and
- acknowledges the importance of children's emotional needs.

An interest in researching children's experience can, therefore, be allied to a moral perspective on the role and status of children which respects and promotes their entitlement to being considered as persons of values and persons with rights.

(Greene and Hogan, 2005: 3)

Loreman (2009: 3) outlines what we mean by respecting childhood:

- To provide children with the basic necessities of life outlined in the United Nations Declaration on the Rights of the Child (1959) and the United Nations International Convention on the Rights of the Child (1989)
- To value children's time, especially in the present
- To value children's enjoyment of childhood
- To value children's relationships with others
- To value children's contributions to family and society
- To value children's individuality and diversity
- To value and accept children' abilities and capabilities.

Early childhood professionals

These principles underpin our approach to studying early childhood and promoting professional values in our work with young children. According to Friedman (2007), professionalism is a complex concept and the discourses of professionalism in relation to early childhood is complicated. Friedman questions the motivations people have and asks how can we contribute to professionalism in the field. She suggests that the components of professionalism (see Figure 1.5) are:

Figure 1.5

Developing professionalism

Early Years Professional Status (EYPS) is a professional status for Early Childhood practitioners who work with children aged from birth to five years. The aim of EYPS was to give qualified early years practitioners the same professional status as primary school teachers. It was introduced by the British Government in 2007, supported by the Children's Workforce Development Council for graduates to obtain professional status through further study and an assessment of their early years practice. Furthermore, early years children's centres and day-care settings will, by 2015, be required to employ at least one Early Years Professional (EYP).

Being a child is no longer, even if it ever was, simply a matter of being shaped by adult-controlled institutions. If individualisation processes continue, then children will become ever more recognised as the active interpreters and co-producers of their own lives and hence of the communities and societies of which they are part (Prout, 2000: 313).

The future of early childhood studies

Having outlined the developments in childhood studies and explored these developments in relation to ECS, this chapter now looks forward to examine where possibilities for future developments may lie. Prout (2005) claims that even recent approaches to childhood are limited by dualist discourse (which gives primacy to researching relations, for example between structure and agency; public and private, etc.). He argued that understanding childhood, a complex phenomenon, is limited by dualistic discourse and that contemporary childhoods in post-modernity are marked by dissolving boundaries and heightened ambiguity and that new conceptual frameworks are required in the study of childhood (Prout, 1996: 198). His suggestion – the adoption of Actor Network Theory (ANT) which draws on semiotics, social constructionism and symbolic interactionism, in order to consider the materials from which social life is produced and the processes by which these are brought into relationship with each other and this concept of *network* – offers a language of ordering that stands between the polar oppositions put forward by modernist social theory (Prout, 2005). That is not to say that ANT has little in common with traditional sociological approaches as it has commonalities with theoretical approaches including social constructionism; symbolic interactionism; semiotics and Foucauldian approaches to power, but it is distinct in one respect in that it rejects the assumptions that society is constructed through human action and meaning alone (Prout, 1996). As ANT aims to be inter-disciplinary to produce a holistic theoretical perspective, it embraces the principles of childhood studies outlined by our book here – advocating the importance of an inter-disciplinary approach based on holistic philosophy. ANT draws on an ethnographic framework, which employs a holistic approach (Sarantakos, 2005) and reveals the complexities of individual and social-group interaction (Frankenberg *et al.*, 2000) which are central in childhood research (James *et al.*, 2010).

Conceptually, therefore, these arguments would appear to be beneficial to supporting some of the key aspects which emerged from within the new social studies of childhood paradigm viewing children as experts in their own lives, the children's rights-based approach to participation and the development of new research methodologies towards such participation and inclusion. Research which gives a voice to children, providing an insight into their subjective world allows children to 'a degree to be "collaborator" in the research process rather than simply study "object"' (Grover, 2004: 81). This acknowledgement of the rise of childhood agency is discussed by James *et al.* (2010: 6) and they outline 'the transition from "the child" as an instance of a category to the recognition of children as particular persons'. It is, therefore, interesting here to consider the answer Latour and Law developed through ANT to the question of agency (Lee, 2001a). It suggests that the more agency and independence a person appears to have, the more dependent they are on a network for their power and identity (Lee, 1998). Similar to Law's (1994: 384) view on agency that it is not something that people possess but an effect generated by a 'network of heterogeneous, interacting materials', Latour (1993) illustrates how the concept of agency and independence is challenged, and paradoxically accounted for, by dependence and incompleteness, and since agency is no longer conceived of as a simple possession it is exposed to empirical study and analysis.

Considering ANT for early childhood.

- Looking back at some of the things you thought about in the learning activity on page 2, consider how they influence childhood experiences.
- Now think about a child you know. Take a while to carefully consider everything that has an influence on that child's life and write them down. Try to think more widely than you did for the first activity and, having read some of the debates presented in this chapter, remember to include international children's rights, national policy, local geographies, access to health care, education and so on. Also think about the more intimate details of a child's family, their relationships with those family members and other people in their lives. What about material goods, access to clean water, paper, pens, television, the internet?
- Then think about the networks that surround some of these actors in children's lives: their family members, where they work; if they work; the professional people that work with young children and how their networks, levels of qualifications and their own experiences also have an impact on young children's lives.
- When you start thinking about it and giving time to really consider the influences on childhood and children's everyday experiences, the complexity of childhood is revealed.

In our attempts to understand childhood, therefore, adopting an ANT approach can help us to see the complexity that surrounds children's everyday lives and their lived experiences of childhood. Thus, by adopting the metaphor of network, childhood can be seen as a 'collection of different, sometimes competing and conflicting, heterogeneous orderings' (Prout, 2005: 71). Childhood is not given but open to continual revaluation and vulnerable to different definitions of what is normal and acceptable, and changing concerns indicate the process of understanding and reconstructing childhood is a continuing but 'continually novel historical phenomenon' (Smith, 2000: 4). In Lee's (2001b) discussion, he illustrates clearly through an ANT approach how children have become separated through a set of practices, people, policies and protecting them from undesirable influences:

> Children under preservation became part of the network that linked them to reasons of state and challenged their agency into their development, socialization and education. The conventional view of children as dependent that emerged was part of this actor network.

(Lee, 2001b: 132)

Lee and Stanner (1999) suggest that ANT is an ethical rather than a moral approach as it incorporates the question of the nature of belonging into different domains and it allows the concepts of dependency and belonging to be applied recursively. Drawing on Latour's (1993) approach to modernity, as a form of belonging, guaranteed through excluding certain characters (hybrids), ANT dissolves boundaries imposed to bring the 'other' back into belonging. ANT endorses democracy (Strathern, 1999), if we recognise that within a network of interdependencies each actant plays a role in the production of reality, we should work towards an inclusive network (Lee and Stanner, 1999). Law (1999: 9) notes 'what is interesting are matters, questions, and issues arising out of, or in relation to, actor-network, and the various approaches to thinking materiality, ordering, distribution and hierarchy with which it interacts'. Recent social changes have, according to Prout (2005) altered the conditions and experiences of childhood, destabilising previous ideas, and the current climate offers a context for understanding the emergence of the children's voice. An awareness of some of these principles of ANT may contribute to allowing the children's voice to come forward. As Latour (1999: 19) observes: 'actors know what they do and we have to learn from them not only what they do, but how and why they do it', thus making it possible for new actors (actants) to define the world in their own terms, using their own dimensions and signs.

Conclusion

This chapter set out to challenge previously held assumptions about early childhood and young children's lives. Childhood studies which began with a critique of the adult ideological viewpoint, 'can become aware of the fact that the erosion of the classic European model of childhood determines the social conditions of the possibility of constituting childhood as an object of knowledge' (Honig, 2011: 730). Currently, the aim of childhood scholarship – to change children's cultural position – is based on a critique of the dominance of developmental psychology from the 19th and early 20th century that had been so influential in shaping common sense approaches to childhood and children's experiences (Lee, 2005). This chapter considered a set of global value principles that might underpin the work of early years professionals. It is important to remember, as Wells (2009b: 16) points out, that 'within any particular historical and social context there will be a normative and hegemonic concept of childhood against which children themselves are compared as individuals and collectives'. This discussion was followed by an overview of the main theoretical perspectives underlying early childhood studies which highlighted how, until relatively recently, childhood has been either neglected by mainstream social theory, or considered from a developmental perspective within areas such as education or the family (Brannen and O'Brien, 1995; Corsaro, 1997). Much of this research has accorded criticism for conceptualising children as incompetent, unreliable and incomplete, as mere objects to be studied (Hill et al., 1996). The adoption of childhood as an interdisciplinary field and the acceptance of the multiple constructions and reconstructions of childhood, as outlined by James and James (2004b), together with the principles set out in the UNCRC provides a theoretical and, widely accepted within social science, rights-based philosophy to underpin ECS. We still, however, have some way to go as we still 'need to cut through the rhetoric of "effective practice", "well-being" and "outcomes", so we are not perpetuating dominant discourses, but deconstructing (and possibly reconstructing) them in order to strengthen our positions as advocates for each other, as well as the children, young people and families that we work with' (Botherton and McGillivray, 2010: 180).

Evaluate your learning

- To what extent do you consider childhood to be a universal, staged process or a social and cultural construction?
- What can understanding the history of childhood teach us about contemporary conceptions of childhood?
- How are children's rights, as set out in the UNCRC, reflected in the current UK legislation on corporal punishment?

References

Alderson, P (2002): Young children's health care rights and consent. In Franklin, B (ed.), *The New Handbook of Children's Rights: Comparative Policy and Practice*. London: Routledge.

Archard, D (2004): *Children Rights and Childhood*, 2nd edn. London: Routledge.

Ariès, P (1962): *Centuries of Childhood*. London: Pimlico.

Backett, K (1982): *Mothers and Fathers: A Study of the Development and Negotiation of Parental Behaviour*. London: Macmillan.

Barker, J and Weller, S (2003): 'Is it fun?' Developing children centred research methods. *International Journal of Sociology and Social Policy* **23**(1–2), 33–58.

Beck, U (1992): *Risk Society: Towards a New Modernity*. London: Sage.

Benton, T and Craib, I (2001): *Philosophy of Social Science*. Basingstoke: Palgrave.

Botherton, G and McGillivray, G (2010): Where are we going? In Botherton, G, Davies, H and McGillivray, G (eds), *Working with Children, Young People and Familes*. London: Sage.

Bourdieu, P and Passeron, JC (1990): *Reproduction in Education, Society and Culture*. London: Sage.

Brannen, J and O'Brien, M (1995): Childhood and the sociological gaze: paradigms and paradoxes. *Sociology* **29**(4), 729–37.

Burr, R and Montgomery, H (2003): Children and rights. In Woodhead, M and Montgomery, H (eds), *Understanding Childhood: An Interdisciplinary Approach*. Chichester: Open University/John Wiley and Sons Ltd.

Christensen, P and Prout, A (2005): Anthropological and Sociological perspectives on the study of children. In Greene, S and Hogan, D (eds), *Researching Children's Experience Approaches and Methods*. London: Sage.

Christensen, PH (2004): Children's participation in ethnographic research: issues of power and representation. *Children and Society* **18**, 165–76.

Clark, A and Moss, P (2001): *Listening to Young Children: The Mosaic Approach*. London: National Children's Bureau.

Corsaro, W (1997): *The Sociology of Childhood*. California: Pine Forge Press.

Crawford, S (2009): The archaeology of play things: theorising a toy stage in the 'biography' of objects. *Childhood in the Past* **2**, 55–71.

Cunningham, H (2003): Children's changing lives from 1800 to 2000. In Maybin, J and Woodhead, M (eds), *Childhoods in Context*. Chichester: John Wiley and Sons In association with The Open University.

Cunningham, H (2005): *Children and Childhood in Western Society Since 1500*. Harlow: Pearson Education.

Drake, RF (2001): *The Principles of Social Policy*. Basingstoke: Palgrave.

Ellis, P (2012): Rights and responsibilities. In Koubel, G and Bungay, H (eds), *Rights, Risks and Responsibilities*. Basingstoke: Palgrave.

Frankenberg, R, Robinson, I and Delahooke, A (2000): Countering essentialism in behavioural social science: the example of 'the vulnerable child' ethnographically examined. *The Sociological Review* **48**(4), 586–611.

Franklin, B (2002): Children's rights and media wrongs. In Franklin, B (ed.), *The New Handbook of Children's Rights: Comparative Policy and Practice*. London: Routledge.

Friedman, R (2007): Professionalism in the early years. In Wild, M and Mitchell, H (eds), *Early Childhood Studies Reflective Reader*. Exeter: Learning Matters.

Goodenough, T, Williamson, E, Kent, J and Ashcroft, R (2003): What do you think about that? Researching children's perceptions of participation in a longitudinal genetic epidemiological study. *Children and Society* **17**, 113–25.

Greene, S and Hogan, D (eds) (2005): *Researching Children's Experience Approaches and Methods*. London: Sage.

Grover, S (2004): Why won't they listen to us? On giving power and voice to children participating in social research. *Childhood* **11**(1), 81–93.

Hart, HLA (1992): Are there any natural rights? In Waldron, J (ed), *Theories of Rights*. Oxford: Oxford University Press.

Hendrick, H (1997): *Children, Childhood and English Society 1881–1990*. Cambridge: Cambridge University Press.

Heywood, C (2001): *A History of Childhood*. Cambridge: Polity Press.

Hill, M, Laybourn, A and Borland, M (1996): Engaging with primary-aged children and their emotions and well-being: methodological considerations. *Children and Society* **10**, 129–44.

Hohmann, U (2010): Tackling inequality in the early years. In Parker-Rees, R, Leeson, C, Willan, J and Savage, J (eds), *Early Childhood Studies*, 3rd edn. Exeter: Learning Matters.

Holland, P (2003): What is a child? Crybabies and damaged children. In Woodhead, M and Montgomery, H (eds), *Understanding Childhood an interdisciplinary approach*. Chichester: Open University in association with John Wiley.

Holland, S (2004): *Child and Family Assessment in Social Work Practice*. London: Sage.

Honig, MS (2011): How is the child constructed in childhood studies. In Qvortrup, J, Corsaro, WA and Honig, MS (eds), *The Palgrave Handbook of Childhood Studies*. Basingstoke: Palgrave.

James, A (2011): Agency. In Qvortrup, J, Corsaro, WA and Honig, MS (eds), *The Palgrave Handbook of Childhood Studies*. Basingstoke: Palgrave.

James, A and James, AL (2004a): Introduction: The politics of childhood – an overview. In Goddard, J, McNamee, S, James, A and James, AL (eds), *The Politics of Childhood*. Basingstoke: Palgrave.

James, A and James, AL (2004b): *Constructing Childhood*. Basingstoke: Palgrave.

James, A, Jenks, C and Prout, A (2010): *Theorizing Childhood.* Cambridge: Polity

Jenks, C (2005): *Childhood.* London: Routledge.

Jordan, TE (1987): *Victorian Childhood Themes and Variations.* New York: State University of New York Press.

Katz, C (2008): Childhood as spectacle: relays of anxiety and the reconfiguration of the child. *Cultural Geographies* **15**, 5–17.

Kaufman, NH and Rizzini, I (2011): Closing the gap between rights and the realities of children's lives. In Qvortrup, J, Corsaro, WA and Honig, MS (eds), *The Palgrave Handbook of Childhood Studies.* Basingstoke: Palgrave.

Kellett, M, Forrest, R, Dent, N and Ward, S (2004): Just teach us the skills please, we'll do the rest: empowering ten-year-olds as active researchers. *Children and Society* **18**, 329–43.

Kirby, P (2002): Involving young people in research. In Franklin, B (ed.), *The New Handbook of Children's Rights: Comparative Policy and Practice.* London: Routledge.

Lancaster, YP (2003): *Listening to Young Children, Promoting Listening to Young Children: The Reader.* Maidenhead: Open University Press.

Lancy, DF (2008): *The Anthropology of Childhood.* Cambridge: Cambridge University Press.

Lansdown, G (2005): Children's welfare and children's rights. In Hendrick, H (ed), *Child Welfare and Social Policy: An Essential Reader.* Bristol: Policy Press.

Lansdown, G (2009): Promoting children's welfare by respecting their rights. In Miller, L, Cable, C and Goodliff, G (eds), *Supporting Children's Learning in the Early Years*, 2nd edn. London: Routledge.

Lansdown, G and Lancaster, YP (2004): Promoting children's welfare by respecting their rights. In Miller, L and Devereux, J (eds), *Supporting Children's Learning in the Early Years.* London: David Fulton in association with the Open University.

Latour, B (1993): *We Have Never Been Modern.* Hemel Hempstead: Harvester Wheatsheaf.

Latour, B (1999): On recalling ANT. In Law, J and Hassard, J (eds), *Actor Network Theory and After.* Oxford: Blackwell.

Law, J (1994): *Organising Modernity.* Oxford: Blackwell.

Law, J (1999): After ANT: complexity, naming and topology. In Law, J and Hassard, J (eds), *Actor Network Theory and After.* Oxford: Blackwell.

Lebegyev, J (2009): Phases of childhood in early Mycenaean Greece. *Childhood in the Past* **2**, 15–32.

Lee, LM (1998): Childhood and self-representation: the view from technology. *Anthropology in Action* **5**(3), 13–21.

Lee, N (2001a): The extensions of childhood technologies, children and independence. In Hutchby, I and Moran-Ellis, J (eds), *Children, Technology and Culture: The Impacts of Technologies in Children's Everyday Lives.* London: Routledge Falmer.

Lee, N (2001b): *Childhood and Society.* Buckingham: Open University Press.

Lee, N (2005): *Childhood and Human Value.* Maidenhead: Open University Press.

Lee, N and Stanner, P (1999): Who pays? Can we pay them back. In Law, J and Hassard, J (eds), *Actor Network Theory and After.* Oxford: Blackwell.

Lewis, C (2009): Children's play in the later medieval English countryside. *Childhood in the Past*, **2**, 86–108.

Loreman, T (2009): *Respecting Childhood.* London: Continuum.

MacNaughton, G, Rolfe, SA and Siraj-Blatchford, I (2001): *Doing Early Childhood Research.* Buckingham: Open University Press.

McLeod, A (2008): *Listening to Children.* London: Jessica Kingsley.

Morgan, M, Gibbs, S, Maxwell, K and Britten, N (2002) Hearing children's voices: methodological issues in conducting focus groups with children aged 7–11 years. *Qualitative Research* **2**(1), 5–20.

O'Brien, C (2003): The nature of childhood through history revealed in artworks? *Childhood* **10**, 362–78.

O'Brien, M, Jones, D and Sloan, D (2000): Children's independent spatial mobility in the urban public realm. *Childhood* **7**, 257–77.

Office for National Statistics (ONS) (2012) *Childhood, Infant and Perinatal Mortality in England and Wales.* (Online). Last accessed 27 August 2012. Available from: www.ons.gov.uk/ons/rel/vsob1/child-mortality-statistics--childhood--infant-and-perinatal/2010/stb-cms-2010.html.

Prout, A (1996): Actor-network theory, technology and medical sociology: an illustrative analysis of the metered dose inhaler. *Sociology of Health and Illness* **18**(2), 198–219.

Prout, A (2000): Children's participation: control and self-realisation in British late modernity. *Children and Society* **14**, 304–15.

Prout, A (2003): Participation, policy and childhood. In Hallett, C and Prout, A (eds), *Hearing the Voices of Children: Social Policy for a New Century.* London: Routledge-Falmer.

Prout, A (2005): *The Future of Childhood.* London: Routledge Falmer.

QAA (2007): *Early Childhood Studies.* (Online). Available from: www.qaa.ac.uk/Publications/InformationAndGuidance/Documents/EarlyChildhoodStudies07.pdf.

Qvortrup, J (ed.) (2005): *Studies in Modern Childhood Society, Agency Culture.* Basingstoke: Palgrave.

Reynaert, D, Bouerne de Bie, M and Vandevelde, S (2009): A review of children's rights literature since the adoption of the United Nations Convention on the Rights of the Child. *Childhood* **18**, 518–32.

Roberts-Holmes, G (2005): *Doing Your Early Years Research Project.* London: Paul Chapman Publishing.

Robinson, K (2010): *Changing Paradigms* (Online). Available from: http://comment.rsablogs.org.uk/videos/page/2/.

Roche, J (1999): Children: rights, participation and citizenship. *Childhood* **6**, 475–93.

Sarantakos, S (2005): *Social Research*, 3rd edn. Basingstoke: Palgrave.

Scott, S, Jackson, S and Backett-Milburn, K (1998): Swings and roundabouts: risk anxiety and the everyday worlds of children. *Sociology* **32**, 689–705.

Smith, R (2000): Order and disorder: the contradictions of childhood. *Children and Society*, **14**, 3–10.

Stainton Rogers, R and Stainton Rogers, W (1992) *Stories of Childhood Shifting Agendas of Child Concern.* Hemel Hampstead: Harvester Wheatsheaf.

Stearns, PN (2006): *Childhood in World History.* London: Routledge.

Strathern, M (1999): What is intellectual property after? In Law, J and Hassard, J (eds), *Actor Network Theory and After*. Oxford: Blackwell.

Taylor, A (2011): Reconceptualising the 'nature' of childhood. *Childhood* 18(4), 420–33.

Thomas, N (2001): Listening to children. In Foley, P, Roche, J and Tucker, S (eds), *Children in Society: Contemporary Theory, Policy and Practice*. Basingstoke: Palgrave in association with the Open University.

Thomas, N and O' Kane, C (2000): Discovering what children think: connections between research and practice. *British Journal of Social Work* **30**, 819–35.

Thornton, S (1998): The vanity of childhood: constructing, deconstructing, and destroying the child in the novel of the 1940s. In Lesnik-Oberstein, K (ed), *Children in Culture Approaches to Childhood*. Basingstoke: Palgrave.

Tomanovic, S (2004): Family habitus as the cultural context for childhood. *Childhood* **11**(3), 339–60.

Turmel, A (2008): *A Historical Sociology of Childhood*. Cambridge: Cambridge University Press.

Twum-Danso, A (2009): International children's rights. In Montgomery, H and Kellet, M (eds), *Children and Young People's World: Developing Frameworks for Integrated Practice*. Bristol: Policy Press.

UNICEF (Online). Available from: www.unicef.org.uk.

van Beers, H and Trimmer, C (2006): *Adults First!* Sweden: Save the Children. (Online). Available from: http://seap.savethechildren.se/upload/scs/SEAP/publication/publication%20pdf/child%20participation/Adults%20first!.pdf.

Veale, A (2005): Creative methodologies in participatory research with children. In Greene, S and Hogan, D (eds), *Researching Children's Experience Approaches and Methods*. London: Sage.

Wells, K (2009a): Children and international politics. In Montgomery, H and Kellet, M (eds), *Children and Young People's Worlds*. Bristol: Policy Press.

Wells, K (2009b): *Childhood in a Global Perspective*. Cambridge: Polity Press.

Wyness, M (2012): *Childhood and Society*, 2nd edn. Basingstoke: Palgrave.

Further reading

Jenks, C (2005): *Childhood*. London: Routledge.

Loreman, T (2009): *Respecting Childhood*. London: Continuum.

Prout, A (2005): *The Future of Childhood*. London: Routledge Falmer.

Turmel, A (2008): *A Historical Sociology of Childhood*. Cambridge: Cambridge University Press.

2 New beginnings: factors affecting health and well-being in the neonate

Heather Passmore and Samantha Chenery-Morris

This chapter aims to:
- consider the nature and impact of early life processes and experiences which might influence the future health and well-being of neonates
- describe the development of the foetus *in utero*
- describe measures to optimise health and well-being in the newborn
- consider the interplay between social and emotional, physical and environmental factors on pregnancy outcome
- consider how early years professionals can help in promoting health and well-being in the newborn.

Introduction

The scope of this chapter is to consider factors affecting health and well-being in the neonate. The neonatal period is the first 4 weeks or 28 days of a child's life. It is during this time that many changes occur rapidly, but as this chapter will demonstrate, it is not only after birth (the postnatal period) that critical events can occur which shape the developing child's life, but preconceptually, antenatally and during birth too. Thus, this chapter will be presented chronologically but there are other factors which influence parental health such as the genetic make up and socio-economic status of the parents, and the environment which all contribute to the healthy development of the neonate. The foundations for life-long well-being are laid down long before birth (Department of Health, 2011a). The physical, mental and emotional health of the woman especially will have a lifelong effect on the neonate (Marmot, 2010).

The income, education and occupation of the parent or parents determine their socio-economic status. Low income and limited education are strongly associated with poorer mental and physical health (Price, 2007). Overall, the health of the nation in the UK has greatly increased over the last 50 years, but the difference between the higher socio-economic groups has increased more dramatically than those of lower status (Marmot and Wilkinson, 2006). Prevalence of smoking and other potentially harmful life-style choices are also higher in lower socio-economic groups, and these factors all impact on the pregnancy and the health and development of the foetus (Agopian *et al.*, in press). Even before conception, the parental genes will each contribute to the unique genetic composition of the baby. The whole process of embryonic and fetal development is dependent on genes, and abnormal genes can cause abnormalities and disease in the newborn. By gaining an understanding of the processes before, during and in the early period following birth we can consider the impact that these may have on future health, growth and development.

Preconceptual care, although offered to women of child-bearing age with existing health conditions such as epilepsy and diabetes, is not the norm within the UK and other countries for many reasons. Some of these reasons include financial and cultural barriers to preconceptual care and, with half of UK conceptions unplanned (Department of Health, 2007b), few women access these services. This chapter will demonstrate that much of the preconceptual care and advice is reiterated or introduced (for those who have had no preconceptual care) in the antenatal period.

There have been many government-led initiatives and policy developments in antenatal and newborn screening and more screening tests are offered to women and their partners earlier than before (NICE, 2008b; UKNSC, 2011). Women are offered screening tests for their own well-being as well as that of their foetus (such as antenatal and postnatal maternal mental health) as these conditions can impact upon the health of the whole family (NICE, 2007).

Optimising maternal health prior to, during and after pregnancy maximises the neonate's well-being. Pregnancy is a normal physiological event and should be viewed as part of life's events. Factors that support health and well-being can be promoted instead of focusing on disease. This approach, termed 'salutogenesis', by Aaron Antonovsky (1979) has been promoted for midwifery practice (Downe, 2008).

A salutogenic approach moves away from a pathogenic disease perspective towards a health and well-being perspective. By promoting a sense of well-being with the parents, this in turn affects the developing foetus and baby. Some researchers suggest that promoting and maximising normal pregnancy and birth has consequences for maternal and infant biochemistry and neuroscience (Downe, 2008). In his theory of salutogenesis, there is a continuum between total wellness and total disease (Antonovsky, 1979). The position of the person, whether they can make sense of their experience, affects the way they see their health. As this chapter focuses on new beginnings and factors that affect new-born health and well-being, this theory has been utilised.

The World Health Organization's (WHO) definition of health has not been amended since it was published in 1946. It states health is a 'complete state of physical, mental and emotional well-being, and not merely the absence of disease and infirmity' (WHO, 1946). When considering the health and well-being of the new-born it is still relevant today, as this definition concentrates on promoting health rather than concentrating solely on the absence of disease and abnormality.

For all prospective parents, pregnancy is an uncertain time and practical considerations also include loss of earnings and need for space, in addition to the responsibility of parenthood.

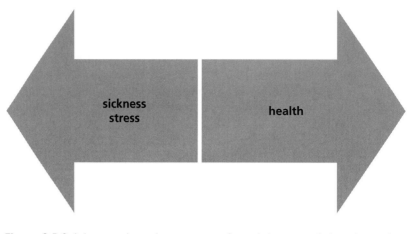

Figure 2.1 Salutogenesis, a change away from sickness and stress towards optimising health

The way in which the prospective parents make sense of this uncertainty and how they use resources available to them can affect their health and that of the developing foetus. If health professionals can promote a salutogenic response to pregnancy, this may be the first of many steps that can improve neonatal health.

From conception to birth

The development of the embryo is a unique and amazing process. Our knowledge of this complex process is increasing with advances in embryological and genetic research and the completion of the Human Genome Project in 2003, yet there is still only a partial understanding of the early period of human experience (HGP, online; Welcome Trust, online). To understand why the period before birth is so significant, and to appreciate the potential impact of factors such as drugs and infections on development, it is necessary to describe briefly the developmental timetable from conception to birth.

The human gestation period is approximately 38 weeks from conception, or 40 weeks from the onset of the last menstrual period. The gestation period is divided into two phases:

1. The *embryonic phase* commences with conception and continues until the end of the 8th week. It is a period of rapid growth and development, and during this phase all of the major organs of the body are formed. The first three weeks following conception are sometimes referred to as the 'pre-embryonic period'.
2. The *fetal phase* comprises the remaining 30 weeks of gestation. It is characterised by growth and further development of the organs and systems established in the embryonic phase.

Development commences at fertilisation when the sperm enters the egg. As soon as fertilisation has taken place, the new cell starts to change. Cells are the basic unit of life and a typical human being is composed of about 350 different types of specialised cell, such as red blood cells and muscle cells (Moore and Persaud, 2003; Carey, 2012). The embryonic cells are initially less specialised, but all cells have basic characteristics and activities. The important activities considered here are cell multiplication, cell differentiation and cell movement.

The process of cell multiplication begins about 30 minutes after fertilisation, when the egg starts to divide into two cells. The cells continue to divide, and by day 4 there is a solid ball of cells known as the 'morula'. The morula enters the uterus and changes into a blastocyst, which is a fluid-filled sphere, containing a group of cells known as the inner cell mass. The inner cell mass will become the embryo, and the trophoblastic cells will form the placenta. At approximately 7–8 days after ovulation the blastocyst will become embedded in the wall of the uterus.

By the third week after ovulation, the inner cell mass has become a disc differentiated into three different types of cells – the ectoderm, mesoderm and endoderm. It is from these cells that the different structures of the body will evolve. At four weeks after fertilisation, the cells have developed to form an embryo approximately 0.5 cm long, and it has a curved form with a head and tail fold. Most of the body systems are now present in a rudimentary form: there is a neural tube, which will form the brain, lung buds which will develop into a respiratory system, and primitive eyes, nose and ears. By this stage, the heart is beating. The changes have been achieved not just by cell differentiation but also by cell movement, which transforms the flat embryonic disc so that the basic body plan is laid down.

By the end of the eighth week, the embryonic phase of development is complete; the embryo is covered with a thin skin. The head has increased greatly in size and is nearly as large as the rest of the body, and the facial features are more distinct. The embryo is making some movements, but at this stage they are not strong enough for the mother to feel them. There is no visible difference between male and female embryos at this stage.

At 12 weeks after fertilisation, the foetus has eyelids which are fused. The kidneys secrete urine, the foetus swallows amniotic fluid and the external genitalia have developed sufficiently for it to be possible to determine the sex of the foetus. At 20 weeks, the foetus looks distinctly human. The body is beginning to be covered by fine hair and a thick greasy substance, known as 'vernix caseosa', which protects the skin from the macerating effects of the amniotic fluid. The fetal movements are now strong enough to be felt by the mother. By 24 weeks, the foetus weighs 550–700 g. The organs have developed and matured to such an extent that the foetus may survive with medical assistance if the birth takes place prematurely. The foetus responds to light, sound and touch, and has developed a sense of taste. It has also developed the ability to feel and respond to pain.

During the remaining weeks of pregnancy, the foetus accumulates fat stores and maturation continues. The lungs, in particular, continue to develop and prepare for function. At birth, the normal baby weighs between 3.0 and 3.5 kg. Although birth is a stage in the developmental process, and rapid changes take place within the baby as it adapts to life outside the uterus, birth does not represent the end of development. Many organ systems do not develop into their final form until puberty or later.

It is important when considering early childhood to remember that the pattern of growth and development from conception reflects the complex interactions between genetic and environmental influences, including nutrient supply on human growth and development (SACN, 2011). Recent research has described how the architecture of the brain is influenced by both genetics and early experience and brain development and developing abilities are built from 'the bottom up' with the most simple circuits laying the foundation and structure for adding more complex advanced circuit and skills (CDC, 2007a; CDC, 2007b; CDC, 2011). Rather like a building, the process of brain development requires a strong foundation, an adequate framing of the structure, wiring the electrical (nervous) system for predictable responses and features that reflect individuality. Toxic shock, for example, in early childhood (including *in utero*), such as exposure to substance misuse or maternal depression, is associated with persistent effects on the nervous system. Stress hormone systems can damage basic brain architecture, with long-lasting results in relation to learning, behaviour, physical and mental health (NSCDC, 2008). This is why it is so important that there is more widespread provision of preconceptual as well as antenatal care.

Learning activity

- Fetal breathing movements commence *in utero*. When do they start and are they of any significance?
- Investigate at what gestation a foetus may feel pain.
- Review the working paper from Harvard University on 'Excessive stress disrupts the architecture of the developing brain' (www.developingchild.harvard.edu) to identify a range of factors that may cause 'toxic shock to the brain'.

Preconceptual care

From the above description, it can be seen that important developmental milestones are reached very early in the embryonic period. At this early stage, the embryo is vulnerable to harm from a variety of sources, yet many women are unaware that they are pregnant when this crucial stage of development is occurring.

There are many interrelated factors that influence health in the newborn, including genetic factors, environmental factors and maternal health. Recent research from the Center for the Developing Child has established the importance of good foundations for the architecture of the brain and principles of care emphasised in recommendations 'Preparing for Birth and Beyond' (see Department of Health, 2011b). To be effective, this approach requires recognition of the complex links between health and social care and the need for interprofessional working, and in the UK this requirement is reflected in the expansion of training for early years professionals.

Widening the provision of preconception care could optimise the health status of child-bearing women through both risk assessment and health promotion strategies to ensure that women are fit to conceive, thereby minimising adverse health consequences for themselves during pregnancy and for the short- and long-term health outcomes for the child. The principle of preconceptional care does require pregnancy to be planned, as well as a strategy to improve the overall health and well-being of child-bearing women, for example, an overall reduction in obesity and the promotion of mental health. The commissioning of care to provide women with opportunities for preconceptual health checks and education at regular intervals from the age of 16 until women choose to 'opt out' may derive both health and social care benefits, with resultant financial benefits. Such a strategy would promote and normalise such health-seeking behaviour rather than leaving it to chance or the domain of more health-motivated couples with higher socio-economic status.

Health centres, including practice nurses and general practitioners, can provide specific advice for women with pre-existing medical conditions, such as diabetes, epilepsy or mental health problems, to ensure stability in their condition with minimal medication or a switch to non-teratogenic prescribing in preparation for conception. Genetic counselling, for individuals with a family history of genetic disorder, provides information about the level of risk, as well as discussing the options open to parents and providing support for couples through the choices they make as a result of being given information. Greater recognition of the potential father's health and life-style habits are also needed, and efforts made to engage him with his partner in positive life-style changes. Smoking cessation and dietary changes are difficult to achieve if the partner does not make a commitment to change as well (Moos, 2004).

However, challenges to comprehensive preconceptual care remain. The difficulties, mainly in engaging families, particularly those from lower socio-economic groups, teenagers and immigrants, can hamper attempts to break the cycle of deprivation. For preconception care to be effective, it needs to be readily accessible and sensitive to the needs of the local population and acceptable to the wide range of religious and cultural groups within contemporary society. The use of health promotion models such as that proposed by Prochaska and DiClemente (1983) to affect behaviour change and motivational interviewing (Rubak et al., 2005) may support the adoption of health care advice and behaviour change. Advice should be non-judgemental and non-directive, so that reproductive decisions are taken by the woman or couple, and not by the healthcare professional. Equally, it should be recognised that preconceptionual care has not failed if the clients do not act on the advice that they receive.

Preconceptual care is, therefore, vitally important. The interaction of genetic and environmental influences on healthy growth and development is well recognised and any determinants of fetal growth are established prior to pregnancy, during the immediate periconceptual period. A woman's nutritional status at the start of pregnancy can determine her ability to meet the needs of the foetus from dietary intake and tissue nutrient reserves. Low maternal status for some micronutrients has characteristic effects, for example folate may increase the risk of congenital anomaly, and for vitamin D an increase in neonatal rickets. Deficits or restriction in maternal nutrient supply will have the greatest impact during high velocity growth and development between conception and two years. As development occurs in an ordered sequence, certain organs and tissues are most vulnerable to nutrient restriction at different times, known as 'critical periods', which can result in irreversible alteration to organ and tissue architecture and function (SACN, 2011).

In the UK, the widespread promotion of folic acid supplementation of 400 µg/day (5 mg/day for women with a previous history of neural tube defect, diabetes, antiepileptic medication and multiple pregnancy), prior to conception for three months and the following three months has demonstrated a reduction in neural tube anomalies (NICE, 2008b). Many women, however, remain unaware of other screening procedures and behaviour modification that would optimise their health for pregnancy and that of their baby. Most environmental hazards, such as lead or mercury exposure, are at their most dangerous when cell division in the embryo is most rapid. By the end of the embryological phase of development, most major structural anomalies that could affect the foetus are already determined (Moos, 2004). A major challenge, therefore, is to provide education in the period before conception, when prospective parents can be offered a series of options that may not be available once pregnancy is confirmed.

Health compromising behaviours like smoking, alcohol use and illicit drug intake can increase the risk of preterm birth; when all three behaviours are combined, it has been associated with a 31 per cent preterm birth rate (Dew *et al.*, 2007). Illicit drug use, such as cocaine, heroin, ketamine and cannabis, may have adverse effects on neonatal growth and neurobehavioural status, though the exclusion of other confounding variables, such as alcohol abuse, smoking, prematurity, socio-economic deprivation and infectious disease associated with lifestyle can make interpretation of precise effects difficult (Klee *et al.*, 2002). There are significant risks to the health and indeed life of a baby if the mother smokes. These include the risk of miscarriage, premature birth and stillbirth, placental abnormalities, low birth weight and, after birth, sudden infant death. A safe level of alcohol intake to prevent any adverse effects on brain development has not yet been established (Tough *et al.*, 2006; NSCDC, 2008; APHO, 2010), so a reduction from the limit of 14 units per week for women towards abstinence is encouraged. Posner *et al.* (2006) and Atrash *et al.* (2006) identify strategies to improve perinatal outcomes through preconception care and Table 2.1 details screening and advice offered to women. The Cochrane Review (Anderson *et al.*, 2010) on preconception life-style advice for people with subfertility reaffirms principles for application to the wider population.

Table 2.1 Summary of pre-conceptual and antenatal advice and care

Topic	Pre-conceptual	Antenatal	Rationale	References
Immunisations	Check rubella status, varicella (chicken pox) and hepatitis B. Immunise if required, avoid pregnancy for three months following immunisation	Check rubella status, for postnatal immunisation if no antibodies. Screening for hepatitis B	The infections of rubella, varicella, hepatitis B, HIV and others can all cross the placenta. Therefore they can infect the foetus or they have teratogenic (harmful) effects including blindness, deafness and others. Prevention is the best treatment	NICE, 2008b
Infectious diseases	Screen for chlamydia trachomatis if <25	Screen for HIV and syphilis and hepatitis B	Treatment of infections reduces the risk of effects on the mother and foetus	NICE, 2008b

(Continued)

Topic	Pre-conceptual	Antenatal	Rationale	References
	Full sexual health screen if woman's request or symptomatic (chlamydia, gonorrhoea, syphilis, HIV, hepatitis B, trichomonas vaginalis, bacteria vaginosis	Chlamydia if woman under 25 years only		
	Toxoplasmosis, cytomegaloviruses	Give advice on toxoplasmosis reduction, hand hygiene prior to preparing food, wear gloves while gardening, wash vegetables, fruit and salad well, avoid cat litter trays or faeces		
Clinical (medical) conditions	Diabetes and epilepsy most frequently associated with poor neonatal outcomes. Pre-conceptual care a priority, altering medicines management may be required. Measurement of HbA1c level for diabetic women	If no pre-existing medical conditions, screen in pregnancy for gestational diabetes, raised blood pressure and pre-eclampsia. Three extra screenings for retinopathy during pregnancy if diabetic	Treatment and additional antenatal care can be tailored to needs in pregnancy	NICE, 2008b
Alcohol intake	To reduce and stop if possible	Avoid drinking alcohol in the first three months of pregnancy. If women choose to drink, no more than 1–2 units once or twice per week. Getting drunk or binge drinking (7.5 units on one occasion) may be harmful to the baby	Risk of fetal alcohol syndrome disorders, including alteration to brain architecture	(NICE, 2008b, NICE, 2010a; Tough *et al.*, 2006)

(Continued)

New beginnings: factors affecting health and well-being in the neonate

(Continued)

Topic	Pre-conceptual	Antenatal	Rationale	References
Smoking	To reduce and stop if possible	Offer individualised smoking cessation programme	A large, rigorous, systematic review concluded that maternal smoking has been attributed to cardiovascular, musculoskeletal and gastrointestinal and facial defects in the developing foetus	NICE, 2010c; Hackshaw et al., 2011
Illicit drug use including cocaine, heroin/ methadone, amphetamines, ketamine and cannabis	Reduce or stop if possible	As pre-conceptual advice	Cannabis is associated with smoking which has detrimental effects on the foetus, discourage women from using cannabis in pregnancy	NICE, 2010a
Prescribed medicines	Medical assessment to determine continued necessity, switch to less teratogenic medicines		Few medicines have been established as safe in pregnancy, limit use to where the benefit outweighs the risk	
Environmental and occupational exposures and teratogens	Mercury and lead: avoid certain fish in diet. Dioxins: reduce dietary fat. Fluoride	As pre-conceptual advice	High fluoride levels have possible adverse effect on children's neurodevelopment	Lu et al., 2006; Choi et al., 2012
Folic acid	400 µg per day 3 months before conception. If obese with a BMI >30, diabetic, epileptic, multiple pregnancy, previous neural tube defect, 5 mg per day at least one month prior to conception	400 µg folic acid supplementation per day until 12 weeks' gestation. If BMI >30, the dose is 5 mg per day. Eat food rich in folate, such as green leafy vegetables, beans, peas, breakfast cereals (these are fortified)	Prevents neural tube defects, such as spina bifida, congenital defects, cleft lip and palates. Neural tube forms on day 26–28 after conception	Wilcox et al., 2007; Wilson et al., 2007; Rasmussen et al., 2008; NHS Choices, 2012
Vitamin A	Avoid vitamin A intakes above 700 µg	As before, foods with high vitamin A, such as liver products, should be avoided	High levels of vitamin A are potentially teratogenic to the developing foetus	RCOG, 2009

(Continued)

(Continued)

Topic	Pre-conceptual	Antenatal	Rationale	References
Vitamin D	Commence vitamin D supplementation 10 µg before or during pregnancy, if women are obese with a BMI >30, women from black and ethnic minorities, women who are socially excluded, women with limited exposure to sunlight, especially those who are housebound	Vitamin D supplementation 10 µg per day as previous	Sunshine is the main source of vitamin D, those with darker skins and who spend long time indoors or covered are at risk of deficiency. This can lead to infantile rickets	NICE, 2008c; RCOG, 2009; CMACE/ RCOG, 2010
Vitamin K	No pre-conceptual care, but advice as antenatal care	Discuss this with women as this supplementation is offered to the neonate following birth	To prevent haemorrhagic disease of the newborn (bleeding). Vitamin K helps clot blood	RCOG, 2009
Diet	Advise client on diet, nutrition and exercise. Achieve BMI in range 20–25	Advise women about food-acquired infections, such as listeriosis and salmonella	Weight management before, during and after pregnancy has significant effects on the developing foetus and the nutritional habits of the family will affect their health. Promote nutritional well-being for optimal family health	NICE, 2008a; NICE, 2008c; NICE, 2010b; NICE, 2010d; CMACE, 2011a
Mental health	Provide care and appropriate referral for improvement, monitor medication and aim to reduce	As pre-conceptual care	Pre-existing mental health conditions are more likely to re-occur	(NICE, 2007; CMACE, 2011a)
Complex social needs	Identify women in this group: asylum seekers, experience domestic abuse, whose first language is not English and women under 20 years	Identify to offer additional support	These groups of women do not always access antenatal care, or their first appointment is later than recommended, (ideally by 10 weeks), therefore a different model of antenatal care is required to meet their needs	NICE, 2010a; CMACE, 2011a

What strategies would you utilise to help a friend adopt the principles of preconceptual care?

Antenatal care

Antenatal care was first introduced in 1915 as a means of improving the health of the mother and the developing foetus. The broad aims of antenatal care are to promote fetal and maternal well-being, to detect and treat deviations from normal, and to prepare the woman and her partner for labour and parenthood. The National Institute for Health and Clinical Excellence offers guidance on antenatal care for women experiencing routine pregnancies and those with complex social needs (NICE, 2008b; NICE, 2010a). The evidence for antenatal care for each of these groups of women is based on cost efficacy, tailoring resources, such as midwifery time, to measurable benefits in maternal and fetal outcomes. Identifying the at-risk cases for whom more supervision is required is a more realistic and valuable use of resources. It is also recognised that antenatal care alone is insufficient to override the problems caused by social deprivation. To make the service more flexible, accessible and appropriate for all women the National Service Framework for Children, Young People and Maternity Services set out a ten-year development plan to improve the services to children, including maternity care (DH/DFeS, 2004). This was subsequently updated (Department of Health, 2007b).

During pregnancy, as well as preconceptually, maternal screening tests and health promotion advice is offered. These aspects of care have been summarised in Table 2.1. In addition to asking whether a woman smokes, in order to promote health by offering a smoking cessation programme, or screening for pre-existing mental health, pregnancy specific and fetal screening is also offered.

Screening during pregnancy

Routinely during pregnancy maternal observations of blood pressure, urinalysis and measurement of the growing uterus, by symphisus fundal height (SFH) are undertaken. They are also indicators of when pregnancy may need extra surveillance or referring to an obstetrician for further tests. Increased maternal blood pressure accompanied by protein in the urine is an indicator of pre-eclampsia; this may impact upon the developing foetus and necessitate pre-term birth. Reduced or increased SFH measurements may also alert midwives to pregnancy issues (Hargreaves *et al.*, 2011). Thus pregnancy observations are a screening tool, instigated to reassure, but they are also indicators of deviations from a normal physiological process, that may need treatment, including early delivery, to maintain the health of the baby.

Specific screening tests are offered to all women during pregnancy. These include sickle cell and thalassaemia screening in early pregnancy, to detect both carriers of the disorder and people with the condition (UKNSC, 2011). Screening for infections, including HIV, hepatitis B and syphilis (detailed in Table 2.1) are offered to detect infections and plan appropriate treatment that minimises the effects of such infections on the mother and reduces transmission to the foetus.

Fetal screening is offered on three occasions in pregnancy: first, an early ultrasound scan from 11 to 14 weeks, second, blood testing from 10 to 20 weeks and finally a further ultrasound scan at 20 weeks' gestation. The first scan is used to confirm the pregnancy duration. It can also detect major structural defects in the developing foetus; however, it is also designed to ensure accuracy of the Down's syndrome screening test. The second of the screening tests, a blood test, is used to detect foetuses at risk of being affected by Down's syndrome (UKNSC, 2011). This is one of the tests where treatment is not available, since the foetus is either affected or not by this condition. What screening in this case offers is parental preparation and choice. The choice is whether to continue with the pregnancy or not and termination of pregnancy for fetal anomalies is offered for this as well as other conditions. The mid-pregnancy (20 week) ultrasound screening offers parents the opportunity to consent to a screening test that detects many congenital structural conditions, such as anencephaly, diaphragmatic hernias and abdominal wall defects. Some of these, such as cleft lip and palate or cardiac defects, can be treated by surgery but not all are detected through ultrasound. Diagnosis can facilitate preparation as to the most suitable place of birth, perhaps a tertiary centre that specialises in neonatal surgery. Most ultrasound scans (95 per cent) show that the foetus is developing normally, because most babies are healthy (UKNSC, 2011). It is also an opportunity for the prospective parents to visualise their unborn child.

The antenatal period, in addition to screening of the mother, pregnancy and foetus, is also a time for parenthood education. This education can assist in the transition to parenthood and preparation for birth.

Influences of birth on neonatal health

Birth should occur between 38 and 42 weeks of pregnancy. Preterm birth occurring before this time can place significant burdens on optimal health for the baby (Table 2.2), and the

Table 2.2 Possible neonatal consequences from birth experience

Preterm birth	The shorter the pregnancy gestation, the greater incidence of intracranial haemorrhage, respiratory distress leading to bronchopulmonary dysplasia, hypoglycaemia, hypocalcaemia, hypothermia, infection, necrotising enterocolitis, jaundice, retinal damage leading to blindness (retrolental fibroplasia) and developmental delay
Birth trauma	Resulting from difficult births, for example intracranial damage resulting from a rapid or poorly controlled delivery of the fetal head, a sternomastoid tumour – muscle damage to the neck during delivery, brachial nerve damage resulting in Erb's palsy following difficulty in delivery of the shoulders, soft tissue damage during a breech delivery or induced trauma during an operative birth, forceps or Ventouse delivery
Birth asphyxia	Regular and careful monitoring of fetal condition is imperative during labour to prevent asphyxia. The condition of the baby is still assessed by means of the Apgar score and cord blood gas measurement for oxygen, carbon dioxide and bicarbonate levels. Babies with an Apgar score below 3 will require greater surveillance during childhood to ensure developmental milestones are reached
Birthweight	Over 4.5 kg – large babies may be as a result of poor maternal glucose regulation during pregnancy. These babies are at risk of hypoglycaemia following birth and may have had a greater risk of birth trauma
	<10th centile for gestational age – these small-for-gestational-age babies are at risk of hypothermia, jaundice, hypocalcaemia, hypomagnesia and developmental delay depending upon severity

shorter the pregnancy gestation, the greater the morbidity and mortality likely to be incurred (Costeloe *et al.*, 2000; CMACE, 2011b). Viability of pregnancy is still defined as 24 weeks of pregnancy in the UK (Department of Health, 1990), although survival is possible for a small minority of babies born before this gestation (Costeloe *et al.*, 2000). This notion of *viability* though is problematic when viewed through a rights lens and is discussed further in the final chapter on children's rights. A WHO report, *Born too Soon* (Howson *et al.*, 2012) postulates that the reasons for the increasing number of global pre-term birth rates include increasing maternal age, chronic maternal health prior to pregnancy, fertility treatments, maternal nutritional deficiencies and infections. It is the responsibility of midwives and obstetricians to plan birth in the appropriate environment according to both maternal and fetal well-being.

Breast feeding

The benefits of breast feeding are well established to confer long-term health benefits for the child (UNICEF, 2012). The type of feeding in infancy can affect growth rate and type of tissue deposited, with growth patterns in breast-fed babies adopted as desirable (SACN, 2011). Breast feeding has also been shown to aid cognitive development (Borra *et al.*, 2012). Initiation of lactation within six hours of birth can reduce the incidence of necrotising enterocolitis among preterm infants. To improve breast feeding rates in the UK, current strategies include raising the rates of and monitoring including:

- breast feeding initiation rate
- breast feeding prevalence at 6–8 weeks
- prevalence of exclusive breast feeding at four months
- percentage of exclusive breast feeding at discharge from neonatal units (Department of Health, 2010).

Learning activity

Find out about what methods have been used to increase the initiation and continuation of breast feeding among teenage mothers.

Postnatal care

During the postnatal period, there are opportunities to teach parents about caring for their babies, including advice on infant feeding, how to recognise if the baby is well and thriving and how and when to seek help, if required. For early years professionals, it is important that support for parents during the neonatal period is directed towards enabling and empowering parents to provide optimum care for their newborn baby. The philosophy of postnatal care is to offer family-centred care (Beckett and Colgan, 2011) and to this end the number of postnatal visits across the UK varies as care should be tailored to the individualised woman's needs (NMC, 2004).

After the baby is born, postnatal care rests on four aspects: two of which are most pertinent to the neonate, i.e. infant feeding and maintaining infant health (NICE, 2006). Parents need knowledge to care for their infant, to promote neonatal well-being and recognise common health problems in their baby. This information is provided by midwives, health visitors and other early years professionals. It is also reiterated in the Department of Health book *Birth to Five* which every prospective parent in the UK is given (Department of Health, 2009). It is very important that postnatal women are asked about their emotional well-being and social support and midwives, health visitors and early years professionals are able to offer parents advice and support on their baby's social capabilities to promote parent–baby attachment (NICE, 2006). The period following birth also offers opportunities to screen the newborn for a variety of disorders and to instigate treatment at an early stage in order to reduce or prevent the potential for harm (UKNSC, 2011).

The UK National Screening Committee (UKNSC, 2011) advocates screening for five congenital conditions (see Table 2.3). This screening is undertaken on day 5–8 following birth and a blood sample is obtained by the midwife via a heel prick, with parental consent. Today, newborn screening is one of the largest screening programmes in the UK and each year over 700 000 newborns are screened. The newborn blood spot screening programme has been, and remains, a very successful screening programme and the uptake of screening tests is high with local figures showing that more than 99 per cent of the babies born each year are being screened. Most babies screened will not have any of the conditions but, for the small numbers that do, the benefits of screening are enormous and a shift from sickness

Table 2.3 Newborn screening programme

Test	Population	Condition and treatment
Congenital hypothyroidism	1 in 4000 UK babies affected	Babies born without enough thyroxine, which is needed for optimal physical and mental development, if detected supplementation of thyroxine enables normal development
Cystic fibrosis	1 in 2500 UK affected babies	Inherited condition which affects the lungs and digestion. Treatment includes high energy diet, chest physiotherapy and medicines
MCADD (medium-chain acyl-CoA dehydrogenase deficiency)	1 in 10 000 UK babies affected	Inherited condition in which babies are unable to break down fat for energy. Regular feeding of special diet required
PKU (phenylketonuria)	1 in 10 000 UK babies affected	Inherited condition where babies cannot process phenylalanine (an amino acid). If untreated, serious mental disability will occur. Treatment is via a special diet that enables babies to thrive and prevents ill effects
Sickle cell disease	1 in 2000 UK babies affected	Disorder of the red blood cells, which transport oxygen around the body. Crises occur when blood cells clump together, causing pain and reduced oxygen and damage to body cells. Treatment includes parental education and prevention of infections with antibiotics. This promotes optimal health

to health can be achieved. Early treatment can improve their health and prevent severe disability or even death.

This is the end of the screening process for the neonate. Care of the family typically transfers to the health visitor between postnatal days 10 and 28. Further screening and development checks, such as hearing and another physical examination of the baby, will occur, with parental consent, at 5 and 8 weeks.

Neonatal mortality

The impact on mothers and their families of having a stillborn baby or death in the first week of life (perinatal mortality) is a tragedy that cannot be overestimated. While the rate of stillbirths and neonatal deaths (deaths in the first four weeks of life following a live birth) has declined significantly in the last 40 years, including the last decade, the rates remain higher in younger women, <25 and over 40 year olds. Having a body mass index (BMI) over 35 (5 per cent of pregnant population) accounted for 10 per cent of perinatal deaths (CMACE, 2010). Women experiencing more socio-economic deprivation and those from Black ethnic origin and to a lesser extent Asian mothers suffer increased rates, though racial differences may reflect confounding variables (CMACE, 2011a). The importance of managing pre-existing medical conditions prior to conception and by booking for antenatal care by 10–12 weeks (Department of Health, 2007a) is emphasised by the increase in stillbirths due to psychiatric disorders, diabetes and endocrine disorders, and neonatal deaths associated with psychiatric disorder, cardiac disease, previous pregnancy problems, for example three or more miscarriages or previous neonatal death (CMACE, 2011b). While the prevalence of smoking and alcohol and substance abuse in the general pregnant population is difficult to measure, there is an increased incidence of neonatal mortality. Babies of multiple pregnancy are at increased risk associated with prematurity, low birth weight and twin specific complications (Garite *et al.*, 2004; Garne and Andersen, 2004). These have shown some reduction with improved neonatal facilities, the use of more advanced technology in monitoring and treatment and policy change on egg replacement for assisted conception. While mortality is measurable, morbidity can be more covert but have a continuing impact on maternal, infant and family well-being.

Conclusion

As stated earlier, the period surrounding birth is important not only in relation to the health of the newborn baby, but also promoting health in later life. The promotion of health begins before we are born, and subsequently it is within the family that the first messages about health are given. The midwife has the opportunity to reinforce positive health messages.

While this may be an aspect for the early years professional to consider, it is also important that there is understanding of the early holistic influences on the children in their care. This understanding may then lead to greater insight into meeting the needs of children who have a congenital abnormality, those who have been born prematurely or of low birth weight, or have been born into poor socio-economic conditions. There are a range of opportunities for healthcare professionals, early years professionals and parents to work in collaboration to provide accessible services to optimise the health and well-being of the newborn.

The salutogenic framework will aid the development of a framework for health promotion; stimulate a culture for change with recognition of the value of optimal health to the individual, to the family and society. A consequence will be reduced health and social care costs. Midwives play a crucial role in improving health and reducing health inequalities as they work with women throughout the pregnancy and after birth. They have the opportunity to raise awareness of lifestyle factors for mothers themselves, their partners and children, which can have a lifelong impact on the health and well-being of their family (Midwifery, 2010).

Learning activity

There is more information and support for parents and early years professionals on the following websites. Access some of these resources to consolidate your learning throughout this chapter:

- The Harvard website Center on the Developing Child: http://developingchild.harvard.edu
- The Department of Health website offers guidance and support to professionals such as Starting Well and Preparing for Birth and Beyond resources: http://www.dh.gov.uk/health/category/starting/; http://www.dh.gov.uk/health/2011/10/preparation-for-birth-and-beyond-resource-pack-to-help-parenthood-groups/

Evaluate your learning

- Discuss the ethical implications for parents and professionals if parents decline advice and screening to promote the health of the newborn.
- To what extent can you develop a salutogenic approach within your practice?

References

Agopian, AJ, Lupo, PJ, Herdt-Losavio, ML, Langlois, PH, Rocheleau, CM and Mitchell, LE (in press): Differences in folic acid use, prenatal care, smoking, and drinking in early pregnancy by occupation. *Preventive Medicine.*

Anderson, K, Norman, R and Middleton, P (2010): Preconception lifestyle advice for people with subfertility. *Cochrane Database of Systematic Reviews* **14**(4), CD008189.

Antonovsky, A (1979): *Health, Stress and Coping.* San Francisco: Jossey-Bass Publishers.

APHO (2010): Smoking in pregnancy 2008/09. In *Health Profiles.* APHO, Association of Public Health Observatories.

Atrash, H, Johnson, K, Adams, M, Cordero, JF and Howse, J (2006): Preconception care for improving perinal outcomes: the time to act. *Maternal and Child Health Journal* **10**(1) 3–11.

Beckett, R and Colgan, G (2011): Family-centred postnatal care. *MIDIRS Midwifery Digest* **21**(1), 77–82.

Borra, C, Iacovou, M and Sevilla-Sanz, A (2012): The effect of breastfeeding on children's cognitive and noncognitive development. *Labour Economics* **19**(4), 496–515.

Carey, N (2012): *The Epigenetics Revolution: How Modern Biology is Rewriting Our Understanding of Genetics, Disease and Inheritance.* London: Icon Books.

CDC (2007a): The Science of Early Childhood Development. Harvard University. (Online). Last accessed 26 March 2012. Available from: www.developingchild.net.

CDC (2007b): A science-based framework for early childhood policy: using evidence to improve outcomes in learning, behavior and health for vulnerable children. (Online). Last accessed 26 March 2012. Available from: www.developingchild.harvard.edu.

CDC (2011): Building the brain's air traffic control system: how early experiences shape the development of executive function. *Working Paper No 11.* (Online). Last accessed 26 March 2012. Available from: www.developingchild.harvard.edu.

Choi, AL, Sun, G, Zhang, Y and Grandjean, P (2012): Developmental fluoride neurotoxicity: a systematic review and meta-analysis. *Environmental Health Perspectives* **120**, 1362–68.

CMACE (2010): *Maternal Obesity in the UK: Findings from a National Project.* London: Centre for Maternal and Child Health.

CMACE (2011a): Saving Mothers Lives: reviewing maternal deaths to make motherhood safer: 2006–08, The Eighth Report on Confidential Enquiries into Maternal Deaths in the United Kingdom. *BJOG* **118**(1), 1–203.

CMACE (2011b): Perinatal mortality 2009 United Kingdom. London: CMACE (Online). Last accessed 12 August 2012. Available from: http://data.parliament.uk/DepositedPapers/Files/DEP2012-1207/HL1520-HL1521-LibDoc.pdf

CMACE/RCOG (2010): *Joint Guideline on Management of Women with Obesity in Pregnancy.* London: CMACE/RCOG.

Costeloe, K, Hennessy, E, Gibson, A, Marlow, N and Wilkinson, A (2000) The EPICure Study: Outcomes to discharge from hospital for infants born at the threshold of viability. *Pediatrics* **106**(4), 659–71.

Department of Health (1990): *Human Embryology and Fertilisation Act.* London: Crown Copyright.

Department of Health (2007a): *Maternity Matters: Choice Access and Continuity of Care in a Safe Service.* London: Department of Health.

Department of Health (2007b): National service framework for children and young people and maternity services. *Standard 6: Pre-conceptual Care.* London: The Stationery Office.

Department of Health (2009): *Birth to Five.* London: Department of Health.

Department of Health (2010): *Healthy Lives, Healthy People: Our Strategy for Public Health in England.* London: The Stationery Office.

Department of Health (2011a): *No Health Without Mental Health: Delivering Better Mental Health Outcomes for People of All Ages.* London: The Stationery Office.

Department of Health (2011b): *Preparing for Birth and Beyond*. London: Department of Health.

Dew, P, Guillory, J, Okah, FA, Cai, J and Hoff, GL (2007): The effect of health compromising behaviors on preterm births. *Maternal and Child Health Journal* **11**(3), 227–33.

DH/DFeS (2004): *National Service Framework for Children, Young People and Maternity Services*. London: Department of Health/Department for Education and Skills.

Downe, S (2008): *Normal Childbirth Evidence and Debate*. London: Elsevier.

Garite, T, Clark, R, Elliott, J and Thorp, J (2004): Twins and triplets: the effect of plurality and growth on neonatal outcome compared with singleton infants. *American Journal of Obstetrics and Gynecology* **191**(3), 700–07.

Garne, E and Andersen, H (2004): The impact of multiple pregnancies and malformations on perinatal mortality. *Journal of Perinatal Medicine* **32**(3), 215–19.

Hackshaw, A, Rodeck, C and Boniface, S (2011): Maternal smoking in pregnancy and birth defects; a systematic review based on 173 687 malformed cases and 11.7 million controls. *Human Reproductive Update* **17**(5), 589–604.

Hargreaves, K, Cameron, M, Edwards, H, Gray, R and Deane, K (2011): Is the use of symphysis-fundal height measurement and ultrasound examination effective in detecting small or large foetuses? *Journal of Obstetrics and Gynaecology* **31**(5), 380–83.

HGP (nd) (Online). Last accessed 16 August 2012. Available from: www.ornl.gov/sci/techresources/Human_Genome/home.shtml.

Howson, CP, Kinney, MV and Lawn, JE (2012): *March of Dimes, PMNCH, Save the Children, WHO. Born Too Soon: The Global Action Report on Preterm Birth*. Geneva: World Health Organization.

Klee, H, Jackson, M and Lewis, S (2002): *Drug Misuse and Motherhood*. London: Routledge.

Lu, M, Kotelchuck, M, Culhane, F, Hobel, C, Klerman, L and Thorp, J (2006): Preconception care between pregnancies: the content of internatal care. *Maternal Child Health Journal* **10**, S107–22.

Marmot, M (2010): Fair society, healthy lives: strategic review of health inequalities in England post-2010. *The Marmot Review*. London: Department of Health.

Marmot, M and Wilkinson, R (2006): *Social Determinants of Health*, 2nd edn. Oxford: Oxford University Press.

Midwifery (2010): *Core Role of the Midwife Workstream Final Report*. London: Midwifery 2020.

Moore, KL and Persaud, TVN (2003): *The Developing Human: Clinically Oriented Embryology*, 6th edn. Philadelphia: Saunders.

Moos, M (2004): Preconceptual health promotion: progress in changing a prevention paradigm. *Journal of Perinatal and Neonatal Nursing* **18**(1), 2–14.

NHSChoices (2012): (Online). Last accessed 16 August 2012. Available from: www.nhs.uk/conditions/pregnancy-and-baby/pages/vitamins-minerals-supplements-pregnant.aspx.

NICE (2006): *Routine Postnatal Care of Women and their Babies*. London: National Institute for Health and Clinical Excellence.

NICE (2007): *Antenatal and Postnatal Mental Health*. London: NICE.

NICE (2008a): *Maternal and Child Nutrition*. London: NICE.

NICE (2008b): *Antenatal Care Routine Care for the Healthy Pregnant Woman.* London: RCOG Press.

NICE (2008c): *Improving the Nutrition of Pregnant and Breastfeeding Mothers and Children in Low-income Households.* London: National Institute for Health and Clinical Excellence.

NICE (2010a): *Pregnancy and Complex Social Factors.* London: National Institute for Health and Clinical Excellence.

NICE (2010b): *Dietary Interventions and Physical Activity Interventions for Weight Management Before, During and After Pregnancy.* London: NICE.

NICE (2010c): *Quitting Smoking in Pregnancy and Following Childbirth.* London: NICE.

NICE (2010d): *Weight Management Before, During and After Pregnancy.* London: NICE.

NMC (2004): *Midwives Rules and Standards.* London: NMC.

NSCDC (2005): Excessive stress disrupts the architecture of the developing brain. *Working Paper 3.* (Online). Last accessed 26 March 2012. Available from: www.developingchild. net.

NSCDC (2008): *Scientific Paper: Even Low Levels of Alcohol During Pregnancy Can Affect Fetal Brain Development.* (Online). Last accessed 8 April 2012. Available from: www .developingchild.net.

Posner, S, Johnson, K, Parker, C, Atrash, H and Biermann, J (2006): The national summit on preconception care: a summary of concepts and recommendations. *Maternal and Child Health Journal* **10**, S197–205.

Price, S (ed) (2007): *Mental Health in Pregnancy and Childbirth.* Edinburgh: Elsevier.

Prochaska, J and DiClemente, C (1983): Stages and processes of self-change of smoking: toward an integrative model of change. *Journal of Consulting and Clinical Psychology* **51**(3), 390–95.

Rasmussen, S, Chu, S, Kim, S, Schmid, C and Lau, J (2008): Maternal obesity and risk of neural tube defects. *American Journal of Obstetrics and Gynecology* **198**(6), 611–19.

RCOG (2009): Vitamin supplementation in pregnancy. *Occasional Paper 16.* London: Scientific Advisory Committee.

Rubak, S, Sandbæk, A, Lauritzen, T and Christensen, B (2005): Motivational interviewing: a systematic review and meta-analysis. *British Journal of General Practice* **55**(513), 305–12.

SACN (2011): *The Influence of Maternal, Fetal and Child Nutrition in the Development of Disease in Later Life.* London: TSO. (Online). Last accessed 12 August 2012. Available from: www.sacn.gov.uk.

Tough, S, Tofflemire, K, Clarke, M and Newburn-Cook, C (2006): Do women change their drinking behaviors while trying to conceive? An opportunity for preceception counseling. *Clinical Medicine and Research* **4**(2), 97–105.

UKNSC (2011): *Screening Tests for You and Your Baby.* London: UK National Screening Committee.

UNICEF (2012): Breast feeding research. (Online). Last accessed 30 July 2012. Available from: www.unicef.org.uk/BabyFriendly/News-and-Research/Research/Breastfeeding-research---An-overview/.

WellcomeTrust (nd) (Online). Last accessed 16 August 2012. Available from: www .wellcome.ac.uk/Our-vision/Research-challenges/Genetics-and-genomics/index.htm?gclid =CIOUo43767ECFVMdtAodRjUAFA.

World Health Organization (1946): Preamble to the Constitution of the World Health Organization as adopted by the International Health Conference, New York, 19–22 June, 1946; signed on 22 July 1946 by the representatives of 61 States (Official Records of the World Health Organization, no. 2, p. 100) and entered into force on 7 April 1948.

Wilcox, A, Lie, R, Solvoll, K, Taylor, J, McConnaughey, D, Abyholm, F, Vindenes, H, Vollset, S and Drevon, C (2007): Folic acid supplements and risk of facial clefts: national population based case-control study. *British Medical Journal* **334**(7591), 464.

Wilson, R, Johnson, J, Wyatt, P, Allen, V, Gangon, A, Langlois, S, Blight, C, Audibert, F, Desilets, V, Brock, J, Koren, G, Goh, Y, Nguyen, P and Kapur, B (2007): Genetics Committee of the Society of Obstetricians and Gynaecologists of Canada and The Motherrisk Program. Pre-conceptional vitamin/folic acid supplementation 2007: the use of folic acid in combination with a multivitamin supplement for the prevention of neural tube defects and other congenital anomalies. *Journal of Obstetrics and Gynaecology Canada* **29**, 1003–26.

3   Embodied childhoods

Jessica Clark

This chapter aims to:
- describe some of the key processes of children's physical growth and development in early childhood
- critically evaluate the dominance of developmental and biological models in understanding children's bodies
- consider the role of culture, society and discourse in young children's embodied everyday lives, while acknowledging young children's potential for embodied agency.

Introduction

The dominant perspective in childhood studies, notably early years care and education, has been to consider that there are universal rules and patterns in the progression of all children that can be discovered, described and understood. Starting in pregnancy (as outlined in the previous chapter), taxonomies of norms, milestones and stages that the majority of children are likely to reach by a certain age or point in growth are used as guidelines for practitioners to ascertain an individual child's developmental progress. The discipline of psychology, notably the areas of developmental psychology and psychoanalysis, has been influential in encouraging the view that experiences in childhood have a profound and long-term impact on individuals into adulthood. It is argued that, in order to enable early intervention, those working with young children should have knowledge of what a child should be doing and/or physically look like at a particular age or stage in their development.

As such, this chapter continues the discussion in Chapter 2 and begins by exploring physical growth in babies and infants, describing why and how this is monitored; then moves on to discuss the development of physical competencies in young children. These explorations are illustrated by examples frequently discussed both by professionals and within popular culture, including the breast- and bottle-feeding debate, physical activity and outdoor play, and childhood obesity. The second part of the chapter then turns to a set of discussions which advocate moving understanding of children's bodies beyond a vessel for the mind and outside of the boundaries of biology and health to consider the impact of socio-cultural influences. Here, readers will be encouraged to critically evaluate the socially constructed nature of both childhood and children's bodies, how children learn to present and use their bodies in '(in)appropriate' ways and how these bodies are simultaneously cared for and controlled through monitoring and surveillance. The examples of gender, disability and obesity, within this section, provide an opportunity to explore the themes above in relation to specific topics.

However, before the 'stage' approach to understanding young children's bodies can be critically evaluated it is important to first understand the basis for such unidirectional maturation models and their use in practice.

Physical growth and development monitoring

It is so often one of the first questions families will be asked of their newborn child – how much does he/she weigh? Regular weighing and monitoring of a child's weight has become an integral part of discussions surrounding 'good parenting' and health professionals spend a great deal of time measuring children, including weight, length and head circumference, comparing these to established norms for a child of that particular age. Screening can facilitate early intervention in potential health problems and the careful collection of physical growth measurements, when plotted onto a centile chart, can allow for early detection of conditions such as coeliac disease.

The centile chart

A centile chart is a device based on a bell curve or distribution which represent boundaries of 'normal' height, weight and head circumference across a population. Charts have historically been based on cross-sectional measurements of large groups of infants and children in the indigenous UK population. Current charts have been developed by the World Health Organization (WHO) using child growth standards and UK90 data for healthy, breast-fed children. These charts differ in that they aim to demonstrate optimal growth rather than average and are based on measurements from children in favourable economic circumstances, carried to term, breast-fed for four months exclusively and with non-smoking mothers. After 15 years of data collection in five countries, WHO published global charts in 2006, recommended for adoption in the UK by the Scientific Advisory Committee on Nutrition (SACN). UK charts were commissioned from the Royal College of Paediatrics and Child Health (RCPCH) to be used in the UK with children born after May 2009 (see the male and female UK-WHO centile charts for children 0–4 years, available at http://www.rcpch.ac.uk/child-health/research-projects/uk-who-growth-charts/uk-who-growth-chart-resources-0-4-years/uk-who-0).

There are critiques which can be levelled at the development of new centile charts by WHO. Despite the use of six centres from which data were collected (Brazil, Ghana,

India, United States of America, Norway and Oman) to represent both rich and poorer countries, the possibility of reflecting the 'realities of these countries' is open to question. As Underdown (2007) argues, the number of obese children is rising in the affluent west, yet average growth is not optimal in the majority of the world, often as a result of malnutrition. It could be difficult to reflect these social 'realities' in the optimal growth curves of a centile chart.

Growth and development data are, in England, recorded and monitored by healthcare and child professionals and held by parents. The latest version of Personal Child Health Records (PCHR) was published in 2009 by the Royal College of Paediatrics and Child Health (RCPCH), taking into account the new UK-WHO centile charts. This document continues to be the base for the recording of measurements of physical growth and development and is held by parents, allowing a variety of professionals including health visitors and general practitioners to plot data on the same chart. These include measurements at birth and a systematic record of contact with health professionals in relation to a child's physical (and social and emotional) development.

Learning activity

Growth and me

Some of you may have your own 'baby books' where your parents, guardians or wider family recorded your early years or you may indeed have one for your own children. See if you can find it and have a look through. Think about the different ways in which we document, seeming to regard as sacred, markers of physical development including many things from locks of hair to photographs and possibly dates of first crawling or walking to the first tooth lost. What might this tell us about how childhood is constructed?

The major physical measurements obtained for infants include:

- **Weight**. Weighing should be done regularly on calibrated scales to ensure accuracy and can be done by midwives, health visitors, nurse practitioners and GPs. Other ways of ensuring accuracy include weighing babies at the same time of day and in the same relation to feeding, just before or after for example. Identification of weight gain patterns is not in itself diagnostic (Wright, 2000), but has the potential to reveal underlying health conditions or problems with feeding practices.
- **Length/height**. There has been disagreement in the benefit of measuring the length of babies and infants, which is done with the child lying on his or her back, the supine position, until they are able to stand, at around 18 months. Fry (1993) maintains the value of this measurement as growth is at its fastest in the first year and a half of life and should be monitored accordingly. The monitoring of length/height is generally not continued after two years of age.

- **Occipitofrontal head circumference**. This measurement is taken at birth, or when swelling has settled after labour, and is typically made again at 6–8 weeks. The data, as with most measurements of physical growth and development, are plotted onto a centile chart, to identify whether a child's head is too large, too small or grows at an unusual rate against normal developmental expectations. It should be noted that it is extremely rare to be able to identify or diagnose serious conditions through measuring head circumference, so further measurement beyond this age is considered to only raise familial anxiety.

Many professionals highlight the importance of this monitoring as a source of reassurance to parents and families. However, concerns have been raised with these kinds of interventions, and more commonly, health promotion strategies in relation to victim blaming and the individualisation of neoliberal approaches to health (for further information on evaluating social policy in early childhood, see Chapter 9). For example, there is a risk that monitoring can, in the case of too frequent screening for example, cause anxiety or contribute to negative feelings and stress. Parents can feel as if they are failing their child by not assuring they fit the designated norm as cultural stereotypes about what constitutes a normally developing body hold great importance for children and families (James, 1993).

Infant nutrition: breast- or bottle-feeding?

The phrase 'breast is best' has been part of official messages surrounding infant feeding for generations. The dominant perspective in contemporary UK society remains overwhelmingly in support of breast-feeding and this is reflected globally with WHO recommending that babies should be exclusively breast-fed until six months of age (WHO, 2002), but despite this it is estimated that worldwide only 34.8 per cent of children are exclusively breast-fed for this time (WHO, 2009). Breast milk, or its substitute, can provide the required nutrients for growth, but there are concerns that the levels of vitamins and protein provided by breast milk alone are unlikely to be sufficient beyond six months (Department of Health, 1994).

Despite official messages which overwhelmingly support breast-feeding, statistics suggest that only 25 per cent of children are still being breast-fed at four months in the UK (UNICEF, 2005). There exist significant differences in breast-feeding among a range of social groups. These include lower rates of breast-feeding among manual social class groups than 'higher occupations' groups, mothers who continued in education until the age of 18 are more likely to breast-feed for longer and children in the south east are more likely to be breast-fed than other UK geographical regions. Reasons for not breast-feeding are diverse and women frequently express their reluctance, citing embarrassment, lack of privacy, fear of under-feeding, inconvenience and a desire to return to work (Hall and Elliman, 2006). It is also important to consider the images surrounding breast-feeding in popular culture as Henderson *et al.* (2000: 1198) point out that:

> Media coverage implies that breast-feeding is problematic, funny and embarrassing … in contrast bottle feeding is socially integrated, highly visible, unproblematic and associated with 'ordinary' families.

The promotion of breast-feeding is a core standard contained within the National Service Framework for Children, Young People and Maternity Services (Department of Health Department for Education and skills, 2004). However, this support and information for families is, as it should be, restricted to the provision of up-to-date information rather than a requirement which can be legislated for. Article 24 of the UNCRC carefully avoids a conflict between maternal and child rights by emphasising women's right to knowledge and information about breast-feeding (Underdown, 2007). There remains a need to recognise both cultural perceptions and individual choice within these discussions. Indeed, findings from the Millennium Cohort Study (Griffiths *et al.*, 2005) suggest that public health strategies aimed at increasing breast-feeding should focus on the support offered to women by partners and wider communities.

Learning activity

(Hidden) spaces of breast-feeding

As you go about your daily lives, meet friends for a coffee or watch television at home look out for discussions of or representations of breast-feeding. Are there spaces available in the café you're in that are designed for breast-feeding mothers? Are we ever presented with breast-feeding soap characters? Think about what this might reveal about dominant understandings of breast-feeding and how this may differ from the messages of official discourses surrounding infant nutrition.

So far this chapter has focused on neonatal and infant growth and associated screening and monitoring; it now turns its attention to physical development beyond infancy. The following sections will explore the development of physical competencies in the early years, considering issues which continue to remain high on contemporary agendas when exploring the lives of young children: physical activity, outdoor play and childhood obesity.

Developing physical competencies

Physical growth is just one of the ways in which young children's bodies are monitored in terms of normal age and stage-based development, with another important area being the development of physical competencies, including:

- **gross motor skills**. Crawling, walking, throwing, catching, climbing stairs
- **fine motor skills**. Fastening buttons, writing, drawing, using gestures
- **everyday manipulative skills** (using both gross and fine motor skills). Cleaning teeth, opening a door, manipulating a keyboard or mouse, using cutlery, riding a bike.

(MacIntyre, 2007: 104)

Figure 3.1

Developmental psychology has tended to gloss over the physical in its explorations, documenting growth or skills and then swiftly moving on (Lindon, 2010). So, apart from the issues relating to health and growth, i.e. birth weight, laid out previously in this chapter, why is the physical so important? Balance, coordination and control of the body are essential in performing tasks and physical competencies make new behaviours possible; thus determining the potential experiences of children in everyday life. Movement and physical activity are considered as key to children's wider learning and development. Goldschmeid and Jackson (2004) support this view that physical development underpins other learning tasks and developed the 'treasure basket' accordingly. The treasure basket contains a collection of everyday, often household objects, made available to babies at a time in their development when they are able to sit up and grasp and explore objects, but a lack of mobility means they cannot yet go rooting around in kitchen cupboards to find saucepans to bang. Goldschmeid and Jackson (2004) argue that this rich variety of everyday objects (none of which should be bought toys) offers stimulus to the senses and in their research observed a striking level of the physical in these explorations, indeed the whole body is involved.

Goddard Blythe (2004, 2009) highlights the first A, B, Cs (attention, balance and coordination), emphasising like Goldschmeid and Jackson (2004) that children learn through embodied investigation. They should not, therefore, be expected to sit still for long periods of time and some early years and educational practices which view learning as taking place indoors sitting at a table have been criticised from this perspective. It can be argued that early years settings have been increasingly measured in terms of academic achievement for children on entering the schooling system and physical development has taken somewhat of a backseat (Lindon, 2010). The profile of physical development received renewed recognition as a result of the *Every Child Matters* (Department for Education and skills, 2004) framework, with staying healthy as one of the five tenets. However, the importance of physical development and activity is not a 21st century invention. Indeed, Margaret McMillan, one of the early education pioneers, placed significant value on the role of physical activity, notably in an outside environment, not just during short designated break times to allow children to 'blow off steam', but as crucial to learning and development in the early years (Wellhousen, 2002), making no distinction between bodily development and intellectual capacity (see also Chapter 7 for further discussion).

Bilton (2002 in Lindon, 2010) highlighted how, as a result of extending outdoor time, children did not have to cram their activities into 15 minutes, there was no mad dash for the doors and activities became less manic and more sustained. Devereux and Bridges (2004 in Lindon, 2010: 112) described in 'the story of the bark chips' how young children became actively involved in the development of an outdoor space when bags of bark were left, after a delivery, on the pavement outside the building. A combination of physical activity, organisation, team work and problem-solving skills were demonstrated as the children independently and spontaneously organised a system for moving the goods to the garden for the next stage of the project. These examples of research support understandings of the value of outdoor play for promoting physical activity, but also for the embodied development of other important skills and children's overall well-being.

Concerns in the 21st century about a lack of physical activity in early childhood and young children's sedentary lifestyles (Lindon, 2010) are considered as particularly problematic in the context of viewing basic physical fitness as laid down during childhood. A recent interest in cases of rickets (Pearce and Cheetham, 2010), a vitamin D deficiency that affects the bones, has led to growing concerns about the lack of time children are spending outside, as vitamin D is synthesised by the skin when exposed to sunlight.

As seen with regards to the impact of birth weight and the monitoring of other growth indicators, discussed earlier in this chapter, childhood behaviours and development are considered to have a long-term impact into adulthood (as outlined in Chapter 1). Just as levels of physical activity are seen to lay the foundation for adult fitness, nutrition in the early years is viewed as impacting on later life, with links between diabetes, coronary heart disease and some types of cancer, with poor diet in childhood. Thus, the status of childhood obesity as one of the key challenges facing the minority world in the 21st century (WHO, 2012) reflects not only a concern as to the physical, social and emotional well-being of young children, but the future health of populations. It is important, however, that in the focus on childhood as laying down physical (and indeed social, psychological and emotional) well-being for adulthood, this does not blind us to exploring the physical, embodied experiences of young children.

Bringing in the social body: evaluating developmental models

There is no doubt that an understanding of how children's bodies grow and change is important for academics, practitioners and policy makers. However, there has been significant critique of unidirectional, maturation models for focusing only on the notion of children as 'becoming' (see Chapter 1 for further discussion) and ignoring the value of children's everyday lives and experiences.

> *Speaking of ages and stages in terms of biological maturation is to make crude assumptions about rates, sequences, sites and constancy of development. Charts of normal growth and development skip over and minimise enormous complexities of variations.*

(Penn, 2008: 64)

The last 30 years have seen increasing research into the capabilities of newborns and infants, and although the significant influence of stage approaches can still be widely seen, there is increasing acknowledgement that the physical development of young children is not unitary and involves both gain and loss. Indeed, contemporary explorations of babyhood (Monaghan, 2012) encourage us to reconsider notions that babies and young children are passive and not agentic. This section of the chapter will explore how increasing critical evaluation of dominant models enables fuller understanding of children's bodies and the embodied realities of children's lives.

The diverse ways in which children's bodies are used, learned, displayed and acted upon, by themselves and by external forces, demonstrates that a single unidirectional model of physical growth and development may not provide a full picture. Taking this further, it can be argued that it is impossible to fully understand children's bodies and physical development without recognising the cultural and historical specificity of such existences and events. A key approach which can help us to explore how children's bodies are thought about and acted upon differently at different points in time and space is 'social constructionism'.

The social constructionist perspective highlighted by Berger and Luckmann (1967) argues that reality is constructed by individuals and social groups in the microprocesses of social interaction. Ariès (1962) highlighted the socially constructed nature of childhood by suggesting that the consciousness of children as different from adults emerged as a result of wider historical and social processes and is not a universal across time and space. Incorporating this perspective into considerations of children's lives was put forward by James and Prout (1997) in *The New Sociology of Childhood*. This new approach signalled a turning point in the academic explorations of childhood, enabling the posing of new questions, emphasising not just how children are controlled by external forces, but also children's agency, cultures, voices and rights (see Chapter 1 for further discussion). They argue that in this new paradigm:

- Childhood is understood as a social construction.
- Childhood is a variable of social analysis.
- Children's relationships and cultures are worthy of study in their own right.
- Children are active social agents.

- Ethnography is a useful method for the study of childhood.
- Studying childhood involves engaging with the processes reconstructing childhood in society.

Embodied agency

Children are viewed not as passive beings, in the new sociology of childhood, but active agents with views and cultures of their own and the power to both articulate these views and take part in the co-construction of culture and society. The primacy of Cartesian dualism, which views the rational powerful mind as separate from and inferior to the body, has sometimes led to agency as a concept being divorced from notions of embodiment. It is our minds that hold and use the power we have to impact our environments. Bodies in this sense are viewed as vessels, not that important in their own right and certainly not as good as the separate and wondrous mind they are made to carry. Recent work, notably from the arena of phenomenology (Merleau-Ponty, 1974) has sought to bring concepts of agency back into the body. All agency, is after all embodied agency, as, at this point in our history, all action (or indeed) action is performed in and through our bodies.

There is now a plethora of research which examines children's perspectives of embodiment which draw, however, broadly from the new sociology of childhood paradigm. Despite both sociology of the body and sociology of childhood perhaps best considered as absent presences (Shilling, 2003) in sociology as a discipline and until recently developing largely on separate tracks (Prout, 2000). Backett-Milburn (2000) examines how children negotiate health messages as part of the embodied management of both public and private spaces and Mayall's (2008) exploration of children's lived bodies in everyday life demonstrates how children are aware, both positively and negatively, of their bodies in the daily encounters of their early years.

Social constructionism and the new social studies of childhood can thus be seen to allow for children's bodies to be thought about as more than just vessels which must grow and develop in particular ways adhering to a pre-assigned sequence of stages. These perspectives offer an opportunity to consider how a culture, at a particular point in its history, views bodies, both as desired and abnormal, as well as how individuals choose to maintain and modify their bodies. However, a focus on the socially constructed nature of childhood and a desire to distance these conversations from previously dominant biological and developmental discourses can result in the bodily dimensions of childhood being neglected in favour of the social dimensions.

This has sometimes resulted in a disembodied picture of childhood (Williams, 2003). Armstrong (1983) uses ideas from Foucault to show the development of paediatric discourses surrounding childhood ('discourse' can be broadly defined as collections of thoughts and ideas or sets of principles which govern social relations and social life). Armstrong (1983) explored how paediatrics transformed from a medical speciality concerned with diseases of children to subsequently concerning itself with child development in general. It studied and measured children's bodies, classifying and categorising them as normal or abnormal. Armstrong's (1983) analysis informs us about the construction of children's bodies within dominant discourses, in this case paediatric, medical discourses. However, as Williams (2003) points out, this kind of approach does relegate the physical body to discourse alone, viewing bodies as disciplined and docile (Foucault, 1980), subject to control by society and inherently lacking acknowledgement of the physical, material 'reality' of the body. In short, as with developmental models of children's bodies, the approach of social constructionism also has limitations.

Care and control of children's bodies

Consideration of bodies as pre-social, a natural given, or as only social, entirely shaped by dominant (or subversive) ideas, means that they have often been skimmed over in critical analysis. A fundamental part of the development of children's bodies not yet discussed within this chapter is how individuals learn the socially 'appropriate' ways to present, modify and use their bodies. As Elias (1978/1939) argues, in order to develop civilised bodies, children must go through a learning process; by doing this their bodies are deemed acceptable and they can become full members of society. Parents, extended family and early years practitioners are often the prime agents involved in educating children about their bodies in accordance with social norms, for example, toilet training or tying of shoe laces. However, it also needs to be recognised that society as a whole impacts parental perceptions and dominant models of professional practice, exerting 'its pressure on the new generation' (Elias, 1978/1939: 140). There has been a surge in research in the late 20th and early 21st centuries highlighting the structures around childhood which seek to both care for and control children's bodies.

Foucault's (1980) work is concerned with the relationship between the body and the powers which act upon it. Particularly he was interested in the micro-physics of power, how institutions in society, such as the education system, shape and control bodies and obviously as a result shape and control individuals. Think for example about the practices of the school classroom in relation to young children's bodies. Children may be requested to line up in single file, are asked to sit 'nicely' at work tables or 'cross-legged' on the carpet for group activities. These school or setting rules are not necessarily designed to facilitate an effective learning environment, although they sometimes do. Rather, using a Foucauldian perspective, they enable children, the future productive citizens in society, to be surveilled, monitored and managed, through surveilling and managing their bodies (for further discussion of Foucault's concept of govermentality, please see Chapter 13). An example of this is seen in The National Child Measurement Programme (NCMP), run by the Department of Health (DH) and the Department of Education (DofE) in England and involves the annual measurement of weight and height for children aged 4–5 and 10–11 years. These individual level bodily measurements are used to inform both individual interventions and wider local planning and delivery of services (NHSIC, 2011).

This management of children's bodies, how they are monitored and attempts made to shape them, is led by the dominant discourses of a particular time and place. This can be seen when thinking about how prevailing views about particular issues in society shift and change through history. For example, the move away from corporal punishment in schools demonstrates a shift in how children are viewed in society. Management and surveillance of children's bodies can be seen not just in educational institutions but in all areas of society which children inhabit. Think back to the discussions at the beginning of this chapter about screening and physical development monitoring. These measurement and intervention techniques facilitate the care of newborns, infants and young children, but they also allow for the monitoring of the bodies of populations. Foucault argues that by increasing interventions into the bodies of individuals and populations, the individuals and institutions in society with power are able to more pervasively control and shape individuals and thus social life itself. For Foucault, the body is not just given meaning through these discourses, but is entirely constituted by them, the body 'vanishes as biological entity and becomes instead a socially constructed product' (Shilling, 2003: 65).

While an understanding of the institutions and discourses which influence children's bodies is crucial to early childhood studies, it is also important to consider the critiques levied at social constructionism and Foucauldian perspectives and not ignore the biological, corporeal, base of the physical body.

Bodies as social ... and biological!

Achieving a balance between biological and social determinism includes an acknowledgement that children do share common experiences of biological and psychological maturation, but that these universal, biological 'facts' are interpreted differently between cultures (James and James, 2004). This middle ground is useful also in thinking about the role of both structure and agency in shaping children's bodies. Prout (2000), for example, draws on Shilling's (2003) view of childhood bodies as both biologically and socially unfinished. This demonstrates a reciprocal and relational relationship between body and society, whereby both are shaped by the other. In her research, James (1993) found that children would show off their old scars, not for sympathy, but as part of a negotiation of their embodied social identities over time, understood through embodied encounters.

Figure 3.2 Social exploration of the physical body

Thus, we begin to consider how children's bodies grow and develop but as part of this process, are also used, presented and shaped by individuals and society. So what about those bodies that do not physically develop according to the normative stages explored previously in this chapter? Or those that do not fit within the cultural boundaries of 'acceptable' or 'normal' children's bodies? The following sections explore how three issues, disability, continuing the theme of nutrition explored earlier in the chapter, obesity, and gender, are understood when exploring the embodied nature of their role both in children's lives and the social construction of childhood itself.

Dis/abled bodies

Understandings of disability in both adults and children have been dominated in research and practice by an individual model which sees disability as inside individuals themselves and caused by physical and medical limitations. This approach places the onus of the disability on the individual, that their body, in the case of physical impairments, is incomplete or abnormal in some way. The result of this has often been that disabled children have been pathologised and considered as unable or unfit to contribute fully to society (see also Chapter 12).

One theorist whose work allows us to explore the processes surrounding how disabled bodies are perceived in society and the subsequent impact of this on children's perception of themselves is Erving Goffman (1959, 1963). Goffman explored the stigmatisation of 'others', individuals whose bodies do not fit within what is categorised as 'normal' by wider society. A physical disability is labelled by Goffman as a visible stigma and he argues that a disabled individual's, in this case a child's, body categorises them as an incomplete or failed member of society. Think back to the point made in the previous section that children's bodies represent their present selves but also the future productive citizen they will become. If a body is viewed as unproductive, an individual considered less than a 'full' person, what does this mean for them?

The relationship between the physical body and a person's identity is seen during this process of stigmatisation whereby children may internalise this negative label, resulting in a spoiled identity. Goffman's earlier work on *The Presentation of Self in Everyday Life* (1959) explored similar issues about how individuals manage their bodies, viewing interactions in daily life, for example in the school classroom, as taking place on a stage. This front stage is where children learn to manage their bodies, according to prevailing social and situational norms. These two aspects of Goffman's work are particularly interesting in the context of exploring notions of disabled bodies and highlight the problems disabled children (and adults) encounter during the work they must engage in, in an attempt to be accepted as full members of society.

An alternative approach that emphasised the rights of disabled people to participate fully in society without discrimination developed in the final decades of the 20th century, the social model of disability. This approach stresses the diversity of humanity, advocating that all children are 'normal' and that disability is not a physical impairment, but actually a failure of society (Oliver, 1996). It is society's unwillingness or inability to enable all individuals that creates disability; in short, children are not disabled, rather society is disabling.

The social model of disability has highlighted a range of salient issues and assumptions about what it is like to live as a disabled child (and adult). Nonetheless, like social constructionism, it is also subject to critique for presenting us with a peculiar disembodied form of embodiment, one which in its very discussions of disability fails to acknowledge the disabled or impaired body itself. Shakespeare and Erickson (2000: 195) argue that what is needed is another model that goes beyond either framework and:

> takes into account ... both the personal and physical experience of disability and the social dimensions ... to recognise the psychological processes and the cultural patterns and representations which influence the way we think about disabled people ... these dimensions of analysis ... produce the disability phenomenon which millions of people experience everyday.

'Weighty' bodies

A significant amount of research suggests that overweight children are more likely to be stigmatised (Goffman, 1963) or bullied by their peers (Cramer and Steinwert, 1998) than children of an ideal or 'normal' weight or body shape. A now somewhat infamous study highlighted by the British Medical Association (BMA, 2005) found that when provided with a series of images of children that they would like to be friends with, obese children were always chosen last, irrespective of other variables such as gender or disability. Indeed, research shows that young children hold negative weight stereotypes about fat bodies (Cramer and Steinwert, 1998).

Pierre Bourdieu (1986) views the body as a bearer of symbolic value in contemporary society; he dubs this value as physical capital. Physical capital in this sense refers to the development of bodies in ways which are recognised as possessing value in social fields. This means that particular kinds of bodies are idealised or more simply promoted in particular societies. Individuals whose physical attributes are seen as mirroring or representing something valued by society are more likely to be positively received; for example, in the context of this discussion thin bodies have more physical capital in contemporary 'Western' societies than bodies considered a larger size. (See Shilling (2003) for more information about Bourdieu's approach to the body). As highlighted earlier when discussing Goffman (1959, 1963), individuals must work to manage their bodies on the stages of social life. This embodied management is in order for bodies and selves to be considered 'normal' or for individuals to pass themselves off as acceptable members of society. Bourdieu also highlights the work, particularly in contemporary society, that individuals undertake to present their bodies, for example, through styles of dress or within body language; this learning, as Elias (1978/1939) states, begins in early childhood. Bourdieu takes this area a little further than Goffman arguing that the physical body is reflective of, or a product of, a person's social class.

Contemporary discourses which desire 'thin' bodies could be argued to be a result of dominant classes not concerned with a body that is useful, for example in manual work, but rather a slim body 'better suited to a world in which economic practice is constituted more strongly by the presentation of self' (Wilkes, 1990: 118). Here, the child's body is represented as subject to control by the individual, malleable as a result of work by a child who is inherently located within a particular social class; so the appropriate body can be achieved through the choice of an appropriate lifestyle.

This focus on bodies as a project to be worked on and part of an individual's identity means that bodies that do not adhere to dominant values are seen as a failure. Those who do not engage with health or self-help regimes so popular in the consumer culture of the 21st century, or who engage in behaviours such as eating unhealthily (or smoking, taking drugs or drinking excessively or while under age) are considered the new moral deviants (Shilling, 2003). This contemporary obsession with the body has been associated with a rise in eating disorders (Grogan, 1999), particularly among young children, as individuals attempt to manage their bodies in line with dominant cultural scripts.

Particular concerns about the role of dolls in children's lives in promoting unachievable and idealised versions of bodies have been raised. Dittmar (2008) highlights that translating the Barbie doll proportions to that of a life-size human shows a body which is not only unattainable but unhealthy. It is important to point out that this issue is by no means limited to girls. Toy dolls or action figures aimed at young boys, such as GI Joe, have bulk and a muscular physique which exceeds even that of body builders (Pope *et al.*, 1999).

In short, contemporary cultural landscapes are perverse and children, it is argued, negotiate a tightrope of the 'normal body', attempting to forge a path between condemnation as fat immoral, deviant and unrealistic, unhealthy and hyper-gendered images of supposedly 'beautiful' bodies.

Gendered bodies

Prendergast (2000) argues that from the moment a child is born they are embodied as a sexed and gendered being. Not only is a child's body viewed as a smaller, incomplete version of that of an adult's they are also, like adults, gendered, resulting in the division of childhood into boy-child and girl-child – what Connell (1987) refers to as the discourses of the pinks and blues. Just as has been argued throughout this chapter, bodies are simultaneously biological and social. Sex is widely considered as referring to the physical differences of sexed bodies and genital anatomy, whereas gender as a concept refers to the socially constructed nature of masculinity and femininity. Cream (1995) demonstrates this with the example of intersex children, through the processes of surgery or other interventions, as a result of parental choice, anatomy that is neither explicitly male nor female can be socially constituted at birth.

Nayak and Kehily (2008) argue for a move away from fixed notions of gender, biologically or as a social category and rather focus on the practice of gender with understandings of gender as a lived process, constantly in flux as it is managed and negotiated. Grosz (1990) understands the way wider discourses impact upon bodies through the concept of body-maps. The child's body in this sense can be viewed as a surface for inscription, both regimes within the wider social order and individual or personal value systems and choices (diet or clothing, for example). These corporeal inscriptions 'make the body into a particular kind of body' (Grosz, 1990: 65). Unlike the criticisms levelled at some Foucauldian perspectives earlier in this chapter, Grosz avoids providing a disembodied picture of gender by acknowledging the presence of what she calls the biological bedrock. This is not fixed either but exists in relation to the social scripts which children learn in relation to manage their bodies in wider society. Lewis (2011) highlights the relationship between gender as social and biological in her explorations of how family relationships and individual bodies are negotiated in the management of privacy in bathroom spaces. As girls reach the end of early childhood (wherever this may be), they must negotiate their changing biological 'feminine' bodies with other family members in the home, revealing how embodied encounters are mediated by both the biological and the socially gendered body, within home spaces. Martin (2008: 211) expands analysis of gendered bodies beyond the home, in research that suggests gendered physical differences are constructed through social institutions and their practices. Through observations in preschool classrooms drawing on activities of dressing up, voices in the classroom and adult bodily instructions, Martin (2008: 211) demonstrates that in early years spaces 'bodies become gendered in ways that are so subtle and taken for granted that to feel and appear natural'.

Judith Butler has become an overwhelmingly influential theorist in this area, stating that 'gender norms are … phantasmic, impossible to embody' (1990: 41). Drawing from arguments around performativity, she puts forward an interpretation of gender that is not a static or pre-assigned category; rather it only comes into being at the point of action (Nayak and Kehily, 2008). That is to say that it is not until we act in a way that is compatible with or subverts the gender order that we are feminine or masculine, a girl or a boy. Butler's work is nuanced and complex in a way that prohibits meaningful further exploration of it here, but as with the critiques levelled at Foucault, earlier in this chapter, there is a risk here of providing a somewhat disembodied perspective of gender.

There does exist a growing body of literature which takes the theoretical contributions of writers such as Grosz or Butler to examine how gender is constructed, negotiated and managed by children. Connell (1995) points to boys displaying proper masculine self-hoods where embodied risk taking is regarded as a key characteristic of masculinity. Green's (1997) research exploring children's accounts of accidents shows that girls talk greatly of responsibility and embodied competence, whereas boys discussed courageous risk taking and how damage to boy's bodies was bravely borne. Here, how the social constructions of gender influence children's embodied lives is revealed.

Learning activity

Bodies in literature

This activity is inspired by a dissertation student I supervised on the BA (Hons) Early Childhood Studies Degree at UCS, who chose for their project to explore representations of overweight characters in children's literature. Read some children's classics, including *Matilda* by Roald Dahl, *Harry Potter and the Philosophers' Stone* by J.K.Rowling and *Blubber* by Judy Blume and consider the words used and attitudes presented towards the 'fat' characters. Think about what this may reveal about wider social attitudes towards weight.

(With thanks to Sarah Hanrahan whose creative ideas inspired this reader activity.)

Conclusion

Throughout this chapter, readers have been encouraged to view children's bodies as simultaneously biological and social, subject to the structures of the wider social order but with children considered as capable of embodied action with the capability of influencing the world around them and with voices that should be heard. Initially, the significant influence of stage-based maturation theories of children's growth and development was presented. Such models, although subsequently subjected to critical evaluation as not as universal as they first appear, should be recognised as forming an important part of early years practice, including screening, growth monitoring and the associated early interventions.

The importance of embodiment is demonstrated by the fact that at this point in human history, all human action and inaction takes place within and through bodies. The concept of the treasure basket is thus illuminated as a mechanism by which children's embodied relationships to spaces and objects can be revealed as a potential tool to enhance children's physical development.

The philosophy of social constructionism and the paradigm of the new sociology of childhood facilitate further engagement with the complex relationship between agency and structure in children's embodied lives. Drawing on the work of Foucault and Elias, the processes by which children's bodies are measured, surveilled and socialised are revealed and, where agency is considered in more detail, children's contributions to such discourses and ability to subvert or negotiate wider social 'body norms' can be shown. The complex interdependencies of nature and culture, and the biological and the social are further interrogated as particular kinds of bodies are considered.

What readers should take away from this chapter, perhaps most importantly, is a recognition of children's bodies as not incomplete or imperfect versions of adults', and we should consider children as 'being' as well as 'becoming', and childhood as conceptually staged but children as active, creative performers (Bluebond-Langner *et al.*,1991).

Evaluate your learning

- How far do physical competencies determine the potential experiences of young children in everyday life?
- Why is the approach of social constructionism often critiqued for providing a disembodied picture of childhood?
- In what environments are young children's bodies likely to be managed and surveilled and why is this?

References

Ariès, P (1962): *Centuries of Childhood*. London: Jonathan Cape.

Armstrong, D (1983): *The Political Anatomy of the Body*. Cambridge: Cambridge University Press.

Backett-Milburn, K (2000): Children, parents and the construction of the 'healthy body' in middle class families. In Prout, A (ed), *The Body, Childhood and Society*. Hampshire: Palgrave Macmillan.

Berger, PL and Luckmann, T (1967): *The Social Construction of Reality: A Treatise in the Sociology of Knowledge*. London: Anchor.

Bluebond-Langner, M, Perkel, D and Goertzel, T (1991): Pediatric cancer patients' peer relationships: the impact of an oncology camp experience. *Journal of Psychosocial Oncology* 9, 67–80.

BMA (2005): *Preventing Childhood Obesity*. London: Board of Science.

Bourdieu, P (1986): The forms of capital. In Richardson, J (ed), *Handbook of Theory and Research for the Sociology of Education*. New York: Greenwood Press.

Butler, J (1990): *Gender Trouble, Feminism and the Subversion of Gender*. London: Routledge.

Connell, R (1987): *Gender and Power*. Oxford: Polity Press.

Connell, R (1995): Boys will be boys? Racism, sexuality and the construction of masculine identities among infant boys. In Holland, J, Mlair, M and Sheldon, S (eds), *Debates and Issues in Feminist Research and Pedagogy*. Berkshire: Open University Press.

Cramer, P and Steinwert, T (1998): Thin is good, fat is bad: how early does it begin? *Journal of Applied Developmental Psychology* **19**, 429–51.

Cream, J (1995): Re-solving riddles: the sexed body. In Bell, D and Valentine, G (eds), *Mapping Desire*. London: Routledge.

DH (1994): *Weaning and the Weaning Diet*. London: HMSO.

Department of Health/Department for Education and Skills (2004): *The National Service Framework for Children, Young People and Maternity Services*. London: Department of Health.

Dittmar, H (2008): *Consumer Culture, Identity and Well Being: The Search for the Good Life and the Body Perfect*. Hove: Psychology Press.

Elias, N (1978/1939) *The Civilising Process, Vol. 1: The History of Manners*. Oxford: Basil Blackwell.

Foucault, M (1980): On governmentality. In Gordon, C (ed), *Power/Knowledge*. London: Harvester Press.

Fry, T (1993): Charting growth: developments in the assessment and measurement of child growth. *Child Health* **1**, 104–09.

Goddard Blythe, S (2004): *The Well-Balanced Child: Movement and Early Learning*. Gloucestershire: Hawthorn Press.

Goddard Blythe, S (2009): *Attention, Balance and Coordination: The ABC of Learning Success*. Chichester: John Wiley and Sons.

Goffman, E (1959): *The Presentation of Everyday Life*. New York: Doubleday Anchor.

Goffman, E (1963): *Stigma: Notes on the Management of Spoiled Identity*. New York: Doubleday Anchor.

Goldschmeid, E and Jackson, S (2004): *People Under Three: Young Children in Day Care*. London: Routledge.

Green, J (1997): Risk and the construction of social identity: children's talk about accidents. *Sociology of Health and Illness* **19**(4), 457–79.

Griffiths, L, Tate, A and Dezateux, C (2005): The contribution of parental and community ethnicity to breastfeeding practices, evidence from the Millennium Cohort Study. *International Journal of Epidemiology* **34**, 1378–86.

Grogan, S (1999): *Body Image*. London: Routledge.

Grosz, E (1990): A note on essentialism and difference. In Gunew, S (ed), *Feminist Knowledge, Critique and Construct*. London: Routledge.

Hall, D and Elliman, D (2006): *Health for All Children*, 4th edn. Oxford: Oxford University Press.

Henderson, A, Kitzingerm J and Green, L (2000): Representations of infant feeding: contents analysis of British media of breast feeding and bottle feeding. *British Medical Journal* **311**, 1196–8.

HSCIC (Health and Social Care Information Centre) (2011) Statistics on Obesity, Physical Activity and Diet: England, 2011. (Online). Last accessed August 2011. Available from: www.ic.nhs.uk/statistics-and-data-collections/health-and-lifestyles/obesity/statistics-on-obesity-physical-activity-and-diet-england-2011.

James, A (1993): *Childhood Identities.* Edinburgh: Edinburgh University Press.

James, A and James, AL (eds) (1997): *Constructing and Reconstructing Childhood,* 2nd edn. Basingstoke: Falmer.

James, A and James, AL (2004): *Constructing Childhood: Theory, Policy and Social Practice.* Basingstoke: Palgrave Macmillan.

Lewis, R (2011): Shutting the bathroom door: parents, young teenagers and the negotiation of bodily boundaries at home. In Holt, L (ed), *Geographies of Children, Youth and Families: An International Perspective.* London: Routledge.

Lindon, S (2010) *Understanding Child Development: Linking Theory and Practice.* London: Hodder Education.

MacIntyre, T and Moran, A (2007): *Understanding Children's Development in the Early Years: Questions Practitioners Frequently Ask.* London: Routledge.

Martin, K (2008): Becoming a gendered body: practices of preschools. In Malacrida, C and Low, J (eds), *The Sociology of the Body: A Reader.* Oxford: Oxford University Press.

Mayall, B (2008): Children's lived bodies in everyday life. In Malacrida, C and Low, J (eds), *Sociology of the Body: A Reader.* Oxford: Oxford University Press.

Merleau-Ponty, M (1974): *Phenomenology, Language and Society.* London: Heinemann.

Monaghan, K (2012): Battling babies: representations of very young children within contemporary parenting literature', unpublished conference paper. *4th International Celebrating Childhood Diversity Conference,* Centre for the Study of Childhood and Youth (CSCY), University of Sheffield.

Nayak, A and Kehily, M (2008): *Gender, Youth and Culture: Young Masculinities and Femininities.* Hampshire: Palgrave Macmillan.

NHSIC (2011): *The National Child Measurement Programme, England: School Year 2010/11.* London: NHSIC.

NHSIC (2012): *Statistics on Obesity, Physical Activity and Diet in England 2012.* London: NHSIC.

Oliver, M (1996): *Understanding Disability: From Theory to Practice.* Hampshire: Palgrave Macmillan.

Pearce, S and Cheetham, T (2010): Diagnosis and management of vitamin D deficiency. *British Medical Journal* **340**, 5664.

Penn, H (2008): *Understanding Early Childhood: Issues and Controversies.* Berkshire: Open University Press.

Pope, H, Olivardia, R, Gruber, A and Browiecki, J (1999): Evolving ideals of male body image as seen through action toys. *International Journal of Eating Disorders* **26**, 65–72.

Prendergast, S (2000): To become dizzy in our turning: girls, body maps and gender as childhood ends. In Prout, A (ed), *The Body, Childhood and Society.* Hampshire: Palgrave Macmillan.

Prout, A (ed) (2000): *The Body, Childhood and Society.* Hampshire: Palgrave Macmillan.

RCPCH (2009): *Personal Child Health Record.* London: RCPCH and Harlow Printing Ltd.

RCPCH (2012): *UK WHO Growth Charts* (Online). Last accessed 13 August 2012. Available from: www.rcpch.ac.uk/growthcharts.

Shakespeare, TW and Erickson, M (2000) Different strokes: beyond biological essentialism and social constructionism. In Rose, S and Rose, H (eds), *Coming to Life.* New York: Little Brown.

Shilling, C (2003): *The Body in Social Theory,* 2nd edn. London: Sage.

Underdown, A (2007): *Young Children's Health and Wellbeing.* Berkshire: Open University Press.

UNICEF (2005) The State of the World's Children – Children under Threat, UNICEF. (Online). Last accessed: June 2012. Available from: www.unicef.org/publications/index_24432.html.

Wellhousen, K (2002): *Outdoor Play Every Day: Innovative Play Concepts for Early Childhood.* Albany: Cengage Learning.

Williams, S (2003): *Medicine and the Body.* London: Sage.

WHO (2002): *Infant and Young Child Nutrition: Global Strategy on Infant and Young Children Feeding: Report by the Secretariat.* 55th World Health Assembly. WHO A55/15.

WHO (2009): *Infant and Young Child Feeding: Model Chapter for Textbooks for Medical Students and Allied Health Professionals.* Geneva: WHO.

WHO (2012): *Prioritising areas for action in the field of population-based prevention of childhood obesity: a set of tools for member-states.* Geneva: WHO.

Wilkes, C (1990): Bourdieu's class. In Harker, J, Mahar, C and Wilkes C (eds), *An Introduction to the Work of Pierre Bourdieu.* Houndsmills: Macmillan.

Wright, CM (2000): Identification and management of failure to thrive: a community perspective. *Archives of Disease in Childhood* **82**, 5–9.

Further reading

Dittmar, H (2008): *Consumer Culture, Identity and Well Being: The Search for the Good Life and the Body Perfect.* Hove: Psychology Press.

Goffman, E (1959): *The Presentation of Self in Everyday Life.* New York: Doubleday Anchor.

Hall, D and Elliman, D (2006): *Health for All Children,* 4th edn. Oxford: Oxford University Press.

Lindon, J (2010): *Understanding Child Development: Linking Theory and Practice.* London: Hodder Education.

Malacrida, C and Low, J (eds) (2008): *Sociology of the Body: A Reader.* Oxford: Oxford University Press.

Prout, A (ed.) (2000): *The Body, Childhood and Society.* Hampshire: Palgrave Macmillan.

Shilling, C (2003): *The Body in Social Theory,* 2nd edn. London: Sage.

Underdown, A (2007): *Young Children's Health and Wellbeing.* Berkshire: Open University Press.

Personal, social and emotional development

Anne Greig

This chapter aims to:

- examine the holistic aspects of personal, social and emotional development within individuals and in reference to the social and cultural systems in which children develop
- introduce and critically evaluate the latest theories on personal, social and emotional development.

Introduction

Often, that sunny autumn, when the weather permitted, the small girls took their lessons seated on three benches arranged around the elm. 'Hold up your books,' said Miss Brodie quite often that autumn, 'prop them up in your hands, in case of intruders. If there are any intruders, we are doing our history lesson ... or our poetry ... English grammar.' The small girls held up their books with their eyes not on them, but on Miss Brodie. 'In the meantime I will tell you about my last summer holiday in Egypt ... I will tell you about the care of the skin, and of the hands ... about the Frenchman I met on the train to Biarritz ... and I must tell you about the Italian paintings I saw. Who is the greatest Italian painter?'

'Leonardo da Vinci, Miss Brodie.'

'That is incorrect. The answer is Giotto. He is my favourite.'

(***The Prime of Miss Jean Brodie,*** **Muriel Spark, 1961/1980: 10–11**)

The fabulous Miss Brodie, above, so obviously 'in her prime' but also, perhaps, a little ahead of her time! Her subversive lessons on matters personal, social and emotional suggested that, in her classroom, the likes of history, poetry and grammar were not everything. Today's reality is that leading authors and researchers are producing convincing evidence that IQ is not, indeed, everything, and that other forms of intelligence, including personal, social and emotional intelligences, are just as important for successful life outcomes (Block, 1995; Gardner, 1993; 2006; Goleman,1996; 1998; 2004; 2007). These other intelligences are now finding their way on to the curriculum, albeit in less significant ways than the traditionally valued intelligences of literacy and numeracy.

In this respect, early years professionals have always been ahead of the times with the established view that early childhood is a period of rapid development of all psychological functions (language, social interaction, physical growth, moral and spiritual intelligences) that are interdependent and best fostered by an holistic approach that is sensitive to the whole child (Hughes and Kleinberg, 1999; see Introduction of this book). Children have to learn to cope with people and settings outwith the family, become increasingly independent, and form positive social relationships, particularly with other children (Howes, 1988; Hartup, 1992; Hay, 1994). To support children through this significant step, we are advised that providing secure, warm and caring relationships, giving praise appropriately, encouraging humour and helping children to feel good about themselves is necessary if children are to have good mental health and be able to take advantage of the learning environment (e.g. Sylva, 1994; Ladd *et al.*, 1999; SCCC, 1999; Trevarthen, 1997; see also government websites for guidance on emotional well-being in the Early Years Foundation Stage (EYFS) and the Curriculum for Excellence on the Scottish Execcutive website, 2012 publications).

Nevertheless, there is considerable evidence of society failing children in exactly this way. Political priorities for raising academic achievement often seemed to render personal, social and emotional (PSE) education the 'Cinderella' of educational and welfare reform, although for several years there has been increased reporting of PSE-related problems in even the youngest children. For example, Campbell (1991) reported that 25 per cent of preschoolers and early primary children met the criteria for oppositional defiant disorder or early-onset conduct problems. More recently, Greig (2004) reviewed the evidence and nature of depression in school children, noting that an estimated eight in every 400 primary school pupils could be depressed at any one time, and two in 100 children aged under 12 years needed psychiatric help (see also Meltzer *et al.*, 2000). Figures for poor areas, difficult social circumstances and during adolescence can be double this (MIND, 2001). Those children with emotional problems were observed to be the least likely to be in contact with services. Subsequent official surveys continued to confirm these alarming statistics and addressed the burden of caring for children with emotional or conduct disorders (Ford *et al.*, 2003; Meltzer *et al.*, 2003, 2011; Meltzer, 2005).

Goodyer (2001) suggested that early years professionals have a key role to play in early detection and intervention. Getting off to a good start does appear to be critical for many children. There is certainly some evidence that criminal actions are carried out to a greater extent by persons who have a history of early childhood aggression (Kazdin, 1995), and many antisocial children remain involved with mental health agencies throughout their lives. Indeed, risk factors identified for youth crime often overlap with mental health and school failure problems (Rutter *et al.*, 1998). As the antisocial acts of a five-year-old may be prototypic of the acts of the delinquent adolescent, the younger the child is at the time of the intervention beginning, the more positive the subsequent adjustment to home and school (Estrada and Pinsof, 1995; Kovacs, 1997).

It is in consideration of these serious consequences of the neglect of the development of the PSE competencies, especially in the early years, that the view is taken here that we ignore them at our peril. It has been noted by Orbach (1997) that:

> ... (society needs to) create an emotionally literate culture, where the facility to handle the complexities of emotional life is as widespread as the capacity to read, write and do arithmetic.

This chapter is an exploration of the other 'literacies': personal, social and emotional (PSE). This includes an examination of the theoretical basis that defines the PSE competencies and a contextual analysis of PSE development in the early years.

A theoretical review of personal, social and emotional (PSE) competence

Although the PSE competencies have been extensively addressed in the literature to date, it has not yet resulted in a single, integrated theory (Guralnick, 1997). Nevertheless, in a research field that is constantly evolving, considerable insights have been gained in recent times. There are several different theories that could be presented, in their own right, as organising constructs for the interactive competencies of early childhood. These include:

- emotional and multiple intelligences or competencies theories
- social competence theory (including self/other, autonomy/connectedness dimensions
- the theory of the development of pro-social competence
- attachment theory
- theory of mind or social understanding
- transactional theories and theories on the influences of systems, ecology and dialectical relationships.

The first two theories are not specifically directed at young children or the developmental precursors of competence. They do, however, potentially inform about the nature of the 'skills' associated with competence. The theories of mind, attachment and pro-social behaviour are developmental and reflect on early socialisation systems, but, until fairly recently, the overlaps in skills, processes and mechanisms common among them have been relatively unexplored. Each theory contains significant elements of the others. Hence, the complex and interacting nature of social, emotional and cognitive functions makes it difficult to ascertain where one theory ends and another begins. The approach taken within this chapter, therefore, is to use the concept of multiple intelligence (Gardner, 1983), and in particular the interpersonal and intrapersonal intelligences (Gardner, 1993), as an organising construct within which to explore the development of the personal, social and emotional competencies which contribute to it.

Defining emotional intelligence and emotional literacy

According to Gardner (1993: 9), emotional intelligence is both inter- and intrapersonal:

Interpersonal intelligence is the ability to understand other people: what motivates them, how they work, how to work co-operatively with them. Intrapersonal intelligence is a correlative ability, turned inward. It is a capacity to form an accurate, veridical model of oneself and to be able to use that model to operate effectively in life.

The meaning of this for early childhood was described by Saarni (1990: 116), who noted that this competency enables children to '… respond emotionally, yet simultaneously and strategically apply their knowledge about emotions and their expression to relationships with others, so that they can negotiate interpersonal exchanges and regulate their emotional experiences'. Nevertheless, in his ancient wisdom in *The Nicomachean Ethics*, Aristotle (cited in Goleman, 1996: 6) lets us know what a tall order this is for anyone, let alone children:

> Anyone can become angry – that is easy. But to be angry with the right person, to the right degree, at the right time, for the right purpose, and in the right way – that is not easy.

In an early childhood context, an 'emotional literacy' interpretation of Aristotle's observations allows us to consider emotional intelligence as a matter of a type of care and education that facilitates the young child's needs to be:

● emotionally reflective about himself/herself and others
● able to regulate emotions
● able to use emotion positively
● responsible for emotional mistakes.

('Antidote', 2003; Steiner and Perry, 1997)

Just as there is evidence of the damage caused by emotional illiteracy, there is growing evidence about the resilience features of emotional competence from longitudinal studies. Children who have good emotion recognition skills at five years are more likely to have good social skills and academic ability at nine years (Izard *et al.*, 2001). As observed by Damasio (1996), a loss of contact with emotions breaks down rationality which (with learning) requires the support of our emotions (Goleman, 1996). Even in the early preschool period, the positive contributions of emotional competence to social competence over the longer term mean that teaching about feelings is important even before the age of four years. Those children who are especially emotional may benefit from learning a means to avoid dysregulated coping and how to respond to the emotions of others prosocially instead of antisocially (Denham *et al.*, 2003).

This brief emotional literacy review illustrates the interdependence of the PSE competencies. This is a broad interpretation of 'intelligence' that presents a useful framework for the exploration of the themes of this chapter:

1. Skills approaches
2. Theoretical approaches – interacting processes (or systems)
3. The developmental progression of personal, social and emotional competences.

Initially, evidence will be drawn from a variety of programmes that mainly targeted older children and teenagers in order to extract skill-based definitions of each competency in isolation from an early childhood developmental model. The general limitations of these approaches will be explored. A brief exploration of the relevant theories will follow. Finally, the personal, social and emotional development of the child in the early years will be mapped out, together with a contextual examination of mediating factors.

Skills approaches

Stone and Dillehunt (1978) chose to emphasise personal skills or 'self-science'. This was broadly defined as 'a sense of self in relation to others', a theme which will presently be seen to recur in other approaches. These skills could be summarised into a few main headings: awareness of self and others; understanding and insight into the thoughts and emotions of self and others; empathy; and cooperation. Although this theory predates the emergence of the theory of mind literature and the theory of pro-social development (see below), it is, in effect, the importance of these that researchers had recognised.

Salovey and Mayer (1990) emphasised the emotional domain skills which can be summarised as including the recognition of emotion, its regulation and management in both self and in relationships with others. As before, the importance of perspective-taking regarding emotional awareness is relevant to the theory of mind literature and implicit is attachment theory (see below) in its recognition of the importance of the emotional quality of relationships.

The Grant Consortium project on the school-based promotion of social competence was both a skill and multi-domain approach (CPPRG, 2002a, 2002b, 2002c; Greenberg and Kusche, 1998). The authors took care to find appropriate skills for the psychological domains of cognition, emotion and behaviour. The skills of 'emotion' could be summarised as the recognition, gauging and management (or regulation) of emotional states. The 'cognitive' skills could be summarised as ways of processing information (or ways of going about understanding the social world and oneself within it). It could be argued here then, that the cognitive dimension includes the understanding and integration of the self and others as already noted in other approaches. Appropriate social 'behaviours' included pro-social responses, positive peer relationships and the skills of verbal and non-verbal communication. Again, the overlaps between many of the skills are apparent; for instance, to what extent is the ability to interpret social cues a cognitive skill or a social skill? The themes of self in relation to others, perspective taking, empathy and quality of relationships are also again evident. More recently, the CPPRG reported the longer-term outcomes for the social competence Fast Track Programme (CPPRG, 2007; 2010a, 2010b).

The final skills approach to be considered at this stage is that of Rose-Krasnor (1997). In defining social competence as 'effectiveness in interaction', Rose-Krasnor begins with the two major domains of the 'self' and 'other' (or autonomy or connectedness). While other approaches have noted the importance of these two domains, they have not been given the same construct status. Hence, the personal 'systems' that support inter- and intrapersonal intelligence could be construed here as the 'self-system' and the 'other system'. Social skills within the self-system could be summarised as a sense of self-efficacy, agency and success in achieving one's own goals. Social skills within the 'other system' could be summarised as quality and status in peer relationships, social responsibility and good social network supports. Behavioural and motivational skills supporting these systems include integration of self and other perspectives, emotional security and regulation, empathy and communicative and problem-solving abilities.

Consistent with all approaches reviewed above, a number of key processes or mechanisms emerge as playing a crucial role in the skills for inter/intrapersonal intelligences. These are understanding of self and others' perspectives and feelings, attachment security including quality of relationships and relating, and pro-social action. These appear to be significant 'within-system (self/other)' skills for the PSE competencies alongside other cognitive skills linked to communication and problem solving. An undue emphasis, however, on skills and specific skill domains may be oversimplifying what is meant by a 'skill', describing each as if they were individually and separately attainable with little attention to developmental processes and interacting mechanisms. Simple lists of underlying social competence 'skills', even if located within a specific 'system', do not address the fact that both skills and systems interact with each other in complex and important ways throughout the course of early childhood development. It also tends to mask the fact that these 'skills' are largely the products of early socialisation (e.g. Hay *et al.*, 1999; Dunn, 1996; Fonagy *et al.*, 1997; Saarni, 1990). These observations serve to illustrate the complex and interdependent nature of these skills (and systems) and suggest that a purely skills-based approach may be of limited help in assisting assessment and intervention.

In general, the 'skills' authors did not seek to address the overlapping nature of skills, systems and developmental progression. Indeed, the above lists of competencies read as a daunting prospect of achievement even for many adults. There is a need to interpret 'skills' in a developmentally appropriate way and in the context of the more recent research on the emergence of children's social understanding, on attachment theory, on the nature of pro-social development and on how these 'domains' actually interact (Hay, 1994; Harris, 1999; Hay *et al.*, 1999; Meins, 1999; Greig and Howe, 2001). In order, therefore, to address the inherent weaknesses of the predominantly 'skills'-based approaches, it is necessary to review other relevant theories in some detail and to consider potential contributions to the bigger picture of personal, social and emotional intelligences. This includes theories of developmental psychopathology, humanism, attachment, social understanding and pro-social development.

Theoretical approaches: interacting developmental processes and mechanisms

The contextualisation of the child, within the home, within the school, within the community and within the culture is crucial in our understanding of how children develop social, emotional and behavioural difficulties and also how some children appear to be either more resilient or vulnerable than others (Bronfenbrenner, 1986; Hinde 1992; 1997). The child's individual biology and psychology, what he brings to any situation in terms of his ability to self-regulate emotion and perceptions is equally important (Bronfenbrenner and Morris, 2006).

Cicchetti (1992) addressed the development of socio-emotional problems within an integrated, multi-causal, developmental and systemic framework. The three principal elements to Cicchetti's theory were causes, developmental tasks and systems. 'Causes', he argued, are not unidimensional. For instance, depression in childhood has a variety of symptom patterns and sources and it is not always possible to determine exact causes. Rather, it is more a matter of contributing factors. This is arguably true of many early childhood personal, social and emotional disorders. 'Developmental tasks' refers to the successful completion or attainment of a number of regulatory functions. These include physiological regulation, affect differentiation, self–other awareness and attachment to caretakers. 'Systems' refers to the fact that the successful attainment of these tasks may become thwarted by dysfunctional systems such as the family, school and society. So, for example, in the case of childhood depression as described by Cicchetti, a dysfunctional family environment (or system) is likely to involve poor parenting, parental mental health problems, low socio-economic status and income, and higher proportions of significant life events, stresses and difficulties such as unemployment, divorce, single-parenthood, etc. A dysfunctional school environment (or system) is likely to have features that increase emotional risks at transition times and to be lacking a caring, nurturing environment that can, in turn, trigger mental health problems. The school is also thought to play a key role in accessing the wider ecology of support services and helping children and families to take advantage of working alongside other service providers. The final, and potentially thwarting, system is that of political forces such as the availability of government resources to prevent or improve children's social and emotional problems. Cicchetti has continued to develop this process, the ecological-transactional model of child development, as a means of understanding the developmental risks and resilience opportunities for children living with maltreatment, chaotic social lives and parental mental illness (Cicchetti and Lynch, 1993; Cicchetti and Toth, 1998; Curtis and Cicchetti, 2003; Davies and Cicchetti, 2004; Mandi and Cicchetti, 2012). An understanding of the systems in which young children are living, as well as what they bring to the situation themselves in terms of biology and temperament, is central to the approach of assessment of risk and resilience (Rutter, 1995; Luther et al., 2000; Masten and Gewirtz, 2006; Rutter, 2012).

Humanism, self-concept and self-esteem

The importance of the healthy development of the self-concept and self-esteem has been established for quite some time by seminal works in social and humanistic psychology. Baldwin's (1906) self-discrepancy theory was an important early Vygotskian reference to self-esteem as being social in origin, and defined as the discrepancy between the perception of an actual self (attributes people believe they possess) and an ideal self (attributes people believe they would like to possess). There is, in addition, an 'ought-self' that refers to attributes people think they ought to possess. The suffering caused by such discrepancies that result in a low self-esteem has been noted to be associated with specific patterns, for example, an actual-ideal discrepancy leads to dejection, disappointment and sadness and an actual-ought discrepancy leads to agitation, apprehension and nervousness (Higgins, 1989). The self-esteem needs of children are therefore crucial for good mental health. Maslow (1954/1970) pointed out that, without healthy self-esteem, children would have impairments in cognitive exploration and aesthetic aspirations that would result in a failure to develop their full individual potential. According to Maslow, an individual child will achieve 'self-actualisation' in all developmental tasks or competencies only if certain successive foundations are successfully laid in early development (see also Chapter 3). In his 'hierarchy of needs', the most basic foundation (level 1) is for physiological or survival needs such as sufficient food and water. Once this is in place, the child needs to feel secure and safe, both physically and emotionally (level 2). Successful attainment in these needs will nurture the needs of love, affection and belonging (level 3). Once these are in place for a child, the need of self-esteem (level 4) can be achieved. Once the conditions of levels 1 to 4 have been met, the child can become self-actualised by an ability to access play and learning opportunities, engaging in the learning process, and having experiences of success and control (level 5). Within a PSE framework, educators have accepted this pivotal, developmental role of self-esteem and are seeking to better assess (Davis-Kean and Sandler, 2001) and promote it in young children (Lawrence, 1987; Mosley, 1996; Emler, 2001; Mosley, 2001; Dalgleish, 2002; Roberts, 2002; Donnellan, 2003). For a recent socio-cultural extension of Baldwin's theory, see Dweck (1999), Bizman and Yinon (2004); and Elliot and Dweck (2005).

Attachment theory

The seminal work of Ainsworth *et al.* (1978) identified three patterns of child behaviour in unfamiliar or fearful situations (which includes learning situations): the secure pattern and two types of insecure patterns, avoidant and ambivalent. Insecure children have developed an insecure, avoidant and coercive strategy using threats, bribes and inappropriate emotional displays. Secure children are better able to use the mother as a secure zone in order to explore and play in the surrounding environment. According to Crittenden (1992), however, the new preschool developmental task associated with attachment involves the adjustment of the partnership towards the potentially differing goals of the child and mother and includes aspects of reciprocity, perspective taking, management of relationships and empathy. Crittenden (1992) identified three strategies and one combination strategy relevant to preschoolers based on studies of children including maltreated and emotionally abused children: secure, insecure-defended, insecure-coercive and insecure defended/coercive (or disorganised). These attachment behaviours are typically manifested during situations of perceived stress or danger.

While the most severely affected children with respect to attachment security will require a multi-agency support system in the way of a planned intervention, other researchers are now beginning to 'take attachment theory to school', documenting the role that teachers and schools play at stressful periods for children, notably transition, and how they can help children to feel more secure (Dunn, 1994). Others have been looking at attachments to day-care workers and teachers as a means of compensating for difficulties elsewhere and at the links between the home and school environments with respect to attachment behaviours and supports (Mitchell-Copeland *et al.*, 1997; Cabello and Terrell, 1999; De Mulder *et al.*, 2000). Early childhood professionals interested in supporting the educational and social interests of vulnerable children, such as children in care or those with emotional disorders, can find the theoretical, assessment and intervention models of attachment in Howe (1995) and Howe *et al.* (1999), and in two of a series of three books by Daniel and Wassell (2002, 2004a, 2004b). For school-based accounts and interventions for attachment issues, there are several helpful publications: *Attachment in the Classroom* by Geddes (2005), *Inside I'm Hurting* by Bomber (2007), *A Short Introduction to Attachment and Attachment Disorder* by Pearce (2009) and finally, the highly successful *Nurture Groups in Schools* by Boxall and Lucas (2010). See also Chapter 5, for more information about attachment.

Social understanding: theory of mind and emotion

In the extensive body of literature now existing, 'theory of mind' refers to the ability to infer other people's mental states such as their thoughts, intentions, desires, feelings and beliefs. The skill is an ability to use this understanding to interpret and make sense of people's actions and predict what they will do next (Dennett, 1978). More recent practical formulations now refer to theory of mind as 'mind-reading' or 'social understanding' (Dunn, 1994; Howlin *et al.*, 1999; Greig and Howe, 2001). Indeed, Howlin *et al.* noted the valuable contribution that the ability to mind-read makes to understanding subtle aspects of communicative intent (including the figurative aspects of humour, irony, sarcasm and metaphor); in deception; in appreciating emotion in others; in self-reflection (thinking about one's own thinking); and in attempting to change the minds of others. Those who are afflicted by the 'mind-blindness' characteristic of autism will suffer from a formidable list of interpersonal problems, including insensitivity to the feelings of other people; the inability to read and respond to what others know, intend or perceive; failure to understand misunderstandings, unwritten rules or conventions, deception and reasons for others' actions. Children progress from the ability to understand what others see, through how things look to others to the significant achievement around three years of age that 'seeing-leads-to-knowing' (the understanding that the child who has seen inside a container will know the contents and the child who touched the container will not know). It is not until about four years of age that children are able to pass the 'theory of mind' test: the false-belief task. In this test, the child is presented with a puppet-play scenario involving Anne who has a box and Sally who has a basket. The child sees how puppet Sally puts a marble into her basket in front of puppet Anne, and then Sally goes away for a walk. When Sally has gone, the child sees Anne take the marble from the basket and put it into her box. Sally comes back and wants to play with her marble. The child is then asked where Sally will look for the marble (in the basket or in the box). By four years of age, most children are able to appreciate that Sally will have a false belief about where the marble is now located (Wimmer and Perner, 1983).

Figure 4.1 Cooperation is an important development milestone

The ability to pass the false-belief task is now known to be influenced by certain socialisation experiences, such as attachment security, symbolic mentalising ability, number of siblings and quality of relationships and pretend play with mothers and siblings (e.g. Perner *et al.*, 1994) (see also *The development of personal, social and emotional (PSE) competence* section below). Researchers are now considering that mind and emotion understanding may be distinct but nonetheless overlapping (Denham *et al.*, 1994; Greig and Howe, 2001), demonstrating that the ability to read the minds and emotions of others is related in complex ways to other psychological processes and mechanisms such as attachment and self-awareness. Indeed, Goodyer (2001) described the development of emotional intelligence as occurring within the development of a theory of mind, and how thinking affects both emotion and behaviour.

He advocates a cognitive-behavioural approach (teaching about the links between thinking, feeling and behaving) to early interventions for children encountering early problems in understanding the minds and emotions of self and other (Webster-Stratton *et al.*, 2006). There are a number of toolkits for schools that are based on these cognitive-behavioural techniques of teaching the whole, school, class or group about the links between thinking, feeling and behaviour (Spence, 2003). Other researchers believe it is possible to teach children emotion and mind-reading abilities (Dunn, 1994; Howlin *et al.*, 1999; Baron-Cohen, 2004; Sharp *et al.*, 2006).

Pro-social development

Being social, getting along with others, cooperating with them and helping them is an important developmental milestone. According to Hobson (2002), thought itself emerges through social relationships. Mind and emotion reading abilities are indeed prerequisites for pro-social action, enabling us to 'empathise' with others and form healthy relationships. Empathy has been defined as 'an affective response more appropriate to someone else's situation than to one's own' (Hoffman, 1987), and is therefore an ability that has the potential to ensure adaptive responses to distress in others. The fact that individuals can vary considerably in their pro-social tendencies has also been linked to experiences of socialisation, such as levels of parental affection, attachment security, parental mental health, family discussion and explanations of feelings of self and of others (e.g. see Denham, 1986; Hay, 1994; Hay *et al.*, 1999 for reviews; Hay *et al.*, 2008; Hay *et al.*, 2010). Hay recommends that the emergence of pro-social competence should not be conceived as a linear, developmental progression but rather as being partly a function of self–other perspective taking, attachment mechanisms and the socialisation experiences that mediate them. Individual difference could be said to be operating with some individuals (and genders) being clearly more caring and sharing than others. Developmentally (see also below), the important, early pro-social milestones include the diminishing of the initial pro-social reflex; the emergence of gender differentiation in pro-social action as a result of socialisation experiences; and the emergence of increasing social understanding. It is Hay's contention that the failure to regulate early pro-social action may lead to later psychopathy. Expanding somewhat on the ideas of both Rose-Krasnor and Cicchetti, Hay recommended the study of long-term, developmental, pro-social changes that span time and consider particular relationships, social contexts and family characteristics, such as parental mental health and numbers of siblings.

Friendship in the early years is crucially important to young children (Howes, 1988; Hartup, 1992), and the ability in the early years to cooperate with others and to form positive peer relationships is known to contribute to emotional, social and academic competence in later childhood; it also serves as a protective factor against externalising problems (Hay and Pawlby, 2003). There can be longer-term mental health problems, however, for children who are highly pro-social and those who consistently fail to establish mutual, positive peer relationships (Hay *et al.*, 2004; Fabes *et al.*, 2006).

To summarise the various theories reviewed, it would appear to be essential for professionals to be aware of the systems that potentially help or hinder the child's successful attainment of the developmental tasks that are required for effective personal, social and emotional competencies. Also required is the appreciation that failure to attain developmental tasks means that certain child needs will simply not be met, thereby increasing the likelihood that the child will fail to thrive personally, socially, emotionally and educationally. Furthermore, what has been repeatedly described are several 'nominally different but clearly overlapping children's abilities, namely, to interpret the mental states of others, to empathise with their feelings, and to adopt their differing social perspectives' (Warden and Christie, 1997). These, in turn, are affected by early socialisation experiences such as early attachment relationships. In order to better understand such competencies, theorists advocate both a developmental and systemic approach. This chapter will therefore conclude with a systemic overview of the development of these personal, social and emotional competencies in the early years.

The development of personal, social and emotional (PSE) competence

Below is a summary of the main developmental milestones and precursors to personal, social and emotional competences in the early years, according to recent research accounts. Each developmental 'stage' description is followed by a brief consideration of the evidence indicating how systems can hinder the development of crucial developmental tasks known to mediate the inter- and intrapersonal intelligences.

First eight months

The first 6–8 months of a child's life is a period of early preverbal communication sequences between infant and carer when they become 'attuned' to each other. This is a basic form of empathic exchanges, during which the child's feelings, such as smiling, are sensed by the parent, played back to the child by the parent in a manner demonstrating that the child's feelings are understood, and reciprocated by the carer (Stern, 1987). Prototypical conversational exchanges occur in the babbling exchanges between infant and carer as the child learns to cooperate in collaborative exchanges and turn-taking with others. This occurs during feeding, caring and playing routines (e.g. Hubley and Trevarthen, 1979; Hay, 1979). Infants also show a form of early empathic reactions by crying when they hear the distress of others, feeling it as if it were their own (Zahn-Waxler and Radke-Yarrow, 1990). An infant this young does not yet have a sense of self-separate-from-others, but nevertheless shows a preference for same-sex faces (Lewis and Brooks, 1974).

Impact of socialisation by 8 months
Early socialisation experiences with carers can disrupt these early, formative, interactive processes. For example, infants of mentally ill, rejecting or neglectful carers may fail to bond or to become attuned. Infants can also 'catch' depression from carers. Thus, early interactive experiences may put a child at a greater risk of later emotional and social disorders (Murray, 1992; Cummings and Davies, 1994; Cummings and Davies, 2002).

12 months

Between 8 and 12 months, the child attains the awareness of object permanence and an associated sense of self as separate from others. Empathically, this means that they begin to understand that others' distress is not their own, yet may react inappropriately (e.g. by wiping their own eyes upon observing another's tears) (Dunn and Brown, 1991). This 'motor mimicry' lasts until the second year. The infant also develops a fear of strangers as a result of the newly developed 'object permanence' of the mother (e.g. Ainsworth *et al.*, 1978).

Impact of socialisation by 12 months

Early socialisation experiences with the carer can lead to the formation of either a secure or insecure attachment to the carer. A parent who is not attuned to the child's fear, who does not return to the child in times of distress and anxiety, creates the possibility of an internal working model of expectations of responses from others (Bowlby, 1980; Stern, 1987; Murray, 1992). Hence, either a secure or insecure behavioural pattern of responding to situations involving the unfamiliar, change, stress or anxiety is established and continued in interactions with others, with pathological outcomes for disorganised infants perhaps even into adulthood (Crittenden, 1992).

18 to 36 months

At around 18 months, the child develops a sense of pretence that enables simple pretend or symbolic play (e.g. a rope is a snake) (Leslie, 1987). A growing vocabulary during the second year creates a new medium for the continuation of attuned (or indeed not attuned) interactive sequences with carers and, by two years, the beginning of the ability to negotiate to achieve self-interests. Children become more self-assertive and begin to develop a sense of guilt or conscience together with self-regulatory capacities (Kagan, 1989; Kochanska, 1993). Gender-appropriate toy preferences and play styles emerge, with boys being notably more aggressive than girls and having a general preference for same-sex playmates (Maccoby and Jacklin, 1980). They may also begin to spend more time with peers and form their first friendships – a social context in which they learn to cooperate with others and jointly solve problems (Howes, 1988). There is an increasing ability to demonstrate actual care or comfort for others in distress and by about three years, it becomes apparent that some children are becoming more caring (Dunn and Munn, 1986) and sharing than others (Hay *et al.*, 1993). Most children of this age are able to cooperate with carers in simple household duties (Hay, 1994) and are becoming aware of the norms in their families and communities that regulate their behaviour, such as teatime rules and moral imperatives (such as no hitting or violence) (Dunn and Munn, 1987).

Impact of socialisation at this stage

Early problems of socialisation, including day-care experiences, mean that some children may, due to insecurity, unregulated fear or anxiety, fail to access and form successful peer relationships. Children whose carers have failed to become attuned to them may lack the interactive skills to positively access others and the strategies to defend themselves from bullies. This is important because there is evidence indicating that the patterns of interaction at preschool associated with later conduct problems, depression and withdrawal may have originated in these very early relationships (Denham *et al.*, 1990; Rose-Krasnor, 1997). Children who do attend day care will be experiencing their first home–care transitions, a potentially fearful encounter for most toddlers (Dunn, 1994). Children whose guilt over their own misdemeanours is mismanaged by carers can develop further emotional and behavioural difficulties later on (Hoffman, 1976; Chapman *et al.*, 1987; Bugental *et al.*, 1992). Fortunately, it has been noted that day care can bring positive experiences to children by facilitating the formation of early friendships and moral reasoning. It is also possible to socially mediate these difficulties because increasing verbal skills mean that children are

Figure 4.2 Gender-appropriate toy preferences and play styles emerge between 18 and 36 months

better able to talk about emotional experiences with parents and other carers (Denham and Auerbach, 1995). Hence, everyday conversations can be used as a means of scaffolding the emotional experiences of the child (Dunn and Brown, 1991).

Figure 4.3 Day care can facilitate the formation of early friendships

36 months to 48 months plus

Between three and four years of age, pretend play becomes increasingly sophisticated with the emergence of role or socio-dramatic play, and perspective taking begins to emerge. That is, the child begins to understand that others have their own thoughts, intentions and beliefs that may be different from their own and that these beliefs may be wrong. They also begin to appreciate that others think and act on the basis of these beliefs, false or otherwise.

This is referred to as a 'theory of mind' in the literature (Lewis *et al.*, 1989; Baron-Cohen, 1993). Effectively, at three and four years, spontaneous pro-social action begins to be replaced by 'the respectable pursuit of self-interest', and this may be linked to gender (Hay *et al.*, 1999). Children should be becoming better able to understand the perspectives of others with respect to feelings and emotions. Most recent findings, however, suggest that an appreciation of the thoughts or beliefs of others need not mean a sound appreciation of another's feelings or of empathic reactions. This is perhaps because the development of the child's understanding of emotions of others is more sensitive to early socialisation experiences than the development of the understanding of logically based beliefs and intentions of others. In this way, children may be more inclined to show developmental lags in understanding emotions rather than intentions (Greig and Howe, 2001). Patterns of secure or insecure-defended or insecure-coercive behaviour are established in the preschool years, as disorganised preschoolers manifest a lack of coherence and positive resolution in their play and interactions (Bretherton *et al.*, 1990; Crittenden, 1992). Also on the increase over this period is the awareness of family and community norms and that transgressions have consequences (Smetana and Braeges, 1990). The appreciation that one is either male or female emerges between the ages of four and seven years, which is also a period during which girls develop pro-social and acceptable means of resolving peer disputes, being better able to pursue self-interests in a more quiet and covert way than boys (Hay *et al.*, 1992).

Impact of socialisation between 36 and 48 months

The impact of early socialisation on the development of social understanding is considerable. Research studies often refer to the skill as 'mentalising ability', and competence in it has been linked to attachment security (Meins, 1999); abilities to reflect about oneself (Fonagy *et al.*, 1991, 1997); number of siblings at home; extent of conversational exchanges at home (Bartsch and Wellman, 1989; Dunn and Brown, 1991); pretend play in the family (Youngblade and Dunn, 1995); and the carer's tendency to treat the child as a 'mentalising' agent (Meins *et al.*, 1998). The early socialisation of emotion understanding is often reported alongside studies on theory of mind (Harris, 1989), but others report emotion understanding as a separate 'skill' (Denham *et al.*, 1990, 1994) that has also been linked to attachment conversational exchanges with carers about conflicts and emotional experiences and parental mental health (Dunn and Munn, 1987; Denham *et al.*, 1994; Denham and Auerbach, 1995). The above review also indicates that children are being exposed to gender socialisation from a very early age. Girls begin to take a more nurturing and pro-social role than boys, and this may put them at risk of later emotional psychopathy (Hay *et al.*, 1999). Socialisation experiences of maternal mental ill-health and insecure attachments may predispose some children to pathological pro-social behaviour and/or more aggression than other children. Furthermore, the manifestations of difficulties associated with early relating may be different for boys and girls. While boys may become more aggressive, girls may be internalising guilt (Zahn-Waxler *et al.*, 1990; DeMulder and Radke-Yarrow, 1991; Hay *et al.*, 1999).

Conclusion

This chapter has considered a range of skill-based definitions of the personal, social and emotional competencies that contribute to a broadly defined personal, social and emotional intelligence. The complex and interdependent nature of the developing personal, social and emotional competencies was also explored. There were several recurring themes that included perspective-taking, or theory of mind, and its associated sense of self and others (autonomy and connectedness), attachment, and pro-social competence. These could be described as mechanisms or processes that underlie most of these competencies and interact in complex ways with early experiences of socialisation. Nevertheless, the fact that the development of these interactional intelligences is so dependent upon the types of experiences children have with significant others, that is, socially mediated, implies that it may possible to socially remedy many of the difficulties.

To conclude, it may be interesting to return to Miss Brodie and her subversive curriculum, for despite her enlightened views on the need to teach about matters that are personal, social and emotional, the character also famously quipped the Watsonian 'blank slate' phrase '… give me a girl at an impressionable age, and she is mine for life'. This chapter has considered how the children we work with do not come to our attention as blank slates. But to what extent can we remedy difficulties that have been socially mediated in the developmental process at impressionable ages? This chapter shows that we are only beginning to really understand the complex nature of personal, social and emotional development and intelligence. How to best teach, support it and to remedy the damage is quite another matter. It is a complex process, and those of us familiar with the fate of Miss Brodie will consider the possibility that even well-meaning, enlightened, middle-class school teachers could get it wrong! But at least she tried. Can any of the rest of us really say the same?

Learning activity

Identify three children of different ages under eight years. By observation of the children or discussion with parents/carers, elicit examples of these children's:

● perspective taking
● attachment to a significant other and
● pro-social competence.

Discuss your findings with a fellow student, colleague or tutor.

Evaluate your learning

● Why is the early socialisation of children so important in their development?
● What might be the signs that a child is not thriving in terms of personal, social and emotional development and what could the reasons for this be?
● Based on what you have learned in this chapter, which theory do you think is most crucial in terms of the underlying developmental processes and mechanisms that lead to the healthy attainment of developmental tasks? Why?

References

Ainsworth, MDS, Blehar, M, Walters, E and Wall, S (1978): *Patterns of Attachment: A Psychological Study of the Strange Situation.* Hillsdale, NJ: Erlbaum.

Antidote (2003): *The Emotional Literacy Handbook: Promoting Whole-School Strategies.* London: David Fulton Publishers.

Baldwin, JM (1906): *Mental Development in the Child and Race: Methods and Processes*, 3rd revised edn. New York: Macmillan.

Baron-Cohen, S (1993): Children's theories of mind: where would we be without the intentional stance? In Rutter, ML and Hay, DF (eds), *Development Through Life: A Handbook for Clinicians.* Oxford: Blackwell.

Baron-Cohen, S (2004): *Mind Reading: The Interactive Guide to Emotions.* Basingstoke: Taylor & Francis.

Bartsch, K and Wellman, H (1989): Young children's attribution of action to beliefs and desires. *Child Development* **57**, 194–201.

Bizman, A and Yinon, J (2004): Social self-discrepancies from own and other stand-points and collective self-esteem. *Journal of Social Psychology* **144**(2), 101–13.

Block, J (1995): On the relation between IQ, impulsivity and delinquency *Journal of Abnormal Psychology* **104**, 395–8.

Bomber, L (2007): *Inside I'm Hurting: Practical Strategies for Supporting Children with Attachment Difficulties in Schools.* Richmond: Worth Publishing Ltd.

Bowlby, J (1980): *Attachment and Loss. Vol. 3: Loss, Sadness and Depression.* New York: Basic Books.

Bowlby, J (1991) *The Making and Breaking of Affectional Bonds.* Oxford: Penguin.

Boxall, M and Lucas, S (2010): *Nurture Groups in Schools*, 2nd edn. London: Sage Publications Ltd.

Bretherton, I, Ridgeway, D and Cassidy, J (1990): The role of internal working models in the attachment relationship. In Greenberg, M, Cicchetti, D and Cummings, EM (eds), *Attachment in the Preschool Years: Theory, Research and Intervention.* Chicago IL: University of Chicago Press, pp. 273–308.

Bronfenbrenner, U (1986): Ecology of the family as a context for human development: research perspectives. *Developmental Psychology* **22**, 723–42.

Bronfenbrenner, U (1992): Ecological systems theory. In Vasta, R (ed), *Six Theories of Child Development: Revised Formulation and Current Issues.* London: Jessica Kingsley, pp. 187–249.

Bronfenbrenner, U and Morris, PA (2006): The bioecological model of human development. In Lerner, RM and Damon, W (eds), *Handbook of Child Psychology. Vol 1, Theoretical Models of Human Development*, 6th edn. Hoboken, NJ, US: Wiley and Sons Inc., pp. 793–828.

Bugental, DB, Blue, J, Cortez, V, Fleck, K and Rodriguez, A (1992): Influences of witnessed affect on information processing in children. *Child Development* **63**, 774–86.

Cabello, B and Terrell, R (1999): Making students feel like family: how teachers create warm and caring classroom climates. *Journal of Classroom Interaction* **29**(1), 17–23.

Campbell, SB (1991): Longitudinal studies of active and aggressive preschoolers: individual differences in early behaviour and outcome. In Cicchetti, D and Toth, SL (eds), *Rochester Symposium on Developmental Psychopathology*. Hillsdale, NJ: Erlbaum, pp. 957–90.

Chapman, M, Zahn-Waxler, C, Iannotti, R and Cooperman, G (1987): Empathy and responsibility in the motivation of children's helping. *Developmental Psychology* **23**, 140–5.

Cicchetti, D (1992): *Developmental Perspectives on Depression*. Rochester, NY: University of Rochester Press.

Cicchetti, D and Lynch M (1993): Towards an ecological/transactional model of community violence and child maltreatment: Consequences for children's development. *Psychiatry* **56**(1), 96–118.

Cicchetti, D and Toth, SL (1998): Development of depression in children and adolescents. *American Psychologist* **53**(2), 221–41.

Conduct Problems Prevention Research Group (CPPRG) (2002a): The implementation of the fast track program: an example of a large-scale efficacy trial. *Journal of Abnormal Child Psychology* **30**(1), 1–18.

Conduct Problems Prevention Research Group (CPPRG) (2002b): Evaluation of the first three years of the fast track prevention trial with children at high risk for adolescent conduct problems. *Journal of Abnormal Child Psychology* **30**(1), 19–35.

Conduct Problems Prevention Research Group (CPPRG) (2002c): Predictor variables associated with positive fast track outcomes at the end of the third grade. *Journal of Abnormal Child Psychology* **30**(1), 37–52.

Conduct Problems Prevention Research Group (CPPRG) (2007): The fast track randomised controlled trial to prevent externalising psychiatric disorders: Findings from grades 3–9. *Journal of American Academy of Child and Adolescent Psychiatry* **46**, 1263–72.

Conduct Problems Prevention Research Group (CPPRG) (2010): Fast track intervention effects on youth arrests and delinquency. *Journal of Experimental Criminology* **6**, 131–57.

Crittenden, PM (1992): Quality of attachment in the preschool years. *Development and Psychopathology* **4**, 209–41.

Cummings, EM and Davies, PT (1994): Maternal depression and child development. *Journal of Child Psychology and Psychiatry*, **35**(1), 73–112.

Cummings, EM and Davies PT (2002): Effects of marital discord on children: Recent advances and emerging process oriented research. *Journal of Child Psychology and Psychiatry* **43**, 31–63.

Curtis, WJ and Cicchetti, D (2003): Moving research on resilience into the 21st century: Theoretical and methodological considerations in examining the biological contributors to resilience. *Development and Psychopathology* **15**, 773–810.

Dalgleish, T (2002): *Self-Esteem: Ages 6–8: Activities to Develop Children's Self-Esteem, Across the Curriculum*. London: A. & C. Black.

Damasio, AR (1996): *Descartes' Error: Emotion, Reason and the Human Brain*. London: Papermac.

Daniel, B and Wassell, S (2002/2004a): *The Early Years: Assessing and Promoting Resilience in Vulnerable Children 1*. London: Jessica Kingsley.

Daniel, B and Wassell, S (2002/2004b): *The School Years: Assessing and Promoting Resilience in Vulnerable Children 2*. London: Jessica Kingsley.

Davies, PT and Cicchetti, D (2004): Towards an integration of family systems and developmental psychopathology. *Development and Psychopathology* **16**(3), 477–797.

Davis-Kean, PE and Sandler, HM (2001): A meta-analysis of measures of self-esteem for young children: a framework for future measures. *Child Development* **72**(3), 887–906.

De Mulder, E and Radke-Yarrow, M (1991): Attachment with affectively ill and well mothers: concurrent behavioural correlates. *Development and Psychopathology* **3**, 227–42.

De Mulder, EK, Denham, S, Schmidt, M and Mitchell, J (2000): Q-sort assessment of attachment security during the preschool years: links from home to school. *Developmental Psychology* **36**(2), 274–82.

Denham, SA (1986): Social cognition, pro-social behaviour, and emotion in preschoolers. *Child Development* **57**, 194–201.

Denham, SA and Auerbach, S (1995): Mother–child dialogue about emotions and preschoolers' emotional competence. *Genetic, Social and General Psychology Monographs* **121**(3), 311–37.

Denham, SA, McKinley, M, Couchoud, EA and Holt, R (1990): Emotional and behavioural predictors of preschool peer ratings. *Child Development* **57**, 194–201.

Denham, SA, Zoller, D and Couchoud, EA (1994): Socialisation of preschoolers' emotion understanding. *Developmental Psychology* **30**(6), 928–36.

Denham, SA, Blair, KA, De Mulder, E, Levitas, J, Sawyer, K, Auerbach-Major, S and Queenan, P (2003): Preschool emotional competence: pathway to social competence? *Child Development* **74**(1), 238–56.

Dennett, D (1978): Beliefs about beliefs. *Behavioural and Brain Sciences* **4**, 759–70.

Donnellan, C (2003): *Self-Esteem.* Cambridge: Independence.

Dunn, J (1988): *The Beginnings of Social Understanding.* Cambridge, MA: Harvard University Press.

Dunn, J (1994): Understanding others and the social world: current issues in developmental research and their relation to preschool experiences and practice. *Journal of Applied Developmental Psychology* **15**, 571–83.

Dunn, J (1996): The Emanuel Miller Memorial Lecture 1995. Children's relationships: bridging the divide between cognitive and social development. *Journal of Child Psychology and Psychiatry* **37**(5), 507–18.

Dunn, J and Brown, J (1991): Relationships, talk about feelings and the development of affect regulation in early childhood. In Garber, J and Dodge, KA (eds), *The Development of Emotion Regulation and Dysregulation.* Cambridge, MA: Cambridge University Press.

Dunn, J and Munn, P (1986): Siblings and the development of pro-social behaviour. *International Journal of Behavioural Development* **9**, 265–84.

Dunn, J and Munn, P (1987): The development of justification in disputes with mother and sibling. *Developmental Psychology* **23**, 791–98.

Dweck, CS (1999): *Self-Theories: Their Role in Motivation, Personality and Development.* Philadelphia, PA: Psychological Press.

Elliot, AJ and Dweck, C (Eds) (2005): *Handbook of Competence and Motivation.* New York: Guilford Press.

Emler, N (2001): *Self-Esteem: The Costs and Causes of Low Self-Worth.* Layerthorpe: Joseph Rowntree Foundation by York Publishing Services.

Estrada, AU and Pinsof, WM (1995): The effectiveness of family therapies for selected behavioural disorders in childhood. *Journal of Marital and Family Therapy* **21**(4), 403–40.

Fabes, RA, Gaertner, BM and Popp, TK (2006): Getting along with others: Social competence in early childhood. In McCartney, K and Phillips, D (eds) *Blackwell Handbook of Early Childhood Development*. Malden, US: Blackwell Publishing, pp. 297–316.

Ford, T, Goodman, R and Meltzer, H (2003): The British Child and Adolescent Mental Health Survey 1999: The prevalence of DSM IV disorders. *Journal of the American Academy of Child and Adolescent Psychiatry* **42**, 1203–11.

Fonagy, P, Steele, M, Steele, H, Moran, GS and Higgitt, AC (1991): The capacity for understanding mental states: the reflective self in parent and child and its significance for security of attachment. *Infant Mental Health Journal* **12**, 201–18.

Fonagy, P, Steele, H, Steele, M and Holder, J (1997): Attachment and theory of mind: overlapping constructs? *Bonding and Attachment: Association of Child Psychology and Psychiatry Occasional Papers No. 14*.

Gardner, H (1983): *Frames of Mind: The Theory of Multiple Intelligences*. New York: Basic Books.

Gardner, H (1993): *Multiple Intelligences: The Theory in Practice*. New York: Basic Books.

Gardner, H (2006): *Multiple Intelligence: New Horizons*. New York: Basic Books.

Goleman, D (1996): *Emotional Intelligence: Why it can Matter More than IQ*. London: Bloomsbury Publishing.

Goleman, D (1998): *Working with Emotional Intelligence*. London: Random House Publishing Group.

Goleman, D (2004): *Emotional Intelligence and Working with Emotional Intelligence*. London: Bloomsbury Publishing.

Goleman, D (2007): *Social Intelligence: The Science of Human Relationships*. London: Arrow Books.

Goodyer, IM (2001): The development of emotional intelligence. In Goodyer, IM (ed), *The Depressed Child and Adolescent*. Cambridge: Cambridge University Press, pp. 24–45.

Geddes, H (2006): *Attachment in the Classroom: The Links Between Children's Early Experience, Emotional Well-being and Performance in School*. Richmond: Worth Publishing Ltd.

Greenberg, MT and Kusche, C (1998): Promoting Alternative Thinking Strategies (PATHS). In Elliott, DS (ed), *Blueprints for Violence Prevention*. Colorado: C&M Press.

Greig, A (2004): Childhood depression – Part 1: Does it need to be dealt with only by health professionals? *Educational and Child Psychology* **21**(4), 43–54.

Greig, A and Howe, D (2001): Social understanding, attachment security of preschool children and maternal mental health. *British Journal of Developmental Psychology* **19**(3), 381–93.

Guralnick, M (ed.) (1997): *The Effectiveness of Early Intervention*. Baltimore, MD: Paul H. Brookes.

Harris, P (1989): *Children and Emotion: The Development of Psychological Understanding*. Oxford: Blackwell.

Harris, P (1999): Individual differences in understanding emotion: the role of attachment status and psychological assessment. *Attachment and Human Development* **1**(3), 307–24.

Hartup, WW (1992): Friendships and their developmental significance. In McGurk, H (ed), *Childhood Social Development: Contemporary Perspectives*. Hove: Erlbaum.

Hay, DF (1979): Cooperative interactions and sharing between very young children and their parents. *Developmental Psychology* **15**, 647–53.

Hay, DF (1994): Pro-social development. *Journal of Child Psychology and Psychiatry* **35**(1), 29–71.

Hay, DF (2009): The roots and branches of human altruism. *British Journal of Psychology* **100**, 473–79.

Hay, DF and Pawlby, S (2003): Pro-social development in relation to children's and mothers' psychological problems. *Child Development* **74**(5), 1314–27.

Hay, DF, Zahn-Waxler, C, Cummings, EM and Iannotti, R (1992): Young children's views about conflict with peers: a comparison of the sons and daughters of depressed and well women. *Journal of Child Psychology and Psychiatry* **33**, 669–83.

Hay, DF, Stimson, CA, Castle, J and Davies, L (1993): The construction of character in toddlerhood. In Killen, M and Hart, D (eds), *Morality in Everyday Life*. Cambridge: Cambridge University Press.

Hay, DF, Castle, J, Davies, L, Demetriou, H and Stimson, CA (1999): Pro-social action in very early childhood. *Journal of Child Psychology and Psychiatry* **40**(6), 905–16.

Hay, DF, Payne, A and Chadwick, A (2004): Peer relations in childhood. *Journal of Child Psychology and Psychiatry and Allied Disciplines* **45**(1), 84–108.

Hay, DF, Caplan, M and Nash, A (2008): The beginnings of peer interaction. In Rubin, KH, Bukowski, W and Laursen, B (eds), *Handbook of Peer Relations*. New York: Guilford Press.

Hay, DF, Hudson, K and Liang, W (2010) Links between preschool children's prosocial skills and their psychological problems. *Early Childhood Research Quarterly* **25**, 493–501.

Higgins, ET (1989): Self-discrepancy theory: what patterns of self-belief cause people to suffer. In Berkowitz, L (ed), *Advances in Experimental Social Psychology*. New York: Academic Press, **22**, 93–136.

Hinde, RA (1992): Human social development: an ethological/relationship perspective. In McGurk, H (ed), *Childhood Social Development: Contemporary Perspectives*. London: Erlbaum.

Hinde, RA (1997): *Relationships: A Dialectical Perspective*. Hove, UK: Psychology Press.

Hobson, P (2002): *Cradle of Thought*. London: Macmillan.

Hoffman, M (1976): Empathy, role taking, guilt, and the development of altruistic motives. In Lickona, T (ed), *Moral Development and Behaviour*. New York: Holt, Rinehart and Winston.

Hoffman, M (1987): The contribution of empathy to justice and moral judgment. In Eisenberg, N and Strayer, J (eds), *Empathy and its Development*. Cambridge: Cambridge University Press.

Howe, D (1995): *Attachment Theory for Social Work Practice*. London: Macmillan.

Howe, D, Brandon, M, Hining, D and Schofield, G (1999): *Attachment Theory, Child Maltreatment and Family Support*. London: Macmillan.

Howes, C (1988): Peer interaction and young children. *Monographs of the Society for Research in Child Development* **53**(1), 94.

Howlin, P, Baron-Cohen, S and Hadwin, J (1999): *Teaching Children with Autism to Mind-Read: A Practical Guide for Teachers and Parents.* Chichester: John Wiley & Sons Ltd.

Hubley, P and Trevarthen, C (1979): Sharing a task in infancy. In Usgiris, IC (ed), *Social Interaction During Infancy.* San Francisco: Jossey-Bass.

Hughes, A and Kleinberg, S (1999): Organisation and management in nursery and infant schooling. In Bryce, TGK and Humes, WM (eds), *Scottish Education.* Edinburgh: Edinburgh University Press.

Izard, CE, Fine, S, Schulz, D, Mostow, A, Ackerman, BP and Youngstrom, EA (2001): Emotion knowledge as a predictor of social behaviour and academic competence in children at risk. *Psychological Science* **12**, 18–23.

Kagan, J. (1989): *Unstable Ideas: Temperament, Cognition and Self.* Cambridge, MA: Harvard University Press.

Kazdin, A (1995): Child, parent and family dysfunction as predictors of outcome in cognitive-behavioural treatment of antisocial children. *Behaviour Research and Therapy* **3**, 271–81.

Kochanska, G (1993): Towards a synthesis of parental socialisation and child temperament in early development of conscience. *Child Development* **64**, 325–47.

Kovacs, M (1997): The Emmanuel Miller Memorial Lecture 1994. Depressive disorders in childhood: an impressionistic landscape. *Journal of Child Psychology and Psychiatry* **38**(3), 287–98.

Ladd, GW, Birch, SH and Buhs, ES (1999): Children's social and scholastic lives in kindergarten: related spheres of influence? *Child Development* **70**(6), 1373–1400.

Lawrence, D (1987): *Enhancing Self-Esteem in the Classroom.* London: Paul Chapman Publishing.

Leslie, AM (1987): Pretence and theory of mind: the origins of theory of mind. *Psychological Review* **94**, 412–26.

Lewis, M and Brooks, J (1974): Self, other and fear: infants' reactions to people. In Lewis, M and Rosenblum, M (eds), *Fear: The Origins of Behaviour, 2.* New York: Wiley.

Lewis, M, Stranger, C and Sullivan, MW (1989): Deception in 3-year-olds. *Developmental Psychology* **25**, 439–43.

Luther, SS, Cicchetti, D and Becker, B (2000): The construct of resilience: A critical evaluation and guidelines for future work. *Child Development* **71**(3), 573–75.

Maccoby, EE and Jacklin, CN (1980): Sex differences in aggression: a rejoinder and reprise. *Child Development* **5**, 964–80.

Mandi, L and Cicchetti, D (2012): Multiple approaches towards understanding antisocial behaviour: current research and future directions. *Development and Psychopathology* **24**(3), 703–4.

Maslow, AH (1954/1970): *Motivation and the Personality*, 2nd edn. New York: Harper & Row.

Masten, AS and Gewirtz, AH (2006): Vulnerability and resilience in early childhood development. In McCartney, K and Phillips, D (eds), *Blackwell Handbook of Early Childhood.* Malden MA, US: Blackwell Publishing, pp. 22–43.

Meins, E (1999): Sensitivity, security and internal working models: bridging the transmission gap. *Attachment and Human Development* **1**(3), 325–42.

Meins, E, Fernyhough, C, Russell, J and Clark-Carter, D (1998): Security of attachment as a predictor of symbolic and mentalizing abilities: a longitudinal study. *Social Development* 7, pp. 1–24.

Meltzer, H (2005): The prevalence of mental health and mental disorders in childhood and adolescence. In Williams, R and Kerfoot, M (eds), *Child and Adolescent Mental Health Services: Strategy, Planning, Delivery and Evaluation.* Oxford: Oxford University Press.

Meltzer, H, Gartward, R, Goodman, R and Ford, T (2000): *Mental Health of Children and Adolescents in Great Britain.* London: The Stationery Office.

Meltzer, H, Gartwood, R, Corbin, T, Goodman, R and Ford, T (2003): *Persistence, onset, risk factors and outcomes for childhood mental disorders.* London: The Stationery Office.

Meltzer, H, Ford, T, Goodman, R and Vostanis, P (2011): The burden of caring for children with emotional or conduct disorders. *International Journal of Family Medicine* EPub ahead of print.

MIND (2001): Children and Young People in Mental Distress. London: MIND.

Mitchell-Copeland, J, Denham, S and De Mulder, EK (1997): Q-sort assessment of child–teacher attachment relationships and social competence in the preschool. Early Education and Development **8**(1), 27–39.

Mosley, J (1996): Quality Circle Time in the Primary Classroom: Your Essential Guide to Enhancing Self-Esteem, Self-Discipline and Positive Relationships. Wisbech, Cambridge: LDA.

Mosley, J (2001): More Quality Circle Time. Wisbech, Cambridge: LDA.

Murray, L (1992): The impact of postnatal depression on infant development. Journal of Child Psychology **33**, 543–61.

Orbach, S (1997): Quoted in the pamphlet *Realising the Potential: Emotional Education for All: An Antidote Report.*

Pearce, C (2009): *Short Introduction to Attachment and Attachment Disorder.* London: Jessica Kingsley Publishers.

Perner, J, Ruffman, T and Leekham, S (1994): Theory of mind is contagious: you catch it from your sibs. *Child Development* **65**, 1224–34.

Roberts, R (2002): *Self-Esteem and Early Learning.* London: Paul Chapman Publishing Ltd.

Rose-Krasnor, L (1997): The nature of social competence: a theoretical review. *Social Development* **6**(1), 111–29.

Rutter, M (1995): Stress research: accomplishments and tasks ahead. In Haggerty, RJ, Sherrod, LR, Garmezy, N and Rutter, M (eds), *Stress, Risk and Resilience in Children and Adolescents: Processes, Mechanisms and Interventions.* New York and Cambridge: Cambridge University Press.

Rutter, M (2012): Annual research review. Resilience: clinical implications. *Journal of Child Psychology and Psychiatry.* Epub ahead of print.

Rutter, M, Giller, H and Hagell, A (1998): *Antisocial Behaviour by Young People: A Major New Review of the Research.* Cambridge: Cambridge University Press.

Saarni, C (1990): Emotional competence: how emotions and relationships become integrated. In Thompson, RA (ed), *Socioemotional Development/Nebraska Symposium on Motivation*, 36. Nebraska: University of Nebraska Press.

Salovey, P and Mayer, JD (1990): Emotional intelligence. *Imagination, Cognition and Personality* **9**, 185–211.

SCCC (1999): *A Curriculum Framework for Children 3 to 5*. Scottish Consultative Council on the Curriculum, Edinburgh: The Scottish Office.

Sharp, C, Fonagy, P and Goodyer, IM (2006): Imagining your child's mind. Psychosocial adjustment and mothers' ability to predict their children's attributional response styles. *British Journal of Developmental Psychology* **24**, 197–212.

Smetana, JG and Braeges JL (1990) The development of toddlers' moral and conventional judgements. *Merrill-Palmer Quarterly* **36**, 329–46.

Spark, M (1961): *The Prime of Miss Jean Brodie*. London: Macmillan.

Spence, SH (2003): Social skills training with children and young people: theory, evidence and practice. *Child and Adolescent Mental Health* **8**(2), 84–96.

Steiner, C and Perry, P (1997): *Achieving Emotional Literacy*. London: Bloomsbury.

Stern, D (1987): *The Interpersonal World of the Infant*. New York: Basic Books.

Stone, KF and Dillehunt, HQ (1978): *Self-Science: The Subject is Me*. Santa Monica: Goodyear Publishing Co.

Sylva, K (1994): The impact of early learning on children's development. In Ball, C (ed), *Start Right: The Importance of Early Learning*. London: Royal Society for the Arts, Manufacturers & Commerce, pp. 84–96.

Trevarthen, C (1997): The curricular conundrum. In Dunlop, AW and Hughes, A (eds), *Preschool Curriculum Policy Practice and Proposals: A Forum for Policy Makers and Practitioners in Scotland*. Strathclyde: Strathclyde University.

Warden, D and Christie, D (1997): *Teaching Social Behaviour: Classroom Activities to Foster Children's Interpersonal Awareness*. London: David Fulton Publishers.

Webster-Stratton, C, Reid, MJ, McCartney, K and Phillips, D (2006): Treatment and preventions of conduct problems: Parent training interventions for young children (2–7 years old). In McCartney, K and Phillips, D (eds), *Blackwell Handbook of Early Childhood Development*. Oxford: Blackwell, pp. 616–41.

Wimmer, H and Perner, J (1983): Beliefs about beliefs: representation and constraining function of wrong beliefs in young children's understanding of deception. *Cognition* **21**, 103–28.

Youngblade, LM and Dunn, J (1995): Individual differences in young children's pretend play with mother and sibling: links to relationships and understanding of other people's feelings and beliefs. *Child Development* **66**, 1472–92.

Zahn-Waxler, C and Radke-Yarrow, M (1990): Origins of empathic concern. *Motivation and Emotion* **14**, 107–30.

Zahn-Waxler, C, Kochanska, G, Krupnick, J and McKnew, D (1990): Patterns of guilt in children of depressed and well mothers. *Developmental Psychology* **28**, 126–36.

Further reading

Barnes, P (ed) (1995): *Personal, Social and Emotional Development of Children.* Milton Keynes: Open University Press.

Cooper, P (ed) (1999): *Understanding and Supporting Children with Emotional and Behavioural Difficulties.* London: Jessica Kingsley.

Greenberg, T (2010): School based prevention: Current status and future challenges. *Effective Education* **2**, 27–52.

Harms, PD and Credé, M (2010): Remaining issues in emotional intelligence: Construct overlap, method artefacts and lack of incremental validity. *Industrial and Organisational Psychology: Perspectives in Science and Practice* **3**(2), 154–58.

Jennings, PA and Greenberg, MT (2009): The prosocial classroom: Teacher social and emotional competence in relation to child and adolescent classroom outcome. *Review of Educational Research* **79**, 491–525.

Roberts, R (2002): *Self-Esteem and Early Learning*, 2nd edn. London: Sage.

Schaffer, R (1996): *Social Development.* Oxford: Blackwell.

Spence, SH (2003): Social skills training with children and young people: theory, evidence and practice. *Child and Adolescent Mental Health* **8**(2), 84–96.

5 Children's relationships

David Rutherford

This chapter aims to:
- explore key issues in the nature and impact of young children's most important relationships with others, as they develop in a variety of parenting, family and social contexts
- examine a broad range of research findings, theories and concepts including family relationships, parenting, family structures and family functioning.

Introduction

Some years ago when I asked our then five-year-old son, Nat, who his important relationships were with he immediately listed his parents, sister, brothers, grandmothers, cousins, aunts and uncles, friends, friends' parents and the cats (but not the goldfish!). I asked him again when he was 14 and his answer was much the same, although the cats had dropped out and his dog, his sister's husband and new baby had replaced them. As a young adult he has many more peer relationships and some of his earlier relationships have weakened or disappeared. Most psychologists would agree that these people are likely to play a significant part in the emotional, social and cognitive development of children in western societies. In all cultures, the survival, health, behaviour and development of skills of children are dependent upon the nurturance, training and control offered by the people with whom they have close relationships (Whiting and Edwards, 1988). The process of socialisation, whereby children are shaped to fit their own particular culture, has traditionally portrayed children as passive recipients of adult influence but, as any parent knows, it is not as simple as that, and children are clearly and determinedly active participants in their own socialisation, constantly modifying and challenging intended influences in pursuit of their own goals and personalities.

The study of relationships is central to social psychology, and in the last few years there has been considerable growth in our knowledge about children's relationships. Currently, theorists from social and evolutionary psychology, ethology, social anthropology and sociology, as well as from developmental psychology, psychiatry and neuroscience, are making significant contributions to our understanding of children's relationships. From the early work of Sigmund Freud and John Bowlby (1953), where the emphasis was almost entirely on the mother–child relationship, there have been some important developments in recent years. First, the whole area has become much more complex, and the multiple interactive nature of children's relationships is being explored. Second, pivotal concepts such as attachment, the family and temperament, continue to be refined and elaborated to reflect the subtlety of relationships. Third, a multicultural perspective has evolved which enables us to examine possible universals of relationships, as well as cultural diversity. Fourth, the significance of a child's relationships with father, siblings, grandparents, other care-givers and friends and peers, is increasingly recognised as being important for that child's future development. Fifth, it is recognised that children's relationships always occur within a social context of already existing relationships which may exert a powerful influence upon the child. Finally, our understanding of the impact upon a child of relationship disturbance, such as parental discord, neglect, or sexual abuse, encourages intervention strategies and ways of improving relationships.

The concept of 'social capital' has emerged as an important idea in recent years and in his book *Bowling Alone*, Putnam (2000: 296) suggests that 'social capital keeps bad things from happening to good kids'. Social capital refers to the resources that are available to people through their social relationships and three types have been identified:

1. **Bonding**. Social capital which comprises the strong connections within a group or family or neighbourhood enabling them to manage or get by on a daily basis.
2. **Bridging**. Social capital is concerned with connections between families and groups and is essential for 'getting ahead'.
3. **Linking**. Social capital describes connections across boundaries between families and formal professional groups within and outside the local community (ResPublica, 2011).

Children living in communities with good social capital do well and are more likely to have better health, be less abused and attain better educational achievement. Recognition of this is apparent in the government's launching of The Big Society policy in 2010, among other things, giving local communities more power and encouraging people to take an active role in their community.

Family relationships

Most children are born into a family. Although there are many problems about defining precisely what comprises a family – ranging from the relatively straightforward conjugal nuclear family to the non-conjugal/reconstituted/extended family – members of families are likely to have persistent relationships involving emotional bonds. That is to say, they belong to a group of interconnected and interdependent people who have psychologically meaningful social interactions (Richards, 1995). In the 21st century, blood ties, common residence or legal connections are not considered necessary for the recognition of a family unit. What is important is that there is mutual recognition of family membership. This allows for the diversity of family units which have developed over the past 50 years, and perhaps 35 different types of family set-up exist in the UK today. Although the traditional nuclear family with both biological parents and two children still exists, the majority of children today are being brought up in families with variable and often changing members. It is possible for some children to have as many as five or six 'parents' (work that out!), several step-parents and siblings, half-brothers and half-sisters and numerous grandparents, whereas others live in lone-parent families with no siblings and little contact with relatives.

Whatever a child's family type, early years professionals, psychologists and lay people all acknowledge the significance of family relationships as sources of socialisation, nurturance, happiness and comfort (as well as irritation, anxiety and frustration). The Good Childhood Report (2012) concludes that most children are happy in their home environment and that there is a strong link with their level of well-being, particularly when their safety, security, privacy and stability are ensured. Life events studies, from the initial work of Holmes and Rahe (1967) onwards, demonstrate that many significant aspects of a person's well-being are related to changes in family relationships. Both major changes (such as the birth of a child into an existing set of family relationships) and minor changes (uplifts and hassles, such as birthdays or tonsillitis) have direct and indirect influences on family members. There is currently a large body of research showing that, in general, our physical and mental health, recovery from illness, and even the number of accidents we have are related to the quality of our close relationships. However, although relationships often provide a buffer against adversity, they can also be sources of severe injury, distress and life-long psychological damage. Also, Lord Laming's report (Laming, 2003) on the inquiry into the death of Victoria Climbié, has generated more than a hundred recommendations for ensuring the care and protection of children in families and institutions throughout the UK.

Parenting

Early research into the ways in which families affect children identified two main dimensions of parental behaviour that were thought to affect a child's subsequent development:

1. The dimension warmth – coldness referred to the amount of affection and playfulness shown towards children
2. The dimension permissiveness – restrictiveness referred to parental toleration of aggressiveness and control of a child's behaviour.

Few associations between parenting styles and children's development were found, but this research paved the way for the influential work of Diana Baumrind (1971), who examined the ways in which different types of relationships between parents and children affect a child's behaviour. Baumrind argues that normal parenting is mainly concerned with influencing and controlling children. Parental 'demandingness' refers to 'the claims parents make on children to become integrated into the family whole, by their maturity demands, supervision, disciplinary efforts and willingness to confront the child who disobeys'. Parental 'responsiveness' is 'the extent to which parents intentionally foster individuality, self-regulation and self-assertion by being attuned, supportive, and acquiescent to children's special needs and demands' (Baumrind, 1991: 62). Following a research tradition in the study of leadership, she identified three parental styles related to three patterns of children's behaviour (Table 5.1).

Table 5.1 Parental styles and children's behaviour

Parental style	Child's behaviour
Permissive	Impulsive–aggressive
Authoritarian	Conflicted–irritable
Authoritative	Energetic–friendly

- 'Permissive' parents have very relaxed relationships with their children and, because they do not believe in restricting their child's independence, they exercise less control and accept lower levels of performance, both cognitively and behaviourally. Often their discipline is inconsistent and a child's freedom of expression is valued highly. The children of permissive parents are often found to be aggressive in their relationships with parents, other adults and other children, unable to control their own feelings of anger, impulsive in their actions and to have low levels of goal-directed achievement orientation.

- 'Authoritarian' parents have very controlling relationships with their children. They tend to restrict a child's activities, set strict rules for the child, and use harsh, punitive discipline for transgressions. They show low levels of affection and are uninvolved in family and cultural events. The children of authoritarian parents are often very vulnerable to stress, fearful and anxious about their relationships and appear moody and unhappy. They react irritably, are rather deceitful, and tend to alternate between sulky, passive withdrawal and overt aggression.

- 'Authoritative' parents achieve a workable balance between setting high and clear standards for a child's behaviour and encouraging independence. Discipline is firm but fair, with the child's viewpoint being taken into consideration and control achieved by reasoning and explaining from an early age. Such parents are warm and committed to the child's cognitive, social and moral development. The children of these parents were found to be energetic and cheerful, to have good relationships with peers and other adults, and purposefully to pursue high levels of achievement. The authoritative style is consistently associated with cognitive and social competence in children at all developmental stages and there are low levels of problem behaviour in girls and boys from infancy to adolescence.

Several independent studies have confirmed Baumrind's findings, and recent work shows that the association between parental styles and children's behaviour persists over the longer term.

A fourth style, the 'Uninvolved', has been identified by other researchers (Maccoby and Martin, 1983). Here, the parents give the minimum of care to maintain the child, and are indifferent to the child's needs. In exteme cases, uninvolved parenting becomes neglect, and the child's social, cognitive and emotional development is very likely to be impaired.

It is important to note that this research is mostly correlational, and that we cannot conclude that parental style causes patterns of children's behaviour (although that is what Baumrind argues). As any parent knows, it is easy to be warmly involved with a child who cheerfully cooperates with parental wishes. The child's characteristics influence the parenting styles as much as the parent affects the child and it may be that parents use the authoritative style because their children are temperamentally cooperative and conforming. Disobedient or disruptive children test the strength and endurance of even the most rational, patient parents.

Critiques of Baumrind's classification of parental styles suggest that identifying only three styles greatly oversimplifies the real situation. Not only do most parents use a mixture of styles, rather than just one, but styles may change over time as children develop. Parents know how impossible it is to achieve absolute consistency with different children at different ages in different situations.

In his book *Paranoid Parenting*, Frank Furedi, Professor of Sociology at the University of Kent at Canterbury, provocatively argues that parenting has become increasingly professionalised because of a culture that denigrates parental competence, and that parents seek more and more expert help to rear their children (Furedi, 2008). Fears of child safety, traffic, stranger danger, abuse, abduction and kidnapping, have led, he believes, to the overprotection of children, the restriction of their play and outdoor activities, with parents driving children to and from school, and a decline in physical activity leading to incompetent, anxious, overweight and unfit children. There is, he says, a general mistrust of adults, particularly of men, which has far reaching implications in diminishing community connections and bonds and leaves parents isolated and anxious, believing that their children are highly vulnerable to their own lack of parenting skills, as well as to almost everybody in the world at large, and needing the help of professionals.

Another aspect of Furedi's ideas is that children are highly resilient and have a great ability to recover from inadequacies in their parent's skills and even major trauma without serious harm being done in the long term. Children, he argues, are not determined by their early experiences; it is not inevitable that poorly parented children will grow into troubled adults. There are many self-righting processes that lead to normal development in all but the most extreme, long-lasting adverse conditions.

Furedi (2008: 196) concludes that 'parenting is not a complex science', but a natural activity, and that as long as parents do their best, without the help of professionals or politicians, but with the advice of friends and family, they will gain the self-confidence to teach children to look after themselves and develop a 'positive vision of humanity'.

Learning activity

In relation to Furedi's ideas, discuss with your parents and grandparents the similarities and differences in parenting that they experienced in comparison with your own.

There has been great progress in our understanding of the factors affecting parenting, and below are some major areas of current interest:

- **Social class.** The different life and working conditions, value systems, educational levels and economic security of middle and working class parents are associated with various differences in child-rearing behaviours.
- **Poverty**. In 2009, it was estimated that 3.9 million children were living in low income households in the UK. That means that about 30 per cent of children are currently living below the poverty line. Although government targets (not fully achieved) actually led to a reduction in children living in poverty between 1998 and 2010, the IFS estimates that current (2012/13) spending cuts in benefits and tax credits will push another 300 000 children below the poverty line in the next three years. These figures have been described as 'appalling'. The impact of poverty on children is profound and denies them good health, power, respect from others, self-esteem, education, decent housing and food, as well as material and social well-being (see also Chapter 8 for a wider discussion on poverty).

Children in poverty are much more likely to suffer chronic ill-health, the effects of which last throughout their lives, and as adults they live about eight years less than better off children ((Layard and Dunn, 2009). Their educational attainment is significantly damaged and they achieve lower scores on many educational measures, such as key stages in English and Maths, and in GCSE grades A*–C. They have limited opportunities for engaging in social activities or community life and have fewer hobbies and holidays. As adults, they are more likely to have mental health problems and have difficulty in gaining paid employment (Power *et al.* 2011). Poverty is obviously very stressful for the parents and may have a negative effect on their behaviour. The likelihood of punitive, non-nurturing parenting, withholding affection and corporal punishment is increased, although there are many other factors that need to be taken into account (Evans, 2004).

- **Ethnicity**. Different ethnic and cultural groups have distinct parenting beliefs and practices, although all cultures are similar in their valuing and respecting children, and many aspects of parenting are common to many societies. Nurturing, teaching, disciplining, monitoring and managing children is universal, and all cultures provide a linguistic and material environment. There are some differences in emphasis which lead to cultural differences in developmental levels. For example, in western societies language skills are highly valued, whereas in some African cultures motor skills are emphasised, and this leads to different levels of development in these behaviours.

  Variations in demandingness occur in different groups. For example, Chinese parents in the United States emphasise discipline, control and respect for elders, whereas in Hispanic families respect for the father's authority is combined with strong maternal warmth. There is evidence that black mothers are more authoritarian and less authoritative than white mothers and spanking is more common in black US families. However, this may occur in the context of warm, nurturing parenting and have fewer negative consequences for their children (Brooks-Gunn and Markman-Pithers, 2005).

  The extended family of African-Americans has for many years been a buffer against the negative forces of racism and poverty, and parents in these families rely on the support and knowledge of grandparents and other kin to enhance authoritative parenting (Barbarin and McCandies, 2002).

- **Single parents**. Although single parents are not a homogenous group, about three-quarters of single parent households are run by mothers. There are a number of problems for mothers raising children on their own and many areas of stress. About half of single mothers are poor and for many families the main source of income is the mother's earnings, which are typically low. Child-care costs are high, and so even if a mother can work to support her family, much of her income is absorbed by day-care costs. It is commonly acknowledged that many single mothers suffer from anxiety, feelings of despair, depression and various health problems, as well as having to cope with low social status, poor quality housing and education, and chronic fatigue, all of which make good quality parenting very difficult. When single parents have adequate income, parenting problems appear to diminish considerably. Single fathers, divorced parents and step-parents affect smaller numbers of children, but there is significant growth in the understanding of the parenting issues in these areas.

- **Gay and lesbian parents**. Lesbian and gay parents are as diverse a group as heterosexual parents, but have been likely to suffer from widespread prejudice and discrimination and have to deal with negative perceptions in many different societies. Systematic research on the children of gay and lesbian parents began in the 1970s and there is now a large body of research into both the parents and the children, clearly showing that the common stereotypes are not supported by the evidence. For example, there is no evidence that children raised by gay and lesbian parents are likely to be sexually abused by adults, ostracised by their peers or isolated in single sex communities. Indeed, the research shows that they have good relationships with peers and engage in the usual social life of family, grandparents, peers and parents' adult male and female friends, just as children with heterosexual parents. The evidence to date shows that gay and lesbian parents provide as good an environment as heterosexual parents for the development and psychological growth of their children and not a single study has found them to be disadvantaged (Patterson, 2009).

There is some evidence that parenting skills are stronger in lesbian couples and parent–child interactions more favourable than in heterosexual couples. In contrast to heterosexual parents, almost no physical punishment is used and reasoning is a preferred method (Johnson and O'Connor, 2002).

Family structures

There are several different models that have been developed over the past 30 years to explain family functioning: structural, systems, contextual and intergenerational models, each with its own emphases and value. Olson's circumplex model identified two main dimensions on which families may be differentiated (Olson *et al.*, 1989). The first of these, namely 'adaptability', refers to the ability of a family to change in response to external or internal demands. The second dimension, 'cohesion', refers to the strength of emotional bonding between family members. On each of the dimensions, a family can be classified into one of four different types, and therefore located on a space on a four-by-four grid (see Table 5.2).

Table 5.2 Cohesion in family structures

		Disengaged	Separated	Connected	Enmeshed
	Rigid	Extreme	Mid-range	Mid-range	Extreme
Adaptability	Structured	Mid-range	Balanced	Balanced	Mid-range
	Flexible	Mid-range	Balanced	Balanced	Mid-range
	Chaotic	Extreme	Mid-range	Mid-range	Extreme

Cohesion

Families located at the extremes of either dimension are postulated to function less well than those that fall in the mid-range or balanced categories. A 'chaotic' family has few clear rules or roles, the children receive little guidance, are inconsistently disciplined and consequently are uncertain about appropriate behaviour and are difficult to control. On the other hand, a 'rigid' family has rules and roles strictly defined, with power exercised by inflexible authoritarian control. In 'structured' and 'flexible' families, rules and roles are negotiated by parents and children democratically, and discipline is firm but fair.

Extremely cohesive families are described as 'enmeshed'. Here family members are so strongly identified and bonded with each other that the outside world is of little significance. 'Disengaged' families have little sense of family identity and each member functions separately without reference to the others. Between the two extremes the members of 'connected' and 'separated' families are bound together by emotional ties, at the same time as maintaining their own individual identity and activity.

Empirical evidence in relation to this model offers clear support for the hypothesis that balanced families function better than other types. They cope with the changing needs of developing children more effectively, with fewer disruptions and less unhappiness than either the mid-range or extreme families (McCubbin *et al.*, 1996).

Balanced, optimal, healthy, energised, well-functioning, effective families

Despite the sometimes hysterical concern expressed by political parties and the tabloid press about the 'breakdown of the family', for example, following the UK riots in the summer of 2011, many families continue to function very well, the members caring for each other with little conflict, and producing responsible, well-adjusted, contributing members of society (Anderson and Sabatelli, 2010).

The following characteristics have been identified by a number of different researchers, and although the list is not exhaustive, it indicates the range of desirable attributes:

- relationships – close and warm
- communication – clear, supportive and empathic; ability to listen
- power – shared but with parental control and parental coalitions
- roles – clearly defined but not rigid or stereotyped
- rules – negotiated and modifiable and related to strong value system
- conflict – regulated and resolved by discussion and negotiation
- world view – collectively agreed and continually reviewed; connected with other social systems
- autonomy – encouraged and accepted.

(**Olsen *et al.*, 2010**)

As anybody who lives within a family knows, these counsels of perfection are easier to state than they are to achieve. Nevertheless, many families do strive to reach the ideals with relatively good success. Some families, however, seem to fail more often than they succeed, and these are identified as dysfunctional families.

Dysfunctional families

Leo Tolstoy wrote in *Anna Karenina*, 'All happy families resemble each other; each unhappy family is unhappy in its own way.' Although the foregoing discussion suggests that he was probably right about happy families, he was clearly mistaken about unhappy families in that they, too, share common characteristics. Whether they are rigid or chaotic, enmeshed or disengaged, they are incapable of consistently dealing successfully with ordinary everyday life and are very likely to do significant harm to the psychological well-being of their members. As can be seen from the Olson model, dysfunctional families are characterised by their extremity. They are extremely rigid or extremely chaotic, extremely disengaged or extremely enmeshed. In terms of the desirable attributes of healthy families, dysfunctional families seem to operate differently, and the following characteristics have been identified:

- relationships – either distant and cold or engulfing, may be abusive
- communication – inadequate, unclear, ambiguous, double-binding
- power – rigid hierarchy, cross-generation alliances
- roles – either inflexibly or poorly defined
- rules – rigidly enforced or very inconsistent
- conflict – frequent destructive clashes without resolution
- world view – idiosyncratic and distorted
- autonomy – either strongly inhibited or irrelevant.

Any family with many of these characteristics is unlikely to provide an adequate environment for its members, particularly for children, and it is likely that at times of stress in particular, one or more of the family members will come to a community's attention as being in need of help in coping with adversity.

Fragile families

In the 1990s, the term 'fragile families' was introduced to describe the new family form that had developed over the previous 50 years, that is, the family of a couple who are unmarried when their children are born. In 2008, 45 per cent of British children were born outside a legal marriage, a rise from 8 per cent in 1971. In the United States, similar patterns have emerged, with 41 per cent of births in 2008 occurring to unmarried mothers, from 11 per cent in 1971. There have been some serious concerns about this new pattern, especially in relation to the well-being of children, and two major studies into fragile families, one in the United States, another in the UK, have examined many aspects of these families (Kiernan *et al.*, 2011).

Data from the Millennium Cohort Study which tracks about 19 000 UK children, and from the Fragile Families Study which follows 5000 children in the United States, contain a wealth of information about parents and children in both countries. Analysis of the data shows that in both countries most of the unmarried parents seem to be in committed romantic relationships and have strong hopes that they will get married, but do not appear capable of maintaining long-term or stable co-parenting relationships. If cohabiting occurs it may be on the 'Swedish model' or 'poor man's marriage' which are the equivalent of married couples families, although they have much lower earning abilities, poor educational backgrounds and have more mental and physical health problems. The stability over time for families with unmarried parents is lower than for married couples, with US couples having much greater instability.

Over time, cohabiting mothers who later marry see their incomes rise similarly to married women, but single mothers and those who end their relationship, have a decline in income and are often impoverished. The contributions of time and money are consistently low among non-cohabiting fathers in the UK, while in the US contributions start high but decline over time as the never-married relationship becomes weaker.

Children born to unmarried parents have more problems than those born into married-couple families and have worse cognitive outcomes, but if the cohabiting family is relatively stable, the children fare better than in unstable conditions. Most fragile family couples are together at the time of a child's birth and have high hopes of a family future together, but many break up in the subsequent years.

Current policies are being developed to focus intensely on the very early 'magic moment' to encourage stable cooperative parenting, responsible sexual behaviour and access to contraception, to increase father involvement, and improving relationship skills (see Chapter 9 for a detailed discussion on social policy in relation to early childhood).

Mothers

More has probably been written about a child's first relationship, usually with his or her mother, than all of the child's other relationships put together. Following the work of John Bowlby in the first edition of his popular classic *Child Care and the Growth of Love* in 1953, there has been a massive development of theory and research evidence in the area, much of it within the framework of two major theoretical positions. *Ethology* adopts an evolutionary, biological perspective and takes the view that the survival of an infant depends upon the inborn behaviour and characteristics of infants (crying, smiling, chuckling, large eyes, round faces) which elicit care-giving behaviour from the mother, such as feeding and comforting. Recent developments in the new discipline of evolutionary psychology suggest that maternal care has evolved to ensure the continuity of her genes (Buss, 2011) and although it is argued that the care-giving behaviours of mothers have a biological basis in humans, they are very significantly modified by cultural learning. The *social learning* approach takes the view that the interaction between biological bases and social environment is best accounted for by principles of reward, punishment, imitation and observation in the relationship between a child and his or her primary care-giver. Mutually rewarding encounters between mother and child begin the process by which an enduring emotional bond is formed, the quality of which is thought by many theorists to be the foundation for all other relationships that the child will develop.

The concept of 'attachment' is central to an understanding of the mother–child relationship. Originally, the term was used to denote an emotional bond of affection for one individual, not interchangeable – an intense driving force towards seeking closeness with another person. This view sees attachment as residing in the individual, whereas more recent researchers have taken the position that attachment refers to a dynamic set of behaviours in the relationship between two people, a transaction in which both child and mother play crucial parts.

Although the newborn baby shows no evidence of attachment, it soon shows preferences – for other people to be nearby, for human faces, for social stimuli and for human voices – which permit the development of attachments. By six weeks, the infant is using its limited repertoire of behaviour to attract attention (smiling or crying), and by three months infants are reacting more positively to their usual care-takers than to strangers. At between six and eight months, the infant begins to show clear evidence of primary attachment, usually – but not always – to the mother. Several factors seem to be important at this stage. First, 'object permanence' emerges as part of the child's cognitive development and the infant realises that someone out of sight still exists. The mother's absence is noticed and 'separation protest' occurs. Fear begins to emerge as a strong emotion and wariness of strangers often causes crying and searching behaviour in the child. Mobility also increases at this stage and the infant now begins to be able to crawl towards the primary care-giver when anxious. After about nine months, attachments begin to be formed with others in the child's environment, such as siblings, the father and grandparents.

Maternal bonding, which is the mother's emotional attachment to the child, begins before the baby is born and continues through the first hours and days of the baby's life. Early contact with the baby, with skin-to-skin touching, is thought by some researchers to be important but not necessary for good bonding to occur (Rode *et al.*, 1981).

Ainsworth *et al.* (1978), using the *Strange Situation Procedure*, have identified three main categories of attachment:

Type B: Secure attachment

This was found in 50–70 per cent of children studied. The child:

- shows a clear preference for the mother
- is outgoing with strangers while the mother is present
- uses the mother as a base for active exploration of the environment
- maintains periodic eye contact with the mother
- shows distress on separation from the mother
- is comforted and warmly greets the mother's return.

The mother:

- is sensitive and responsive to the baby's needs
- encourages exploration and communication
- is warm and emotionally expressive.

Type A: Anxious – avoidant attachment

This was found in 20–25 per cent of children studied. The child:

- ignores the mother
- is not especially wary of strangers and ignores them
- shows little exploration when with the mother
- is not distressed upon separation
- avoids the mother upon her return.

The mother:

- is rigid and self-centred
- is cold and uninvolved with the baby
- avoids physical contact
- tends to be intolerant and irritable
- is unresponsive to the baby's needs.

Type C: Insecure – ambivalent attachment

This was found in 10 per cent of children studied. The child:

- is sometimes clinging and sometimes rejecting
- is reluctant to explore

- is very wary of strangers
- becomes very distressed at the mother leaving
- both seeks and rejects comfort upon reunion.

The mother:

- is inconsistent in her care-giving
- has difficulty in interpreting the child's needs
- attempts close physical contact
- has difficulty synchronising with the baby.

Learning activity

Consider Ainsworth's attachment patterns with a person from a different cultural backgound from your own. Identify any differences in maternal behaviour that you have experienced.

Subsequent studies have found a fourth pattern, namely 'disorganised' attachment, which occurs in high-risk families and where the child appears confused and apprehensive about his or her relationship with the mother (Main and Solomon, 1986).

There is some clear evidence that the quality of the primary attachment has significance for a child's subsequent relationships in childhood, and even later. Securely attached infants are likely to become more confident, skilful, socially orientated, cooperative and outgoing, and to be more popular and to have more friends (La Freniere and Sroufe, 1985). There is also evidence that poor-quality attachment between mother and child is linked to the mother's own insecure attachment as a child. Both security and insecurity may be transmitted from one generation to the next. The Adult Attachment Interview was developed by Mary Main and is seen as a major breakthrough in attachment research in recent years (Cassidy and Shaver, 1999). It is suggested that autonomous parents who have a positive view about their own childhood attachments are better able to respond to their children's needs than are dismissive or preoccupied parents who, because of unresolved attachment issues and memories, are unable to focus on their own infant.

Cross-cultural studies have shown that attachment theory, which has a clear western bias and values autonomy, exploration and independence, may nevertheless be applied to many different cultures with different values, although with a need for caution. Some cultures seem not to have children who fall into some of the attachment categories. In the Dogon people of Mali, for example, 87 per cent of the children were secure and none at all were avoidant or ambivalent, although 13 per cent were disorganised (True et al., 2001). The attachment categories are broad and may not therefore always identify subtle variations in attachment behaviours. For example, secure Japanese children cry less than secure German children on separation from their mothers, but both have the same secure classification. In some cultures, the ability to anticipate a child's needs is valued highly, though this is not actually measured in much western research which is concerned with anxiety that has already occurred. These and other controversial aspects of attachment theory will receive further research attention as the importance of cross-cultural understanding is recognised (Music, 2011).

Early Childhood Studies: A Multidisciplinary and Holistic Introduction

Fathers

In the last 25 years, research into fathers has increased considerably in both the US and Europe, led by the influential work of Michael Lamb and his colleagues.

These authors identified three main dimensions of parental involvement:

1. **Engagement:** The time spent interacting with a child on a one-to-one basis, for example, while reading a story.
2. **Accessibility:** The parent is occupied but available to respond to the child if necessary, for example, while reading the newspaper.
3. **Responsibility:** The parent is accountable for the everyday care and welfare of the child, for example, feeding, clothing.

In two-parent families where mothers are not employed, fathers appear to spend about 25 per cent of the time that mothers do *engaged* with their children; 30 per cent of the time mothers that are *accessible* to their children and take perhaps 10 per cent of the *responsibility* for child care. Many fathers, however, take essentially no responsibility for their children's care. For example, it is almost always mothers who stay at home with ill children or take them to the doctor. Levels of paternal responsibility have very slowly increased over 30 years, but mothers still do the majority of the work associated with children. In families where the mother goes out to work, fathers spend a slightly higher proportion of time with their children, but this is not because fathers are doing more, it is because employed mothers do less (Lamb, 1997).

Research by Parke and his co-workers (Parke, 1996) has shown that, with newborn infants, fathers were just as involved as mothers in interaction with their babies and nurtured, touched, looked at, kissed, talked to and held them equally. In only one behaviour – smiling – did mothers surpass the fathers. However, in the earliest days, even with bottle-fed babies, fathers spent less time than mothers in feeding and related care-taking activities, which suggests that parental role allocation operates from the beginning of a child's life.

Beyond the newborn period, fathers spend less time feeding and care-taking than mothers, and spend more time in play activities. Whereas mothers pick children up for care-taking activities such as nappy-changing, fathers pick them up to play with them. Not only do fathers play more with their children, but they also play differently to mothers. From as early as eight months, fathers engage in physical play, lifting, pushing and rough-and-tumble activities, while mothers engage in toy-stimulated play and reading to their children. These differences seem to be consistent throughout the early years and lead to a preference for fathers as playmates, with more than two-thirds of children choosing to play with their father rather than their mother. Research shows that the quality of the father's social, physical play is significantly related to the cognitive development of boys, while the quality of the father's verbal interactions with girls is important in female cognitive development.

It is important to note that the most recent research in this area shows that fathers and mothers are more similar than different in their influence upon children. It is warmth, security, closeness and sensitive support that are important, not whether it is the father or the mother who provides it (Lamb, 2010).

The absence of a father is likely to be significant in a child's life. Apart from the poverty frequently found in families headed by a single mother, there is some evidence that IQ scores are lower, that achievement at school is poorer and that 75 per cent of the children whose parents divorce feel rejected by their fathers even when the fathers visit frequently (Wallerstein and Kelly, 1996). There is also some evidence that a father's absence is associated with psychiatric problems, lack of self-control and violent behaviour, particularly in boys. Girls seem to be less affected in this way.

Recent research in father involvement with young children in the UK has shown that there are some significant benefits for children later in their lives. Eirini Flouri, at London University's Institute of Education, has produced over 100 papers, articles, chapters and books in the past ten years, based on the National Child Development Study of children born in 1958, and has shown that a strong father figure improves children's later mental health, makes anti-social behaviour (and for boys, trouble with the police), less likely, and makes young people more likely to gain A-level or higher qualifications and to have more satisfactory partnerships in adult life (Flouri, 2010). The four key criteria for gauging father involvement were reading to the child, taking the child on outings, taking an interest in the child's education and an equal role in managing the child. It is important to note that it is the continued presence of a father figure that matters. The family structure, whether he lives with the mother or not, whether he is the biological father or not, did not make a difference. An older brother, an uncle, even a friend may suffice when the involvement is of good amount and of quality (Flouri and Buchanan, 2003).

Despite the strong evidence on the benefits to children of good quality father involvement, it is important to recognise that not all fathers are the same and that violent fathers are harmful to the safety and well-being of their children. Research in Sweden shows that about 10 per cent of children are affected by violent fathers and although there is a lack of evidence in the UK, the figures are probably similar. The recent Department for Children, Schools and Families (DCSF) estimate of 200 000 children affected by physical domestic violence is likely to be an underestimate (DCSF, 2010). These children, living in households with a violent father, who are either abused directly or observe violence towards their mother, are likely to be very distressed, to be highly anxious and to have significantly worse developmental outcomes. Apart from disruption to sleep, to general educational progress and to social relationships with other children, children at primary school may copy the father's behaviour in aggressing girl pupils and female teachers and there is evidence that many areas of later emotional disturbance are the result of early experiences of violence (Stanley, 2011). There is also growing evidence that the development of the brain is adversely affected by prolonged exposure to violent fathers (Hester *et al.*, 2007). It is important to note that this work challenges the idea that violent fathers may be good enough fathers. They are not. In her recent book, Lynne Harne argues that the ideal of father involvement should not compromise a child's safety or well-being (Harne, 2011).

One of the areas thought to be very important in relation to fathers is that of sex-role development. First, fathers appear to prefer boys, and from birth onwards actually treat boys and girls differently. They encourage boys to be more 'masculine' and consistently pay more attention and give more stimulation to boys than to their daughters (although they cuddle their daughters more than their sons). They also appear to discriminate more than mothers in the treatment of male and female children, and seem to have somewhat rigid views about what constitutes appropriate sex-role behaviour, which they communicate to boys by providing masculine role models. Interestingly, boys who live in households without fathers generally show fewer sex-typed behaviours and attitudes than boys who live in intact families. The role of fathers is clearly important in a number of areas, yet there is also a pronounced discrepancy between popular cultural beliefs and actuality. To bring the two closer together, cultural support systems designed to encourage fathers' involvement, clearer role allocation and expectations and better early socialisation of males in nurturance and responsibility-taking, are all needed for the benefits to be realised.

Sibling relationships

The birth of a second child into a family is of significance not only to the parents but also to the first-born child. Until the early 1980s, there were few systematic studies of sibling relationships (except for birth-order effects and sibling rivalry), but since then there have been major developments in our understanding of the impact of a second child on the family, how sibling relationships develop and change, the links between parent–child relationships, and the effects of early relationships upon a child's later friendships and adjustment. The leading instigator of these developments was Judy Dunn (Dunn and Kendrick, 1982), and she continues, with her co-workers, to make important advances in this area (see Dunn (2002) and Jenkins and Dunn (2009)).

The commonly held view that a first-born child's reaction to a new baby will create behavioural problems, jealousy and rivalry seems to be borne out. Increased disturbance of bodily functions, anxiety, withdrawal and dependency are among the immediate consequences to have been noted. Although hostility may occur, first-born children show a range of reactions, ranging from interest, concern and empathy, through ambivalence to outright aggressiveness. In general, however, first-borns are keen to help to care for the new baby and to cuddle and play with him or her. One of the factors that influences the beginning of a sibling relationship is the way in which the mother talks to the first-born about the new baby before it is born. When mothers make reference to the expected baby, relationships between the siblings are subsequently much more friendly than when the newcomer has not been introduced in discussion. Also, positive feelings between siblings are more likely when the parents have a positive relationship with each other.

The birth of a second child changes the existing relationships within a family. Mothers may reduce the amount of time spent with the older child while they concentrate on the baby, and fathers often spend more time with the older sibling, while both parents have less time for each other. Same-sex siblings seem to develop friendly relationships with each other, particularly in families with first-born boys. Older children seem to become particularly vigilant about the mother's interactions with a new baby and often demand absolute equality of maternal attention. The second-born child is also very vigilant in monitoring the mother's relationships with her older children, and it is out of this interest that a child's social understanding develops.

In the early years, siblings serve a number of functions for each other. They provide affection and security, companionship and intimacy. They give support and help to each other, provide models for imitation and the learning of both skills and language, and through conflict and cooperation develop their own internal working model of relationships and an understanding of the feelings of others.

Figure 5.1

In her recent book, Claire Hughes, of Cambridge University's Centre for Family Research, suggests that there is good evidence in the Toddlers Up Study that sibling interactions lead to accelerated social understanding and better awareness of others' mental states even when teasing and rivalry are present (Hughes, 2011).

There is some evidence that the quality of sibling relationships is associated with the security of attachment each child has to its mother. That is, securely attached older and younger siblings are likely to have friendly relationships with each other, whereas insecurely attached children are more likely to have antagonistic relationships with one another. Although it is plausible that maternal attachment provides a template for subsequent relationships, we must note that the evidence is correlational and as yet does not indicate a causal effect between attachment and the quality of sibling relationships.

One of the areas of sibling research that has received considerable attention in recent years is concerned with differential parental treatment of children, especially the notion of favouritism towards one of the siblings. Many adults who report a poor sibling relationship in childhood often attribute this to their parents either positively favouring one of the children or scapegoating one of them. An early study found that mothers were less affectionate and had less social interaction with second children than with first-born children (Jacobs and Moss, 1976), but in an even earlier study, Lasko (1954) found that parents were less warm and more coercive towards their first-born children. Recent studies show a high level of consistency of treatment by mothers at 12 and 24 months, although in one study there was a sizeable group of mothers (34.5 per cent of

Early Childhood Studies: A Multidisciplinary and Holistic Introduction

the sample) who appeared to treat their children differently (Ward *et al.*, 1988). This, of course, may be because their children's temperaments need differential treatment. At a given point in time with, say, a 12-month-old boy and a 24-month-old girl, maternal treatment may be quite different because of the age-determined or temperamental needs of the children.

What seems to be important in the different treatment of children by their parents is the discrepancy between one child and another. Bryant and Crockenberg (1980) found that, even when a child's own needs were being well met, if there was a discrepancy of treatment by the mother, that child would show more hostility and negative behaviour towards his or her sibling. Hetherington's (1988) study showed that it is the relative treatment of children that is significant, rather than the absolute parental behaviour that affects children most deeply. A sibling treated less warmly, less affectionately, more irritably or more punitively is likely to behave more aggressively and with less affection towards the other sibling. The favoured child is also more aggressive and unaffectionate towards the sibling. The favouritism–hostility hypothesis would seem to be supported. Recent research suggests that some children are particularly susceptible to differential treatment by parents. This seems to be related to the child's perception of having less responsive or unfair parents. The child attributes a negative meaning to parental actions and may create a situation in which it is almost impossible for the parents to be perceived as fair. There is a growing research interest in this aspect of a child's interpretations of reality and there are many questions yet to be answered about the effects of perceptions upon the child's future development. Conley (2004) argues that every family has a pecking order and that in a complex, multilayered way, families select the most potentially successful sibling and invest considerably in their development.

One final point is that in many cultures around the world, siblings provide and receive a great deal of care-giving, and therefore their socialisation, from their siblings and not from adults which is the usual pattern in western societies. The implications of this will undoubtedly be explored as our knowledge of other cultures expands especially through the increase in anthropological studies.

Learning activity

For at least 30 minutes, observe the interaction between two or more siblings under the age of eight years of age. Identify instances of affection, empathy, concern, support, help, jealousy, rivalry, aggression.
Consider your observations in the light of theory from this chapter and discuss with a tutor, colleague or fellow student.

Grandparents

About 30 000 years ago, human beings began to live significantly longer and for the first time grandparents were still around when their children had children of their own. Before this, most of our ancestors died of famine, disease, childbirth or injury before the age of 30 and were not alive as the next generation were born and grew up. Caspari (2011) argues that the newly surviving grandparents were able to help their own daughters gather food, look after the young children and that they were able to pass on knowledge about food and water resources and skills in tool making. In terms of survival, this gave a huge adaptive advantage to children helped by grandparents, and our ancestors flourished as other early humans, such as the Neanderthals, died out.

Although the extended family, with three generations living together, diminished significantly in the 20th century, there is growing evidence that grandparents increasingly play an important part in children's lives. Throughout Europe and North America, increasing life expectancy means that many children are growing up in four or even five generation families and have the opportunity to form long-lasting relationships with their grandparents. In many countries, the increase in numbers of working mothers, higher divorce rates, more cohabiting parents and children born outside marriage, as well as more one-parent families, means that grandparents increasingly participate in the care of their grandchildren.

A recent study in Europe found that 58 per cent of grandmothers and 49 per cent of grandfathers had provided regular or occasional childcare in the past year and in the United States 43 per cent of grandmothers report giving regular child care (Hank and Buber, 2009). There are, however, wide variations between different ethnic groups, between southern and northern European countries, and in the UK, a mother's qualifications and level of poverty affect the amount of grandparent care provided. Grandparents are particularly helpful in the care of children at times of stress, such as during and after divorce. For example, Bridges *et al.* (2007), found that closeness to grandparents was helpful in the adjustment to parental separation, and that children saw their grandparents as important to confide in. They are also found to be supportive to parents of children with special needs or disabilities, providing care, support and advice, as well as financial and practical help. Maternal grandmothers, as in many aspects of grandparent support, are often seen as the most important resources.

As grandparents of six grandchildren, in the past year, my wife and I have been to parks, pantomimes, art galleries, to birthdays, Easter, Christmas and wedding parties, to church, school fairs, libraries, museums, the beach, swimming pools and on holiday with grandchildren. We have picked them up from school, babysat, watched TV, read, drawn and written letters to them, talked on the phone and spent countless hours playing with dolls, stickers, cars, trains, Lego, animals, dinosaurs and musical instruments. Sometimes, we have cooked with them, bathed them, read stories and put them to bed. We have fed fish, birds, dogs, frogs, ducks, goats, pigs and horses together, and eaten in restaurants, pubs, ice cream parlours and supermarkets. What amazing developments we have seen and how rewarding it is for us all.

These activities probably illustrate grandparent relationships with children in separate, intact two-parent families, where treats and fun are most common and basic care-giving is only occasional. There are, however, recent studies showing that there has been a rise in the numbers of children who grow up in households headed by grandparents in which the parents are absent or unable to look after their children, and the grandparent has the role of primary care-giver. There is evidence indicating that such intensive grandparent involvement is connected with poor psychological outcomes for the children, possibly due to the severe family problems that led to the grandparent's involvement in the first place, and the poverty that is often found in these circumstances (Glaser, 2010).

Although there is some good evidence that grandparents are beneficial in many ways, there is still much to discover, and it must be concluded that the role of grandparents is under-researched and much more work needs to be done.

Friends

In adults, friendships are based on the reciprocal exchange of benefits between equals, in which there is a sense of commitment and affection. Friendships are special in a way that simple peer interactions are not. Young children are clearly primarily attached to their parents in the first year or so of their lives, but they show increasing interest in other children, and by the age of four or five years most children have formed a special relationship with at least one other child. At school, they develop relationships with about five children, a figure which continues into adolescence.

Children's conceptions of friendship begin somewhat simply and become more elaborate and differentiated as the child grows older. Infants' conceptions are likely to focus on concrete aspects ('he lets me play with his toys'), whereas older children will use more complex and abstract ideas. Many psychologists argue that these differences are related to the general cognitive and language development of the child (Dunn, 2004).

Identification of a child's friendships has been attempted by several different methods:

- asking children to indicate their best friends
- asking children who they 'like especially'
- observing the proximity between children.

In general, the level of agreement between these methods, although not perfect, has been very high. Frequently, a friend identified by a child will also be identified by a parent or a teacher, and the two children will clearly prefer to play together.

Children's friendships, like those of adults, move through a series of 'stages' (Levinger, 1983). A necessary condition for a child to begin a friendship is proximity – that is, being in the same place at the same time. However, this is not sufficient for the establishment of a friendship, because if the initial encounter is not rewarding at a superficial level, the relationship is unlikely to develop. At the second stage, the build up of the relationship is characterised by repeated encounters which are mutually rewarding, in which the children communicate with each other and establish common interests by exchanging information and beginning the process of reciprocal self-disclosure. The consolidation of a friendship is marked by the development of a 'we' feeling, where the two children develop a commitment to one another and stable patterns of conflict resolution and successful management of the relationship occur. Sometimes, the deterioration of a friendship happens when clear disagreements or conflicts are not successfully resolved. However, children's friendships often end without any clear argument and seem simply to fade away because the children stop interacting with one another, presumably because the interaction is no longer mutually satisfying. The ending of a child's friendship usually results in the children avoiding one another, reduced interaction and dependence and usually little recrimination or conflict.

The functions of friendship in children probably vary with the age of the child, but a number of areas have been identified as important in child development. First, friendships are significant in the development of social competence. Howes (1983) found that, in children aged four to nine months, social behaviour with friends (as opposed to non-friends) was more elaborate, play was more cooperative, emotional exchanges were more positive and vocalising was increased. Friends are both cognitive and emotional resources for each other. They provide information about the world (not always accurately, e.g. 'My dad's a millionaire') and the opportunity for cooperative learning where, because of the nature of the relationship, the quality of the learning is likely to be better and problem-solving capacities are maximised. There is some evidence that friends increase the amount of laughing, talking, smiling and looking, i.e. positive emotional feelings, and that they also increase a child's sense of security in a strange situation. A recent Ofsted report found that having lots of friends was the second highest contributer to a child's happiness, after having lots of fun (Morgan, 2012). Studies of adult relationships strongly suggest that friendships provide a buffer against the adverse effects of stressful life events, such as divorce or a death in the family. Those with good-quality close relationships seem to suffer fewer physical illnesses or psychological disturbances than more isolated individuals. It would seem likely that this is true for children as well. Friends are judged second only to parents as sources of emotional support and their value increases as children get older.

Studies of adult friendship indicate that one of the major factors in the formation and continuation of relationships is 'similarity'. Not only do we develop relationships with and eventually marry people similar to ourselves, but children, too, base their choices of friends upon similarity. Although choices are sometimes made on the basis of dissimilarity, for example, higher status or more attractive or more popular children may be sought as friends, there is strong evidence of similarity between friends on a number of dimensions. From early childhood to adolescence, children have friends of similar age. To some extent, this is determined by the age structure of nurseries and schools and imposed by adults, but when given a free choice, most children usually form friendships with those of the same age. This is probably because of the egalitarian, horizontal power distribution between friends.

From preschool years onwards, same-sex friendships predominate and opposite-sex friendships are rare until adolescence, although even then only 5 per cent of friendships are with the opposite sex. Studies indicate that race, educational aspirations, attitudes towards achievement and children's culture (e.g. music and sport) are all found to be similar between friends. Not only do children choose friends similar to themselves, but they actually become more similar to one another over time. Finding someone who is very like oneself is obviously highly rewarding and the potential risks of conflict created by dissimilarity are significantly reduced.

The overall outcome of children's friendships is that they are important, if not absolutely necessary, for optimal development in a number of areas. Hartup and Rubin (1986) argue that most of the benefits of friendship may be achieved by other relationships – with parents, siblings or other family members. However, there is a developmental advantage for a child with friends. Perspective-taking, cooperation, altruism, social competence and adjustment and conflict management are all best learned within friendships.

A number of studies show that being without friends is connected to less desirable developmental outcomes, to having more emotional problems, to being less sociable, less well-adjusted to school and to making less good educational progress. However, some friendless children seem to have no need for friendship and have healthy psychological development (Schaffer, 1996).

Research into popularity shows that intellectual ability and physical attractiveness are important in a child being liked by other children. The 'beautiful is good' stereotype seems to operate from an early age and it appears that the positive responses bright, attractive children get from birth onwards helps them to develop friendly, cheerful behaviours and skills which enable them to initiate interaction with other children, to maintain that interaction with sensitive communication, and to resolve conflict with agreeable and fair strategies. Popular children have more friends and generally have high global self-worth scores (Berndt, 2002). Unpopular children may be either rejected or neglected by their peers. Those who are rejected are often argumentative and anti-social, unwilling to share or cooperate, and are often inappropriately overactive and talkative. Neglected children are often withdrawn, non-assertive and shy, with much solitary behaviour. Both groups seem to lack the social skills which bring positive reactions from their peers. However, it is the rejected group which are of serious concern as there is growing evidence that they are likely to develop problems of adjustment as they grow older, particularly in aggressive, anti-social behaviour, drug abuse and criminality (Mikami *et al.*, 2010).

Conclusion

In reviewing the ideas, theories and evidence discussed in this chapter, the importance of a child's relationships is apparent. Relationships of high quality, whether they are with mother, father, siblings, friends or grandparents, have a profound and long-lasting beneficial effect on the emotional, cognitive and social development of children, and poor quality or abusive relationships are likely to have severe adverse consequences. Although all children have their own unique characteristics, they are very responsive to the influences of their culture, their socioeconomic circumstances, their family, and all of those with whom they interact. Widening our understanding of the reciprocal nature of these interactions and revealing the complex subtleties of a child's relationships are tasks which are now well established, though incomplete. Enriching our understanding through the growth of new knowledge of values and practices from the fascinating and diverse cultures of the world is the next major task and will undoubtedly modify our views of what is right or best in relationships for children's psychosocial development.

Evaluate your learning

- How can early years professionals help increase a child's social capital?
- Can good parenting be taught and learned? Justify your answer with some examples from published research.
- Is attachment a valuable concept in relation to child care or schooling? Can you find any evidence of some criticisms in relation to attachment theory?

References

Ainsworth, MD (1978): *Patterns of Attachment: A Psychological Study of the Strange Situation.* Hillsdale, NJ: Erlbaum.

Anderson, S and Sabatelli, R (2010): *Family Interaction*, 5th edn. London: Pearson.

Barbarin, O and McCandies, T (2002): African American Families. In Ponzetti, J, Hamon, R, Kellar-Guenther, Y, Kerig, PK, Laine Scales, T and White, JM (eds), *International Encyclopaedia of Marriage and Family*, 2nd edn. New York: Macmillan.

Baumrind, D (1971): Current Patterns of Parental Authority. *Developmental Psychology Monographs* **4**, 1–103.

Baumrind, D (1991): The influence of parenting style on adolescent competence and substance use. *Journal of Early Adolescence* **11**(1), 56–95.

Berndt, TJ (2002): Friendship quality and social development. *Current Directions in Psychological Science* **11**, 2–10.

Bowlby, J (1953) *Child Care and the Growth of Love.* Harmondsworth: Penguin.

Bridges, LJ, Roe, AEC, Dunn, J and O'Connor, TG (2007): Children's perspectives on their relationships with grandparents following parental separation: a longitudinal study. *Social Development* **16**(3), 539–54.

Brooks-Gunn, J and Markman-Pithers, L (2005): The contribution of parenting to ethnic and racial gaps in school readiness. *The Future of Children* **15**(1), 138–67.

Bryant, B and Crockenberg, S (1980): Correlates and dimensions of prosocial behaviour. *Child Development* **51**, 529–44.

Buss, DM (2011): *Evolutionary Psychology: The New Science of the Mind,* 4th edn. New Jersey: Prentice Hall.

Caspari, R (2011): The evolution of grandparents. *Scientific American* **305**, 44–9.

Cassidy, J and Shaver, P (1999): *Handbook of Attachment Theory, Research and Clinical Applications.* New York: Guilford Press.

Conley, D (2004): *The Pecking Order: Which Siblings Succeed and Why.* New York: Pantheon Books.

Department for Children, Schools and Families (DCSF) (2010): *Support for All.* London: DCSF.

Dunn, J (2002): Sibling relationships. In Smith, PK and Hart, CH (eds), *Blackwell Handbook of Childhood Social Development.* Malden, MA: Blackwell Publishers.

Dunn, J (2004): *Children's Friendships: The Beginnings of Intimacy.* Malden, MA: Blackwell.

Dunn, J and Kendrick, C (1982): *Siblings: Love, Envy and Understanding.* London: Grant McIntyre.

Evans, GW (2004): The environment of childhood poverty. *American Psychologist* **59**(2), 77–92.

Flouri, E and Buchanan, A (2003): The role of father involvement in adolescents. *British Journal of Social Work* **33**, 399–406.

Flouri, E (2010): Fathers' behaviors and children's psychopathology. *Clinical Psychology Review* **30**, 363–9.

Furedi, F (2008): *Paranoid Parenting.* London: Continuum.

Glaser, K, Montserrat, E, Waginger, U, Price, D, Stutchbury, R and Tinker, A (2010): *Grandparenting in Europe.* London: Grandparents Plus.

Hank, K and Buber, I (2009): Grandparents caring for their grandchildren, findings from the 2004 Survey of Health, Ageing, and Retirement in Europe. *Journal of Family Issues* **30**(1), 53–73.

Harne, L (2011): *Violent Fathering and the Risks to Children, The Need For Change.* Bristol: The Policy Press.

Hartup, WW and Rubin, Z (eds) (1986): *Relationships and Development.* Hillsdale, NJ: Erlbaum.

Hester, M, Pearson, C, Harwin, N and Abrahams, H (2007): *Making an Impact: Children and Domestic Violence*, 2nd edn. London: Jessica Kingsley.

Hetherington, EM (1988): Parents, children and siblings. In Hinde, RA and Stevenson-Hinde, J (eds), *Relationships within Families*. Oxford: Open University Press.

Hill, AC (1987): Affiliation: people who need people. *Journal of Personality and Social Psychology* **52**, 1008–18.

Holmes, TH and Rahe, RH (1967): The social readjustment rating scale. *Journal of Psychosomatic Research* **11**, 213–18.

Howes, C (1983): Pattern of friendship. *Child Development* **54**, 1041–53.

Hughes, C (2011): *Social Understanding and Social Lives*. Hove: Psychology Press.

Jacobs, BS and Moss, HA (1976): Birth order and sex of siblings. *Child Development* **47**, 315–22.

Jenkins, J and Dunn, J (2009): Siblings within families. *New Directions for Child and Adolescent Development* **126**, 79–93.

Johnson, S and O'Connor, E (2002): *The Gay Baby Boom: The Psychology of Gay Parenthood*. New York: New York University Press.

Kiernan, K, McLanahan, S, Holmes, J and Wright, M (2011): *Fragile Families in the US and UK Fragile Families*. Working Paper WP 11-04-FF. Center for Research on Child Well-Being, Princeton University.

La Freniere, P and Sroufe, LA (1985): Profiles of peer competence in the pre-school: interrelations between measures, influence of social ecology, and relation to attachment history. *Developmental Psychology* **21**, 56–9.

Lamb, ME (1987): *The Father's Role: Cross-cultural Perspectives*. Hillsdale, NJ: Erlbaum.

Lamb, ME (ed) (1997) *The Role of the Father in Child Development*. New York: Wiley.

Lamb, ME (ed) (2010): *The Role of the Father in Child Development*, 5th edn. New Jersey: Wiley.

Laming, H (2003) *The Victoria Climbié Inquiry*. London: The Stationery Office.

Lasko, JK (1954): Parent behaviour toward first and second born children. *Genetic Psychology Monographs* **49**, 97–137.

Layard, R and Dunn, J (2009): *A Good Childhood*. London: Penguin Books.

Levinger, G (1983): Development and change. In Kelley, H, Berscheid, E, Christensen, A, Harvey, JH and Huston, TL (eds), *Close Relationships*. New York: Freemans.

Maccoby, EE and Martin, JA (1983): Socialisation in the context of the family. In Mussen, PH and Hetherington, EM (eds) *Handbook of Child Psychology*, 4th edn. New York: Wiley.

Main, M and Solomon, J (1986): Discovery of a disorganized/disorientated attachment pattern. In Brazelton, TB and Yogman, MW (eds), *Affective Development in Infancy*. Norwood, NJ: Ablex.

McCubbin, HI, Thompson, AI and McCubbin, MA (1996): *Family Assessment : Resiliency, Coping and Adaptation*. Madison: University of Wisconsin Publishers.

Mikami, AY, Lerner, MD and Lun, J (2010): Social context influences on children's rejection by their peers. *Child Development Perspectives* **4**, 123–30.

Morgan, R (2012): *Measuring Happiness*. Manchester: Ofsted.

Music, G (2011): *Nurturing Natures*. Hove: Psychology Press.

Olson, DH and McCubbin, HI (1989): *Families: What Makes Them Work.* Beverley Hills, California: Sage.

Olson, DH, DeFrain, J and Skogrand, L (2010): *Marriage and Family: Intimacy, Diversity and Strengths,* 7th edn. Columbus, OH: McGraw-Hill.

Parke, RD (1996): *Fatherhood.* Cambridge, MA: Harvard University Press.

Patterson, C (2009): Children of lesbian and gay parents: psychology, law, and policy. *American Psychologist* **64**(8), 727–36.

Power, A, Willmot, H and Davidson, R (2011): *Family Futures: Childhood and Poverty in Urban Neighbourhoods.* Bristol: Policy Press.

Putnam, RD (2000): *Bowling Alone.* New York: Simon and Schuster.

ResPublica (2011): *Children and the Big Society.* London: Action for Children.

Richards, M (1995): Family relations. *The Psychologist* **8**, 70–2.

Rode, S, Chang, P, Fisch, R and Sroufe, LA (1981): Attachment patterns of children separated at birth. *Developmental Psychology* **17**, 188–91.

Schaffer, HR (1996): *Social Development.* Oxford: Blackwell.

Stanley, N (2011): *Children Experiencing Domestic Violence: A Research Review.* Dartington: Research in Practice.

The Good Childhood Report 7 (2012). The Children's Society: London.

True, M, Pisani, L, Fadimata, O (2001) Infant–mother attachment among the Dogon of Mali. *Child Development* **72**(5), 1451–66.

Wallerstein, JS and Kelly, JB (1996): *Surviving the Breakup.* New York: Basic Books.

Ward, MJ, Vaugh, BE and Robb, MD (1988): Social-emotional adaptation and infant-mother interaction in siblings. *Child Development* **59**, 643–51.

Whiting, BB and Edwards, CP (1988): *Children of Different Worlds.* Cambridge, MA: Harvard University Press.

Further reading

Bornstein, MH and Lamb, ME (eds) (2011): *Developmental Science.* Hove: Psychology Press.

Cassidy, J and Shaver, P (eds) (2008): *Handbook of Attachment,* 2nd edn. New York: Guilford Press.

Flouri, E (2005): *Fathering and Child Outcomes.* Chichester: John Wiley.

Knox, D and Schacht, C (2010): *Choices in Relationships,* 11th edn. Belmont, CA: Wadsworth.

Lamanna, M and Riedmann, A (2011): *Marriages, Families and Relationships,* 11th edn. Belmont, CA: Wadsworth.

Roffey, S (ed) (2012): *Positive Relationships.* London: Springer.

6 Play, language and learning

Anne Greig

This chapter aims to:
- explore the nature of, and interrelationship between, play, language and learning.

Introduction

Consider the following scene from a Wendy house, involving Simon and Rebecca, both aged four years, who are not friends:

S: *Oh, it's half-past one! Cor, I think it's time we've to go to bed!*

R: *(Ignores him)*

S: *Goodnight! I'm going to bed.*

R: *(Ignores him)*

S: *I'm going to bed!*

R: *But mummies and daddies stay up for late … take a book to bed … let's take our babies to bed!*

S: *I'm going to sleep, I won't bother (mutters).*

R: *(Follows him). It's time to go to sleep now.*

S: *Come on, shut the curtains shall we? I'm going to have some water and then I put some aspirin in a cup. I got a poorly head.*

(Extract from Greig, 1993)

According to Garvey (1991), we may regard this play-scene as charming, silly or disturbingly perceptive in its portrayal of adult behaviour. However, for the serious student of the child, there is much more to discern and discover. It can tell us, for instance, about relationships on many levels – between the children themselves, with adults at home, and in the little cultural rituals of going to bed. It tells us about their communicative and social competencies and also how they think, learn and feel. Researchers from a variety of disciplines that include child development, anthropology and psychotherapy, examine hundreds of such encounters between children in order to detect the patterns and rules which govern their interaction and communication (for recent accounts, see Goodwin, 1997; James, 1998; Blatchford, 1998; Howe *et al.*, 2002; Pellegrini *et al.*, 2004).

In this chapter, we shall explore the nature of this play with its associated language and learning, and examine their role in early childhood. We shall also focus on the complex and special relationship between these three aspects of early childhood. Our approach to early childhood has been expressed as an holistic one and the nature of the relationship between play, language and learning is an example, par excellence, of the holistic nature of the child. Children play, learn, talk, build relationships – and more besides – all at once, making the child observer's task a difficult one. In addition, specifying the exact nature of interacting elements is often contentious. For instance, does the child develop language after, before or in parallel with the development of cognition? The relationship between play, language and learning is of this highly complex and contentious nature. An apt analogy to introduce the nature of the relationship comes from Bjørkvold (1987), who describes the Swahili concept of 'ngoma'. This is a special word meaning 'dance-ritual-song', activities which in the Swahili culture are inseparably moulded together – no song without dance, no dance without words and song. It is a nice idea, and in considering the play of Simon and Rebecca, it is apparent that their play, language and learning are inextricably linked, but would we go so far as to say 'no play, no language, no learning' or 'no language, no play, no learning'? Clearly there are links, but to what extent and in what way? Finding the answers to these questions is the ongoing and daunting task of both theoreticians and practitioners.

The study of language is a very large, well-defined research area in itself, including specialised research on acquisition, including literacy, oracy, reading, bilingualism, linguistics, psycholinguistics, sociolinguistics, applied linguistics, grammars, phonology, syntax and semantics, language and mind, semiotics and signs, non-verbal communication and paralinguistics (see Whitehead, 1990; Chapman, 2000, Wells, 2007; Wells, 2009) for a contemporary analysis. Learning theory has a variety of perspectives and it has been claimed that, although research on play has produced some valuable results, the overall pattern is disconnected, much of it not following a clearly thought-out or promising agenda (Nicolopoulou, 1993; Hunter, 1998). Our agenda is to introduce the available theoretical approaches to play, language and learning. The field will also be delimited in that we are focusing on early childhood and the relevant theorists (mainly Piaget and Vygotsky) who, in addition to being learning theorists, subscribe to theories on play and the role played by language. Consequently, the chapter will have a theoretical flavour, with less attention being given to more applied, practical specialisms.

Special issues and influential theories on play, language and learning

As we do not have to whip children into playing and learning how to say 'mama', most people would be happy to agree that play, language and learning are all spontaneous activities. None the less, they need examination with regard to the influences of genes, environment or both. For example, are cognition and language both natural and equally spontaneous activities? That is, to what extent is each innate or acquired? Consequently, the nature–nurture controversy will be a recurring theme in this chapter (see also Chapter 1).

In addition, the special relationship between language and learning promotes a debate as to which one has supremacy. Does language determine thought or is it a byproduct of the learning process? Both language and learning are relatively easy to define and research on language usually refers either dircctly or indirectly to research on learning and vice versa. They need not, however, refer to play. 'Play' seems to be one of those words, like 'beautiful' or 'pornographic', that you know when you see it, but that is difficult to define (Goodman, 1994). There is an emerging consensus that, given the width of the concept of play within and across cultures, it is important not to be bound by limited definitions of play (Hunter, 1998; James, 1998) and, despite passionate writings on the subject, there remains a need for more systematic research into the functional aspects of play (Scott, 1998).

In this section, we shall focus on play, language and learning, together with their special issues. Furthermore, because play is usually viewed as the context for the display or improvement of learning and language, the sequence of discussion will be learning, followed by language and finally play. Towards the end of the chapter, consideration will be given to the relationship between play, language and learning.

Special issues in learning

The question of how children learn has been much studied. The first few years of a child's life are a period during which the child will learn more than in the rest of his or her lifetime. The early years, including the time in the womb, are regarded as critical in terms of vulnerability to infection, damage and environmental modification. Consequently, it is important to understand this early learning process so that we are in a position to enhance it, intervene and develop new theories. In essence, learning theories occupy various positions in the nature–nurture controversy. As you will already be aware, these positions are known as nativist, empiricist and constructivist views.

Nativists are biologists who argue that the child is genetically pre-programmed to unfold in certain ways and that attainment of knowledge takes place only gradually and via inherent maturational mechanisms. (For a contemporary, nativist approach to the genetic pre-wiring of cognitive processes, see Karmiloff-Smith, 1995; Karmiloff-Smith, 2006.) Empiricists argue that the child is not born with genetic blueprints, but is instead a 'tabula rasa' or blank slate which is filled only as a consequence of environmental experience. This is the approach of behaviourists such as Pavlov and Skinner, who believed that learning is the process of forming associations between external stimuli and internal responses. This type of learning is mainly passive, with the child responding to the environment, although operant conditioning sees the child or organism as operating on the environment. Constructivists represent a combination of both genetic pre-programming and environmental adaptation or experience. The child actively constructs a version of reality from his or her unique experiences. It is this approach which has been most influential in educational research and has greater holistic relevance.

Influential learning theories

The constructivists Piaget, Vygotsky and Bruner all share an interest in the relationship between the inner, biological, individual child and the outer, environmental, social child – that is, the extent to which a child's knowledge is determined biologically and culturally, compared with the child's freedom to act independently and creatively. All three theorists agree that the child is both determined and a determiner of knowledge and understanding. Where they differ is in the emphasis that they each place on the direction of the relationship.

In the process of learning, Piaget's child is an isolated individual who attempts to adapt to the world around him or her. This process of adaptation takes place via four important processes: schemas, assimilation, accommodation and equilibration. Schemas are present from the start and are initially purely physical or sensory actions. The infant does not plan, intend or internally represent objects by means of mental pictures, but instead responds only to stimuli that are immediately available. For instance, the infant will have a looking schema, a holding schema and a grasping schema. As the child develops, he or she acquires more obviously mental schemas, such as categorisation and comparison of objects. After further maturation, more complex schemas are added, such as deductive analysis. It is, however, the three basic processes of assimilation, accommodation and equilibration which enable development from the simple action schemas of infancy to the increasingly complex mental schemas of later childhood. Assimilation involves taking in and absorbing experiences into existing schemas. Thus, when a child already knows how to pick up one object, new objects and situations can be acted out and understood within the existing schema. There is also room for subjectivity in the process, because a child may assimilate a roundish object into a round schema and remember it as being more round than it actually is.

Accommodation occurs when the child changes an existing schema as a result of new information taken in by assimilation. For instance, a child will have a sucking schema for the breast which will have to be adapted to a new form of action in order to cope with a bottle, and subsequently to drink from a cup. Subtle sensorimotor changes will be necessary in order to cope with the less familiar objects. In this way, accommodation is crucial for the developmental progress. As the child adapts existing schemas to new ones presented in the environment, Piaget believed the child to be seeking a balance in his or her understanding of the world, and this he termed 'equilibration'. The child strives to create a coherent and internally consistent understanding and knowledge. According to Piaget, there are four crucial stages when the child is faced with challenges resulting in disequilibrium, after which, through adaptation, the balance is restored and the child achieves a significant shift on to a higher level of understanding. In essence, then, the child is inner, biological and individual – many adults and educators have believed that they must wait for the child to reach the appropriate level of development before they can enhance his or her emerging capabilities. While such a strict interpretation of the theory has not been advocated recently in practice, the Piagetian approach does, to a considerable extent, place the responsibility for learning on the child who develops in isolation, making and testing theories as he or she constructs understanding by operating or acting on his or her environment. Piaget's child therefore becomes social only gradually as his or her cognitive capacity to do so matures.

Vygotsky's child, by contrast, is the child in society. The social nature of the child is present right from the beginning when the infant arrives into a complex world of social relationships and culture – a culture which itself has an historical development. Vygotsky proposed two lines of development for the child: the natural line of organic growth and maturation and the line of cultural improvement of the psychological functions. At a certain point, they meet up, mediated by speech (Vygotsky writes about speech rather than language) and external, cultural knowledge becomes internal. While Vygotsky viewed individual forces and cultural forces of development as being equally important, his general emphasis is often regarded as being on the impact of culture on the child. Vygotsky does not accept that a child is in the position of creating a conceptual world 'from scratch', but believes that they need instead to appropriate the conceptual resources of the pre-existing cultural world which are transmitted to them by parents, adults and peers. He argued that psychological functions originate in interaction with other people and therefore such knowledge appears initially in interaction with others or interpersonally, and only later becomes intrapersonal (within the child). The example of this cited in *Mind in Society* (Vygotsky, 1978) is the development of pointing, highlighting the importance of gesture and communication in cognitive development.

> Initially, this gesture is nothing more than an unsuccessful attempt to grasp something … At this initial stage, pointing is represented by the child's movement … that and nothing more … When the mother comes to the child's aid and realises his movement indicates something, the situation changes fundamentally … Pointing becomes a gesture for others … consequently, the primary meaning of that unsuccessful grasping movement is established by others.

(Vygotsky, 1978: 56)

The facilitative role for the more competent other is further developed by Vygotsky in his theory of the zone of proximal (next) development. He complained about the generally accepted method of assessing a child's level of development using standardised tests, because these do not differentiate between the child's actual developmental level and what he or she might reasonably achieve with some assistance (see also Chapters 3 and 7). In this situation, individual children will demonstrate greater interpersonal variation in terms of potential development. According to Vygotsky, then, the zone of proximal development (ZPD) is:

> … the distance between the actual developmental level as determined by independent problem solving and the level of potential development as determined through problem solving under adult guidance or in collaboration with more capable peers.

(Vygotsky, 1978: 86)

Vygotsky's child is therefore a social, outer, culturally determined child. Nonetheless, through the ZPD, any child is capable of making a unique contribution to his or her learning, knowledge and understanding.

Bruner's approach to learning was influenced by both Piaget and Vygotsky, but ultimately owes more to Vygotsky. Bruner's child assimilates and accommodates, but the nature of mental representation is crucially influenced by the child's social interactions and environment. Children learn to think in actions (enactively), in pictures (iconically) and in words (symbolically), because actions, pictures and words are used by people around them. That is, learning and knowledge are social in origin and, although the developmental sequence is enactive, then iconic and finally symbolic, Bruner believes that all three remain available to adults. Although he has not presented a unified theory of learning, his work has formalized many of Vygotsky's ideas into educational strategies such as 'scaffolding' (a culturally imposed framework for learning) and the 'spiral curriculum' (the notion that any subject can be taught effectively in some intellectually honest form to any child at any stage of development) (Bruner, 1972, 1990; for a critical review, see Newman and Holzman, 1993).

Special issues in language

In defining language, in order to be consistent with our holistic views elsewhere, it is necessary to make our definition in the broadest sense of both verbal and non-verbal communication. Smith *et al.* (2003; 2011) discuss how communication systems exist within almost all species, yet what sets humans apart is the creative flexibility of generating new meaningful utterances, communication of ideas, shared thoughts and consideration of themes that are remote in time and place. As such, communication is an excellent example of complex human behaviour, recruiting information processing to the full. The fact that children have already quickly mastered the complexities of communication by the preschool years is an ongoing research interest. Are children born pre-programmed to learn language? What is the effect of the environment? How does language develop? These questions are directly relevant to learning and the nature versus nurture issue already mentioned.

The recognition that there is a fundamental connection between language and thinking has existed since the time of Aristotle. However, the general claim that thought and language are intrinsically related raises a number of questions. Can there be thought without language? Do different languages reflect different ways of thinking? Do different languages cause differences in the ways in which people think? The view that language determines thought and mentality is traditionally known as linguistic determinism, and consistent with this is linguistic relativity, which means that differences in languages cause differences in thinking. From a developmental point of view, there has always been some debate about which develops first – thought or language – and the exact nature of the interdependence between them. The contention that it is language which dictates thought has serious implications for children and their free will – children will be socialised into a restricted world view, habitual patterns of language use in some subcultures will disadvantage children educationally, thought will not exist without language, thought will not develop before language and communication across cultures will at best be limited. Such views have been attacked as being narrow and pessimistic and a number of alternatives have been in circulation for some time (Mead, 1934; Piaget, 1959; Vygotsky, 1962; Chapman, 2000). Other theorists have examined cognitive development empirically and have

Figure 6.1 Vygotsky considered language and adults to be crucial for the development of cognitive processes

Early Childhood Studies: A Multidisciplinary and Holistic Introduction

differing notions of the role played by language, culture and social relationships. The two main approaches could be described as western (Piaget, 1959) and eastern (Vygotsky, 1962). Piaget and Vygotsky agree that thought does not originate in language. However, Piaget virtually ignored language except in relation to the unsocial nature of egocentric speech – a view he later revised – and how the child's stage of cognitive development is manifested in the language of the child. This egocentric speech reflects the child's cognitive developmental level as being unable to take the 'social' point of view of others. While acknowledging the importance of peers over parents for cognitive development, because of the opportunity they present for interaction on an equal footing, Piaget none the less gave the child's inherent creativity and individuality precedence over social factors in cognitive development. Vygotsky, on the other hand, considered both language and adults to be crucial for the development of cognitive processes.

Language and thought, which are initially separate functions, join forces at about two years of age to transform the inner mental life of the child. A child initially uses overt speech (egocentric) to organise the inner mind and the overt speech then becomes covert or inner thought. Speech is a powerful source of signs and empowers the child to restructure his or her environment. In addition, language is an important feature for internal cognitive restructuring – as the child plays, he or she will often maintain a monologue on what he or she is doing. The outer speech is not unlike the commentary that adults provide for very young children, for example counting out loud as the child climbs the stairs '… one … two … oops … two … three'. Such monologues represent over-socialised speech, which eventually becomes internal or silent inner speech, thus enabling verbal thought (for a modern account of egocentric speech, see Bråten, 1991; Diaz and Berk, 1992).

The ideas from the seminal works of interactionists such as Donaldson (1978), Youniss (1980) and Trevarthen (1987), taking account of both individual and social influences on language and thought, continue to be well represented in modern developmental research (e.g. Trevarthen and Aitken, 2001; Wells, 2007; 2009; Bus and Out, 2009).

Influential language theories

The main theoretical approaches to language acquisition are:

- learning
- nativist
- cognitive
- social interactionist.

The learning theory or behaviourist approach to language explains acquisition as a matter of imitation and reinforcement. As an infant says 'goo goo', babbles, etc., the sounds are shaped by adults until they become words. It is also argued that when a child imitates an adult, the adult rewards the child, and these words will then be learned and used again under similar stimulus conditions. While one can readily find examples of imitation, reinforcement and shaping in language, they do not necessarily occur in all utterances. It is too simplistic to account for the child's spontaneous, original speech efforts and their sensitivity to the regularities of speech evident from their systematic errors as they try to generate meaningful utterances.

The nativist view of Chomsky is one in which infants are pre-programmed to learn a language and are highly sensitive to the linguistic features of their environment. As Chomsky was concerned with the mental structures within the mind, he spoke of an internal language acquisition device (LAD), namely the mental apparatus that supposedly innately programmes human beings to a universal grammar, thus making it possible for them to speak and comprehend language. Examples of the evidence which suggests that children do generate their own language around rules might include their tendency to over-generalise a rule such as plurals (e.g. 'mans') and tenses (e.g. 'goed'). The traditional cognitive (Piagetian) view of language acquisition is that it is seen as part of general cognitive development. In effect, language acquisition must wait for sensorimotor thinking to develop first.

The importance of the role played by adult and child relationships in learning has, however, been applied to the study of language acquisition. As a social interactionist, Bruner proposed, in addition to the LAD, a 'sister' known as a language acquisition support system (LASS).

> If there is a language acquisition device, the input to it is not a shower of spoken language but a highly interactive affair shaped … by some sort of an adult language acquisition support system.

(Bruner, 1983: 39)

This approach is pragmatic in that it emphasises language use and its social functions. According to Bruner, the LASS is not exclusively linguistic, but forms part of an overall system for passing on the culture of which language is both instrument and creator – passed on through a complex system of rules (for a critical analysis, see Newman and Holzman, 1993).

Aitchison (1983) proposed that something specific to language is innate, even though we are not entirely sure what that 'something' consists of. Neither can language be explained as a general offshoot of general intelligence, although we undoubtedly use it when we speak in an as yet undefined way. Aitchison considers learning theories, such as those of Skinner, to have failed dismally as an explanation of how children acquire language. Chapman (2000) gives an interesting account of language learning which is 'interactionist'. He argues that, in light of improved methodologies and shifts in our understanding of children's general cognitive development (e.g. integration of infancy research with later childhood, thinking as a collaborative process and theory of mind, to name a few), language learning needs to be reconceptualised as an integration of learning in multiple domains:

> Much of what appears given or innate in young children's developing cognition and language, may on closer inspection, be shown to arise from the statistical structure of the encountered world and the correlations arising in action upon it, in a manner shared with other species … Such an enterprise is initially discomfiting, in a world of narrow and traditional disciplines of study and discourse; it suggests a reality so multi-layered and complex that it is dizzying to think about.

(Chapman, 2000: 45)

There have been many studies of the relationship between language and learning (see, for example Roskos and Christie, 2000; Bus et al., 2008; Wells, 1987, 2007, 2009).

Special issues in play

Play and childhood usually go together. Indeed, much of what children do is regarded as play. However, much of what children do is also clearly not play (Garvey, 1991). Different cultures may view play and childhood differently (see Introduction and Chapter 9 for further discussions around this topic; also see James, 1998). In the Greek language, for example, the word for play comes from the word for child, and a separate word is used for organised games or contests, mostly associated with adult life. The English 'play' comes from the Anglo-Saxon 'plega', which referred to play or rapid bodily movement and was also used to mean performing with musical instruments. However, Roman languages (e.g. French and Italian) do not distinguish between play and games and use one word for both.

Although play has been passionately and widely studied, authors have repeatedly noted that the most troublesome aspect of studying play arises from the fuzziness of the concept and the lack of a precise behavioural definition (e.g. Fein, 1981; Pelligrini and Smith, 1998; Scott, 1998). There are many ways of approaching play and there are also many different kinds of play (see Pelligrini and Smith, 1998; Smith *et al.*, 2003), so it is perhaps unsurprising that a firm working definition eludes us. Consider a baby babbling in his or her cot or shaking a rattle, or two boys chasing each other and wrestling on the floor, or the elaborate role play of four-year-old doctors and nurses. Play may be viewed differently depending on personal characteristics, such as age, gender, culture, social class, features of the environment (e.g. space, weather and equipment) and cultural factors (e.g. behavioural conventions and fashions). These are some of the factors which are known to influence play and the difficulty in defining it. Consequently, while authors agree that it is best not to define play, most of them have attempted to identify the general characteristics of/criteria for play (Hunter, 1998; Lillemyr *et al.*, 2001). It is generally agreed that play is non-literal, that is, a non-serious attitude to reality (Garvey, 1974) and that play is pleasurable, enjoyable and indexed by laughter. Other more contentious characteristics include freedom from extrinsic motivation; that is, play is unconstrained by external rules or social demands, but is engaged in for its own sake (Bruner, 1976); the flexibility of play in utilising alternatives for action, which means variation in the form and content of the play, and play as having a means rather than ends orientation (e.g. Hutt, 1979; Smith *et al.*, 2011). Sutton-Smith and Kelly-Byrne (1984) accuse researchers and practitioners alike of over-emphasising the importance and positive aspects of play. Instead, they remind us that play can be non-egalitarian (e.g. dominance and conflict), may not be voluntary, spontaneous or intrinsically motivated (obligation to and the power of friends and restricted environments), often manifests negative affect (fighting, brutal teasing) and finally, can be dysfunctional. Smith (1993) urges theoreticians, practitioners and students of play to proceed with caution and to take a balanced view of play and its value and relationship to children. It is both ambiguous and paradoxical and the preferred definitional common ground noted above remains unsteady. None the less, most practitioners are convinced of the empowering potential of play for developing language and learning, and this view has been reflected in the burgeoning interest in play in the fields of psychology, education, anthropology and sociology, and also in the recommendations of policy-makers and practitioners (e.g. Lillemyr *et al.*, 2001).

Mellou (1994), in a review of play theories, prefers to view them as either classical (early) theories (e.g. surplus energy theory, recreation/relaxation theory, practice theory, recapitulation theory) or modern theories (e.g. psychoanalytical theory, metacommunicative theory, cognitive theory). More will be said about these theories later, but Mellou is keen to point out that the much-criticised early theories actually provide a basis for the modern theories. In all theories, she claims, there is a duality in the process of play in terms of personal expression versus social adaptation.

Influential play theories

The forum for the discussion of the nature and purpose of play was opened by the German poet and philosopher, Schiller, in the 18th century with his letters on the *Aesthetic Education of Man*. He was responsible for formulating the evolutionary-type theory, notably what became known as the 'surplus energy' theory of play, according to which the young of both animals and humans have large quantities of superfluous energy that are invested in the aimless activity of play. Smith *et al.* (2011) cite the classic theorists on play (Spencer, Lazarus, Patrick, Hall and Groos). Spencer's (1873) elaboration of this notion included classification of types (e.g. sensorimotor, artistic-aesthetic, memetic, games) of play. Other evolutionary/ biological theories include those of recreation and relaxation (Lazarus, 1883) and Patrick (1916), who argued that play was needed by adults and children as a natural consequence of experiencing fatigue. Thus, the function of play was to renew the organism by way of its alternative and more primitive source of energy. An extreme evolutionary theory is Hall's recapitulation theory, in which the development of the individual mimics the development of the species. In this way, children's play was seen to represent the evolutionary history of our species. For example, climbing was related to the early animal stage of mankind, while playing with dolls was linked to a later agricultural/patriarchal stage. One particularly influential evolutionary theory was that of Groos (1901). Under a Darwinian influence, he proposed practice theory, according to which the young of various species went through more or less extensive periods of immaturity during which they had the chance to practise skills that would prove indispensable to them in adult life. These included the practice of physical, mental and social skills. The results of such playful activities were regarded as being of secondary importance, as what mattered most was the behaviours involved in the process. For a critical appraisal on the types and functions of play, see Pelligrini and Smith (1998) and Smith *et al.* (2011).

Many widely accepted theories of play are of a more psychological nature, dealing with the emotional, social and cognitive functions. First, play is presented as being important in the emotional life of individuals – it helps to overcome problems of reality and it satisfies basic emotional needs. Second, the social functions of play, normally studied by sociologists or social anthropologists, are what could be described as 'affiliative' in that play is akin to ritual in social groups and contributes to a temporary inversion of reality and of given social structures, offering a sense of 'togetherness'. This approach is still only represented by a few studies in developmental research (e.g. Corsaro, 1979). The social function of play is perhaps more commonly studied in conjunction with cognition (socio-cognitive) as, for example, in the work of Leslie (1987), Bateson (1955), Bruner (1976) and Vygotsky (1967), or in conjunction with emotion (socio-emotional), as in the work of Freud (1920). Third, the purely cognitive function of play is the domain of Piaget, who differs from the socio-cognitivists noted above, not only with regard to their interest in the social context, but also in the role that language plays in the development of the cognitive function. We shall now consider each of these approaches to play in slightly more detail.

For the psychoanalysts, play has an important role in resolving the emotional conflicts that arise as a consequence of the child's relationships with others. Children and adults alike are subject to anxiety and neuroses, the foundations of which begin in childhood and persist into later life. Psychoanalysts therefore view childhood as critical and the role of play as therapy as particularly important (Alvarez and Phillips, 1998; Woolgar, 1999). For psychotherapists, play is a serious business (Winnicot, 1971). For children who have been deprived of a normal access to play, there can be serious consequences (e.g. Levin, 2002).

Play that is therapeutically facilitated by adults can give these troubled children a sense of emotional 'containment' (Bion, 1962). This refers to an emotional 'gathering together' of the child who is distressed, so that emotions can be managed, the child has the security of being heard and learns a model of how to deal with distress and think about feelings. The need to feel secure in order to play productively is a crucial concept in attachment theory (see also Chapters 4 and 5). It is this psychoanalytical approach to play which has established the play therapy system currently used for highly disturbed children, although there are many different therapeutic approaches (e.g. Erikson, 1963). Erikson argued that children are partners with their futures in play because their 'as-if' play seemed to serve as a metaphor for their lives. When children grow up, their adult life-style will have been implicit in their childhood free-play. It is through play that they learn to deal with disappointment and failure and learn to approach life with a sense of increasingly focused purpose.

Piaget considered play to be characterised by the primacy of assimilation over accommodation – the child incorporates events and objects into existing mental structures. As the child evolves through cognitive developmental stages, there is an equivalent manifestation in play behaviours. First, sensorimotor play is practice play involving repetitive actions which gradually become purposive. When language and representation emerge, the child is able to play symbolically. However, this is a solitary affair, directed initially towards self, and is a simple ability, for instance, to pretend to go to sleep out of the context of reality. Soon, the child will move from this self-reference to other-reference – for example, he or she will put dolly to sleep (Figure 6.3). This is followed by the ability to use objects symbolically; for example, a peg serves as a substitute for a doll. Finally, the child is able to make sequential combinations – that is, a whole play-scene. Socio-dramatic play is evident between four and seven years, when the child engages in pretend-play with others. Between 7 and 11 years, the child moves into the realm of collective symbols, rules and games with rules, and it is this play which marks the transition to a socialised individual.

Figure 6.2 Piaget's primacy of assimilation – the child incorporating events and objects into existing mental structures

Figure 6.3 Putting dolly to sleep: children move from self-reference to other-reference

Play thus moves from purely individual, idiosyncratic, private processes and symbols to social play and collective symbols. As play is about assimilation, pretend play serves to enable the child to relive past experiences, rather than to create possible future ones.

The other play theorists who have been concerned with cognition have, without exception, also addressed how language and the social environment interact with the child's learning or developing cognitive abilities. Vygotsky discussed play as arising from social pressures, that is, for social and emotional needs. For Vygotsky (1967), play is always a social symbolic activity. Even when a child plays alone, there will be implicit socio-cultural themes; for example, toys are cultural inventions and role-play entails socially constructed rules for behaviour and interaction. Vygotsky believed that solitary play was a later development than social play, and that genuine play emerged at about three years of age. Genuine play has two main characteristics, namely the imaginary situation and the rules implicit in that imaginary situation. For example, a child playing as a 'mother' can freely select her behaviour, but must also follow the rules of maternal behaviour as she understands them, and this entails cognitive effort. Later on, pretend-play with games and rules, such as chess, involves explicit rules but an imaginary situation. The function of play is socio-emotional – the child desires to act in the ways of an adult, but is not yet able to do so. This need can be satisfied through fantasy. Furthermore, in submission to implicit and explicit rules, children are empowered with self-control over their impulsive desires. Importantly, play also contributes to cognitive development rather than simply reflecting it. It is through early play that the child first creates the zone of proximal development:

> *In play a child is always above his average age, above his daily behaviour; in play it is as though he were a head taller than himself.*

(Vygotsky, 1967: 6)

Consider also a pretend world in which a piece of wood can be used as a substitute for a doll or a horse or a car. This is the creation of a world dominated by meanings – one in which action arises from ideas rather than from objects – and this paves the way for abstract internalised thought (for a critical review of Piaget and Vygotsky, see Nicolopoulou, 1993).

Bruner (1976), clearly influenced by Groos and Vygotsky, noted that the increased dominance of play during immaturity among higher primates serves as practice for the technical social life that constitutes human culture. He also realised the practical educational implications of his theory and the role played by others (especially adults), in particular, referring to interactional routines such as 'peek-a-boo' as 'scaffolding'. It is such conventional routines and formats of games which prepare children to take their place in society and culture.

The remaining socio-cognitive theorists have developed further the importance of communication and language in play or, more precisely, pretend-play, for the development of knowledge and understanding. There is more consideration given to the nature of mental representation and the child's ability to comprehend his or her own understanding and that of other people. Bateson (1955) was interested in the 'not really serious' aspect of play which presupposes that children are well able to distinguish between what is play and what is not. This ability to stand back from their activities and represent it as 'not serious' is a particular type of higher understanding between players which Bateson termed 'metacommunication'. Play behaviour signals convey the message 'what I am about to say is not to be taken exactly as I say it'. Thus, it is in play that a child learns about the different ways in which social rules can be 'framed' and 'reframed'. According to Bateson, then, what a child actually learns in play is about learning itself.

In a similar vein, Leslie (1987) focused on pretend-play as a means whereby a child develops knowledge about his or her own and other peoples' thinking or metacognition. When children engage in imaginary role-play, some statements may be true (e.g. 'this cup is empty') and others false (e.g. the imaginary tea 'is cold') (where both statements are used with reference to a child's empty play cup). Children know that, while it is true that the cup is empty, any tea in the cup will be imaginary. Thus, pretend-play is about the overall understanding of the situation and not the truth value of statements within the situation. Consequently, the emergence of pretend-play between 18 and 24 months can be seen as the development of the faculty of metarepresentation.

The most influential of these theorists for educational policy and reform have been Piaget, Vygotsky and Bruner. However, these theorists are essentially psychologists. There is another species of theorist for whom the philosophy of education is the direct and principal concern, including Froebel (1782–1852), McMillan (1860–1931), Dewey (1859–1952) and Isaacs (1885–1948). Another way in which these theorists differ from those already mentioned is in their eclectic approach to the holistic well-being of the whole child – physical, mental, emotional, social and spiritual (for a detailed overview, see Bruce, 1991). Froebel believed play to be a unifying mechanism which integrated the child's learning, and as the highest phase in the child's functioning, viewed play as a spiritual activity. McMillan developed the free-play side of the curriculum, seeing greater cohesion between Froebelian ideas and practical application. In the 20th century, Dewey helped teachers to take play seriously in the classroom, while Isaacs was more specific about the emotional nature of the child and how play helps to meet his/her emotional needs. Despite the views of these leading educational minds, the emotional, spiritual and playful dimension to learning is still a much neglected area of early childhood provision.

Summary and interplay of the theories

A discussion of the interplay between play, language and learning presents a considerable challenge. The task is a thesis in itself and specific research on this complex three-way relationship is scant. However, if we turn to developmental psychology, we find many exciting and relevant developments. In her 1996 review of theory and research, Dunn (1996) describes the links between emotion, cognition and interpersonal relationships. This work illustrates what is currently missing from many traditional, early education-based programmes which feature play, language and learning as a single unit. Leading researchers are now integrating the play, language and learning notion in a 'play and literacy in early childhood' approach (Roskos and Christie, 2000, 2001). We now also know much more about the social and emotional lives and abilities of young children, and so cannot ignore their obvious impact on children's play, language and learning (see Chapter 4 for a detailed discussion). Indeed, an holistic approach to child development and behaviour demands that we paint on a much broader canvas.

In summarising this chapter, some of the common ground shared by classical and modern theories of play includes the following:

- The categorisation of types of play (e.g. functional, sensorimotor, artistic-aesthetic, memetic, games), all of which appear in the work of Spencer and Piaget in various forms.
- The non-literal ('as-if') nature of play. This is crucially important for all modern cognitive theorists, such as Bateson and Leslie, as well as for the classical theorists.
- The importance of the lengthy period of childhood for the purpose of practising skills through play features in the work of Groos, Piaget and Bruner.
- The emotional functions of play. Interestingly, a diversity of authors agrees on this. Piaget (1962) describes play as 'pleasure in mastery ... illusion of omnipotence', while Vygotsky (1962) describes play as 'wish-fulfilment' after having experienced early disappointment. For psychoanalysts, play is described as the only remedy that children (and sometimes adults) have at their disposal after confronting the real side of living with others. The views of Piaget, Vygotsky and Freud have been seized upon by the holistic education theorists.

Those features of play which relate closely to learning include play as pressure-free – in that the consequences of success or failure are very different in play and in reality, play as symbolic and play as interactive. Such theories include ideas from cognitive science, such as script theory – knowledge acquisition through social interaction (Nelson, 1981) – and schema theory (Athey, cited in Nutbrown, 1993), which is based on Piagetian concepts. From sociology comes the frame analysis of Goffman, which has a dramaturgical approach, sharing much with script theories. There is a body of literacy-play research (e.g. Butterworth, 1993) in which the social constructivist theory helps to show that play and literacy share certain mental processes such as representational and narrative abilities (Meek, 2000). Narrative approaches to early literacy learning (Fein *et al.*, 2000; Roopnarine *et al.*, 2000) argue that children have an abundant store of narrative tools for narrative organisation that pave the way for language acquisition (Bruner, 1990; Pellegrini and Galda, 2000). For young children, literacy certainly involves the ability to talk about and reflect on oral and written language and this is often represented in the narrative genre (Fein *et al.*, 2000). Higher-order abilities of metacommunication and metarepresentation, such as thinking about thinking, thinking about talking and thinking about reading, playing and learning are also noted as important for positive outcomes (Howe *et al.*, 2002).

Additionally Meek (2000: viii) reminds us that:

> literacy is neither a single entity nor a cloistered individual virtue. Its labyrinthine past locates it in recurrent social practices and conventions related to textual transmission before printing ... it is helpful to remember that cognitive aspects of literacy are always deeply entwined with cultural ones.

Since play is evident before speech and language, it is apparent that children enjoy the ludic nature of words from the start. Meek refers to classic studies on children's delight at word play and the strange, incongruous worlds of stories and nursery rhymes, humour and teasing (for more recent accounts, see also Smith *et al.*, 2011).

Most developmentalists stress the importance of relationships and the interpersonal context in which language, imagination and cognition flower (e.g. Hobson, 1989; Williams and

Rask, 2003; Wells, 2007; Mol *et al.*, 2008, 2009). In addition to relationships with parents, children form friendships, have siblings and spend a great deal of time with peers at school. If this context is not there or is maladaptive, there will be consequences for the child and for society, because it is in these early social interactions that children first learn to partake in their culture (Trevarthen and Hubley, 1978; Stern, 1985; Smith, 2009; Wells, 2009). Other studies express the importance of practitioner attitudes towards play at school and the impact of play on children's learning (e.g. Blatchford, 1998; James, 1998; Pellegrini *et al.*, 2004; Saracho and Spodek, 2006; Tsao, 2008; Carroll *et al.*, 2010). The importance of adult mediation in the playground and at home in order to scaffold social problem-solving with peers and siblings has also been noted (Levin, 2002; Howe *et al.*, 2002; Bus and van Ijzendoorn, 1992; Bus, 1995, 2001a, 2001b; Pellegrini *et al.*, 2004; Giles and Wellhousen 2005; Davidse *et al.*, 2011). Finally, a number of researchers are bringing the links between play, language and learning into the 21st century by exploring the role of interactive multimedia and technology in the play, language and learning of children (van der Kooy-Hofland *et al.*, 2011; van Dijken *et al.*, 2011).

It is interesting that, despite clear indications by leading educational thinkers and practitioners of the importance of emotional and spiritual development in children's play, language and learning, there has been a glaring gap in relevant research and practice for quite some time. This topic, however, is pursued in detail in Chapter 4.

Conclusion

Simon and Rebecca could be anywhere one might expect to find children playing – in their own home, at preschool, in a hospital, in a care facility or with a child-minder. What do all of these theories and special issues on play, language and learning mean for them and the adults who are caring for or studying them? At once, it is clear that children are both fascinating and complex individuals and, given the holistic nature of the child, it is important to concede that no single special issue or theory is absolutely correct and able to account for the total complexity of behaviour involved in play, language and learning.

Learning activity

Observe a group of young children at play. Use the narrative report technique to record their actions and utterances. Afterwards, analyse the children's language and play, identifying ways in which the two are linked, and noting any learning that occurred as a result of the language and play.

References

Aitchison, J (1983): *The Articulate Mammal: an Introduction to Psycholinguistics*, 2nd edn. London: Hutchison.

Alvarez, A and Phillips, A (1998): The importance of play: a child psychotherapist's view. *Child Psychology and Psychiatry Review* 3(3), 99–103.

Bateson, GA (1955): A theory of play and fantasy. *Psychiatric Research Reports* **2**, 39–51.

Bion, WR (1962): *Learning from Experience*. London: Heinemann.

Bjørkvold, JR (1987): Our musical mother tongue – world-wide. In Soderbergh, R (ed), *Children's Creative Communication*. Lund: Lund University Press.

Blatchford, P (1998): The state of play in schools. *Child Psychology and Psychiatry Review* 3(2), 58–67.

Bråten, I (1991): Vygotsky as precursor to metacognitive theory. II. Vygotsky as metacognitivitist. *Scandinavian Journal of Educational Research* **35**, 305–20.

Bruce, T (1991): *Time to Play*. London: Hodder Education.

Bruner, JS (1972): *The Relevance of Education*. London: Allen & Unwin.

Bruner, JS (1976): Functions of play in immaturity. In Bruner, JS, Jolly, A and Sylva, K (eds), *Play: its Role in Evolution and Development*. New York: Basic Books, pp. 28–64.

Bruner, JS (1983): *Child's Talk: Learning to Use Language*. New York: W.W. Norton & Co.

Bruner, JS (1990): *Acts of Meaning*. Boston, MA: Harvard University Press.

Bus, AG (1995): Joint book reading makes for success in learning to read: A meta-analysis on intergenerational transmission of literacy. *Review of Educational Research* **65**, 1–21.

Bus, AG (2001a): Early book reading in the family: A route to literacy. In Neuman, S and Dickinson, D (eds), *Handbook of Research in Early Literacy*. New York: Guilford Publications, pp. 179–91.

Bus, AG (2001b): Parent-child bookreading through the lens of attachment theory. In Verhoeven, L and Snow, C (eds), *Creating a World of Engaged Readers*. Hillsdale, NJ: Lawrence Erlbaum.

Bus, AG and Out, D (2009): Unraveling genetic and environmental components of early literacy: A twin study. *Reading and Writing* **22**(3), 293–306.

Bus, A and van Ijzedoorn, M (1992): Patterns of attachment in frequently and infrequently reading mother-child dyads. *Journal of Genetic Psychology* **153**, 395–403.

Bus, AG, de Jong, TM and van Ijzendoorn, MH (2008): Social aspects in language and literacy learning: Progress, problems and interventions. In Spodek, B and Saracho, O (eds), *Contemporary Perspectives on Social Learning in Early Childhood Education*. Charlotte, NC: Information Age Publishers, pp. 243–58.

Butterworth, G (1993): Context and cognition in models of cognitive growth. In Light, P and Butterworth, G (eds), *Ways of Learning and Knowing*. Hillsdale, NJ: Lawrence Erlbaum Associates.

Carroll, JM, Bowyer-Crane, C, Duff, FJ, Hulme, C and Snowling, MJ (2010): *Developing Language and Literacy: Effective Interventions in the Early Years*. London: John Wiley and Sons.

Chapman, RS (2000): Children's language learning: an interactionist perspective. *Journal of Child Psychology and Psychiatry* **41**(1), 33–54.

Corsaro, WA (1979): We're friends, right? Children's use of access rituals in a nursery school. *Language in Society* **8**, 315–36.

Davidse, NJ, de Jong, MT, Bus, AG, Huijbregts, SCJ and Swaab, H (2011): Cognitive and environmental predictors of early literacy skills. *Reading and Writing* **24**(4), 395–412.

Diaz, RM and Berk, LE (1992): *Private Speech: From Social Interaction to Self-regulation*. Hillsdale, NJ: Lawrence Erlbaum Associates.

Donaldson, M (1978): *Children's Minds*. London: Fontana.

Dunn, J (1996): The Emmanuel Miller Memorial Lecture 1995. Children's relationships: bridging the divide between cognitive and social development. *Journal of Child Psychology and Psychiatry* **37**, 507–18.

Erikson, E (1963): *Childhood and Society*. London: Routledge and Kegan Paul.

Fein, G (1981): Pretend play in childhood: an integrative review. *Child Development* **52**, 1095–118.

Fein, G, Ardila-Rey, AE and Groth, LA (2000): The narrative connection: stories and literacy. In Roskos, KA and Christie, JF (eds), *Play and Literacy in Early Childhood: Research from Multiple Perspectives*. Abingdon: Routlege, pp. 27–43.

Freud, S (1920): *Three Contributions to the Theory of Sex. Nervous and Mental Disease Monographs No. 7*. New York: Nervous and Mental Disease Publishers.

Garvey, C (1974): Some properties of social play. *Merrill-Palmer Quarterly* **20**, 163–80.

Garvey, C. (1991): *Play*, 2nd edn. London: Fontana.

Giles, RM and Wellhousen, K (2005): Reading, writing and running: Literacy learning in the playground. *The Reading Teacher* **59**(3), 383–5.

Goodman, JF (1994): 'Work' versus 'play' and early childhood care. *Child and Youth Care Forum* **23**, 177–96.

Goodwin, M (1997): Children's linguistic and social worlds. *Anthropology Newsletter* **38**, 1–4.

Greig, A (1993): *Communication at Playgroup: A Relationships Approach*. Unpublished doctoral dissertation, Cambridge University.

Groos, K (1901): *The Play of Man*. New York: Appleton.

Hobson, P (1989): Beyond cognition: a theory of autism. In Dawson, G (ed), *Autism: Nature, Diagnosis and Treatment*. New York: Guilford Press.

Howe, N, Rinaldi, CR, Jennings, M and Petrakos, H (2002): 'No! The lambs can stay out because they got cosies': constructive and destructive sibling conflict, pretend play, and social understanding. *Child Development* **73**(5), 1460–73.

Hunter, M (1998): Play across the spectrum. *Child Psychology and Psychiatry Review* **3**(3), 115.

Hutt, C (1979): Play in the under-fives: form, development and function. In Howells, JG (ed), *Modern Perspectives on the Psychiatry of Infancy*. New York: Brunner/Marcell.

James, A (1998): Play in childhood: an anthropological perspective. *Child Psychology and Psychiatry Review* **3**(3), 104–9.

Karmiloff-Smith, A (1995): *Beyond Modularity: a Developmental Perspective on Cognitive Science*. Cambridge, MA: MIT Press.

Karmiloff-Smith, A (2006): The tortuous route from genes to behaviour: A neuroconstructivist approach. *Cognitive, Affective and Behavioural Neuroscience* **6**(1), 9–17.

Lazarus, M (1883): *Die Reize des Spiels*. Berlin: Fred. Dümmlers Verlagsbuchhandlung.

Leslie, A (1987): Pretence and representation: the origins of 'theory of mind'. *Psychological Review* **94**, 412–26.

Levin, DA (2002): Aggression in the playroom. In Render-Brown, C and Marchant, C (eds), *Play in Practice: Case Studies in Young Children's Play, Early Childhood Consortium*. St Paul, MN: Redleaf Press.

Lillemyr, OF, Fagerli, O and Søbsted, E (2001): *A Global Perspective on Early Childhood Care and Education: A Proposed Model*. Paris: UNESCO.

Mead, GH (1934): *Mind, Self and Society*. Chicago: University of Chicago Press.

Meek, M (2000): Foreword. In Roskos, KA and Christie, JF (eds), *Play and Literacy in Early Childhood: Research from Multiple Perspectives*. Abingdon: Routledge, p. viii.

Mellou, E (1994): Play theories: a contemporary review. *Early Child Development and Care* **102**, 91–100.

Mol, SE, Bus, AG, de Jong, TM and Smeets, DJH (2008): Added value of dialogic parent-child book readings: A meta-analysis. *Early Education and Development* **19**(1), 7–26.

Mol, SE, Bus, AG and de Jong, JM (2009): Interactive book reading in early education: A tool to stimulate print knowledge as well as oral language. *Review of Educational Research* **79**(2), 979–1007.

Nelson, K (1981): Social cognition in a script framework. In Flavell, J and Ross, L (eds), *Social Cognitive Development*. New York: Cambridge University Press, pp. 97–118.

Newman, F and Holzman, L (1993): *Lev Vygotsky: Revolutionary Scientist*. London: Routledge.

Nicolopoulou, A (1993): Play, cognitive development and the social world: Piaget, Vygotsky and beyond. *Human Development* **36**, 1–23.

Nutbrown, C. (1993): *Threads of Thinking*. London: Paul Chapman Publishing.

Patrick, GTW (1916): *The Psychology of Relaxation*. New York, Houghton: Mifflin.

Pellegrini, AD and Smith, PK (1998): The development of play during childhood: forms and possible functions. *Child Psychology and Psychiatry Review* **3**(2), 51–7.

Pellegrini, AD and Galda, L (2000): Cognitive development, play and literacy: issues of definition and developmental function. In Roskos, KA and Christie, JF (eds), *Play and Literacy in Early Childhood: Research from Multiple Perspectives*. Abingdon: Routledge, pp. 63–74.

Pellegrini, AD, Blatchford, P, Kentaro, K and Baines, E (2004): A short-term longitudinal study of children's playground games in primary school: Implications for adjustment to school and social adjustment in the USA and the UK. *Social Development* **13**(1), 107–23.

Piaget, J (1959): *The Language and Thought of the Child*. London: Routledge and Kegan Paul.

Piaget, J (1962): *Play, Dreams and Imitation in Childhood*. New York: Norton and Co Inc.

Roopnarine, JL, Shin, M, Donovan, B and Suppal, P (2000): Sociocultural contexts of dramatic play: implications for early education. In Roskos, KA and Christie, JF (eds), *Play and Literacy in Early Childhood: Research from Multiple Perspectives*. Abingdon: Routledge, pp. 205–20.

Roskos, KA and Christie, JF (2000): *Play and Literacy in Early Childhood: Research from Multiple Perspectives*. Mawah, NJ: Lawrence Erlbaum Associates.

Roskos, KA and Christie, J (2001): Examining the play-literacy interface: A critical review and future directions. *Journal of Early Childhood Literacy* **1**(1), 59–89.

Saracho, ON and Spodek, B (2006): Young children's literacy and related play. *Early Child Development and Care* **176**(7), 707–21.

Scott, S (1998): Forum on play: introduction. *Child Psychology and Psychiatry Review* **3**(2), 50–1.

Smith, PK (1993): Play and the uses of play. In Moyles, JR (ed), *The Excellence of Play*. Buckingham: Open University Press, pp. 15–26.

Smith, PK (2009): *Children and Play: Understanding Children's Worlds*. Oxford: Wiley-Blackwell.

Smith, P, Cowie, H, and Blades, M (2003): *Understanding Children's Development: Basic Psychology*. London: Blackwell Publishers.

Smith, PK, Cowie, H and Blades, M (2011): *Understanding Children's Development*. London: John Wiley and Sons Ltd.

Spencer, H (1873): *The Principles of Psychology*. New York: Appleton and Co.

Stern, D (1985): *The Interpersonal World of the Infant*. New York: Basic Books.

Sutton-Smith, B and Kelly-Byrne, D (1984): The idealisation of play. In Smith, PK (ed), *Play in Animals and Humans*. Oxford: Basil Blackwell, pp. 305–21.

Tsao, YL (2008): Using guided play to enhance children's conversation, creativity and competence in literacy. *Education* **128**(3), 515–20.

Trevarthen, C (1987): Infants trying to talk: how a child invites communication from the human world. In Soderbergh, R (ed), *Children's Creative Communication. Fourth International Congress for the Study of Child Language*. Lund: Lund University Press, pp. 9–31.

Trevarthen, C and Hubley, P (1978): Secondary intersubjectivity: confidence, confiding and acts of meaning in the first year. In Lock, A (ed), *Action, Gesture and Symbol: The Emergence of Language*. London: Academic Press.

Trevarthen, C and Aitken, KJ (2001): Infant intersubjectivity: research, theory, and clinical applications. *Journal of Child Psychology and Psychiatry* **42**(1), 3–48.

van der Kooy-Hofland, Kegel, C and Bus, AG (2011): Evidenced-based computer interventions targeting phonological awareness to prevent reading problems in at risk young students. In Neuman, S and Dickensen D (eds), *Handbook of Early Literacy Research*, vol. 3, New York: Guilford Press, pp. 214–27.

van Dijken, M, Bus, AG and de Jong, MT (2011): Open access to Living Books on Internet: A new chance to bridge the linguistic gap for at-risk preschoolers. *European Journal of Special Needs Education* **26**(3), 299–310.

Vygotsky, LS (1962): *Thought and Language.* Cambridge, MA: MIT Press.

Vygotsky, LS (1967): *Play and its role in the mental development of the child. Soviet Psychology* **3**.

Vygotsky, LS (1978): *Mind and Society.* Cambridge, MA: Harvard University Press.

Wells, G (1987): *The Meaning-makers: Children's Learning, Language and Using Language to Learn.* London: Heinemann.

Wells, G (2007): Semiotic mediation, dialogue and the construction of knowledge. *Human Development* **50**, 244–74.

Wells, G (2009): *The Meaning Makers: Learning to Talk and Talking to Learn*, 2nd edn. Bristol: Multilingual Matters.

Whitehead, MR (1990): *Language and Literacy in the Early Years: An Approach for Education Students.* London: Paul Chapman Publishing Ltd.

Williams, M and Rask, K (2003): Literacy through play: How families with able children support their literacy development. *Early Childhood Development and Care* **173**(5), 527–33.

Winnicot, D (1971): *Playing and Reality.* London: Tavistock.

Woolgar, M (1999): Projective doll play methodologies for preschool children. *Child Psychology and Psychiatry Review* **4**(3), 126–34.

Youniss, J (1980): *Parents and Peers in Social Development. A Sullivan–Piaget Perspective.* Chicago: Chicago University Press.

Further reading

Dietze, B and Kashn, D (2011): *Playing and Learning in Early Childhood Education.* Canada: Pearson.

Kane, SR and Furth, HG (1993): Children constructing social reality: a frame analysis of social pretend play. *Human Development* **36**, 199–214.

Lee, V and Das Gupta, P (1995): *Children's Cognitive and Language Development.* Oxford: Basil Blackwell in association with the Open University.

Mead, GH (1932): *The Philosophy of the Present.* La Salle, IL: Open Court Publishing Company.

Meadows, S (2006): *The Child as Thinker: The Development and Acquisition of Cognition in Childhood*, 2nd edn. London: Routledge.

Moll, LC (ed) (1992): *Vygotsky and Education: Instructional Implications and Applications of Socio-historical Psychology.* Cambridge: Cambridge University Press.

Moyles, JR (1989): *Just Playing.* Milton Keynes: Open University Press.

Moyles, JR (2010): *The Excellence of Play.* Milton Keynes: Open University Press.

Nelson, K (ed) (1989): Monologues in the crib. In Nelson, K (ed), *Narratives from the Crib.* Cambridge, MA: Harvard University Press.

Nelson, K and Seidman, S (1984): Playing with scripts. In Bretherton, I (ed), *Symbolic Play.* London: Academic Press Inc., pp. 45–71.

Whitehead, M (2007): *Developing Language and Literacy with Young Children.* London: Sage Publications.

Early childhood education and care

Beverley Nightingale and Sally Payne

This chapter aims to:

- contextualise early childhood education within an historical, legal and socio-cultural framework giving both definitions and purpose and the underpinning principles and philosophies
- present a broad overview of education and care provision across the United Kingdom including how children learn, the roles and responsibilities within settings and across early years provision and the curriculum frameworks and approaches outlined in Scotland, Wales, Northern Ireland and England
- promote reflection related to early childhood education and care, including what is understood by high quality, international perspectives and emerging influences.

Introduction

This chapter presents an overview of education and care in the United Kingdom giving consideration to origins of the current provision and contemporary issues. Early childhood has had many definitions. For the purposes of this chapter and giving recognition to the symbiosis of education and care as standard, we define it from conception to eight years.

Education and care – definitions and purpose

The United Nations (UN) (1989) Convention on the Rights of the Child (UNCRC) affirms children's fundamental right to education and care (Articles 3 and 28) (see www.unicef.org. uk/CRC).

Care is described by the United Nations Children's Fund (UNICEF, online – see www. unicef.org/earlychildhood/files/Guide_to_GC7.pdf) as ensuring and promoting children's 'survival, protection, growth and development in good health with proper nutrition … in a safe environment that enables them to be physically healthy, mentally alert, emotionally secure, socially competent and able to learn.' The concept of care starts before birth (see Chapter 2 for a further discussion on care before birth) and is life-long with most individuals assuming greater responsibility for their own care over time. The philosophy of holism and the link with education underpin its importance.

Education seems a little more complex to define. It is the means of developing every child's potential and transmitting culture within society. The Organisation for Economic and Cultural Development (www.oecd.org/site/educeri21st/40554299.pdf) suggests education should prepare children to cope effectively with the changing demands of society with an emphasis on learning how to learn. UNICEF concentrates on health and nutrition interventions but also add early stimulation and interaction. Ensuring that young children are developmentally ready for school is an integral part of UNICEF's education priority (UNICEF, 2012).

UNESCO (United Nations Educational, Scientific and Cultural Organisation) depicts early childhood education as a means of improving children's development, well-being, health, self-esteem and learning (http://unesdoc.unesco.org/images/0021/002122/212270e.pdf). There is a clear merging of education and care underpinned by the holistic philosophy and with clear benefits for children and society.

The benefits of good quality early childhood education and care (ECEC) are:

- recognised human rights
- developmental advantages
- improved academic achievement
- societal advantages.

The publication of *Supporting Families in the Foundation Years* (DfE with DoH, 2012) epitomises the importance of considering education and care together during the early years as a basis for later achievement, not only for individuals and families, but also for society (Field, 2010; Allen, 2011; Tickell, 2011).

Underpinning values, principles and philosophies

If you are working with young children, it is important to have a set of values and principles which guide what you do in practice. Values are fundamental beliefs of a person or group in which they have emotional investment. Values held by individuals may come from personal experience or from ideas or theory which have been commonly accepted or agreed within society. Principles are generalisations which are accepted as true and valid. Both values and principles govern behaviour. A philosophy is a 'set' of values which influence and guide action or behaviour and there is a more detailed discussion on principles and values in Chapter 1.

Learning activity

Look at the table in Chapter 1 (see p.9) and identify your personal values and principles about working with young children. Why do you have these and where do they come from?

Underpinning principles are stated in many of today's early years governing frameworks such as the Early Years Foundation Stage (EYFS) (DfE, 2012; DCSF, 2008a). In the EYFS, there are principles with practice examples given to demonstrate how they can be achieved. Many of the principles stem from an early childhood tradition in education (Bruce, 1997) which is still of relevance today. Educational pioneers such as Friedrich Froebel (1782–1852), Rudolf Steiner (1861–1925) and Maria Montessori (1869–1952) have been influential internationally and central in highlighting the common beliefs, values and principles about children which still hold true. For instance, Froebel (1907) saw the family as the most important first educator of the child. He also believed that early years experiences determined how the child progressed. These ideas came from his practice with children and informed his theoretical stance and writings. He was influenced by previous educational thinkers, such as Johann H Pestalozzi (1746–1827) and Jean-Jacques Rousseau (1712–78), and they in turn were influenced by others making it possible to go back to the likes of Comenius (1592–1670) who was considered the father of modern education. It is important to note that Montessori and Steiner nurseries and provision flourish internationally, extending choice to parents.

Today, in addition to what educational theorists have given us, there is a growing body of research in such areas as brain studies and neuroscience, in provision and practices and in policy effects. These all impact on our understandings, our principles and philosophy, either strengthening our position or making us reconsider our stance. We must understand why we practice in a particular way and to recognise what has influenced it (see also Chapter 1).

It is useful to think about the principles of organisations as you are developing your knowledge and understanding. For instance, there is considerable consensus among educators of the benefits to young children of a climate of respect in their ECEC setting (Smidt, 2010). Respect is related to educators being sensitive and responsive to children's needs, interests, motivation and circumstances and being attuned to each as an individual. It would be evident in interactions and in the way individuals are treated and treat others. Respect features in many official policy and advisory documents and sets of principles (e.g. UNCRC, 1989; UNESCO, 2001; DCSF 2008a; Ofsted, 2009).

The EYFS states that by the end of the Foundation Stage, children should have 'a developing respect for their own cultures and beliefs and those of other people' and understand that 'they can expect others to treat their needs, views, cultures and beliefs with respect' (DCSF, 2008a: 2.8). Recognising cultural diversity is crucial in this. The Parents Early Education Partnership (PEEP) *Room to Play Study* (Evangelou *et al.*, 2008) also highlights the benefits of creating respectful, reciprocal and responsive relationships with all children and parents.

A fundamental principle is a commitment to inclusion and equality of opportunity. Equality of opportunity is often misunderstood; it is about treating all children as individuals, *not* about treating all children exactly the same. It reflects our holistic approach of sensitive, responsive and, as far as possible, individualised ECEC according to need. It is about entitlement and social justice. All children must feel they are being treated fairly and equitably. Early years are, after all, the years when discriminatory concepts, attitudes, images and language can develop (Wall, 2011). Consequently, early childhood must be a crucial period for supporting children in developing positive self-concepts and bias-free attitudes, unlearning prejudiced views and behaviour and learning effective ways to challenge discrimination and counter the distorted realities associated with prejudice. ECEC educators must facilitate intercultural and inclusionary understanding; as Baldock (2010: 123) suggests, 'it must be in the ability of early years practitioners to understand how young children learn and the best ways of supporting them in that'.

Naturally it is essential that early years educators understand fully their own attitudes and are able to confront instances of discrimination firmly, but tactfully. Of especial significance for educators in pursuit of equality of opportunity is the context-sensitive ecological model of ECEC (see Bronfenbrenner, 1989) illustrating how we cannot understand a child's needs in isolation from one another or from his/her family, culture, community, group, society, etc. The holistic approach and collaboration with parents and communities are, therefore, essential as many theorists have indicated (for example, Evangelou and Sylva, 2008; Nutbrown *et al.*, 2008; Pound, 2011).

Professor Lilian Katz (2003: 14) summarises the situation in the early 21st century:

> *'... no-one today with serious educational and social policy-making responsibility for a community or a country all round the world would now argue against the proposition that the experiences of the early years of life have a powerful influence later on'*

Also, going to preschool has a positive impact '... compared to not going at all' (Siraj-Blatchford, 2003: 11).

Learning activity

Access the findings about preschool provision in the EPPE (2003) Research Brief RBX 15-03 online (http://eppe.ioe.ac.uk/eppe/eppepdfs/RB%20summary%20findings%20from%20 Preschool.pdf).

Another principle of close collaboration between educators and families is now widely accepted evidence that indicates that effective home-setting links can have a positive impact on children's achievement, development, behaviour, attitudes to school and continuity. Additional benefits to parents/carers include increased confidence and self-esteem and greater insight into children's development and ECEC experiences.

While most early years professionals value the role and contribution of parents and accept that parents have rights, there may be difficulties and tensions. There is, however, general agreement that partnerships/collaboration might be developed and/ or strengthened via:

- respect for parents, their views, the role they play in children's lives, their home culture, religious beliefs, choices and decisions
- commitment to the partnership/working together and an obvious sense of equity and active listening
- home-visiting schemes, perhaps when children start nursery
- support for parents, such as books, leaflets, website, meetings, support groups, workshops
- recognition and utilisation of parents' skills and expertise.

Working in partnership with parents or their primary carers is not new; Froebel placed great importance on parents as educators and believed it was teachers who should promote and support this. Successive governments have demanded closer working with parents, and thus enabled many parents to take a more active role in the education of their children. This is based on the premise that if a child realises that his or her parents are enthusiastic about education, he or she is more likely to view his/her schooling in a positive light.

How children learn

Children can learn from everything they experience, whether planned or not. The context a child exists in is subject to influences both external and internal (see Chapter 6 for a more extensive discussion). For this reason, parents and practitioners must observe, listen and respond to the needs and interests emanating from the child. The interaction of the 'who', 'where', 'what', 'when' and 'how' culminates in learning. Each area is individual and needs exploration. Permutations are exponential:

- 'who': stage of development, interest, motivation, disposition, culture, background, needs
- 'where': the context and environment; physical, emotional, outdoors, indoors
- 'what': physical, emotional, social, intellectual, natural progression or that required by society
- 'when': immediate, delayed, after repetition and consolidation
- 'how': as a 'lone scientist' (see Piaget, cited in Gray and McBlain, 2012), through social constructivism (see Vygotsky and Bruner in Waller *et al.*, 2011) or observation (see Bandura and Skinner, cited in Gray and McBlain, 2012) play, child-initiated and adult-led activities.

It is challenging to find a way through the complexity and provide successful opportunities to maximise children's potential. It is very much a minefield (see Figure 7.1). Adults must ensure a child is not inhibited, 'turned off' or prevented from learning.

Learning activity

Research the following key learning theorists:
- Piaget
- Vygotsky
- Bruner.
How do their theories inform the adult role in teaching and learning?

Developmentally appropriate practice (DAP) has been influential in ECEC for several years – a largely Piagetian constructivist approach portraying the child learning through play in an environment tailored to his/her developmental stage and needs (Rodger, 2012). DAP has been challenged for its failure to take sufficient account of children's social and cultural contexts and zone of potential development (ZPD). However, contextually appropriate practice would emanate from children's developmental needs and interests, as well as from their familial, social and cultural environments. Early years practitioners need to be sociologists, psychologists and philosophers to best negotiate opportunities for each child.

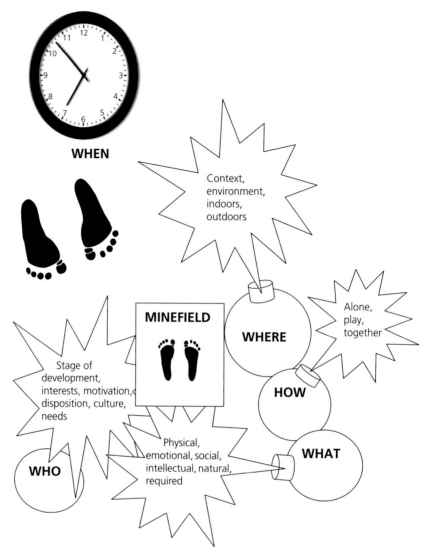

Figure 7.1 The minefield of children learning

Learning activity

Consider the importance of context on learning. If young children lived in a country where they regularly had to collect water from a source and carry it home for use, do you think they would know more about volume and weight of water than a child living in a home with water taps? Should developmentally appropriate practice (DAP) be developmentally and contextually appropriate practice (DeCAP)?

The learning environment

This is an important aspect of the offered curriculum and must be devised to promote and support children's all-round development and learning. Children learn from their environment by taking an active and independent role which will give them the confidence to assume and seek further knowledge. Environments will change as children gain mobility and competence. Figure 7.2 illustrates the prominence of choice within and between activities in order to foster a child's independence.

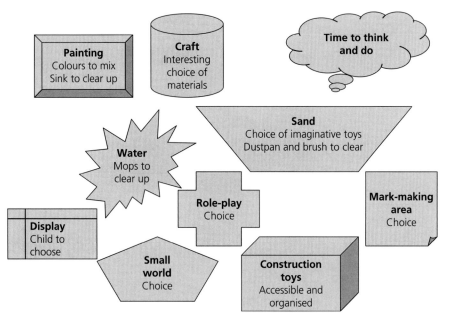

Figure 7.2 Choice within an early years setting

It is important to recognise the importance of outdoor learning. Whatever can be learnt indoors can also be learnt outdoors, in fact there is greater potential in the natural environment. The curriculum can be enriched and holistic learning enhanced by careful use of the outdoor environment. In addition, traditional playground games, hop-scotch, sand/water trays, climbing frames, role-play areas, water-mark making on a hot sunny day, environmental art, wheeled bikes and toys can contribute to an exciting outdoor extension to the curriculum and classroom environment – given appropriate organisation and resourcing. The outdoors also allows children to learn by working on a larger, more active scale than is (often) possible indoors. Extensive activity in an outdoor environment facilitates children's learning about risk (see Figure 7.3). Approaches such as 'forest schools' have been imported and adapted from Scandinavia. The Early Years Foundation Stage promotes children's 'free flow' indoors and outdoors.

Learning activity

Research forest schools and consider the application of this approach in the UK.

Figure 7.3 Outdoor play

Roles and responsibilities within settings and across provision

In 2008, the government in England published the Children and Young People's Workforce Strategy 2020 with the vision that by 2020 everyone working with children should be ambitious for them; should be excellent in their practice; committed to partnership and integrated (inter-agency) working; and be respected and valued as professionals. This strategy was to facilitate the five outcomes of the *Every Child Matters* agenda from the Children Act (2004), for children and young people to be safe, stay healthy, enjoy and achieve, make a positive contribution and achieve economic well-being.

Stakeholders in ECEC settings would be children, parents/guardians, the workforce and also any community involvement. Therefore, the workforce could include early years professionals, practitioners, teachers, plus ancillary staff and community representatives, for example from the local education authority (LEA), local schools, preschools, early years and childcare partnerships, or SureStart children centres.

There are many factors that may result in a variety of education and care support staff and adults working alongside professionals and teachers. The effects of government funding for young children, the funding formula in schools, inclusion, labelling and workforce remodelling are just some of the reasons. Various degrees of assistance both professional and voluntary may come from:

- nursery nurses
- teaching assistants and learning support assistants
- other teachers in parallel or adjacent classes, headteacher or deputy headteacher.
- breakfast and afterschool club staff
- early years advisors, consultants and advisory teachers
- professionals from outside agencies, such as speech and language therapists, educational psychologists, social workers, health visitors, physiotherapists and police
- volunteers, students and visitors.

Learning activity

How has the government responded to the final report of the independent review of early education and childcare qualifications, *Foundations for Quality* by Professor Nutbrown (2012)?

Lead professionals working with young children need to organise and manage the learning environment; they need to be able to work with other adults, while ensuring the effective utilisation of these human resources; they need sound managerial skills and the ability to use their own and others' strengths to the best advantage (Drake, 2009).

To benefit all those involved and especially the children, it is important there is:

- thorough observation and planning
- clear and open communication in a supportive environment
- knowledge of the skills and interests of each person and the use of these to the learning environment – all to be valued, acknowledged and used effectively
- modelling of certain behaviours
- opportunities for constructive feedback
- monitoring and evaluation of roles.

Hayes (2012: 141) recognises that in schools the most successful 'are usually those in which there is a high level of collaboration and a good team spirit'. This is important in every type of setting which children attend. Ensuring that each team member understands policy and procedures, the ethos and aims of the school or setting, will support collaborative working and avoid the risk of any enterprise being a disheartening and unprofitable experience for all concerned.

Many support staff are closely involved in planning alongside the professionals, a co-operative venture that benefits all concerned (Ofsted, 2010). The accompanying sharing of knowledge, skills and understanding will, of course, support the strategies employed in the process of children's learning and also the analysis and enhancement of practice. Regular meetings will be necessary for such activities, and particularly important for disseminating learning, passing on significant information and sharing relevant matters of import and concern.

Multi-agency working

The United Kingdom now has many integrated centres offering education and care, family support, health and welfare services and adult training, meaning the workforce is increasingly diverse and may well be working across professional and organisational boundaries (Aubrey, 2011: 103). A partnership approach is important in working to a holistic philosophy and can provide opportunities for professionals to develop shared training and values for the benefit of the child (Robbins and Callan, 2009). Working with outside agencies requires a focus on collaborative working with the child and/or family at the centre. This inter-disciplinary practice received an increased emphasis under the *Every Child Matters* 2003 agenda and then the Children Act 2004, emphasising coordinated planning, commissioning and delivery of education, health and social welfare services for children and families. Accordingly, this integrated practice demands early years professionals and support workers who understand children's all-round needs and development, as well as the complexities and socio-cultural contexts of their lives. Crucially, these adults must also be capable of genuine cooperation with relevant others in the best interests of children's welfare and education.

Continuing professional training and development is a quality indicator and can be helpful in this endeavour for everyone working with young children in whatever capacity; they can be supported in acquiring or enhancing the necessary skills and knowledge, particularly as roles and responsibilities change and evolve in the early years environment. According to Blandford and Knowles (2009: 368), 'Services should adopt a flexible child-centred approach to service delivery to ensure the changing needs and priorities of the child and their parents can be met at any given time.' Attendance at multi-agency training sessions (involving a range of relevant professionals) can be particularly valuable for encouraging stronger and more effective inter-professional working with and for children and their families. In practice, multi-agency teamwork can be challenging as it requires time, money, training and a commitment to collaboration for it to be effective. Obviously, the coordination of such a wide range of expertise could, with strong commitment and adequate resourcing, take settings closer to providing the ideal of integrated ECEC.

Learning activity

Think about and identify the challenges of working in a multi-agency team. How might these be alleviated?

Educator knowledge, understanding, skills and attitudes

Sylva *et al.* (2004: 4) found in the Effective Provision of Pre-School Education project (EPPE) that there was a 'positive relationship between the qualification levels of the staff and the ratings of centre quality. The higher the qualifications of the staff, particularly the manager of the centre, the more progress children made.'

Another key finding was the quality of adult–child interactions as they engage in 'sustained shared thinking' (Sylva *et al.*, 2004: 4). Responding to and extending child-initiated interactions were found to be important, as were open-ended questions that stimulate debate, higher-level thinking, problem-solving and questions from the child. Discussions, debating stories, adults answering 'why' questions, how things work, helping children explore their thoughts and feelings, cooperative play, explaining adult modelling and one-to-one situations were also identified as beneficial in terms of children's cognitive development. Siraj-Blatchford *et al.* (2002), in their *Researching Effective Pedagogy in the Early Years* (REPEY), conclude that good outcomes for children are linked to educators having sound knowledge of the ECEC curriculum and child development and developing shared aims with parents. Providing formative feedback to children during activities and having clearly thought-out behaviour policies also had positive effects. Sensitive, developmentally appropriate interaction, in a supportive and stimulating environment was highlighted in *Every Child a Talker* (ECAT) (DCSF, 2008b). Research and concerns from educators about the number of children who were not being immersed in a rich environment of words, sounds, rhythm, verbal and non-verbal expression from birth prompted this initiative.

Rodger (2012: 69) considers the professional standards for leading provision (leadership) by qualified teachers and those with the Early Year Professional Status (EYPS). These standards relate to professional knowledge, understanding and skills, to planning, assessing and evaluating learning opportunities, to creating a safe, supportive and challenging environment, to having a commitment to professional development, to establishing effective relations with stakeholders and parents and ensuring anti-discriminatory practice.

Particularly important for educators is understanding how young children learn, referring naturally to an holistic view of learning relating to all aspects of development – for example, intellectual, linguistic, emotional, physical, social, cultural, gender-related, moral and spiritual. Vygotsky (1978) advocated that educators encourage children's learning via social interaction and apprenticeship-type relationships with a more cognitively skilled other, and also through play, instruction, first-hand experience, observation, imitation and practice. Planning and organising for holistic and educative play is another essential and exciting (but never easy) aspect of the educator's role, even though it may appear quite effortless in the hands of a skilled practitioner.

The *National Strategies: Early Years 'Learning, Playing and Interacting'* (DCSF, 2009: 5) practice guidance document recognises the value of play in children's learning and from a policy perspective is in tune with the widespread acceptance of the benefits of play and play-based approaches for children's learning (Drake, 2009; Smidt, 2011; Macintyre, 2012; Broadhead and Burt, 2012).

Reflecting on and developing practice as a matter of course is an essential skill. Identifying what has gone well, in addition to not so well, is important. Recognising what developments are necessary and how they relate to existing practice to achieve improvement can be challenging.

Curriculum frameworks and approaches in the UK

Since devolution, education policy in the four constituent countries of the UK has diverged: for example, England has pursued reforms based on diversity of school types and parental choice; Wales (and Scotland) remain more committed to the concept of the community-based school. Systems of governance and regulation – the arrangements for planning, funding, quality-assuring and regulating learning and for its local administration – are becoming increasingly differentiated across the four home countries.

Scotland

Education Scotland is the key national body supporting quality and improvement in Scottish education (www.scotland.gov.uk):

> *The national guidance and multimedia resource, Pre-Birth to Three: Positive Outcomes for Scotland's Children and Families was revised by Education Scotland in collaboration with key partners to support and inform practice across Scotland. It includes current research to improve evidence-based practice and important information on pre-birth and brain development. It reflects the principles and philosophy which underpin the Early Years Framework (2008) and Curriculum for Excellence.*

The Curriculum for Excellence is Scotland's curriculum for children and young people from 3 to 18 years. It replaces the Curriculum Framework for Children 3 to 5 and the 5 to 14 curriculum. Curriculum for Excellence builds on the solid foundations developed in the critical years of pre-birth to 3 years which is supported by the new National Pre-Birth to Three Guidance.

The early level of Curriculum for Excellence spans preschool and primary as it is designed to meet the needs of most children from three years until the end of primary school. Many of the core messages of Curriculum for Excellence relate to the importance of:

- active, experiential learning
- a holistic approach to learning
- smooth transitions
- learning through play.

Children start primary school aged between 4 years and 6 months and 5 years and 6 months depending on when the child's birthday falls. Pupils remain at primary school for seven years. Secondary school starts at 12 years.

The eight curriculum areas are:

- Expressive arts
- Health and well-being
- Languages (French, German, Spanish or Italian) in later primary
- Mathematics
- Religious and moral education
- Sciences
- Social studies
- Technologies.

Education Scotland believes the key to achieving transformational change in the long term is the re-aligning of services towards early intervention as opposed to crisis management. It stresses that all relevant services work together to identify and meet the needs of individual children, in line with the principles of 'Getting it right' for every child (see www.childreninscotland.org.uk).

Wales

In Wales, the Welsh medium education is used by over 20 per cent of primary schools; lessons in the language itself are compulsory for all pupils until the age of 16 years. In 2008, the Foundation Phase was implemented for 3–7 year olds (www.wales.gov.uk). It is based on experiential learning, in small groups, with a teacher ratio of 1:8 for the youngest ages.

The Welsh National Curriculum focuses on active involvement and developing each child's:

- skills and understanding
- personal, social, emotional, physical and intellectual well-being so as to develop the whole child
- positive attitudes to learning so that they enjoy it and want to continue
- self-esteem and self-confidence to experiment, investigate, learn new things and form new relationships
- activities in the outdoors where they have first-hand experience of solving real-life problems and learn about conservation and sustainability
- creative, expressive and observational skills to encourage their development as individuals with different ways of responding to experiences.

Northern Ireland

The Northern Ireland Executive's Department of Education (DENI) is responsible for the country's education policy until higher education. In Northern Ireland, educational services are administered by regional education bodies known as Education and Library Boards (ELBs) (www.northernireland.gov.uk). There are five of these and their function is similar to that carried out by local education authorities (LEAs) in England and Wales.

All schools in Northern Ireland follow the Northern Ireland curriculum which is based on the National Curriculum used in England and Wales. At all three key stages, children build and improve their personal, social, intellectual, physical and emotional skills. In their earliest school years, well-planned, hands-on and challenging play is used to follow interests and encourage natural curiosity. In Northern Ireland, the school starting age is four (compared to five in England and Wales), with nursery provision offered to three-year-olds. The Primary Phase is divided into three stages:

1. Foundation Stage, P1–P2, ages 4–6 years
2. Key Stage 1, P3–P4, ages 6–8 years
3. Key Stage 2, P5–P7, ages 8–11 years.

An emphasis on the development of necessary skills is included, such as:

- controlling feelings and emotions
- being able to work with others

- talking and listening
- reading and writing
- maths
- problem-solving
- how to use ICT.

There are six areas of learning comprising:

1. Language and literacy (talking, listening, reading and writing)
2. Mathematics and numeracy (numbers, measures, shape, space, sorting, patterns and relationships)
3. The arts (art and design, drama, music)
4. The world around us (geography, history, science and technology) (learning interdependence, place, movement and energy, change over time)
5. Personal development and mutual understanding (personal development and health, mutual understanding in the local and wider community)
6. Physical development and movement (athletics, dance, games and music) plus religious education.

England

In England, the reformed Early Years Foundation Stage (Department for Education, 2012), takes forward the government's changes to the 2008 framework as recommended by the 2011 Tickell Review (implementation from September 2012).

There are three prime areas of learning and development:

1. Communication and language
2. Physical development
3. Personal, social and emotional

and four specific areas to meet 17 early learning goals:

1. Literacy
2. Mathematics
3. Understanding the World
4. Expressive Arts and Design

The Early Years Foundation Stage (DfE, 2012) also:

- requires a review of a child's progress every 2–3 years to be shared with parents
- encourages providers to be responsible for determining the balance between play and teaching, child- and adult-led activities
- requires opportunities to develop English skills for children with English as an additional language
- releases settings from EYFS requirements if children attend for limited time
- highlights safeguarding and welfare requirements. The importance of safeguarding is stressed by including examples of signs of abuse and neglect, requirement for policies covering use of mobile phones and cameras, providers to check suitability of managers,

staff development, child-minder EYFS training, clarification of exceptions to staff:child ratios and provider responsibility for recording risk assessments.

The EYFS reforms which slim down previous procedures for practitioners have been well received, however, the focus on children's readiness for school has been met with the cry 'schools should be ready for the child not the other way round!'

Each learning area has a set of early learning goals to be achieved by most children by the end of their reception year and formulated to inform planning, lay the foundations for future learning and aid transition into Key Stage 1 of the National Curriculum. To support practitioners, development statements have been given as guidance. These are deemed not to be age-related, but indicate a typical range of development. Any specified curriculum needs to be made personally relevant to individual children with their own experiences, natural interests and enthusiasms applied to the learning in an enjoyable and meaningful way. Quality learning must also be realistically challenging.

Much emphasis has been placed on the development of personal, social and emotional aspects in the early years. Figure 7.4 illustrates one pathway through the personal, social and emotional map to the corresponding early learning goal – echoing the emphasis on children developing a sense of community and the importance of respecting others.

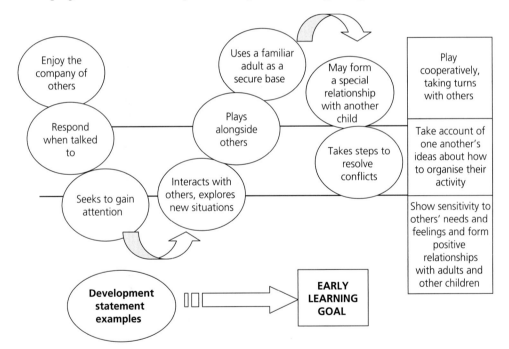

Figure 7.4 Physical, social and emotional development: making relationships

Learning activity

Compile a table of the four UK countries to compare provision and curriculum content. Reflect on similarities and differences.

The rolling planning process of the early years foundation stage journey

Provision for young children must be planned using curriculum guidance and knowledge about individual children (see earlier section entitled 'How children learn').

'Plan–do–review' is the simple version of the planning cycle. This becomes more complex but more meaningful when it includes assessment, reflection and evaluation with the planning cycle as an on-going or rolling process and the all-important observation of children informing each aspect (see Figure 7.5).

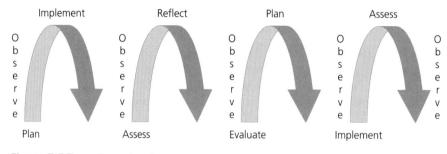

Figure 7.5 The rolling planning process

Most pupils will have commenced their 'journeys' in some form of preschool provision. Several will have travelled far and some will just be beginning – the teacher must take each child forward by building on the child's current level of knowledge, understanding and abilities. Documentation may well have accompanied a child from a previous setting and this may be useful in assessing where he or she is on the map and, therefore, where he/she will start the next stage of his/her 'journey'. There is little doubt, however, that observation and knowing each child and his/her family are the key tools to ensuring the planned (and hopefully delivered) curriculum meets individual needs. The responsibility for planning each child's 'journey' lies with the teacher or early years practitioner, often in consultation with colleagues and parents.

While support for planning is available in many forms (e.g. development matters (www.foundationyears.org.uk), books, journals, online resources), professional expertise is essential when decisions are taken, for example what to include, omit or amend; how to implement plans to maximise the opportunity for each child in terms of benefit and achieving his/her potential; how to individualise and differentiate each child's journey; how to enthuse children and encourage their involvement and interest.

It is also vital that professionals understand how children think and learn. Educators will naturally pose questions derived from theories of learning, for example:

● How do I organise the children?
● Does this activity need children to work together to maximise their zone of proximal development?
● What is the role of the adult?

- Is scaffolding required to provide suitable steps to achievement?
- Does the activity need modelling, or will that stifle creativity?
- Are appropriate resources provided with which the child might experiment?
- Is there space to work?
- Is there time to listen and encourage?
- Are there opportunities for the child to make decisions and become an independent learner?
- Are the teaching and learning styles appropriate for the child/children and to the activity?
- Will each child be involved, engaged, motivated and interested by the activity?

It must also be noted that children learn from the offered curriculum, which is wider than the nationally prescribed curriculum, and encompasses all of a child's experiences: intellectual, creative, physical, emotional, social and spiritual. The offered curriculum may be different from the received curriculum – that is, what the children actually learn from the provision. There is also the hidden curriculum which includes all that is learned by the children that was not planned or part of the designated curriculum (e.g. values and attitudes of those around them).

Assessment to inform individual journeys

As children progress on their individual journeys, there is a need to evaluate and assess their achievements. Assessment, as demonstrated in the rolling planning process, is integral to a successful 'journey'. This assessment may be 'formative', to inform the next step, 'diagnostic' to determine specialist requirements and interventions, or 'summative' to take stock of children's attainment at the end of the year. Encouraging self-assessment increases children's understanding of their learning journey and personal self-awareness. Limited or speedy progress may indicate the need for specialist provision. This may take the form of special educational needs (SEN) or inclusion in 'gifted and talented' groups.

In the final term of the year in which a child reaches age five, the EYFS profile must be completed for each child demonstrating their readiness for year 1. It must reflect ongoing observation and any relevant records and indicate whether children are meeting, exceeding or not yet reaching ('emerging') expected levels of development.

Transition to Key Stage 1

It is expected that most children will achieve the early learning goals by the end of the reception year; some will have gone beyond, others may still have some way to travel. Children moving from reception to year 1 might experience a change in environment and ethos. The play approach of many reception classes may be entirely or largely replaced by more of a sit and work approach which may inhibit learning. There may be the necessity for children to learn as a whole class for inappropriate periods of time. In practice, and as an ideal, the experienced professional in the enlightened and sufficiently resourced school maintains a smooth transition over whatever time is needed to prepare children for the less play-oriented approach of subsequent primary school years.

The teaching team must make certain that children participate in a wide range of planned activities to ensure their development and learning are holistic and the full statutory curriculum is covered – sound reasons for organising activities that are stimulating and enticing!

A thorough and considered planning process is equally crucial at KS1 of the National Curriculum. Teacher assessment continues with observation and record keeping, supported by examples of children's work, providing evidence of their progress and informing the planning process. Targets (derived from the scheme of work) are often shared with children so that they know what is expected and are involved and empowered. This can encourage development of responsibility, reflection and evaluation on their part.

The National Curriculum

The National Curriculum (www.education.gov.uk) for England for education in maintained (not independent) schools provides an entitlement and statutory framework. It outlines what must be taught and specifies attainment targets for children's learning at each of the four key stages. Year 1 and 2 of primary school are known as Key Stage 1, years 3 to 6 as Key Stage 2. Compulsory National Curriculum subjects are the same for both key stages: English, maths, science, design and technology, information and communication technology (ICT), history, geography, art and design, music, physical education, plus non-statutory religious education, citizenship, modern foreign languages (MFL) and personal, social and health education (PSHE) (www.direct.gov.uk). Programmes of study specify what should be taught within each subject at each key stage, while the attainment targets set out the knowledge, skills and understanding pupils must achieve in each subject by the end of each key stage.

Identification of a need to improve standards of literacy and numeracy from an accumulation of inspection, research and test evidence has resulted in concentration on these areas; the Primary Framework for Literacy and Mathematics was introduced in 2006 to raise standards and complement the National Curriculum. A variety of approaches to teaching are encouraged and although there are regular dedicated lessons ensuring focus on, for example phonics and mental maths, there was also a recognition that these skills can be developed across the curriculum.

In January 2011, the Secretary of State for Education announced a review of the National Curriculum in England. Draft National Curriculum documents for English, mathematics and science were published as a starting point for discussion with key stakeholders and followed by full public consultation towards the end 2012.

The English National Curriculum has been criticised for being too prescriptive and assessment-driven, for the arbitrariness of the attainment targets and for its potential detriment to pupils' motivation. This is allied to the long-standing debate in the UK which has centred on the age at which a more formal style of teaching should be introduced to young children (see Figure 7.6). This has undoubtedly influenced the Early Years Foundation Stage curriculum (www.foundationyears.org.uk/early-years-foundation-stage-2012) which is not intended to be formal and indeed mirrors many aspects of the preschools of Europe. These follow an informal, play-based curriculum where young children are encouraged to make sense of the world in which they live. Recent emphases on literacy, numeracy and the raising of standards in primary education have meant that many teachers – with the exception of the most confident, competent and creative – may be introducing too much formal learning too soon. In addition, greater accountability and the pressure on teachers to meet targets have led to instances of children's entitlement to a broad and balanced foundation stage being eroded (House, 2011). This should also be considered alongside the fact that children normally start school when they are four years old (due to government funding), despite the statutory requirement to begin in the term following their fifth birthday. In other European countries, compulsory schooling starts later, at six or seven years.

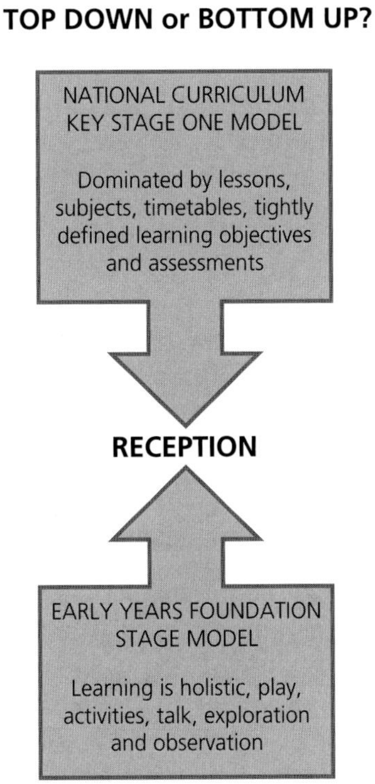

TOP DOWN or BOTTOM UP?

NATIONAL CURRICULUM
KEY STAGE ONE MODEL

Dominated by lessons, subjects, timetables, tightly defined learning objectives and assessments

RECEPTION

EARLY YEARS FOUNDATION
STAGE MODEL

Learning is holistic, play, activities, talk, exploration and observation

Figure 7.6 Top down or bottom up?

High quality education and care

Quality is easy to recognise but difficult to define in a concise straightforward way! Quality has become a national buzz-word and a universal business and educational aim. Policy documents often present quality as objective, real, universal and knowable, but there is broad agreement that quality is a socially constructed, culturally bound, context-specific and dynamic concept. Quantitative measurements are easily made and understood, for example staff:child ratio, however it is the qualitative aspects, for example positive relationships, which can demonstrate greater significance to the stakeholder(s) (child, parent, practitioner, community).

To begin to understand quality in relation to early years practice, differing perspectives may be considered (Dahlberg *et al.*, 2007).

Experiential education

Laevers (1994, 2000) and his experiential education purports to evaluate as well as improve quality. He specifies three dimensions:

1. **Context/treatment variables**. For example, the classroom environment, programme content, teacher style, level of training and educator/child ratios.
2. **Effects or outcomes of ECEC programmes**. While undoubtedly valuable, this does not actually improve the quality of experience for children currently in the settings.
3. **Process variables**. These are considered to describe, as well as improve, quality by focusing on the extent of children's emotional well-being and their level of involvement in activities. Children's involvement is characterised by Laevers as concentration, persistence, motivation, fascination and intensity of experience, leading to deep learning and development. The provision of appropriately challenging activities is deemed imperative, as are positive relationships and children being happy and secure in a stable, caring and stimulating environment.

SureStart

From an examination of cross-national evidence from 15 countries, Mooney *et al.* (2003) developed a set of three inter-dependent indicators of quality to support SureStart ECEC programmes which is a UK Government programme encouraging integration of education, health and family support services for young children and families:

1. **Structural features**. For example, adequate funding, equity of access, affordability, staff qualifications and training, staff–child ratios and group size.
2. **Process features**. For example, developmentally appropriate activities, sensitive interactions between children and adults.
3. **Outcomes**. For example, cognitive development, school readiness, academic skills, parents' satisfaction with provision.

Self-evaluation and partnership with parents were also deemed significant elements of quality and, together with the above features, seemed to be correlated with higher quality ECEC.

Starting strong (early childhood education and care)

Improving the quality of ECEC is a major priority for the Organisation for Economic Cooperation and Development (www.oecd.org). Starting strong (OECD, 2001) made a broad holistic comparison of early years policy and practice in 12 countries. While much attention is given to acknowledging and reconciling diversity in the range of contexts, values and perspectives, a consensus quality framework emerged and similarities with the models of Laevers and SureStart can be detected.

There are four elements:

1. **At systemic level:** sufficient investment, efficiently coordinated management structures, adequate staff training and conditions, clear pedagogical frameworks; procedures for monitoring and evaluation.

2. **At programme level:** duration and intensity of programmes, favourable group size and adult–child ratios, suitable environment and equipment.
3. **Process variables:** sensitive adult–child interactions, active partnership with parents, effective learning and social opportunities.
4. **Outcome variables:** short- and long-term measurement of, for example, children's development and achievements.

Studies I (OECD, 2001) and II (OECD, 2006) culminate in Starting Strong III, A Quality Toolbox for ECEC (OECD, 2012) where the OECD identifies effective policy 'levers': goals and regulations, curriculum standards, qualifications, training and working conditions, engaging families and communities and research and monitoring.

Children's views

Children's views on what constitutes quality are important. Mooney and Blackburn (2003) were commissioned by the Department for Education and Skills (DfES) to ascertain children's views to inform consultation for Investors in Children. They reviewed much literature, surveyed early years development and childcare partnership consultations and consulted with children from different ECEC settings. They summarise children's views on quality:

- Friendships should be encouraged and supported.
- A wide range of activities, regularly changed to suit children's interests and needs with sufficient indoor and outdoor space.
- Children and staff should have fun, with staff facilitating activities.
- Staff show respect for children, are caring, take time to listen, avoid raising their voices and interact sensitively with children.
- There is a choice of attractive, enjoyable food with ready access to drinks.
- Children's views to be regarded seriously and children encouraged to participate in programme decisions.

(Adapted from Mooney and Blackburn, 2003).

Most of these indicators could be accommodated within the earlier quality frameworks described above, and of course they accord with the UN Convention on the Rights of the Child (1989), Article 12 – acknowledging and responding to the voice of the child.

Quality early childhood education and care probably should:

- adopt an holistic philosophy and an integrated/multi-professional approach to the education and care of young children
- create an atmosphere of respect that values each child, ensures children's social and emotional well-being and is anti-discriminatory
- make certain that educators have the appropriate knowledge, understanding, skills and attitudes to interact and work effectively with young children, providing a range of appropriate and challenging learning activities. The Nutbrown Report (2012) puts forward some interesting proposals
- work in partnership with children's families
- enhance quality through reflective practice and evaluation

- maintain a rich, stimulating, child-focused learning context with adequate indoor and outdoor space, equipment/materials and time for a wide range of activities
- be adequately funded with a favourable ratio of educators to children
- promote effective leadership and management of highly trained educators who are given regular opportunities for continuing professional development.

This consensus does not constitute a check-list, but rather a framework from which to develop a rich understanding of quality. By entering into a dialogic process with stakeholders and taking account of the range of perspectives, educators can work more democratically towards contextually appropriate quality (CAQ) within their particular setting. Evaluation is an essential aspect of quality in any ECEC programme – essential, that is, in enhancing provision and achieving high standards and best outcomes for children and their families.

Evaluation

The Office for Standards in Education (Ofsted) is responsible for inspecting funded nursery provision for young children, child-minding and day care. They have established formal criteria and processes for these inspections. The documents are publicly available and early years professionals are obliged to pay careful attention to the specified requirements (www.ofsted.gov.uk). Helpful as inspection can be, to achieve real quality within an inclusionary paradigm, we must go beyond these procedures.

Learning activity

Access and compare two Ofsted reports of early years settings you are familiar with: www.ofsted.gov.uk/inspection-reports/find-inspection-report.

Evaluation should be applied to all the dimensions of quality in any setting and there is strong consensus that multiple perspectives, including children's views are significant. Evaluation strategies might include:

- formal and informal observations
- asking questions, informally or via interviews/questionnaires, of all participants to elicit views
- listening carefully to children, parents, colleagues, inspectors, advisors, managers and head teachers
- asking and answering questions of ourselves
- comparing our provision and practice with that of others (via visits or reading)
- sharing views, discussing educational ideas and practice with others
- process evaluation: observing day-to-day activities and evaluating particularly in terms of involvement, exploration, mental effort, challenges, matching child's capabilities, task orientation and engagement, quality of interactions
- product evaluation: evaluating the outcome of activities in terms of development, changes in children's awareness, attitudes, interests, understanding, knowledge, learning, behaviour, skills and competencies

- partnership evaluation: how effective are partnerships with parents, stakeholders, other professionals, the community
- using formal and standardised procedures for assessing children's experiences and learning outcomes (e.g. Laevers' (1994) Leuven Involvement Scale for Young Children (LIS-YC); the Early Childhood Environment Rating Scale (ECERS-R 2003, ITERS-R 2006).

Most crucially, practitioners must act on the results of evaluative procedures, especially when aspects of practice have been identified in need of improvement. Indeed, evaluation must be viewed as integral to the regular planning cycle. This reflective practice requires us to reflect on our observations and evaluations; to discuss them with colleagues, other professionals, parents and children; and to study relevant research and so develop an informed action plan to improve elements of our provision in need of enhancement or enrichment. Through such a process, evaluation emerges as an extremely important strategy for working towards and improving quality in our ECEC provision.

International perspectives

It is human nature to compare and contrast what you do with what others do. As globalisation becomes the byword for the 21st century, it is not uncommon for governments, societies, organisations, communities and individuals to compare, contrast and discuss education systems, approaches, processes and outcomes they are familiar with, sharing with others things that work well and those they may find challenging. A cautionary note is that it is always important to ensure that information given or shared is accurate, reliable and valid as there can be an overenthusiastic urge to present systems of education in the best possible light. The cultural differences of countries must also be considered as this means systems can never be transplanted but need to be adapted to the specific context. In this way, education models and practices are shared and interpreted, grasped, modified or rejected. For the most part, the sharing of ideas has resulted in many improvements to education systems in developing and developed countries.

Many countries can be identified as having useful education systems or curricula approaches, but it depends on what and how the judgements or measurements are made. It could be reading, literacy, numeracy or even gender parity of access. The Organisation for Economic Co-operation and Development (OECD, 2011) and United Nations Educational, Scientific and Cultural Organisation (UNESCO, 2011: S1.1, 9–15) and United Nations Children's Fund (UNICEF, 2008) are three organisations that provide some statistical evidence on education and care.

Some countries' early childhood education stands out and has attracted attention from around the world. These include Scandinavian countries, such as Denmark and Sweden. The two included below have impacted on many countries around the world.

Early childhood services in Reggio Emilia (a city in northern Italy) are recognised as a source of inspiration for early years educators worldwide. Many have sought to capture the essence of their quality (e.g. Dahlberg *et al.*, 2007; Thornton and Brunton, 2009). Reggio Emilia adopts a social-constructivist approach, with children regarded as active, rich and competent co-constructors in their own development. Relationships with children, families, other educators, community members and between children are considered crucial to positive educational and developmental outcomes; consequently they are carefully nurtured. There is a strong emphasis on multiple forms of knowing and on the symbolic representation of ideas and feelings through the famous 'hundred languages' (Malaguzzi, cited in Fillipini and Vecchi, 1997) which children possess. There is no predetermined curriculum; the understanding, experiences and interests that children bring to the setting constitute the starting points for learning, where they are supported in developing critical thinking and abilities to enable them to contribute fully to a democratic society. A stimulating environment, sensitive interaction and responsiveness are much emphasised in the teaching and learning process with considerable use of projects, thoughtful observing of children and careful documenting of their progress and activities, well supported by the shared reflective practice of stakeholders (Rinaldi, 2006). While the lack of a specified curriculum has led to criticism on grounds of accountability, advocates cite in defence the detailed recording undertaken by educators. The numerous international early years professionals who visit the centres and maintain links or work collaboratively with the educators bears testimony to the value this approach has been given.

The New Zealand early childhood framework (www.educate.ece.govt.nz) includes a range of diverse services all connected by the Te Whariki curriculum which was introduced in 1996 and is partly written in Maori. It is a socio-cultural framework that endeavours to meet the needs of all children from diverse social or cultural backgrounds. It promotes the attitudes and customs of both its minority and majority nationalities and was developed to ensure key guiding principles were addressed, such as partnership with parents, and keeping family and community central.

Its four key principles are empowerment, holistic development, family and community and relationships. These, together with the five strands of well-being, belonging, contribution, communication and exploration, enable educators to focus their support for young children. The Maori weaving metaphor (Whariki) a 'woven mat for all to stand on' takes the perspective that everything is interconnected and learning takes place in the social world. A project-based approach using children's interests determines the content of the children's educational experiences. It has many strengths, including its holistic and inclusive approach. Educators can develop or weave the curriculum based on the children they have, so it has the potential for rich developmental experiences vital for stimulating learning. However, bringing together diverse services, health, care and education can be challenging as can an approach that does not stipulate specific content to be covered or skills to be learned. Pressure from governments over accountability mean this type of approach is much more difficult to measure.

Similarities between Reggio Emilia and Te Whariki can be seen. They both have a clear set of principles and a principled approach to the curriculum which advocates social justice. They are child-centred and consider children learn best when they are interacting with the environment and other people. The child as an active explorer is central and this requires the adult to be the facilitator, guide and co-constructor of knowledge.

Both approaches document or provide a narrative of the children's learning and include emotional aspects or children's feelings as part of the process. Partnership with parents underpins the whole philosophy of both approaches as does respectful, knowledgeable educators.

Learning activity

Choose either the Reggio Emilia or the Te Whariki approach and distinguish where it could have influenced UK curricula.

Emerging influences

The guidance for the education and care of young children is continually developing as a result of research or reflection by professionals, politicians and parents and the advent of new technology – the rolling planning process or reflective practice on a grander scale. New problems and issues constantly emerge; for example, there has been a great deal in the media about children not being sufficiently fit and healthy, with blame being attributed to an unhealthy diet and sitting too much in front of TVs or computer screens. Such issues lead to new initiatives, for example a stronger emphasis on physical activity in curricula and healthy eating initiatives. Importantly, a greater recognition of the need for local authorities, relevant agencies, organisations and practitioners to collaborate (to provide an integrated service for young children and families) is much emphasised. The primary school may find itself the base for a multi-professional workforce (health, education and social care) that can better ensure holistic and optimum provision to promote young children's all-round development and well-being and support their families, thus giving our children the best possible start in life. However, with the emergence of independent academies and free schools, education and care may become fragmented or priorities changed by governments in their attempts to drive up educational standards.

Education in inextricably linked to politics. Research commissioned by the government is useful in determining developments necessary and influencing policy. The Department for Education's current research includes:

- Nutbrown, C. (2012) The final report of the independent review of early education and childcare qualifications: Foundations for Quality. London: Department for Education.
- SureStart National Evaluation by Birkbeck College due to be completed end of 2012.
- Evaluation of pilot for free early learning and childcare for two-year-old children, with follow up at age five, ended in May 2012 by National Centre for Social Research.
- Effective Pre-School, Primary and Secondary Education 3–14 (EPPSE) – Continuation to Age 16.
- University of London (IoE – SSRU) 2008–end 2013.

Learning activity

Find out about the following early childhood pioneers: Margaret McMillan, Friedrich Froebel, Maria Montessori, Robert Owen, Susan Isaacs and Johann Heinrich Pestalozzi. Identify similarities and differences:
- in their backgrounds
- in their theories of education (e.g. role of play, involvement of parents)
- in the application of their theories to early years settings
- with early childhood education today.
Share your findings with a fellow student/peer.

Conclusion

This chapter has contextualised early childhood education and care within an historical, legal and socio-cultural framework. It has usefully included definitions and purpose and considered underpinning principles and philosophies. A broad overview of early childhood education provision across the United Kingdom has been presented with emphasis on how children learn, as well as adult roles and responsibilities. Reflection on quality provision has been discussed, international perspectives identified and emerging influences deliberated.

Evaluate your learning

- Why is it important to have principles to inform your practice?
- Why is quality of ECEC difficult to define?
- What is the point of considering educational provision and practice in other countries?
- Why is research important in providing for evidence-based practice?

References

Allen, G (2011): *Early Intervention: The Next Steps.* London: HM Government.

Aubrey, C (2011): *Leading and Managing in the Early Years*, 2nd edn. London: Sage.

Baldock, P (2010): *Understanding Cultural Diversity in the Early Years.* London: Sage.

Blandford, S and Knowles, C (2009): *Developing Professional Practice 0–7.* Harlow: Pearson Education.

Broadhead, P and Burt, A (2012): *Understanding Young Children's Learning Through Play.* Abingdon: Routledge.

Bronfenbrenner, U (1989): *The Ecology of Human Development.* Cambridge, MA: Harvard University Press.

Bruce, T (1997): *Early Childhood Education*, 2nd edn. London: Hodder Education.

Dahlberg, G, Moss, P and Pence, A (2007): *Beyond Quality in Early Childhood Education and Care: Policy and Practice.* London: Sage.

DCSF (Department for Children, Schools and Families) (2008a): *Statutory Framework for the Early Years Foundation Stage.* Nottingham: HMSO.

DCSF (Department for Children, Schools and Families) (2008b): *Every Child a Talker.* Nottingham: DCSF.

DCSF (Department for Children, Schools and Families) (2009): *Learning, Playing and Interacting.* London: QCA.

Department for Education (2012): *Early Years Foundation Stage.* London: HMSO.

Department for Education with Department of Health (2012): Supporting families in the foundation years. (Online). Last accessed July 2012. Available from: www.education.

gov.uk/home/childrenandyoungpeople/earlylearningandchildcare/early/a00192398/ supporting-families-in-the-foundation-years.

Drake, J (2009): *Planning for Children's Play and Learning.* Abingdon: Routledge.

EPPE (2003) RESEARCHBriefRBX15-03. (Online). Available from: http://eppe.ioe.ac.uk/ eppe/eppepdfs/RB%20summary%20findings%20from%20Preschool.pdf.

Evangelou, M and Sylva, K (2008): *Supporting Parents in Promoting Early Learning: The Evaluation of the Early Learning Partnership Project.* Oxford: Department of Education, University of Oxford and Department of Social Policy and Work, University of Oxford.

Evangelou, M, Coxon, K and Sylva, K (2008): *Room to Play PEEP Study.* Oxford: University of Oxford.

Field, F (2010): *The Foundation Years: Preventing Poor Children Becoming Poor Adults.* London: HM Government.

Fillipini, T and Vecchi V (eds) (1997): *The Hundred Languages of Children: Narrative of the Possible.* Reggio Emilia: Reggio Children.

Froebel, F (1907): *The Education of Man.* Translated by WN Hailmann. New York: Appleton & Co.

Gray, C and MacBlain, S (2012): *Learning Theories in Childhood.* London: Sage.

Hayes, D (2012): *Foundations of Primary Teaching,* 5th edn. Abingdon: Routledge.

House, R (ed) (2011): *Too Much, Too Soon? Early Learning and the Erosion of Childhood.* Stroud: Hawthorn Press.

Katz, LG (2003): The right of the child to develop and learn in quality environments. *International Journal of Early Childhood* **35**(1), 2.

Laevers, F (1994): The innovative project: experiential education and the definition of quality in education. In Laevers, F (ed), *Defining and Assessing Quality in Early Childhood Education.* Leuven: Leuven University Press, pp. 159–72.

Laevers, F (2000): Forward to basics: deep-level-learning and the experiential approach. *Early Years* **20**(2), 20–9.

Macintyre, C (2012): *Enhancing Learning Through Play,* 2nd edn. Abingdon: Routledge.

Mooney, A and Blackburn, T (2003): *Children's Views on Childcare Quality.* London: DfES.

Mooney, A, Cameron, C, Candappa, M, McQuail, S, Moss, P and Petrie, P (2003): *Early Years and Childcare International Evidence Project: Quality.* London: DfES.

Nutbrown, C (2012): The final report of the independent review of early education and childcare qualifications. Foundations for Quality. London: Department for Education.

Nutbrown, C, Clough, P and Selbie, P (2008): *Early Childhood Education: History, Philosophy and Experience.* London: Sage.

Ofsted (2009): Childcare Groups: A Passion to be outstanding. Available from: http://www. ofsted.gov.uk/resources/childcare-groups-passion-be-outstanding

Ofsted (Office for Standards in Education, Children's Services and Skills) (2010) Workforce reform in schools: has it made a difference? (Online). Last accessed July 2012, Available from: www.ofsted.gov.uk/publications/080263.

OECD (2001): *Starting Strong: Early Childhood Education and Care.* Paris: OECD.

OECD (2006): *Starting Strong II: Early Childhood Education and Care.* Paris: OECD.

OECD (2011): Education at a Glance 2011: OECD Indicators. Paris: OECD Publishing. (Online). Available from: www.oecd.org/dataoecd/61/2/48631582.pdf.

OECD (2012) Starting Strong III – A Quality Toolbox for Early Childhood Education and Care. Paris: OECD.

Pound, L (2011): *Influencing Early Childhood Education: Key Figures, Philosophies and Ideas.* Maidenhead: OUP/McGraw-Hill Education.

Rinaldi, C (2006): *In Dialogue with Reggio Emilia.* London: Routledge.

Robbins, A and Callan, S (eds) (2009): *Managing Early Years Settings.* London: Sage.

Rodger, R (2012): *Planning an Appropriate Curriculum in the Early Years,* 3rd edn. Abingdon: Routledge.

Siraj-Blatchford, I (2003): *Supporting Children's Learning: The EPPE Project.* Report of the Nottingham Early Years Conference, September 2002.

Siraj-Blatchford, I, Sylva, K, Muttock, S, Gilden, R and Bell, D (2002): *Researching Effective Pedagogy in the Early Years.* London: Department for Education and Skills.

Smidt, S (ed) (2010): *Key Issues in Early Years Education,* 2nd edn. London: Routledge.

Smidt, S (2011): *Playing to Learn.* Abingdon: Routledge

Sylva, K, Melhuish, EC, Sammons, P, Siraj-Blatchford, I and Taggart, B (2004): The Effective Provision of Pre-School Education (EPPE) Project: Technical Paper 12 – The Final Report: Effective Pre-School Education. London: DfES/IOE, University of London.

Thornton, L and Brunton, P (2009): *Understanding the Reggio Approach,* 3rd edn. Abingdon: Routledge.

Tickell, C (2011): *The Early Years Foundations for Life, Health and Learning.* London: Department for Education.

United Nations (1989): Convention on the Rights of the Child (UNCRC). (Online). Available from: www.unicef.org.uk/CRC.

UNICEF (2008): The Childcare Transition: A league table of early childhood education and care in economically advanced countries Innocenti Report Card 8. Florence: Innocenti Research Centre.

UNICEF (2012): Unicef in Action. (Online). Last accessed July 2012. Available from: www.unicef.org/earlychildhood/index_action.html?p=printme.

UNESCO (2007): A Human Rights Based Approach to Education For All. Available from: http//unesdoc.unesco.org/images/0015/001548/154861e.pdf.

UNESCO (2011): Global Education Digest 2011: Comparing Education Statistics Across the World. Montreal, Canada. (Online). Available from: www.uis.unesco.org/Education/Documents/ged-2011-en.pdf.

Vygotsky, L (1978): *Mind in Society.* Cambridge, MA: Harvard University Press.

Wall, K (2011): *Special Needs and Early Years,* 3rd edn. London: Sage.

Waller, T, Whitmarsh, J and Clarke, K (2011): *Making Sense of Theory and Practice in Early Childhood.* Maidenhead: Open University Press.

Websites

www.bernardvanleer.org

www.childreninscotland.org.uk

www.directgov.uk

www.educate.ece.govt.nz

www.education.gov.uk

www.eppe.ioe.ac.uk

www.foundationyears.org.uk

www.northernireland.gov.uk

www.oecd.org

www.ofsted.gov.uk

www.scotland.gov.uk

www.unesco.org

www.unicef.org.uk

www.wales.gov.uk

Further reading

Evangelou, M, Sylva, K, Kyriacou, M, Wild, M and Glenny, G (2009): *Early Years Learning and Development Literature Review.* Oxford: University of Oxford.

James, A, Jenks, C and Prout, A (1998): *Theorizing Childhood.* Cambridge: Polity Press.

8 Understanding childhood in late modernity

Emma Bond and Stuart Agnew

This chapter aims to explore:
- the relationship between early childhood and late modernity
- early childhood in relation to the risk society
- children's experiences of new media technologies.

Introduction

It is not unusual for students to draw upon their own life experiences when embarking upon an academic degree, especially when the subject area is one that can be closely related to their own lived reality, such as early childhood. Although such experiences do provide an insight, we should not assume that they are the norm against which others can be compared. The use of our own life experiences should be seen in terms of common sense, a subjective interpretation of reality based on cultural traditions and assumptions. However, by utilising sociological perspectives, we can begin to question beliefs and values that seem common sense or natural and give academic consideration to the social influences acting on early childhood. Recent developments in childhood studies (as discussed in Chapter 1) and the emphasis on understanding children's experiences have led to a new interest in exploring the relationship between young children, early childhood and society.

Sociology is interested in understanding wider social changes and in light of recent technological advances, a chapter on sociological approaches to understanding early childhood and young children's everyday experiences would not be complete without a discussion of the relationship between young children, technology and new media. Additionally, technological advances in recent years make it more difficult for adults to compare current childhood realities to those of their own childhood experiences. This chapter introduces some of the key factors influencing contemporary childhoods through a discussion of the work of Beck (1992) and Giddens (1990, 1991) and an examination of 'risk', 'late modernity' and the relationship between childhood and new media technologies.

Understanding childhood

Corsaro (2011) suggests that until recently, children and childhood were not seen as a worthy topic to explore, investigate or theorise within sociology, primarily due to children being seen not as autonomous actors that influence society, but as being subservient to adults. However, as the academic study of children and childhood grew, initially linking research to pre-existing debates in relation to families and schools, sociology stopped marginalising children, producing a multitude of theoretical conceptualising of childhood (see Corsaro, 2011 and James *et al.*, 2010) and 'children have become a source of our concerns about the nature of identity in a rapidly changing world' (James *et al.*, 2010: 205). Recently, research has been undertaken to explore the concept of risk within children's experiences and Scott *et al.* (1998) suggest that risk is central to the social construction of childhood.

James *et al.* (2010) suggest that in late modernity, the child remains a victim of public space where the outside is considered a risky place to be and this section explores some of the issues that may be relevant to childhood and contemporary children's lives. Indeed, Furedi (2002: 199) goes so far as to argue the development of the culture of what he terms 'paranoid parenting', and he claims that our anxiety to keep children safe is 'likely to be more damaging to them than the risks they encounter in their daily interactions with the world'. The concepts of the child and childhood in late modernity shape our understanding of children and influence adult control over children's social worlds. Research, which explores children's own understanding and management of risk and its impact upon their everyday lives, suggests that children themselves are reflexive in their conceptualisation of risk and actively negotiate boundaries imposed upon them by adults. Childhood is identified and constructed as a time of innocence, vulnerability and dependence (Jenks, 1996) and such images of childhood are influential in shaping children's identities in public life (Harden, 2000).

James and James (2001) argue that contemporary moral discourses are tightening the net of social control on children's lives to the extent that children have increasingly become the subjects of overt and covert regulation and, consequently, opportunities for children to be relatively free from adult control have been greatly reduced (Valentine, 1996). A central feature of modernity has been the idealisation of the private sphere of the home (Slater, 1998) and a key element of this has been the expulsion of children from the public sphere and the segregation of children and childhood into the home (Roche, 1999). In the United Kingdom, a hierarchy of mobility in relation to public space appears to have emerged towards late modernity and many social theorists have commented on the disappearance of children from the street (James *et al.*, 2010). Roche (1999) suggests that children, despite being social actors, are often rendered silent and invisible by the attitudes and practices of adult society. Although the rights of children, as articulated in the United Nations Convention on the Rights of the Child (UNCRC) (United Nations, 1989) and the Children Act 1989, would seem to suggest that children's status as citizens is unequivocal, children continue to be marginalised (James and James, 2001). Holloway and Valentine (2001) highlight the debates about spatiality in childhood that are associated with places, sites in everyday life and the spatial imagery in ideologies of childhood generally (see also Chapter 13, *Children's geographies*). Public space has come to be defined as adult space and young children's participation in public space is controlled and limited by adults in a number of ways, from formal, often legal restrictions on where children are allowed to go, parental restrictions on children's participation in and access to public life, restrictions on children's behaviour in public spaces, and many public amenities are geared towards adult use in terms of size (Harden, 2000).

Jenks (1996) develops Foucault's ideas of spatial control to suggest that the exercise and manipulation of space is a primary example of adults controlling the child's world. Conceptually, the shift in social control processes and in the nature and targets of social reactions are probably the most significant sociological developments associated with the risk society (Ungar, 2001). It is interesting to note from James and James (2001) that the net of social control has increasingly tightened around childhood during the 1990s under New Labour and the control of children's behaviour is increasingly a focus for policy initiatives. The Crime and Disorder Act (1998) introduced increased powers for the police to stop children who are outside school during school hours and enabled courts to 'require the parent of every convicted juvenile offender to attend parenting programmes and if necessary to control future behaviour' of the child (Arthur, 2005: 235). The availability of such policies signifies an increase in the breadth and depth of the surveillance of childhood and reflects the extension of a pseudo-parental responsibility to the community as a whole outside the family and works to deny children's autonomy and their right to be responsible and govern their own behaviour (James and James, 2001).

Controlling children

Hendrick (2008) identifies historical developments, both in terms of policies and specific events that have transformed political and public perceptions of children from innocent angels to potential menacing devils. Furthermore, Jewkes (2011) highlights how the media direct both public and political attention on children, constructing them as evil monsters or tragic victims dependent upon social and political focus at the time. The tragic events in 1993, resulting in the death of Jamie Bulger, increased growing anxieties over children and young people at that time, however, the age of the perpetrators escalated those concerns as this introduced the idea that young children can be a danger to wider society. The images presented by the press of an innocent 'blond-haired, blue-eyed Jamie as an epitome of an ideal child' reinforced his status as a victim (Jewkes, 2011:105). A more recent example occurred in 2009 when two young boys aged 9 and 11 years were taken to waste ground in Edlington, South Yorkshire and subjected to a 90-minute sustained attack by two brothers aged 10 and 11. Although serious assaults by children on other children are rare occurrences (Muncie, 2009), this did not prevent the popular media presenting it as another example of 'broken Britain'. Yet this dichotomy of the innocent/dangerous child is nothing new. Pearson (1983) identifies various stages throughout history when children and young people were viewed as dangerous; the late modern arguments are a replication of old themes.

Chapter 1 discussed developments surrounding welfarism and children's rights, however, society can also be measured against how it responds to those who transgress social norms. As such, children regularly receive a vast amount of negative publicity from politicians, criminal justice agencies and the media relating to their behaviour in public places. Traditionally, responses fall into two main perspectives – the welfarist perspective (as discussed in Chapter 1) that focuses upon the best interest of the child and the justice perspective where 'responsibilisation' is placed both on the child and their parents for the deviant behaviour. There is no doubt that the Crime and Disorder Act 1998, with its abolition of *'doli incapax'*, translated as incapable of evil (this was a presumption held by the courts that children under 14 did not fully understand the consequences of their actions and as such should not normally face criminal prosecution except in exceptional circumstances) and the introduction of populist punitive controls over children's behaviour falls clearly into the justice model.

Serious offending behaviour by children is thankfully very rare (Muncie, 2009), however, by using our sociological imagination we are able to consider challenging behaviour in a different light. Emile Durkheim (1858–1917), highly regarded as one of the most influential sociologists ever (Stones, 2008) posits that deviant or challenging behaviour can also have a useful function for society. In essence, he suggests that society can learn from deviant activities as it helps reinforce moral values and social norms, providing an opportunity to reflect upon itself (Carrabine *et al.*, 2009).

Learning activity

Consider the tasks below.

Scenario 1

A child has been drawing pictures but when left alone for a few minutes, draws upon the walls.
Using the principles discussed above, what learning occurs for both the child and the adult?

Scenario 2

Two children have a fight over a toy at playgroup. By reflecting on this situation what learning could result from it?

As these scenarios demonstrate, Durkheim's belief that deviancy, or in this case minor behavioural issues, can offer a function to society beyond the actual event.

Late modernity and the family

According to Giddens (1999: 60) attitudes towards having children have also changed and now 'it is a decision guided by psychological and emotional needs'. In late modernity, family structure has altered as a consequence of individualisation and people are driven into bonding in a partnership, which is not a primeval need, but one which grows with the losses that individualisation brings (Beck, 1992). Beck (1992: 118) suggests that the child is the 'source of the last remaining, irrevocable, unexchangeable primary relationship' and 'becomes the final alternative to loneliness'. Late modern society appears to have re-adopted the child as the site or the relocation of discourses concerning stability, integration and the social bond, and 'children are now seen not so much as "promise", but as primary and unequivocal sources of love, but also partners in the most fundamental, unchosen, unnegotiated form of relationship' (Jenks, 1996: 107). Parents who recollect a childhood unhindered by many of the concerns facing today's parents are anxious about traffic and stranger danger and, indeed, worry about most aspects of their children's lives (O'Brien *et al.*, 2000). However, as

Furedi (2002) suggests, many aspects of paranoid parenting have little to do with the reality of children's lives arguing that:

This obsessive fear about the safety of children has led to a fundamental redefinition of parenting. Traditionally, good parenting has been associated with nurturing, stimulating, and socializing children. Today, it is associated with monitoring their activities. An inflated sense of risk prevails, demanding that children should never be left on their own and that preferably they should be within sight of one of their parents at all times.

(Furedi, 2002: 5)

In individualised society, qualitatively new types of personal risk arise and today's risks derive from internal decision that depends simultaneously on scientific and social construction (Beck, 1992). Increasingly, in the UK, letting children roam or play out unaccompanied is becoming a marker of neglectful or irresponsible parenthood (O'Brien *et al.*, 2000) and Scott *et al.* (1998) suggest that discourses around parental responsibility heighten parental anxiety as parents are held responsible for their children's well-being and conduct and are, thus, held accountable if their children are victimised or if they victimise others.

Discourses on risk are located principally in the public sphere rather than the private sphere of the family (Harden, 2000) and findings from Hood *et al.*'s (1996) study indicate that parents view the home as a safer place than outside because of pollution, traffic and potential violence. Parents are becoming increasingly afraid about a diversity of social and environmental dangers to their children lurking in the public realm, not least dangers from other children, which means that parents are now seeking to prevent their children from having contact with anything but the most controlled and sanitised of public spaces (Philo, 2000). However, it is important to note Arthur (2007), who proposes that although the dominant belief regarding the safest environment for children is the private sphere of the home, for many children home can be a place of turmoil, family discord and potentially an abusive environment. This is supported by the ever-growing evidence highlighting dangers within the home (Office for National Statistics, 2012) for example in 2010/11, of the 56 incidents of homicides of children under 16, 64 per cent were committed by a parent or step-parent and children under one year of age are statistically the most at risk group of being a victim of homicide (Smith *et al.*, 2012). Baby Peter, who died in 2007 aged 17 months, was the subject of a child protection plan and his name had been on Haringey's child protection register under the category of physical abuse and neglect since December 22, 2006. The NSPCC (2012) highlight the lack of any one specific source that monitors child homicides which makes it challenging to grasp the overall extent of serious dangers facing children.

Risk anxiety, engendered by the desire to keep children safe, frequently has negative consequences for children themselves and curtails children's activities in ways which may restrict their autonomy and their opportunities to develop the necessary skills to cope with the world (Scott *et al.*, 1998). However, Prout (2000) observes that only a few children are so tightly controlled in this process and suggests that, for many children, it involves a high degree of negotiation with parents keen to protect their children from the real and supposed dangers of the street, but also anxious to maximise their children's accumulation of informal cultural and social capital. According to Brannen and O'Brien (1995), through individualisation, young children have or can make choices but the opportunities for choice are increasingly standardised in modern societies, while the process of globalisation means that many of the cultural and leisure options available to children have become similar.

The independent child in late modernity

Towards the end of the 20th century, the representation of children as having a right to a life of their own became commonplace in social analysis and legal discourse (Beck, 1998). Prout (2000) suggests that, in spite of the greater surveillance, control and regulation of children, there is an increasing tendency to recognise children as people in their own right, as individuals with a capacity for self-realisation (a notion embraced by modernity) and, within the limits of social interdependency, autonomous action. A tension between self-realisation and control has always been a feature of modernity (Giddens, 1990, 1991) and a pattern is emerging in which public institutions are more concerned with the control of children, while the private sphere is constituted as the place where children are more allowed to express choice, exercise autonomy and work towards their individual self-realisation (Prout, 2000). Brannen and O'Brien (1995) note how the discourses which govern western models of parenting children are individualised and children are encouraged to become representative of themselves, to develop individual identities and to 'negotiate' their relationships with their parents – children enter into the public realm through a complex interaction of constraint and choice. Although much of adult–child negotiation of boundaries is likely to be framed in terms of potential risk, we cannot assume that children are always willing to be bounded, either by definitions of them as dependent and lacking in adult competencies, or by attempts to curtail their activities and, while boundaries are primarily established and maintained by adults, they may be tested and challenged by children (Scott *et al.*, 1998). This view is further developed by Harden (2000), whose research indicates that children do not simply accept the limitations on their participation in public life, may be critical of formal restrictions, may employ strategies for subverting legal and parental restrictions and are active in their negotiation of boundaries with their parents.

The globalisation of children's rights has had an impact on all aspects of children's lives, from their relationship with their parents to their participation in school and other social institutions, and the paradigm of childhood sociology emphasising children's position as social actors, as creative and inventive users of the world around them, has nurtured a blossoming conceptual and empirical exploration of children's competency and agency in a range of diverse settings (O'Brien *et al.*, 2000). Children generate their own understandings of the world and of culture in response to the structures and images which surround them (James *et al.*, 2010). Much literature explores how children see the world, their values and priorities and the ways in which they themselves feel marginalised – the child has become a research subject (Roche, 1999). However, Scott *et al.* (1998) point out that children's participation in constructing their own everyday world takes place within the constraints set by their subordinate location in relation to adults, as children's understanding of what it means to be a child has been shaped by their interaction with more powerful, adult social actors with pre-existing, albeit negotiable, ideas about childhood and children.

In everyday life, abstract ideas of the child come up against the actuality of children of different ages and genders, with a range of attributes and capacities (Backett, 1982). Research reflects how contemporary young children's everyday social worlds are bound up in differences defined by age, gender, unique personality, culture, family circumstance and personal environment. By the last year of primary school, a significant majority of children in O'Brien *et al.*'s (2000) study reported a fair degree of independence in their daily life, such as being allowed to go to the local shops without an adult, to play out on the streets without an adult and to go to and come home from school without an adult. However, their findings highlight key differences in contemporary children's use of public spaces as linked to variations in age, gender, family culture and ethnicity and to the physical environments of the neighbourhoods or settlements where they live. Girls were more restricted, had a narrower and more constrained home range and spent less time in public urban settings than boys when they were out and were more likely to be supervised by adults than boys. O'Brien *et al.* (2000) are, therefore, critical of assumptions of a unitary public child.

Risk and early childhood

While anxieties about risk may be shaped by public discussions, it is individuals that cope with these uncertainties and central to this is the individual reflexive monitoring of risk. However, it is possible to question, in relation to children, whether all individuals are regarded as equally reflexive. Public debates on risk rarely include children's own opinions and risks to children are defined and managed by adults on children's behalf and, therefore, the element of choice, responsibility and reflexivity accredited to adults in relation to risk is denied to children (Harden, 2000; Roche, 1999).

Learning activity

List a variety of examples that demonstrate the way that a parent/guardian may control a child's life and how these measures are amended over time as the child grows up.

For example, looking at the time a child goes to bed, how does this change over time and why? Could there be some form of negotiation regarding this as the child gets older? Is it predominantly the child's choice or is it normally set by the adult, if so, why?

In contemporary society, we live our everyday lives amidst the almost constant reflexive monitoring of risk, which pervades our sense of how to manage ourselves and the world (Scott *et al.*, 1998). Research indicates that both parents and children conceptualise public space in terms of risk. Parents balance and negotiate the immediate with the longer-term risks in managing and controlling their children's lives (Hood *et al.*, 1996) and children are concerned about moving outside the private and local spheres (Harden, 2000; O'Brien *et al.*, 2000). James *et al.* (2010) suggest that the opportunities for contemporary young children to mix, socialise and learn are restricted to institutional settings, which may have a profound effect on children's social interaction and social learning. However O'Brien *et al.* (2000) argue that, although modes of parental sponsorship create a closeted lifestyle, where children are spatially segregated and chaperoned, this is one of the adaptations particular parents and children make to living in a more insecure world and the general elaboration of the modern home has created a socio-sphere of enrichment rather than entrapment for many contemporary children. Indeed, 'the importance of the child is rising' (Beck, 1992: 118), but childhood remains constructed as a time of innocence, vulnerability and dependence (Jenks, 1996). Young children, the object of a great deal of social concern and increasing anxiety about risk, superimposed upon a protective discourse, are viewed as vulnerable innocents to be shielded from the dangers of the wider social implicitly adult world (Scott et al., 1998).

While the child in late modernity remains a victim (James et al., 2010), a review of the recent research which explored children's own understanding of risk in their everyday lives, suggests that they actively negotiate the boundaries imposed on them by adult control, are critical of formal restrictions and are reflexive in their own conceptualisations of risk (Harden, 2000; O'Brien et al., 2000). It is, furthermore, apparent from the literature that the process of individualisation is reflected in contemporary children's lives and it could, therefore, be argued that the child is not a passive victim, as risk management and understanding may be an important part of children's identity both as individuals and as members of cultural groups (Green, 1997). The very notion of the child, therefore, fails to consider that children are not one homogenous group but are individuals with unique personalities, different ethnic and cultural backgrounds, ages, gender, family circumstance and environment.

Given the range of competencies and functions required of a complex modern society, children must be encouraged to develop a range of evaluative and interpretative skills (Smith, 2000). Green (1997) suggests that to deny responsibility for risk management would be to deny competence as an individualised expert in the risk society. Yet, as Keen (2007) observes, the technological contexts of contemporary everyday lives are blurring the boundaries of the notion of expert. Roche (1999) argues that children are social actors with much to contribute here and now, and that the language of children's rights is about respecting and valuing the contribution children make, and have to make, to the world children and adults share, a world hitherto defined and imagined primarily in adult terms – it is about power.

Being a child is no longer, even if it ever was, simply a matter of being shaped by adult-controlled institutions. If individualisation processes continue, then children will become ever more recognised as the active interpreters and co-producers of their own lives and hence of the communities and societies of which they are part.

(Prout, 2000: 313)

Theorising risk

Based upon the central claim that society is in an era of dramatic change in modernity and the consequences of industrialisation are impacting on the social world in the form of risks, the work of Beck (1992) and Giddens (1990, 1991, 1999), has altered the worldview of risk (Culpitt, 1999). Beck (1992) describes how risk is not only national but global, in relation to the impact on individuals' lives, and how the production of risks is unpredictable and crosses traditional boundaries, international borders, space and time to affect everyone now and in future generations. An atmosphere of uncertainty in society is emerging – the *Risk Society*. Giddens (1991) suggests that the interrelated processes of social reflexivity, globalisation and detraditionalisation are changing social life dramatically and that social and political institutions cannot respond to the increasing risk and proliferation of lifestyle choices (Penna et al., 1999). For sociologists, 'the interest in risk lies in its potential to bridge the gap between individuals, communities and the larger social structure' (Hart, 1997: vii). Theoretical approaches to risk specify social change in different ways. Lupton (2006) identifies the three major theoretical approaches to risk, each with a specific viewpoint, within sociology: risk society (which has been highly influential and adopts a fairly realistic approach), cultural/symbolic and governmentality (which is more concerned with the regulation of modern societies). There are various approaches to explanations from the cultural-theoretical perspective of Douglas (1992) (and how socio-moral environments react to risks which focuses on the explanation of resistance against social change); more recent culture theory approaches which develop beyond the structural-functionalist perspective and are influenced by a cultural or qualitative change in social sciences, to Foucault's perspective on governmentality, that in individualised neo-liberal morals of self-creation and self-responsibility, individual interests and desires link with governmental impositions (Zinn, 2007).

Beck's (1992: 19) argument is summed up in his opening lines:

> In advanced modernity the social production of wealth is systematically accompanied by the social production of risks. Accordingly, the problems and conflicts relating to distribution in a society of scarcity overlap with the problems and conflicts that arise from the production, definition and distribution of techno-scientifically produced risks.

Beck's (1992) claim that modernity is radically changing from an industrial society to a risk society stems from two historical developments: first, that genuine material need is reduced with human and technical productivity and through legal and welfare state provisions. Second, Beck argues that manufactured risk is an unintended consequence of industrialisation, as production in modernisation has led to unfamiliar hazards and potential threats. Beck (1992) introduces his thesis of two interrelated issues, reflexive modernisation and risk, and contrasts it with traditional analyses before exploring its application in the context of class, family and work, and finally discusses the political implications on science and technology.

There are remarkable similarities between the work of Beck (1992) and Giddens (1990, 1991, 1999). In their analyses of reflexive modernisation, both describe high consequence risks which are 'not only undelimitable in space and time, but also in their incidence across social and economic divisions as characteristic of this historical phase' (Benton, 1999: 50). In *Consequences of Modernity*, Giddens (1990) concentrates on the central themes of security versus danger and trust versus risk and outlines institutional transformations associated with modernity. Modernity refers to 'modes of social life or organisation which emerged in Europe from about the 17th century onwards and which subsequently became more or less worldwide in their influence' (Giddens, 1990: 1). Giddens (1990) describes the greater opportunities created by social institutions within modernity but, under a greater threat of conflict, as a double-edged phenomenon.

Giddens (1991), in *Modernity and Self-Identity*, explores these themes further, arguing that globalising tendencies of modern institutions are accompanied by a transformation in social life with profound implications for personal activities. He describes how institutionally structured risk environments, with rapidly developing and often contradictory specialised knowledge portrayed through media channels, contribute to the risk society. As awareness increases with the dynamic nature of knowledge, the notion of risk becomes central to society and to individuals as they reflexively construct their own life biographies. Risk is 'a more or less ever-present exercise, of a partly imponderable character … the risk climate of modernity is thus unsettling for everyone; no one escapes' (Giddens, 1991: 124). Giddens

(1999) distinguishes two types of risk: external risk (for example, nature) and manufactured risk, which includes risks of marriage and family, which he claims concern society now. Specifically, Wyness (2012) highlights individualisation and late modernity has created opportunities for choice, but that these opportunities are adult-centric. Although there may be some reconceptualisation for adults within late modernity, 'there is no new conceptual space for children' (Wyness, 2012: 58).

Both Beck (1992) and Giddens (1990, 1991, 1999) suggest that modernity is a risk culture and contrast traditional with modern societies in terms of the hazards to which they are vulnerable. Beck (1992) proposes that although, through individualisation, social classes lose their social identity, inequalities remain redefined as an individualisation of social risks perceived as personal failings and anxieties. Individuals disembedded from primary relationships is linked by Giddens (1991) to the problem of 'risk versus trust' to form the most urgent of the several uncertainties of modern life (Lemert, 1999). Giddens (1991) discusses how, through media influence, ecological risks and catastrophes form an inevitable part of people's lives. Self-identity, structured through the consideration of risks, becomes a reflexively organised behaviour in which individuals make choices about lifestyle and life plans. To prevent the generalised risk climate from impinging upon life circumstances, individuals develop a protective cocoon of basic trust (Giddens, 1991). He develops Goffman's notion of *Umwelt*, which corresponds to a system of references to describe how the protective cocoon of trust is constructed by individuals. Through risk profiling, sometimes deferring in space and time, individuals deflect potentially hazardous consequences and maintain a viable *Umwelt* (Giddens, 1991).

Risk, new media technologies and early childhood

Although early childhood (0–8 years) is under-researched compared to other age groups (Lankshear and Knobel, 2003), it is important to remember that 'children acquire a significant part of their knowledge of the world through the media' (Süss *et al.*, 2001: 28). Postman (1983: 97) argues that in having access to information children are 'expelled from the garden of childhood', but Orleans and Laney (2000) suggest that teachers and parents take a less apprehensive and more integrated view of the social effects of children's computer use. Süss *et al.* (2001) highlight how new media technology does not substitute for communication and interaction with people and is integrated into social settings with friends.

The UK Government's current drive to further IT in education emphasises the perceived power of technology and its benefits, but this vision, Holloway and Valentine (2003) suggest, is technologically deterministic. Unlike educational settings, contemporary technologies use a combination of visual, text and aural forms and young children are very familiar with computer popular culture, developing expertise by learning from informal settings that are different from what is expected in schools (Cross, 2004). Tapscott (1998) claims that the internet gives children back playspace, albeit virtual, and Steinke (2004) suggests that the interactive features of the web may be one strategy to increase interest among girls in science and technology. While Buckingham (1998) is critical of such approaches, he suggests that what Postman (1983) and others have done is raise questions about conceptions of childhood and the changing nature of children's experiences with the media.

Livingstone (2003b) suggests that the nature of children's use of media technologies and use of the internet generates public anxieties which both guide and undermine research, making the study of children within the private sphere of the family home a complex issue, theoretically and practically. 'Children, as symbols of the future themselves, are seen to have the most to gain or lose as we enter the information age' (Valentine and Holloway, 2001: 59).

> *The electronic media play an increasingly significant role in defining the cultural experiences of contemporary childhood. Children can no longer be excluded from these media and the things they represent; nor can they be confined to the material that adults perceive to be good for them. The attempt to protect children by restricting their access to media is doomed to fail. On the contrary, we now need to pay much closer attention to how we prepare children to deal with these experiences; and in doing so, we need to stop defining them simply in terms of what they lack.*

(Buckingham, 2000: 16)

Social change, early childhood and new media

Livingstone (2002: 1–3) examines the complicated interplay between social change, children, public anxieties and new media, and suggests that the growing body of research in this area is increasingly informed by children themselves, yet the terms associated with work in this area – audiences, children and early childhood, users and contexts of use and new media, for example – remain somewhat contested. She emphasises the complexity of contemporary media environments and children's everyday lives:

> *We can no longer imagine living our daily lives – at leisure or at work, with family or friends – without media or communication technologies. Nor would we want to. As we enter the 21st century, the home is being transformed into the site of a multimedia culture, integrating audiovisual, information and telecommunication services. There is much more discussion of the potential benefits of the ever-more significant, ever-more multifunctional electronic screen. Media headlines regularly focus on the possible consequences – e-commerce, the virtual classroom, global consumer culture, cyber-democracy, and so forth. And public anxieties keep pace, reflecting a widespread concern with the kind of society that today's children will grow up to live in as adults. Hence, there is a speculation about 'the digital generation', 'children in the information age', 'computer nerds', 'innocents on the net', the 'digital divide' and 'addicted surfers'.*

The interest in the use of ICTs in educational settings and the recognition that ICTs have the 'potential to transform social and organisational life' is not new (Hemmings *et al.*, 2001: 110). The media play a central role in everyday life in western information societies and their importance is still increasing (Süss *et al.*, 2001). However, Hutchby and Moran-Ellis (2001) suggest that in many sociological studies of technology, little account has been taken of young children in analyses of major technological changes and their impact on everyday social and economic life. 'Much of the academic and lay writing that is available on young people's use and understanding of new technologies of communication, information, and entertainment is often impressionistic and oversimplistic' (Thurlow and McKay, 2003: 95).

Buckingham (2000) offers a comprehensive account of children and media and discusses various alternative perspectives in considerable detail. He is critical of the many accounts of technology which take an essentialist view of childhood, arguing that they reflect a sentimentality about childhood that fails to recognise the diversity in children's lived experiences and in their relationships with media technologies. Buckingham's (2000) claim is apparent in Postman's (1983: 80) suggestion that:

The new media environment that is emerging provides everyone, simultaneously, with the same information. Given the conditions I have described, electric media find it impossible to withhold any secrets. Without secrets, of course, there can be no such thing as childhood.

Recently, a more positive aspect of the relationship between children and technology has begun to emerge and, rather than passive victims, the notion of children possessing media literacy has received much attention. However, while much more positive about the impact of the media and digital technology than Postman (1983), these more optimistic accounts, such as Tapscott (1998), are also technologically deterministic as technology remains perceived as instrumental in bringing about changes in many aspects of children's lives (Buckingham, 1998). Valentine and Holloway (2001) suggest, therefore, that the child is portrayed as technically competent but immature – a biologically essentialist approach (see Jenks, 1996). Selwyn's (2003: 351) analysis of discursive constructions of the child computer user identifies six themes to argue that the 'emblematic role of the child has been exemplified in ongoing debates concerning the increasing role of technology in society and the perceived shift of countries such as the UK into a post-industrial era and associated "information age"'. The emerging picture from the literature is one of a somewhat polarised view of technology, positive in terms of employment and the development of technological skill and simultaneously negative with regard to the perceived detrimental effects on intellectual development and social relations (Lenhart *et al.*, 2001; Thurlow and McKay, 2003).

Poverty or inequality?

Discussions of poverty are complex and frequently start with questioning what is meant by poverty. The debate often hinges around 'absolute' poverty in comparison to 'relative' poverty. Absolute definitions focus on the idea of subsistence when even the basic survival needs, namely water, food and shelter, are absent. Relative poverty considers the standard in a particular society at a particular time. A family who cannot afford (rather than choose not to have) a fridge, car, television or holiday may be seen and see themselves as poor in some social settings, but not in others. Both definitions of poverty rely on criteria for labelling an individual or family as poor. Official bodies and research on poverty use differing criteria for measuring poverty and in any study on rising or falling poverty, it is worth considering the definition used and checking that the same definition has been used at different points in time.

Rather than setting a particular figure, the two most frequently used approaches are counting those on Income Support or below the average income with a check to ascertain whether or not this is before or after the deduction of housing costs. These are, however, measures that are relative to rising costs and inflation and allow comparison of some kind. The Child Poverty Act 2010 requires the government, among other things, to report on their performance in reducing child poverty. The report produced on behalf of the Department of Work and Pensions and the Department for Education, highlighted that the previous government's target of reducing the number of children living in relative income poverty by half in 2010 was not achieved (Crown, 2012). The report noted that approximately 2.3 million children currently live in poverty in the UK; however, the authors challenge the traditional approaches to measuring poverty as they fail to acknowledge important aspects of social engagement and what it feels in reality to be poor. Irrespective of whether a family earns more than the national average income or they receive Income Support, in late modernity, the emphasis placed upon participating with new technologies, whether it is having a mobile phone or internet access, suggests that this area of life is increasingly becoming a necessity rather than a luxury (Davis *et al.*, 2012).

An alternative approach to measuring poverty can be seen using the Minimum Income Standard (MIS) as developed by the research conducted by the Joseph Rowntree Foundation. Originally conducted in 2007/2008, this standard is based upon what people from diverse backgrounds, supported by experts in the area of nutrition and heating for example, identified as being essential for them to have an acceptable standard of living. This is not an attempt to over-simplify the complexities that are associated with poverty, which can be seen when considering only some of the diverse factors impacting upon individuals, such as ethnic and regional variations, family make up and employment status (Wyness, 2012), but it provides a reality check upon theoretical propositions. The MIS therefore provides a 'way of monitoring how the incomes required to participate in society evolve as society changes' (Davis *et al.*, 2012: 5). Specifically, the MIS originally covered needs not wants and as such luxury goods have never been included; also the over-arching principle is to understand what it took to be able to have choices, participate within society and have an acceptable standard of living. The 2012 findings offered some differences from the original research, most notably the perception by participants that having a computer and internet access was a minimum requirement and that due to an increase in the income required to meet minimum standards together with challenges facing families with children, some 'children will grow up in families where they or their parents will have to do without essentials' (Davis *et al.*, 2012: 5).

Extend your knowledge

Visit the Joseph Rowntree Foundation website and download Davis *et al.*'s study, *A Minimum Income Standard for the UK in 2012: Keeping Up in Hard Times*, from http://www.jrf.org.uk/sites/files/jrf/minimum-income-standards-2012-full.pdf (http://www.jrf.org.uk/). Draw up a list of what you think is essential for a family, based upon the principles incorporated by the report.

What could you do without if you had to and what would the impact be?

Rhetoric or reality?

An important resource for both academics and students is the Ofcom (2011: 7) report, *UK Children's Media Literacy*, which provides a comprehensive analysis of 'media literacy among children and young people aged 5–15 and their parents/carers' in 2010 (Table 8.1). The report demonstrates the extent of media technology use among very young children and young people. The table below indicates a selection of findings related to the different uses of technology by children, clearly demonstrating the extent media technology is ingrained with the lived realities of children in late modernity.

Table 8.1 Selected key findings relating to media technology use by age range in UK 2010.

Age range (years)	Home internet access (%)	Smartphone ownership (%)	Play on gaming device (%)	Hours online per week (%)
5–7	67	3	82	5.2
8–11	82	13	94	8.4
12–15	90	35	91	15.6

Source: Ofcom (2011)

Although homes with children lead in gaining internet access, socio-economic differences remain marked and Facer *et al.* (2001) also suggest that children's access to a home computer is patterned along socio-economic trends. 'We also need to locate children's uses of these media in relation to broader social, economic and political forces' (Buckingham, 2004a: 112) and the 'digital divide' has gained the attention of politicians and philanthropists both in America (Attewell, 2001) and the UK (Buckingham, 2004b; Livingstone and Bober, 2004). This recognition, Attewell (2001: 257) argues, 'is the latest effort to encourage our reluctant social and political leaders to ameliorate inequality and social exclusion'.

Protection and participation

Postman (1983: 45) draws on Elias' civilising process argument to claim that, as the concept of childhood developed, society began to 'collect a rich content of secrets to be kept from the young: secrets about sexual relations, but also about money, about violence, about illness, about death, about social relations'. Livingstone (2003a) discusses the notions of secrecy and surveillance and the use of filters has grown significantly in internet-using households during the early part of the 21st century. However, recent figures have suggested that there has been a reduction in households with internet access using internet controls or filtering software from 43 per cent in 2009 to 37 per cent in 2010 (Ofcom, 2011). Parents also employ other methods to promote safe internet use, such as locating the computer in a public area of the house and attempt to monitor their children's use of the internet (Livingstone and Bober, 2004; Lenhart, 2005). However, moves to encourage parents to protect children or control their use of the media grants children themselves little or no independent agency, yet children's understanding and skill with new technologies enables them to access culture and communication that 'largely escape parental control' (Buckingham, 2000: 5).

This is supported by Ofcom (2011) as overall 48 per cent of parents in their study believed that their children knew more about the internet than they did. This figure rose significantly (70 per cent) when the age of the children was between 12 and 15 years. Holloway and Valentine (2001) suggest adults and children have very different perspectives on ICTs and, while adults are concerned about the future, children are interested in the present and the social relationships within which they have to manage their own identities. It is, therefore, interesting to note from Roberts *et al.* (2005: 60) that 'despite concerns that parents often express about the impact of media on their children, the kids themselves do not report much parental effort to monitor or curb their media consumption'.

Learning activity

How much protection is really offered?

Think of your own home or that of someone you know well that has a child or children and consider the following in light of the previous discussion.

- How many 'media technologies' are there in the home? (game consols, phones, TV, radio, etc.)
- Where are they located (in which rooms)?
- Can adult content be viewed, read or heard on them (after the watershed, on Anytime, on demand, the internet)?
- Are any of them internet enabled (phones, games console, laptop, tablet)?
- Can and do children have unsupervised access to these technologies?
- Are there any restrictions in place regarding the use of the technologies?

If yes, what are they and why?

If no, why?

Buckingham (1998: 560) highlight's Katz's attitude to the authoritarian attitudes to children's access to technology, such as blocking software, 'as fundamental attacks on children's freedom'. Katz's argument, Buckingham (1998: 561) claims, is based on 'notions of children's rights' and challenges dominant views on the negative impact and potential harm of technology on children's lives. While Postman (1983) argues that the conception of children's rights rejects adult supervision and control of children and provides a philosophy to justify the dissolution of childhood, the situation is clearly rather more complex than he appears to acknowledge. Hick and Halpin (2001: 56) explore both the positive and negative aspects of the internet from a global perspective to suggest that the internet is having 'a profound impact on children's rights around the world, and whilst the internet has been a valuable tool in connecting children and promoting awareness of children's rights, it has simultaneously been a "destructive" and "hard-to-control" force'.

Conclusion

Although children are not a central feature in Beck's individualisation discourse, recent research suggests that the findings indicate that the individualisation of young children's lives is present across a wide range of socio-economic backgrounds. Buckingham (2000: 15) argues that 'the dominant construction of children as pre-social individuals effectively prevents any consideration of them as social beings, or indeed citizens'. The construction of the child in previous debates that view childhood as a time of innocence which should not be corrupted or exploited does not 'match the reality of many children's lives and fails to acknowledge that children are active participants' (Selwyn, 2000: 148). Recent theoretical advances and related research, however, is beginning to effectively challenge this perspective and offers evidence to support developments in the new paradigm of sociology of childhood that children are, indeed, active social beings and attempt to understand the diversity of the realities of children's lived experiences. Children have become consumers from a very early age (Selwyn, 2000) and the complex interaction between late modernity, new media technologies and early childhood and the increasing recognition of children as consumers has further influenced contemporary views of children as being capable of maintaining independence and impact upon the economy (Lee, 2001).

Livingstone (1998) stresses the importance of contextualising new media in relation to the contexts of young children's lives, including pre-existing media; theorising media use in relation to modernity and both being informed by and informing academic study of childhood. Much recent research on a wide variety of media technologies highlights gender, age and socio-economic differences in children's access to, perceptions and use of technologies and these marked divisions are giving rise to further concerns of technological inequalities, access to information and potential exclusion.

As this chapter has highlighted, being a child in late modernity poses a multitude of challenges and opportunities to children and their parents. Young children's experiences are affected by wider socio-economic conditions and political conditions. Understanding the relationship between 'risk', 'late modernity' and childhood is essential for early childhood scholars in order to gain further knowledge of societal reactions to children, whether due to inappropriate behaviour or the use of new media technologies. In this period of rapid social change, opportunities for learning and researching abound and there has never been a more exciting time to study early childhood.

Evaluate your learning

- To what extent are children's everyday experiences controlled and managed by adults as a consequence of risk anxiety?
- Should poverty be measured using the Minimum Income Standard (MIS) or based upon welfare benefit entitlement?
- What is the relationship between contemporary social constructions of childhood and new media technologies?

References

Arthur, R (2005): Punishing parents for the crimes of their children. *The Howard Journal* 44, 233–53.

Arthur, R (2007): *Family Life and Youth Offending: Home is where the Hurt Is.* London: Routledge.

Attewell, P (2001): The first and second digital divides. *Sociology of Education* **74**, 252–9.

Backett, K (1982): *Mothers and Fathers: A Study of the Development and Negotiation of Parental Behaviour.* London: Macmillan.

Beck, U (1992): *Risk Society Towards a New Modernity.* London: Sage.

Beck, U (1998): The democratization of the family. In Beck, U (ed), *Democracy Without Enemies*. Cambridge: Polity Press.

Benton, T (1999): Radical politics – neither left nor right? In O'Brien, M, Penna, S and Hay, C (eds), *Theorising Modernity: Reflexivity, Environment and Identity in Giddens' Social Theory*. Longman: London.

Brannen, J and O'Brien, M (1995): Childhood and the sociological gaze: paradigms and paradoxes. *Sociology* **29**(4), 729–37.

Buckingham, D (1998): Review essay: Children of the electronic age? Digital media and the new generational rhetoric. *European Journal of Communication* **13**(4), 557–65.

Buckingham, D (2000): *After the Death of Childhood Growing Up in the Age of Electronic Media*. Cambridge: Polity Press.

Buckingham, D (2004a): New media, new childhoods? Children's changing cultural environment in the age of digital technology. In Kehily, MJ (ed), *An Introduction to Childhood Studies*. Maidenhead: Open University Press.

Buckingham, D (2004b): Keynote opening address. Digital generations: children, young people and new media conference. London: LSE, July 2004.

Carrabine, E, Cox, P, Lee, M, Plummer, K and South, N (2009): *Criminology: A Sociological Introduction*, 2nd edn. London: Routledge.

Corsaro, W (2011): *The Sociology of Childhood*, 3rd edn. London: Sage.

Cross, B (2004): Split frame thinking and multiple scenario awareness: how boys' game expertise reshapes possible structures of sense in a digital world. Paper presented at Digital generations: children, young people and new media. London, LSE, July 2004.

Crown (2012): Child poverty in the UK: The report on the 2010 target. London: Stationery Office.

Culpitt, I (1999): *Social Policy and Risk*. London: Sage.

Davis, A, Hirsch, D, Smith, N, Beckhelling, J and Padley, M (2012): A minimum income standard for the UK in 2012: keeping up in hard times (online). Available from: www.jrf.org.uk/sites/files/jrf/minimum-income-standards-2012-full.pdf.

Douglas, M (1992): *Risk and Blame: Essays in Cultural Theory*. London: Routledge.

Facer, K, Furlong, J, Furlong R and Sutherland, R (2001): Home is where the hardware is. Young people, the domestic environment and 'access' to new technologies. In Hutchby, I and Moran-Ellis, J (eds), *Children, Technology and Culture The Impacts of Technologies in Children's Everyday Lives*. London: RoutledgeFalmer.

Furedi, F (2002): *Paranoid Parenting. Why Ignoring the Experts May Be Best for your Child*. Chicago: Chicago Review Press.

Giddens, A (1990): *The Consequences of Modernity*. Cambridge: Polity Press.

Giddens, A (1991): *Modernity and Self-Identity: Self and Society in the Late Modern Age*. Cambridge: Polity Press.

Giddens, A (1999): *Runaway World: How Globalisation is Shaping Our Lives*. London: Profile Books Ltd.

Green, J (1997): Risk and the construction of social identity: children's talk about accidents. *Sociology of Health and Illness* **19**, 457–79.

Harden, J (2000): There's no place like home: the public/private distinction in children's theorizing of risk and safety. *Childhood* **7**, 43–59.

Hart, G (1997): Introduction. In Green, J (ed), *Risk and Misfortune: The Social Construction of Accidents*. London: UCL Press.

Hemmings, TA, Clarke, KM, Francis, D, Marr, L and Randall, D (2001): Situated knowledge and virtual education. In Hutchby, I and Moran-Ellis, J (eds), *Children, Technology and Culture: The Impacts of Technologies in Children's Everyday Lives*. London: RoutledgeFalmer.

Hendrick, SH (2008): Constructions and reconstructions of British childhood: an interpretative survey, 1800 to the present. In Muncie, J, Hughes, G and McLaughlin, E (eds), *Youth Justice: Critical Readings*. London: Sage.

Hick, S and Halpin, E (2001): Children's rights and the internet. *Annals of the American Academy of Political and Social Science* **565**, 56–70.

Holloway, SL and Valentine, G (2001): 'It's only as stupid as you are': Children and adults' negotiation of ICT competence at home and at school. *Social and Cultural Geography* **22**, 25–42.

Holloway, SL and Valentine, G (2003): *Cyberkids: Children in the Information Age*. London: RoutledgeFalmer.

Hood, S, Kelley, P, Mayall, B, Oakley, A and Morrell, R (1996): *Children, Parents and Risk*. London: Social Science Research Unit.

Hutchby, I and Moran-Ellis, J (2001): Introduction: relating children, technology and culture. In Hutchby, I and Moran-Ellis, J (eds), *Children, Technology and Culture: The Impacts of Technologies in Children's Everyday Lives*. London: RoutledgeFalmer.

James, A and James, A (2001): Tightening the net: children, community and control. *British Journal of Sociology* **52**, 211–88.

James, A, Jenks, C and Prout, A (2010): *Theorizing childhood*. Cambridge: Polity Press.

Jenks, C (1996): *Childhood*. London: Routledge.

Jewkes, Y (2011): *Media and Crime*, 2nd edn. London: Sage.

Keen, A (2007): *The Cult of the Amateur*. London: Nicholas Brealey Publishing.

Lankshear, C and Knobel, M (2003): New technologies in early childhood literacy research: a review of research. *Journal of Early Childhood Literacy* **13**(1), 59–82.

Lee, N (2001): The extensions of childhood. Technologies, children and independence. In Hutchby, I and Moran-Ellis, J (eds), *Children, Technology and Culture: The Impacts of Technologies in Children's Everyday Lives*. London: RoutledgeFalmer.

Lemert, C (1999): A world of differences: What if it's so? How will we know? In O'Brien, M, Penna, S and Hay, C (eds), *Theorising Modernity Reflexivity, Environment and Identity in Giddens' Social Theory*. London: Longman.

Lenhart, A (2005): Protecting teens online. Pew Internet and American Life Project. (Online) Available from: www.pewinternet.org.

Lenhart, A, Raine, L and Lewis, O (2001): Teenage life online: The rise of the instant message generation and the internet's impact on friendships and family relationships. Pew Internet and American Life Project. (Online). Available from: www.pewinternet.org/reports.

Livingstone, S (1998): Mediated childhoods: a comparative approach to young people's changing media environment in Europe. *European Journal of Communication* **13**(4), 435–56.

Livingstone, S (2002): *Young People and New Media*. London: Sage.

Livingstone, S (2003a): Speaking at Children, Mobile Phones and the Internet: the Mobile Internet and Children. Proceedings of the Experts' Meeting, Tokyo, Japan, 6–7 March 2003, (Online). Available from: www.iajapan.org/hotline/2003mobilepro-en.html.

Livingstone, S (2003b): Children's use of the internet: reflections on the emerging research agenda. *New Media and Society* **5**(2), 147–66.

Livingstone, S and Bober, M (2004): UK Children Go Online. Surveying the experiences of young people and their parents. [Online]. Last accessed 7 November 2004. Available from: www.children-go-online.net.

Lupton, D (2006): Sociology and risk. In Mythen, G and Walklate, S (eds), *Beyond the Risk Society: Critical Reflections on Risk and Human Security*. Maidenhead: Open University Press.

Muncie, J (2009): *Youth and Crime*, 3rd edn. London: Sage.

NSPCC (2012): Child homicide statistics January 2012. (Online), Available from: www.nspcc.org.uk/inform/research/statistics/child_homicide_statistics_wda48747.html.

O'Brien, M, Jones, D and Sloan, D (2000): Children's independent spatial mobility in the urban public realm. *Childhood* **7**, 257–77.

Ofcom (2011): UK children's media literacy. (Online). Available from: http://stakeholders.ofcom.org.uk/binaries/research/media-literacy/media-lit11/childrens.pdf.

Office for National Statistics (2012): Injury and poisoning mortality, England and Wales 2010. (Online). Available from: www.ons.gov.uk/ons/dcp171778_254689.pdf.

Orleans, M and Laney, MC (2000): Children's computer use in home: isolation or socialization? *Social Science Computer Review* **18**(1), 56–72.

Pearson, G (1983): *Hooligan: A History of Respectable Fears*. Basingstoke: MacMillan Press.

Penna, S, O'Brien, M and Hay, C (eds) (1999): *Theorising Modernity: Reflexivity, Environment and Identity in Giddens' Social Theory*. Harlow: Addison Wesley Longman.

Philo, C (2000): The corner-stones of my world. Editorial introduction to special issue on spaces of childhood. *Childhood* **7**, 243–56.

Postman, N (1983): *The Disappearance of Childhood*. London: WH Allen.

Prout, A (2000): Children's participation: control and self-realisation in British late modernity. *Children and Society* **14**, 304–15.

Roberts, DF, Foehr, UG and Rideout, V (2005): Generation M: Media in the lives of 8–18 year olds. Kaiser Family Foundation. (Online). Available from: www.kff.org/entmedia/entmedia030905pkg.cfm.

Roche, J (1999): Children: rights, participation and citizenship. *Childhood* **6**, 475–93.

Scott, S, Jackson, S and Backett-Milburn, K (1998): Swings and roundabouts: risk anxiety and the everyday worlds of children. *Sociology* **32**, 689–705.

Selwyn, J (2000): Technologies and environments: new freedoms, new constraints. In Boushel, M, Fawcett, M and Selwyn, J (eds), *Focus on Early Childhood Principles and Realities*. Oxford: Blackwell Science.

Selwyn, N (2003): Doing IT for the kids: re-examining children, computers and the information society. *Media, Culture and Society* **25**, 351–78.

Slater, D (1998): Public/Private. In Jenks, C (ed), *Core Sociological Dichotomies*. London: Sage.

Smith, K, Osborne, S, Lau, I and Britton A (2012): Homicides, Firearms Offences and Intimate Violence 2010/11: Supplementary volume 2 to Crime in England and Wales 2010/11. (Online). Available from: www.homeoffice.gov.uk/science-research.

Smith, R (2000): Order and disorder: the contradictions of childhood. *Children and Society* **14**, 3–10.

Steinke, J (2004): Science in cyberspace: science and engineering. World wide web sites for girls. *Public Understanding of Science* **13**, 7–30.

Stone, J (2004): Buzz in the playground: mobile phone brands say they don't target under-16s but phone ownership by children as young as seven is on the rise. Are youths being exploited? *Marketing Week* **27**(39), 37.

Stones, R (ed.) (2008): *Key Sociological Thinkers*, 2nd edn. Basingstoke: Palgrave MacMillan

Süss, D, Suoninen, A, Garitaonandia, C, Juaristi, R and Oleaga, JA (2001): Media childhood in three European countries. In Hutchby, I and Moran-Ellis, J (eds), *Children, Technology and Culture. The Impacts of Technologies in Children's Everyday Lives*. London: RoutledgeFalmer.

Tapscott, D (1998): *Growing Up Digital: The Rise of The Net Generation*. New York: McGraw Hill.

Thurlow, C and McKay, S (2003): Profiling 'new' communication technologies in adolescence. *Journal of Language and Social Psychology* **22**(1), 94–103.

Ungar, S (2001): Moral panic versus the risk society: the implications of the changing sites of social anxiety. *British Journal of Sociology* **52**, 271–91.

United Nations (1989): The Convention on the Rights of the Child. (Online). Available from: www.unicef. org/crc/crc.htm.

Valentine, G (1996): Children should be seen and not heard? The role of children in public space. *Urban Geography* **17**, 205–20.

Valentine, G and Holloway, SL (2001): 'Technophobia': parents' and children's fears about information and communication technologies and the transformation of culture and society. In Hutchby, I and Moan-Ellis J (eds), *Children, Technology and Culture: The Impacts of Technologies in Children's Everyday Lives*. London: Routledge.

Wyness, M (2012): *Childhood and Society*, 2nd edn. Basingstoke: Palgrave MacMillan.

Zinn, J (2007): Risk, social change and morals: conceptual approaches of sociological risk theories. Working Paper 17. (Online). Available from: www.Kent.ac.uk/scar/papers.

Further reading

Ariès, P (1962): *The Centuries of Childhood*. London: Cape.

James, A, Jenks, C and Prout, A (2010): *Theorizing Childhood*. Cambridge: Polity Press.

Woodhead, M and Montgomery, H (eds) (2003): *Understanding Childhood: An Interdisciplinary Approach*. Chichester: John Wiley & Sons/Open University.

Wyness, M (2012): *Childhood and Society*, 2nd edn. Basingstoke: Palgrave MacMillan.

Children and social policy: an introduction

Sarah Richards

This chapter aims to:
- outline the academic discipline of social policy applied to children and their families
- consider the contested meanings of social policy welfare
- explain why childhood is such a significant area in welfare provision
- explore the sustained state interest in shaping children's lives.

Introduction

This chapter will outline the academic discipline of social policy applied to children and their families. It will start by defining social policy and clarifying the term 'welfare'. It is worth bearing in mind as you begin to explore this discipline that many of the terms used are contested. As Carney (2005: 191) eloquently depicts, they are 'fat' words: 'they conceal many (sometimes even incompatible) shades of meaning'. Part of your role as a student is not to select one meaning over another, rather it is to be aware of what these contested meanings are and how each application may impact upon the lives of children. Having outlined the term 'social policy', this chapter will explain why childhood is such a significant area in welfare provision. By the end of this chapter, the reader should know what social policy is, be aware that there are philosophical and ideological values which underpin the implementation of social policy and have begun to explore the sustained state interest in shaping children's lives.

It should not be assumed that interest in children on the part of the state is consistent or uniform (Hendrick, 2005). There are alternative perspectives as to the appropriate role that the state should play in the lives of citizenry. These different perspectives shape the development of social policy and encompass competing political agendas. It is necessary for students of early childhood to be able to recognise these different philosophies in order to be able to unpack the ideas which underpin the extensive social provision surrounding children. There is also an important relationship between the sociology of childhood (see Chapters 1 and 8) and social policy which needs consideration in this introductory discussion. The social context where social policy is differentially experienced by social groups is not separate from the policy itself and, therefore, social policy has to be understood in part through the groups receiving welfare. Ideas found in the sociology of childhood are inextricably linked to the welfare provided for children. Social values about what children should be, or could be in the future, and indeed should not be, are important in the study of children and social policy. In the sociology of childhood, these ideas are theoretically explored and in social policy it can be argued that they become realised. Prevalent ideas about children are explored as part of this discussion and linked with examples of policy for further illustration.

Finally, this chapter will outline some of the dominant areas which social policy has intervened into the lives of children. Here, philosophies of welfare and ideas about children and childhood will be used to introduce students to how the study of social policy can offer insight into the lives of children and the aspirations of the state through such intervention.

Children and their relationship with the state

What is social policy?

Students new to the discipline of social policy can sometimes be confused by the term. As an academic discipline within the social sciences, it is an umbrella term for the study of services which are organised to provide welfare. The study of social policy explores how, why and to whom welfare is delivered and this academic study can often be used to inform practice (Alcock, 2008: 2). While this chapter confines the discussion to the UK, it is worth reiterating Alcock's point that contemporary analyses of social policy frequently compares approaches found in different countries and, as such, social policy as an academic discipline is not always restricted to nation-state boundaries. If social policy is the study of the processes of organising and delivering welfare, then the term 'welfare' requires explanation.

What is welfare?

'Welfare' is a broad term which commonly refers to the support for citizens, typically encompassing health, education, housing and social security provision. While few would argue about the need to provide some level of support to citizens and individuals, welfare becomes contested as it develops into a wider discussion about who is entitled to receive support, what they should receive and for how long. The term is also used in alternative ways in different countries (see Deacon (2002: 4) for a useful and broad discussion on the inconsistencies of the term welfare). Entitlement to welfare is a controversial and ongoing debate as is the issue of who should provide it and how it is funded. One of the common perceptions around the provision of welfare is that it is only provided by the state and paid for by the redistribution of resources through taxation. The term 'state' is clarified by Spicker (2008: 70) as frequently being used very 'loosely' in context-specific ways, but generally meaning the way in which governmental power is exercised. This power might have a central governmental origin, but is variously delivered through local authorities and structures across the country. In reality, a variety of informal welfare provision also exists which includes the family, charitable organisations, religious institutions and community groups and the market (see Alcock (2008) for a comprehensive discussion of this mix in welfare). Consider the variety of ways that working parents organise holiday childcare. Some use private or community clubs, some rely on friends, some employ nannies or make informal arrangements through family, such as grandparent support. Private, state and voluntary arrangements are all evident depending on personal choice, finance and availability. This is a simple example of a welfare mix.

The extent of provision by different political parties has fluctuated historically and continues to do so. Traces of this historical welfare pluralism remain in social policy today:

- **Friendly Societies**. Declared legal in 1793, these historically provided sickness insurance by offering support for loss of income, old age and disability. This role can be linked to national insurance that we recognise as being part of welfare in contemporary terms. Cordery's (2003) discussion of Friendly Societies is useful here.
- **Voluntary Hospitals**. These flourished in the mid-18th century, relied financially upon philanthropy and were administered locally by unpaid volunteers. Incorporated into what we now recognise as the NHS in the mid-1940s, some of the hospitals that we recognise today, such as Bart's in London and Addenbrooke's in Cambridge, began as voluntary hospitals. For further discussion, see www.hospitalsdatabase.lshtm.ac.uk/the-voluntary-hospitals-in-history.php.
- **National Society for the Prevention of Cruelty to Children (NSPCC)**. This organisation began in the late 19th century after local initiatives in Liverpool and London developed by local businessmen and philanthropists highlighted the plight of children.

Under the current Coalition Government, the nature and extent of this mix is currently topical. Questions about how to facilitate a larger role for community groups and volunteers are being asked, and, in consequence, the idea of a smaller role for the state is explored (Ellison, 2011: 45). Such attempts, however, do not necessarily reduce welfare spending. This combined approach can be referred to as 'welfare pluralism'. Nevertheless, in this chapter, we predominantly focus on the state role of providing welfare for children and their families.

Why has the state taken a sustained interest in young children? The care of children is predominantly recognised as being the responsibility of parents, taking place in the private, idealised and privileged institution known as the family. In consequence, it can be challenging to view children as individuals due to the extent to which society emphasises this familial approach. Social policy specifically (though not exclusively) has reflected this position. Children and childhood have become inseparable from the institution of the family (Hendrick, 2005). State intervention into the lives of children extends throughout childhood, the very length of which in part is politically determined through social policies. Motivation for this interest is an important consideration. Some have argued that it is coercive (see Donzelot (1980), for example). It certainly cannot simply be taken as 'an expression of our collective good will' (Frost and Stein (1989: 9), cited in Hendrick (2005: 33)). Perhaps an appropriate stance to initially take is to recognise that the welfare of children is not simply about the benevolent care of children, but also about meeting contingent needs and values of society. Recognising what those needs and values are is part of understanding the form of social policy as it relates to children.

The language in social policy towards children is mostly (though not exclusively) one of care. It evokes the perception that the well-being and best interests of children are of paramount importance and the driving force behind provision. This care towards children should not be casually disputed, but neither should it be taken as being the whole story. The current practice of social policy shows children being recognised and encouraged, as social actors, to participate in the decision making that affects their lives in part to acquire the skills currently needed for an autonomous adulthood (Lewis, 2010). A significant contemporary influence on this increased focus on the rights and participation of children has been the European Convention on Human Rights brought into UK law through the Human Rights Act 1998 (Kay *et al.*, 2011). However, the study of social policy can also demonstrate continued objectification of children through provision where their care is part of a wider social and political agenda (Skevik, 2005: 339). An example of this is found in the extensive provision now in place for the care of young children prior to school. The socialisation of children and the development of preschool skills available through attendance at day care are emphasised, though contested (Williams, 2004). The development of such preschool provision also facilitates greater employment opportunities for women. Providing places for young children to be cared for enables more women to work and potentially rely less upon economic support from the state (Williams, 2004).

The historical development of health and education provision cannot simply be viewed as state interest in the well-being of children and must be seen in the wider context of future investment for society. Intervention in the lives of children on the part of the state can, therefore, have diverse social and political agendas. The following extract identifies some of the issues facing adults which the state has interest in addressing through social policy. It reveals how children are seen as a potential cost where preventative intervention can be effective in reducing the intergenerational consequences of some complex social issues.

> *Poverty and worklessness, lack of qualifications, poor health, insufficient housing and poor parenting can cast a shadow that spans whole lifetimes and indeed passes through generations. These problems can be multiple, entrenched and mutually reinforcing. And some family experiences can make things worse. They can limit aspiration, reinforce cycles of poverty, and provide poor models of behaviour that can impact on a child's development and well-being, with significant costs for public services and the wider community.*

(Social Exclusion Task Force, 2007: 1)

The above quotation speaks directly about families in poverty. However, it also offers insight into the relationship between children, parents and the state more generally. This interest is informed by ensuring the development of citizens for the future and reducing adult reliance on the state to meet their needs (again a contested term and worthy of some reading around, see for examples *Taxonomy of Social Need* (Bradshaw, 1972) or Spicker's clarification). It is important to recognise the wider social and political interests in children which also influence how and why we shape their lives through extensive social provision. As Spicker (2008) argues, there is a liberalist argument that children should be the responsibility of their parents, but there is also the perception that children are everybody's interest. Recognition of children's place being in the care of their family, with parents ultimately responsible for this care and well-being, is an orthodoxy that is rarely challenged. It is also controversial to disrupt, for example, removing children from the care of their biological parents. However, the state requires children to grow up with the skills and attributes necessary to be active citizens and meet the needs of a global economic and democratic society. Balancing the autonomy of the family (and the rights of those within it) and shaping the family to meet the wider social and political interests can be difficult.

The shape and extent of intervention into the lives of children and families has varied historically based on specific need and circumstance. It has also been based upon changing social values, ideas of what makes a good society and to what extent it is up to the state to provide. The underpinning philosophies and ideologies of welfare are important aspects of understanding social policy in relation to the child and are introduced in the next section.

Learning activity

Write a short paragraph for each of the following questions:
- What is 'social policy'?
- Why is the term 'welfare' contested?
- What interests does the state have in providing welfare to children?

Values and ideologies of welfare

This section begins with some of the fundamental values evident in historical and contemporary social policy. Spicker's (2008) cautionary note about the danger of over-simplifying these concepts is useful here, for (as he points out) each of the following remain ambiguous and 'essentially contested'. Each also deserves much greater consideration than is available here and for a wider discussion of these values, see Spicker's (2008) comprehensive introductory text.

Freedom

Freedom in welfare can be outlined from two alternative positions (Spicker, 2008). The first is an 'individualist' one where freedom is valued as the capacity to be independent, independent as a family unit and as a citizen, independent from excessive obligation to distribute wealth to others in society. The greater the role of the state to provide welfare the more this freedom is reduced. In this position, social welfare is seen as a challenge to freedom. The second perspective of freedom is a 'social' one where it is suggested that freedom comes from the interdependence of individuals where social welfare enables people to be free from the constraints of poverty, for example. The individualist versus the social debate is not restricted to how freedom is realised, but extends more broadly across social policy.

Solidarity

The basis of solidarity is one of mutual obligation (Spicker, 2008). It involves a reciprocal exchange between people. However, solidarity is limited in that it is usually restricted or exclusive to a particular group, such as citizens for example. In order to enjoy the full benefits of reciprocity you need to belong to the group.

Rights

In welfare, rights are often linked to citizenship and therefore, like solidarity, rights can be exclusive to a particular group or membership (Spicker, 2008). In the past, citizenship has been constructed and understood through these rights or entitlements. TH Marshall famously outlined three sets of rights within citizenship as civil, political and social. However, citizenship has become increasingly associated with responsibilities too (Lister, 2011). Rights to welfare should therefore be understood as contingent.

Justice

This value is fundamentally a distributive principle. It concerns the proportions in which people should contribute to and receive things from society. Corrective justice means that the punishment should fit the crime; distributive justice means that people should have fair shares (Spicker, 2008). It is the distributive element that is most relevant to discussions about social policy and childhood.

Democracy

This term can suggest a system of elected government, a means of participating in governance and a description of a society where the citizens have political rights (Spicker, 2008: 88).

Having outlined some fundamental (if contested) values which can be found in social policy, it is important to introduce some of the perspectives or positions which become evident in analysis of social policy with particular reference to children. These positions are socially, politically or ideologically derived and are based upon ideas of what good welfare is, what a good citizen is (in the case of children, a good future citizen) and how individuals can be moulded to reflect these values and in turn, can shape a good society. The debate about whether a good society is achieved through the intervention of the state or from the role of the free market or a combination of both is current and unresolved. The following four approaches outline ideas about how to respond to children and their needs (or assumed needs) through policy. Each perspective situates children within the family and recognises the need and potential social investment in children and the necessity of policy to realise this investment. However, the position of children varies in each. Some of these perspectives are more recent and emerging, such as children's rights, while others are more longstanding, such as laissez-faire (see Fox Harding (1991) and Hendrick (2005) for further explanation).

Children's rights perspective

From this position, the child is afforded subject status with 'agency'. This term remains ambiguous in how it is used and what it can mean but is evident in current welfare development. The greater participation of children in decision making reflects this perspective. However, while the language of this perspective is found extensively in recent policy both nationally and internationally, it is also evident that it is frequently subordinate to other approaches and for some falls far short of rights afforded to adults.

Parental rights perspective

This position emphasises the rights and role of the birth family. To that end, disadvantaged families receive financial support to reduce the inequality of the market. Protecting and defending parental rights was a significant area of policy interest during the establishment of the welfare state, where an expansive role for the state in supporting the rights of individuals and families was established.

State paternalism

Here the state takes an interventionist, paternal role towards children. Policy from this perspective seeks to compensate for the limitations of the family and poor parenting. Intervention into the family by professionals to ensure the nurture and protection of children is the focus. Some argue that this undermines the autonomy of the biological family and that the child is socially constructed as passive and vulnerable. The financial assistance provided in supporting children can also be regarded as both caring and controlling.

Laissez-faire

Also sometimes referred to as the New Right, this position argues for minimum state intervention. This position has been dominant historically (prior to the establishment of the welfare state), but continues to have contemporary relevance. The family in this perspective has been constructed as patriarchal and autonomous. This organisation of male power within the family reflected traditional, hierarchical power structures and gender divisions. However, the contemporary emphasis here promotes autonomy and independence from the state whatever the structure (see Fox Harding (1991) and Hendrick (2005) for further explanation).

It is important to recognise that these perspectives are not exclusive or entirely discrete. There can be (and often are) considerable overlaps in policy that reflect more than one perspective. Although the perspectives outlined above focus on approaches towards children, they are also part of much wider philosophical debate about the extent and structure of welfare and its delivery. Children are increasingly recognised as consumers of welfare, as well as holding the future potential to deliver an economically successful society. What form intervention takes can reflect particular values and ideas about the social construction of childhood and it is these ideas which are explored in the next section.

Learning activity

Consider which of the approaches outlined above most reflects your view on welfare for children.

The welfare of children is depicted as an important and appropriate role for social policy. Children are situated within the family and it is frequently through this institution that intervention occurs. Taking each perspective in turn outline a welfare response towards children in a family where no adults are currently working.

Social construction of childhood

On to the child we heap the thwarted longings of decaying societies and try to figure something better. It's a hard burden for children to carry.

(Burman, 2001: 11)

Historically, emerging state interest in children and the use of social policy to intervene in their lives, either to address a specific need or to enhance their well-being, has corresponded with the changing needs and anxieties of the wider society. Indeed, what we recognise as the 'child' has in part been created by the welfare provision developed around children (Platt, 2005). For example, the introduction of compulsory education in part corresponded with a philanthropic concern about children in the public sphere, as well as the need for the country to remain economically competitive beyond its predominance of the industrial revolution (see also Chapter 13 *Children's geographies*). More currently, the relationship between education and the economy is clear. While an emphasis on education being in the best interest of children is not contested, the economic benefit for wider society is also part of the need for educating children. Tomlinson (2005: 405) explores this connection through discussion of a 'knowledge intensive' economy.

Education is a crucial type of investment for the exploitation of modern technology. In advanced industrial societies, it is inevitable that the education system should come into a closer relationship with the economy ... as the proportion of the labour force engaged in manual work declines and the demand for white-collar, professional and managerial worker rises (Halsey *et al.*, 1961: 1–2, quoted in Tomlinson, 2005: 405).

Varied and emerging interest in children has also generated a large workforce of professional experts with specialist knowledge to care for children through a range of provision to address health, development and protection (Hendrick, 2005). This surveillance of children by 'experts' can represent care, however, when children are viewed through developmental models explanation of their failure to comply with expected goals are looked for. Monitoring welfare for children can therefore represent control for parents and their families. It can also confine how we see children, reducing the many narratives of childhood to linear models, developmental goals and educational attainment. Increased scientific approaches and modern technology along with a romantic view of children has led to an unrealistic perception of children as vessels to address the problems in society (Hatch, 1995).

The notion was that if we can somehow intervene in the lives of children, then poverty, racism, crime, drug abuse and any number of social ills can be erased. Children become instruments of society's need to improve itself, and childhood became a time in which social problems were either solved or determined to be unsolvable (Hatch, 1995: 119).

Moss and Petrie (2005: 85) argue that, 'Our construction of childhood and our images of the child represent ethical and political choices, made within larger frameworks of ideas, values and rationalities'. There are dominant narratives which are evident in policy development and held more generally in society, and these inform how we think, speak and act towards children (Moss and Petrie, 2005). These ideas influence policy development which in turn continues to shape the childhood that children experience. Social constructions stem from 'a set of social relationships or they are the consequence of specific social arrangements', these arrangements can include welfare (Spicker, 2008: 53). The dominance of these contradictory ideas explains (at least in part) why there is no one coherent policy approach towards children (Hendrick, 2005). The social arrangements made around children and the idea that intervention may prevent social problems is evident in the dichotomies explored below, as is the relationship between sociology of childhood and social policy in early childhood studies.

Care versus control

Modern childhood is argued to be a time of extensive surveillance. The monitoring of children's development, education and behaviour begins in the family through expectations ascribed to the parental role and the observation by professionals, such as health visitors, general practitioners and social workers. Early years professionals and teachers monitor and oversee the benevolent care of children. The nurture of children through this professional focus is evident in policies such as *Every Child Matters* (DfES, 2003) where the focus on health, protection, achievement, contribution and economic well-being brought diverse agencies together to work more effectively as partners to prevent and tackle issues which impede the well-being of children and ensure their future prosperity. However, this benevolent surveillance can also be construed as state control into the lives of children and their parents (Donzelot, 1980). Children at risk of failing to meet their potential can experience a more overt form of control. Cunningham and Tomlinson (2005: 91) suggest that 'punitive policies have frequently been introduced alongside progressive measures'. Muncie (1999) argues that the rhetoric of care cloaks the more punitive approach.

The Crime and Disorder Act (1998) demonstrates the moral anxiety about children and young people participating in activities which undermine social order and cohesion. Within this Act, local authorities and police held the power to sanction children and their parents. The punishment of children through the imposition of curfews and anti-social behaviour orders and of their parents in failing to prevent children behaving badly, were regarded as preventative measures to deter disorder and foster a cohesive sense of community. These aspirations were part of the social and political agenda for the New Labour Government elected in 1997. The approach towards children, however, neglected to account for adverse life circumstances and unequal social structures which may have been contributing factors, such as poverty. The control of parents through Parenting Contracts and Orders emphasises their obligation to control children and is indicative of a punitive approach towards children and their families, an increase in the surveillance of and reduction in the privacy of the family (Shaw, 2010).

Dependent versus independent

The dependency of children is a prevalent idea which derives from but then extends developmental assumptions of immaturity and incompetency (see Chapter 3, *Embodied childhoods*, for further evaluation of developmental models used to structure childhood). Children are dependent in part because they are required to attend compulsory education and are situated within the family where their economic inactivity makes them financially reliant upon their parents and the state to meet their needs. As Spicker (2008: 53) suggests, children are dependent because 'they are required to be'. Children's rights legislation demonstrates this dependency and specifically positions children within the family where it is their right to receive love and nurturance and their dependence upon adults for this love and care are maintained. The contemporary language of rights for children, however, also speaks about their responsibility. Agency and independence are characteristics that adults are assumed to have and that children are encouraged to acquire through increased participation in social structures, such as school councils. Children's participation in school councils emerged from *Every Child Matters* (DfES, 2003) and is part of an active contribution which speaks specifically to the rights and obligations of citizenship. The prevalence of school councils is seen variously as part of children's role in the democratic process, as a shift in power from adult to child. However, Lewis (2010) sees such activity as the expectation of children to learn the required skills of citizenship before they are deemed rational and old enough to attain the status (see Lister (2003) for further discussion on children and citizenship).

Victim versus threat

Children are precious. The world they must learn to inhabit is one in which they will face hazards and obstacles alongside real and growing opportunities. They are entitled not just to the sentiment of adults but a strategy that safeguards them as children and realises their potential to the very best of their ability (DfES, 2003: 4).

The epigraph succinctly encapsulates the idea of the child as future investment, their vulnerability and the role of the state to protect and ensure their safety so that their potential is reached. The protection of children and prevention of harm, either on the part of their parents or others, is a theme which receives extensive attention in policy development. Public interest and anxiety in protection issues remains high, though the efficacy of policies and those who implement them remain publically debated with each failure. This is not to suggest that non-intervention is appropriate but reflects the challenges in shaping effective policy. Child protection as a theme (either implicitly or explicitly) is widely evident in historical and contemporary legislation. However, risk to children in society (which legislation seeks to reduce), like dependency (explored above) cannot simply be put down to biological vulnerability but is also part of the social construction of childhood. Childhood is constructed as a time of dependence, passivity and innocence where children are supposed to be unencumbered by specific areas of knowledge, particularly sexual knowledge. Protecting children and maintaining the dominant ideas found in the social construction of childhood is a challenging balance. We situate children within the private space of the family where abuse is frequently found; and yet it remains idealised as a place of safety and harmony. Arguably, however, greater surveillance (outlined above under Care versus control) of the family can increase the detection of such abuse. Paradoxically the propensity of socially held ideas about the child as vulnerable is complicit in the need to develop interventions to protect them from the consequences of this vulnerability.

There is a flip side of the risk for children from society – the risk to society from children. The idea that children can threaten the social order, like the idea that children are vulnerable, is recurrent and normative. Young people were publically labelled as 'feral' in the English riots of 2011; the term encapsulates the concern about deviant, poorly socialised children who grow up to threaten the safety of the streets (Shaw, 2010). There are examples of approaches used to inhibit children and young people's use of public space. The 'Mosquito' has been used as an anti-loitering device which emits a high frequency noise designed to move young people on. There are also clear examples of particular groups of children being socially constructed as a greater risk at various times, children of the underclass whose parents are deemed to be incapable, unworthy, or immoral, the poor child, the boy child, the black child (Cunningham and Tomlinson, 2005; see also Williams, 2004; Jones, 2002). Franklin (1995: 4) sums up this particular dichotomy by suggesting that children have gone from innocent 'sugar and spice angels to inherently evil demons who, typifying Britain's declining moral standards, seem incapable of distinguishing right from wrong'. However, both ideas have variously been emphasised at particular social and historical moments. The impact of these dual ideas should not be underestimated if we are to understand social policy in relation to children. Hendrick (2003) calls for recognition of the extent to which 'protective legislation' towards children and young people is about the management of their potential threat.

Learning activity

Using recent newspaper articles about children or childhood, identify how often you can recognise examples of the ideas outlined above. Consider the influence of these ideas in shaping children's lived experiences. What purpose do these ideas serve?

Alternative ideas about children

The emergence of children as beings rather than becoming and the demand for them to be seen in their own right, rather than hidden in the family or school, has focused recent sociological attention on children's experiences. A more focused children's policy approach attending to issues specifically related to children as users of welfare has gradually emerged as separate to the family (Kay *et al.*, 2011). The focus in policy to shape and train children for a future time, however, remains a dominant focus with associated aspirations and anxieties which accompany it. Examples of policy which focus on the child as an investment include financial support introduced by New Labour such as Child Trust Funds and Educational Maintenance Allowance for older children (Churchill, 2011). Recent developments aimed at coordinating and joining up provision established through *Every Child Matters* (DfES, 2003) and The Children Act 2004 have reinforced the separation of childhood from adulthood (Alcock, 2008). The notion of children and adults as interdependent with shared needs who are jointly being shaped and shaping culture as capable and active participants in their own right, remains elusive in policy development. Williams (2004) suggests that while recent policy and legislation has restructured the relationship between children, their families and the state, it has neglected to facilitate the value of respect for children and young people though recent emphasis on well-being does acknowledge children's subjectivity. The ideas expressed below, which Moss and Petrie (2005) argue are found in what they term a 'good childhood', are also commonly neglected in policy.

Joy, spontaneity, complexity, desires, richness, wonder, curiosity, care, vibrant, play, fulfilling, thinking for yourself, love, hospitality, welcome, alterity, emotion, ethics, relationships, responsibility – these are part of a vocabulary which speaks about a different idea of public provision for children, one which addresses questions about a good life, including a good childhood, and starts with ethics and politics (Moss and Petrie, 2005: 104–5).

Figure 9.1

Children's need and capacity to relate to adults interdependently, to socially belong and be recognised for such qualities has not yet been fulfilled in policy. In this section, we have seen how children are ascribed the aspirations and anxieties of society through ideas about what children should be or could be and not be, often at the expense of real children's experiences and interests. The final section uses this and the previous content of the chapter to explore areas of policy which have recently dominated policy development around children.

Prevalent areas of intervention

... the history of children and childhood is inescapably inseparable from the history of social policy. We cannot hope to understand the former without an appreciation of the latter.

(Hendrick, 1994: xii)

So far in this chapter we have explored the contested nature of social policy and what concepts like 'welfare' can mean. We have identified that there are social and political values and ideologies which underpin policy development and ways in which we socially construct childhood which also influence the development of social policy. This last section explores some of the recent key areas of intervention but should not be assumed to be an exhaustive list. The last decade has represented a significant time of policy development into the lives of children with the prevailing theme of prevention and intervention to deter social problems and enhance social cohesion. The social investment into childhood is related to wider problems in society, such as the negative impact of poverty, unemployment and dysfunctional families. As you read, it is worth taking note of the overlap in these areas. For example, tackling poverty is related to education policy, supporting the family is linked to the health and well-being of children and effective education seen as essential to the economic prosperity of individual adults and the nation state. These individual areas are connected in welfare provision as they are in children's lived experiences. And these lived experiences of children are directly linked to the adults they become and the society that they in turn shape.

The family

The family as an institution enables adults to be economically active and children to be socialised and educated (McKie and Callan, 2012). It is seen as a basic building block upon which a stable society is built (Shaw, 2010). Although it may be perceived as a private institution, the social, economic and political contribution of family members ensures that the family is an important location for social policy and as an institution is the recipient of many diverse services. Like childhood, however, the family can be seen as either a social investment or a potential threat to society. What constitutes a dysfunctional family is contingent and varies politically and historically. Some recognisable and notorious examples have included the lone parent family (most commonly female-headed), the workless family, and increasingly, the family which allows children to truant and behave in an anti-social way. Just as the 'problem family' has varied, so has the policy response to address it; but shaping the family to ensure stability and appropriate contribution to society is a longstanding aim of those developing social policy.

Economic support of families has been an obvious and significant area of intervention. Universal child benefit offered to all families (regardless of income) to financially support child rearing was introduced as Family Allowance in 1945 and 'established unequivocally the state's acknowledgement of some responsibility for the welfare and costs of children' (Platt, 2005: 85). It formed part of the comprehensive Beveridge welfare reforms after the Second World War. More recent examples include Child Tax Credits and subsequently the Working Family Tax Credit scheme, introduced by New Labour as part of an 'opportunity enhancement' strategy from 1997 (Page, 2007: 115). The aim of these subsidies based on income has been to provide targeted economic support, focused on particular families with an emphasis to promote child well-being, reduce child poverty and to encourage the economic activity of adults (Churchill, 2012). You might be able to recognise state paternalism here, but the political agenda is also concerned with reducing the long-term high costs associated with non-intervention. Recent policy has been aimed at tackling 'high levels of benefit dependency and poverty and the potentially negative outcomes for children' through the care and control of the family (Bradshaw, 2003: 147). Enabling adults to carry out their economic responsibility is part of a wider social and political agenda, thereby reducing reliance upon state welfare which is indicative of laissez-faire values. This approach connects the good citizen with the rights and responsibilities and encourages adults to foster these values and socialise children through them. New Labour assumed a more 'neutral' approach to family formation than previous political administrations had done (Haux, 2011: 148). Enabling all families to work (regardless of formation) was a driving aim behind the National Childcare Strategy, tax credits, SureStart, wrap-around school child care and greater access to adult education to increase skills and qualifications for the workplace. However, debate concerning the 'ideal' family formation and how to support it continues (see, for example, Shaw, 2010; Haux, 2011; Churchill, 2012). The current Coalition Government's concern over the decline in marriage is indicative of traditional values towards the stability and privilege of this type of family which reflects not only a laissez-faire approach, but also promotes parental rights. However, more overt 'pro-marriage' reforms have currently been muted by Liberal Democratic influence in the Coalition Government (Churchill, 2012: 41).

Every child matters

Lauded as representing the 'most comprehensive reform of child welfare services for 30 years' (Hendrick, 2005: 59), *Every Child Matters* (Department for Education and Skills, 2003) came out of the Lamming Report (2003) in Parton (2006) which focused on child protection following the murder of Victoria Climbié. The subsequent Children Act 2004 provided the legal framework for greater communication and coordination among disparate welfare services involved in the care of children. A partnership approach towards the well-being and welfare of children at local authority level was established through the Children Act 2004 with an emphasis on the five key outcomes outlined in *Every Child Matters*: enjoy and achieve, economic well-being, being healthy, staying safe and making a positive contribution. The Ministry for Children, Young People and Families was established in 2007 as part of this coordinated approach, subsequently incorporated into the Department for Education in 2010. Churchill (2012) suggests this reflects a return to a key value of education for the Coalition Government (elected in 2010).

You will note that being healthy is one of the five key outcomes of *Every Child Matters* and has always been a prominent area of welfare development. As with other areas in policy, keeping children healthy is part of what is considered to be in the 'collective interests' of society, as well as an individual child's (Alcock, 2008: 53).

Health and well-being

Health policy mainly focuses on prevention, surveillance and risk. Hendrick (2005) reminds us to acknowledge the concept of health as socially constructed. What we understand by the term 'health' reflects our collective and contingent knowledge, values and social anxieties. Buckingham (2008: 19) points out that as citizens of a western nation we are enjoying good health as a result of advances in medicine and the control of infectious diseases. However, public anxieties about health, and risks to it, remain high. What is meant by illness can be equally ambiguous. Traditionally, health has simplistically been defined as the 'absence of illness' (Kay and Tisdall, 1979 cited in Hendrick, 2005). However, it was defined by the World Health Organization (1946) as more than being the absence of disease, and inclusive of physical, mental and social well-being, and the term now encompasses a broader understanding. The current emphasis on well-being in relation to health and childhood however, emerged in part from the UNICEF (2007) report on the well-being of children and young people. It was identified through indicators on material, education, health, safety, family, peer relationships, behaviour and risk. The UK did not fare well in this report and was found to be in the bottom third of rankings for five out of the six dimensions (Shaw, 2010: 125).

Historically, monitoring the health of children has been prevalent and remains evident in welfare provision. Hill and Tisdall (1997: 2005) suggest that policy currently concentrates on educating children and families about good health and lifestyles, while also monitoring the health of children through surveillance structures (health visitors, schools, medical profession in health centres). Health care has two distinct areas: responding to illness and facilitating wellness through the prevention of illness. The second theme is one most pertinent to children where prevention of ill health through surveillance programmes (such as immunisations) and educating children in health maintenance for adult life are seen as important areas of provision. This preventative focus is evident in the Children Act (2004) by the coordination of services and the support of well-being through the facilitation of Child and Adolescent Mental Health Services (CAMHS). Examples of historical development of health provision include:

- **Public Health Act 1847**. Established community health services which improved health through enhancing environmental conditions such as poor sanitation (Alcock 2008: 57).
- **Public Health Act 1875**. Local authority role in public services such as water supply and sewerage.

- **National Health Service Act 1948**. Provided comprehensive and universal provision, free at the point of delivery, developed vaccination programmes as preventative measure against the spread of disease.

While policy emphasises the role of educating individuals to make a 'healthy' lifestyle choice, the role of the state to intervene is regarded by some as a further erosion of the public/private divide and intrusion on the part of the state into the private life of the individual (Shaw, 2010). Contradictions are also evident in health messages aimed at families. Home-cooked meals are promoted as being a better alternative to processed and convenience food, yet the expectation of parents to work ensures that many have less time and opportunity to prepare such meals. Intervening in the private role of the family though contentious is commonplace, in part to seek to address the rise in levels of childhood obesity, seen as being a significant health risk. The health impact of obesity is problematic for children and adults and is commonly construed as being a self-inflicted lifestyle choice (Shaw, 2010). The responsibility of parents is taken as self-evident, with a poor nutritional diet as a result of obesity now being discussed in terms of child neglect (Horwath, 2007).

Figure 9.2

The school is seen as a location for educating children about nutrition, balanced diet and exercise which has widened the remit of the teacher's role. The expectation upon schools to deliver healthy meals has also increased where cost-effectiveness of provision alone is no longer sufficient, and nutritional value must also be considered. However, the individual health of children relies on many contributing factors perhaps not immediately associated with the term. Ill health is empirically linked to poverty, poor housing, low educational attainment, geographical location and ethnicity (Bradshaw, 2003). Tackling poor health therefore requires a broader welfare approach than those found specifically in the preventative measures of vaccine programmes, access to GPs and promotional initiatives to change behavior, such as 'Change4Life'. Despite extensive policy towards children in recent decades, the wider policy approach has been a shrinking role for the state and a greater role for the individual (laissez-faire). Addressing the structural inequalities associated with ill health by increasing the role of the state is now viewed as politically undesirable, economically unsustainable and paternalistic towards autonomous citizens. Recognition of the negative impact on children's health and well-being, however, requires a policy response. New Labour introduced SureStart in 1998 as a means to tackle the negative impact of poverty on health and educational attainment through targeted intervention into specific families. Education remains an area of policy seen as being instrumental in elevating children out of poverty, and the associated consequences of it, such as poor health.

Education

Like other areas of provision covered in this section, this brief discussion of education is not intended to be a comprehensive and historical account, but aimed at encouraging students to recognise that the kind of education children receive is a political debate linked to the perspectives and ideas about children and society. The education landscape is changing, with new providers emerging alongside the local authorities; however, the long-standing interest in shaping education policy on the part of the state remains. The establishment of free schools is a recent example of the role of the market (laissez-faire) in education though these remain funded by the state. Currently, teachers, parents and private businesses can set up a school and run it, independent of the local authority. This was made possible in 2010 by the Coalition Government and emerged out of the establishment of academies which was introduced by the previous Labour administration with the intention of addressing the problem of 'failing schools'. Other examples of the market in state education include publishing school performance tables so that parents (as the consumers of education) can determine school choice for their children. The establishment of a national school curriculum by the Conservative Government in 1988 provided a standardisation of education, making it easier for parents to determine the quality of education offered in their local area and encouraged schools to improve and compete. A focus on parent's rights is also clear here.

Education is constructed as a right in the United Nations Convention on the Rights of the Child (UNCRC). For the individual child, education represents the opportunity to climb out of poverty and disadvantage and for personal development. A children's rights perspective is relevant to review these ideas through. However, historically education was not simply introduced as a response to welfare need and it remains the location where equipping children with appropriate skills for the social and economic prosperity of the wider society occurs. In consequence, education might not always exclusively promote a rights perspective but reflect other values too. Ideas about the 'child as investment' and, in consequence, as threat through a failure of education are relevant. Educating the child as a social investment is well demonstrated in the current focus on early years education.

Early years education

Traditionally, nursery education has not been an area where local or national government has had much interest. In the past, children of three and four years of age have been firmly located at home in the care of family rather than in formal education. However, public nursery provision has expanded considerably in recent years, though it is still not comprehensive or compulsory (Alcock, 2008: 37). This emergence of state interest in nursery education has been in part to intervene earlier into the lives of children as a preventative measure and also as part of enabling adults to work and must be seen in relation to welfare-to-work programmes developing at the time. There has been a significant expansion in private nurseries providing day care, as well as publicly funded nursery provision which young children are now entitled to. The 2006 Childcare Act tasked local authorities with providing sufficient places, information to parents and support for providers. The same Act also provided a framework for the inspection of this provision through the Office for Standards in Education (Ofsted) (Alcock, 2008). As part of a wider agenda of tackling child poverty and increasing the life chances of disadvantaged children, the role of preschool education has been widely recognised as beneficial intellectually, socially and emotionally (Churchill, 2012) (see Chapter 7 for a full discussion of preschool and early years provision).

Primary education

Primary education is formalised (compulsory) from the age of five years in the UK. This is earlier than in other countries and the effectiveness of starting so young is contested (Riggall and Sharp, 2008). The focus is on numeracy, literacy and science. A Nationalised Curriculum was established through the Education Reform Act (1988). However, the establishment of academies and free schools suggests a move away from a centralised curriculum. Schools are inspected through Ofsted. Education in early childhood has been developed through the discipline of child psychology (see the Plowden Report, 1967). The ages and stages of childhood shape a child's educational experience and the ways in which appropriate knowledge is delivered in a child's life course. The structure of education should be considered in relation to developmental models of childhood (see Chapter 4, *Personal, social and emotional development*). Education is separated into three stages: the Foundation Stage (preschool), Key Stage 1 (5–7 years) and Key Stage 2 (7–11 years). This compartmentalisation reflects social assumptions of the 'becoming' child developing towards adulthood. It does not necessarily reflect their ability but provides the structure through which children are processed and given the opportunity to acquire relevant personal, social and economic skills. Dahlberg and Moss (2005) argue that current education produces a narrow depiction of childhood where the language of the market (laissez-faire) speaks of early intervention as a mechanism for dramatic future financial savings and a good return on investment.

- **1870:** local school boards established.
- **1880:** compulsory attendance for children between 5 and 10 years old.
- **1944 Education Act:** extended compulsory education up to the age of 15 years. Established the tripartite system and outlined the role of local education authorities as representative of the state in delivering a national education system.
- **1967 Plowden Report:** identified the importance of relationship between home and school.

- **1978 Warnock Inquiry:** highlighted special educational needs.
- **1988 Education Reform Act:** encouraged schools to act competitively through the introduction of national standards and league tables.
- **1998 The Crick Report:** led the way to citizenship on the curriculum.
- **2011 Tickell Review:** independent report on Early Years Foundation Stage (EYFS).

Poverty

As you read about policy responses to poverty, reflect on your ideas developed by doing the earlier activity about responding to children's need through the family. Consider Platt's (2005: 3) argument that '[c]hild poverty can only be recognised as a particular social problem once childhood is acknowledged as having a sacrosanct claim to interest, regardless of parental behaviour or economic position'. Some intervention aimed at children is delivered through the family, such as financial support; other examples are directed to the individual child such as education. The debate about how to successfully resolve the need to care for children as a central aim, without condoning the perceived poor choices of inept or feckless adults, remains difficult and contentious to achieve. This balance is influenced by the perspectives outlined earlier where determining those deserving and undeserving of support (sometimes referred to as 'less eligibility') is also dependent upon ideological ideas about the role of the citizen, the state and where responsibility for welfare should lie.

Anxiety about the impact and consequences of poverty for children is evident historically and remains topical (see Chapter 8, *Understanding childhood and late modernity*, for a further discussion on poverty). Blaming the poor for their poverty is a theme found in the New Poor Law (1834) and remains present in policy discourse. However, an emphasis on poverty is not historically consistent and is also politically expedient (Platt, 2005). Tackling child poverty was placed high on the political agenda by the Labour administration in 1997 with the claim to halve it by 2010 and eradicate by 2020. Prevention of the debilitating personal and social consequences of poverty through early state intervention into children's lives was seen as a legitimate role for the state by the Labour Government. Attempting to achieve this aim encompassed a broad range of policies to increase household income, such as Child Tax Credit (introduced in 2001), while also working towards improving the life chances of children through education, early years provision and family support, SureStart, established in 1998 being an example of this approach. Churchill (2011), however, reminds us that this commitment to tackling child poverty did not prevent withdrawal of benefit from those deemed undeserving through anti-social behaviour and those with restricted access to benefit, such as asylum seekers and refugees.

The Coalition Government states that it remains committed to taking the legislated steps outlined in the Child Poverty Act (2010) towards the eradication of child poverty by 2020/21 (Stewart, 2011). This involves the regular production of child poverty strategies and includes a relatively low income target. However, the consequences of the current recession in the UK (at time of publication) coupled with a political administration ideologically predisposed to reducing the welfare role of the state, is not yet apparent. An increase of targeting children's benefit (means testing) however, is evident. Child benefit will be means tested in 2013 rather than being available to all, along with restricting eligibility for Child Tax Credit and SureStart. A benefit cap of £26 000 is also planned for 2013. In an *Independent Review on Poverty and Life Chances*, Field (2010) argues that greater emphasis on good parenting and quality early years provisions are effective anti-poverty strategies. Identification of better parenting, however, potentially places the responsibility on to the shoulders of parents where blame for failure easily follows. Stewart (2011: 182) suggests that children have experienced a treble blow through, 'the continuing impact of the recession, the need to reduce the structural deficit and the arrival of a new government committed to particularly steep cuts to public spending and placing lower priority both on income poverty and on children'.

What happens to the welfare of children in times of austerity?

As well as targeting certain benefits, the Coalition Government has begun to identify specific families they label as 'troubled'. This family is categorised as having one or more of the following indicators (previously identified by Social Exclusion Task Force (2007)). Low income, no working adults, poor housing, parents with no qualifications, a mother with a mental health problem, a parent with a long-standing illness or disability and a family where there is an inability to afford basics such as food or clothing. It is suggested that local councils, led by a Troubled Families Team, are to be paid by results for an integrated approach to reduce the anti-social behaviour argued to be caused by these families. The Community Secretary, Eric Pickles, has claimed that these families need less understanding and greater public recognition for trouble that it is suggested they cause in the community (Chorley, 2012). Critics of this approach suggest that many of the issues used to define these families are indicative of structural inequality and beyond their control and should not be used to apportion blame.

In 2010, the Coalition Government outlined their intention to introduce Universal Credit from 2013 to replace the current structure which, they suggest, impedes people's capacity to move away from benefit and into work, while the cost of administering the current benefit system remains high. The current emphasis on measuring well-being is also indicative of a move away from a specific focus on income poverty. Churchill (2011: 213) suggests that the spending cuts of the coalition do not 'equate to family-friendly economic and social policies' and that these cuts will have a disproportionate impact on lone parent families, women and families headed by young parents. Children in these families are likely to experience considerable hardship, while the general public attitude to welfare continues to favour its reduction.

Learning activity

There are two photographs included in this chapter. Both images are here to encourage reflection on the wider themes discussed in this chapter. The first shows a number of children with their faces obscured. Use this photograph to consider whether, despite varied social and political interest in children, we can or should assume to know children and be experts of their worlds. The second image depicts a child eating with an adult in close proximity. Using this image, consider the extent to which the adult surveillance is representative of care or control.

Conclusion

The aim of this chapter has been to introduce the study of social policy and childhood. To achieve this, the terms 'social policy' and 'welfare' along with some of the underpinning values and perspectives in welfare were outlined. Ideas about childhood ascribed to children at various social and political times were also outlined before going on to discuss some significant areas of recent welfare provision. The contingent nature of social policy can initially make the study of it challenging, just as you learn about a particular policy approach, its aim, focus, strengths and limitations, another political administration or social need comes on the scene and the policy landscape shifts. However, it is important to remember policy is not created in a vacuum, but always developed on previous policy and always reflective of wider social and political values about a society and its people. The tools of the trade in the study of social policy are found in embracing this contingency while recognising recurring themes evident in welfare development and their position in historical and current policy.

Evaluate your learning

- To what extent is childhood shaped by contemporary welfare provision?
- Evaluate the extent to which ideas about childhood influence the care and control of children through social policy.
- Do you suggest that welfare provision is always in the best interests of the child?

References

Alcock, P. (2008): *Social Policy in Britain*. Basingstoke: Palgrave Macmillan.

Bradshaw, J (1972): A taxonomy of social need. *New Society* **496**, 640–3.

Bradshaw, J (2003): Child poverty and child health: an international perspective. In Hallett, C and Prout, A (eds), *Hearing the Voices of Children: Social Policy for a New Century*. London: RoutledgeFalmer.

Buckingham, A (2008): Doing better, feeling scared: health statistics and the culture of fear. In Wainwright, D (ed), *A Sociology of Health*. London: Sage.

Burman, E (2001): Beyond the baby and the bathwater: postdualistic developmental psychologies for diverse childhoods. *European Early Childhood Education Research Journal* **9**(1), 5–22.

Carney, T (2005): Liberalism or distributional justice? The morality of child welfare laws. In Hendrick, H (ed), *Children and Social Policies, Child Welfare and Social Policy*. Bristol: Policy Press.

Churchill, H (2011): *Parental Rights and Responsibilities: Analyzing Social Policy and Lived Experiences*. Bristol: The Policy Press.

Churchill, H (2012): Family support and the Coalition: retrenchment, refocusing and restructuring. In Kilkey, M, Ramia, G and Farnsworth, K (eds), *Social Policy Review 24: Analysis and Debate in Social Policy*. Bristol: Policy Press.

Cordery, S (2003): *British Friendly Societies 1750–1914*. Houndsmill: Palgrave Macmillan.

Cunningham, S and Tomlinson, J (2005): Children, social policy and the state: the dichotomy of care and control. In Lavalette, M and Pratt, A (eds), *Social Policy: Theories, Concepts and Issues*, 3rd edn. London: Sage.

Dahlberg, G and Moss, P (2005): *Ethics and Politics in Early Childhood Education (Contesting Early Childhood)*. Routledge: London.

Deacon, A (2002): *Perspectives on Welfare Ideas, Ideologies and Policy Debates*. Buckingham: Open University Press.

Department for Education and skills (DfES) (2003): *Every Child Matters*. London: The Stationery Office.

Donzelot, J (1980): *The Policing of Families: Welfare versus the State*. London: Hutchinson.

Ellison, N (2011): The Conservative Party and the Big Society. In Holden, C, Kilkey, M and Ramia, G (eds), *Social Policy Review 23: Analysis and Debate in Social Policy 2011*. Bristol: Policy Press.

Field, F (2010): *The Foundation Years: Preventing Poor Children Becoming Poor Adults*. The report of the Independent Review on Poverty and Life Chances, December. London: HM Government.

Fox Harding, LM (1991): *Perspectives in Child Care Policy*. London: Longman.

Franklin, B (ed) (1995): *The Handbook of Children's Rights: Essays in Comparative Policy and Practice*. London: Routledge.

Hatch, JA (1995): *Qualitative Research in Early Childhood Settings*. Westport, CT: Greenwood Press.

Haux, T (2011): Lone parents and the Conservatives: anything new? In Holden, C, Kilkey, M and Ramia, G (eds), *Social Policy Review 23: Analysis and Debate in Social Policy 2011*. Bristol: Policy Press.

Hendrick, H (1994): *Child Welfare: England 1872–1989*. London: Routledge.

Hendrick, H (2003): *Child Welfare: Historical Dimensions, Contemporary Debate*. Bristol: Policy Press.

Hendrick, H (ed) (2005): Children and social policies. In Hendrick, H (ed), *Child Welfare and Social Policy*. Bristol: Policy Press.

Hill, M and Tisdall, K (1997): Children and health. In Hendrick, H (ed), *Child Welfare and Social Policy*. Bristol: Policy Press.

Horwath, J (2007): *Child Neglect: Identification and Assessment*, Basingstoke: Palgrave Macmillan.

Chorley, M (2012): *IoS Exclusive: Problem families told – 'Stop blaming others', Independent*. (Online). Last accessed 26 July 2012. Available from: www.independent.co.uk/news/uk/politics/ios-exclusive-problem-families-told--stop-blaming-others-7834235.html.

Jones, C (2002): Voices from the front line: state social workers and New Labour. *British Journal of Social Work* **31**, 547–62.

Kay, E, Tisdall, M and Hill, M (2011): Policy Change Under Devolution: The Prism Of Children's Policy. *Social Policy and Society* **10**(1), 29–41.

Lewis A (2010): Silence in the context of child voice. *Children and Society* **24**, 14–23.

Lister, R (2011): The age of responsibility: social policy and citizenship in the early 21st century. In Holden, C, Kilkey, M and Ramia, G (eds), *Social Policy Review 24: Analysis and Debate in Social Policy, 2012.* Bristol: Policy Press.

Lister, R (2003): Investing in the citizen-workers of the future. *Social Policy and Administration* **37**(5), 427–43.

McKie, L and Callan, S (2012): *Understanding Families: A Global Introduction.* London: Sage.

Moss, P and Petrie, P (2005): Children – who do we think they are? In Hendrick, H (ed), *Child Welfare and Social Policy.* Bristol: Policy Press.

Muncie, J (1999): Institutionalised intolerance: youth justice and the 1998 Crime and Disorder Act. *Critical Social Policy* **19**(2), 147–75.

Page, RM (2007): *Revisiting the Welfare State.* Maidenhead: Open University Press.

Parton, N (2006) *Safeguarding Childhood.* Basingstoke: Palgrave Macmillan.

Platt, L (2005): *Discovering Child Poverty: The Creation of a Policy Agenda from 1800 to the Present.* Bristol: Policy Press.

Plowden Report (1967) Children and their primary schools. Last accessed 14 November 2012. Available from: www.educationengland.org.uk/documents/plowden.

Riggall, A and Sharp, C (2008): *The Structure of Primary Education. England and Other Countries (Primary Review Research Survey 9/1).* Cambridge: University of Cambridge Faculty of Education.

Social Exclusion Task Force (SEFT) Cabinet Office (2007) *Reaching Out: Think Family: Analysis and Themes from the Families At Risk Review*, Cabinet Office. (Online). Last accessed 28 September 2008. Available from: www.cabinetoffice.gov.uk/media/cabinetoffice/socialexclusion_task_force/assests/think_families/pdf.

Shaw, S (2010): *Parents, Children, Young People and the State.* Maidenhead: Open University Press.

Skevik, A (2005): Children of the welfare state: Individuals with entitlements or hidden in the family? In Hendrick, H (ed), *Child Welfare and Social Policy.* Bristol: Policy Press.

Spicker, P (2008): *Social Policy Themes and Approaches.* Bristol: Policy Press.

Stewart, K (2011): A treble blow? Child poverty in 2010 and beyond. In Holden, C, Kilkey, M and Ramia, G (eds), *Social Policy Review 23: Analysis and Debate in Social Policy, 2011.* Bristol: Policy Press.

Tomlinson, S (2005): Education and the economy. In Hendrick, H (ed), *Child Welfare and Social Policy.* Bristol: Policy Press.

UNICEF (2007) An overview of child well-being in rich countries. Last accessed 14 November 2012. Available from: www.unicef.org/media/files/ChildPovertyReport.pdf.

Williams, F (2004): What matters is what works: why every child matters to New Labour. Commentary on the DfES Green Paper Every Child Matters. *Critical Social Policy* **24**(3), 406–27.

World Health Organization (1946): Preamble to the Constitution of the World Health Organization as adopted by the International Health Conference, New York, 19–22 June, 1946; signed on 22 July 1946 by the representatives of 61 States (Official Records of the World Health Organization, no. 2, p. 100) and entered into force on 7 April 1948.

Further reading

Alcock, P (2008) *Social Policy in Britain.* Basingstoke: Palgrave Macmillan.

Churchill, H (2011) *Parental Rights And Responsibilities: Analyzing Social Policy and Lived Experiences.* Bristol: The Policy Press.

Hendrick, H (ed) (2005) *Child Welfare and Social Policy.* Bristol: Policy Press.

Spicker, P (2008) *Social Policy Themes and Approaches.* Bristol: Policy Press.

10

The multidisciplinary child protection system: current policy and practice

Jackie Plenty

This chapter aims to:
- explore the legal and policy framework underpinning the child protection system
- identify the signs and symptoms of physical, sexual, emotional abuse and neglect; and consider prevalence
- consider the child protection system and signpost to further information
- critically analyse inter-agency collaboration and partnership working.

Introduction

Working with abused children and safeguarding children from abuse and neglect is a fundamental aspect of early childhood studies. All professionals who provide care for children have child protection responsibilities and need to have knowledge of the legal and policy framework underpinning child protection procedures. They also need to remain acutely aware of the challenges that can emerge in the face of managing painful emotions that can impact on all those involved in a child protection investigation. Child abuse by its very nature can evoke strong feelings of anger, fear, frustration, mistrust, sadness, helplessness and even repulsion. Regardless of our training and readiness for managing the complexity surrounding child abuse and child protection work, we can find ourselves exposed to over-identifying with victims, withdrawing or becoming too systematic in our approach, over-reacting or moving away from our need to remain child-centred and losing focus on the child.

We need to strive to protect family life, draw out strengths and positive factors, empower and work in partnership, remaining sensitive, supportive and empathic, deploying honesty and transparency at the same time as being rigorous and focused on safeguarding, and managing and assessing risk. We also need to follow procedures and gather evidence that can at times feel over-methodical, bureaucratic and highly intrusive. This is not an easy balancing act to maintain when we are also expected to uphold public trust and work holistically with other professionals from a variety of disciplines and avoid getting caught up in the turmoil and crisis that can be experienced by vulnerable children and their families.

The historical development of legal and policy frameworks

Over the course of more than 30 years, the abuse of children has been constructed as one of the major problems of our time. This is not because child abuse is a new phenomenon as it has existed for centuries, but society has struggled to recognise, acknowledge and accept it as a problem. Historically, the existence of child mistreatment is indisputable. Across the 17th and 18th centuries, severe physical punishment, child prostitution, abandonment, infanticide and harsh labour were not uncommon. State concern centred on street children, young offenders, children at work and those looked after by poor law institutions. Church and community patrols and court hearings were the general response to public concerns around the immorality and exploitation of children. The emergence of the National Society for the Prevention of Cruelty to Children (NSPCC) in the 1880s, shifted the response from rescuing children outside their families, to rescuing children living in their homes, although it was not until the passing of the 1889 Prevention of Cruelty to Children Act that need to protect children became mandatory. Numerous Acts followed, extending the original Act, and by 1908 the main components of child protection law and policy were set and mirror those that exist today (Corby, 2006).

The denial of abuse continued in the early part of the 20th century, when Freud's accounts of women who had been sexually abused within their families failed to be acknowledged and were recounted and reinterpreted as fantasy. This was despite the punishment of incest being enshrined in law in 1908 (Reder *et al.*, 1993). It was the medical profession that then began to acknowledge physical abuse in the mid-1900s and Caffey (1946), a paediatric radiologist from the United States, described bone lesions and subdural haematomas resulting from trauma. This was followed by the US paediatrician, Kempe and colleagues in 1962 publishing their work on the 'battered child syndrome' (Kempe *et al.*, 1962. 'Non-accidental injury' became the accepted medical term adopted in the UK, with police, social workers and doctors becoming more involved in working together to detect it (Polnay and Polnay, 2007). Parton (1979) provided detailed accounts of the development of child abuse as a social problem through the previous two decades, but it was not until the 1980s that it was widely accepted that familial child sexual abuse had been taking place as opposed to the long-held previous conception that this only happened with strangers unknown to the child.

Following the Second World War, there was greater societal interest in the welfare of deprived children. The Curtis Committee (1946) inquired into children who had been separated from their parents, providing a detailed account of child-care concerns. At the same time, the inquiry into the manslaughter of 12-year-old Dennis O'Neill, by his foster father, influenced the emergence of the 1948 Children Act (Home Office, 1945). Bowlby's (1951) studies into maternal deprivation as a result of institutional care were also highly influential. The link between delinquency and neglect was the key focus during this period which was reflected in the 1963 Children and Young Persons Act that also provided material and financial assistance to allow children to remain in their family homes. The need for more of a 'family-focused' professional response was supported in the Seebohm (1968) report that led to the Health and Welfare and Children's Departments becoming unified social services departments under the local authority in 1970. Further cases of child abuse began to be exposed in numerous inquiries, reports and investigations and were characterised by disbelief, denial, conflict and scandal.

The Maria Colwell Inquiry (DHSS, 1974) highlighted numerous health and welfare workers who failed to notice the ill-treatment that seven-year-old Maria endured through much of her young life, resulting in gross malnourishment and injuries from severe beatings by her step-father that led to her death. The inquiry, followed by a series of government reports and circulars, led to the setting up of the child protection system that currently exists today, providing a more thorough system for monitoring children at risk, with a focus on ensuring that a prompt response was made to allegations of abuse and that inter-agency collaboration would improve.

Despite this, a further 26 inquiries into the abuse and deaths of children through to 1981 were undertaken, the majority of which highlighted that health and welfare professionals were already involved in the case (Corby *et al.*, 2001).

The Department of Health and Social Security publication (DHSS, 1985) highlighted an over-use of statutory powers and a lack of focus into the needs of families by social workers. At the same time the Beckford Inquiry (London Borough of Brent, 1985) that examined the death of four-year-old Jasmine horrifically beaten by her step-father and only seen once by her social worker during the last ten months of her life, made 68 recommendations highlighting 'over-optimistic social workers'. Although other professionals were also to blame, Brent Council was deemed to be at fault. The inquiry stated that social workers needed to employ the full force of the law and make child protection their primary focus. This became the statutory obligation of local authorities and area review committees and child abuse registers became child protection committees and child protection registers, referred to today as 'child protection plans'. This re-affirming of the key role of social service departments and the use of the term 'child protection' in the renaming of registers, led to a dramatic increase in registrations through the period 1984 and 1991 (Corby, 2006: 117). A further 12 child death inquiries followed in the lead up to the publication of the Children Act 1989.

The Children Act 1989

The Children Act 1989 which came into force in 1991 was considered to be an important and far-reaching reform of the law in respect of safeguarding children, introducing comprehensive changes to legislation in England and Wales. While it mandated compulsory intervention, it also heralded the idea of working in partnership with children and families, as well as taking a supportive approach with an ethos that centred on children being cared for and brought up in their own families where possible. The Act reinforced the autonomy of families through definition of parental responsibility and provided support from local authorities for families where children were considered be 'in need' (Section 17) or who may be suffering or are likely to suffer significant harm (Section 47). Ultimately, it aimed to bring private and public law together in one framework, while trying to achieve a better balance between protecting children and enabling parents/carers to challenge state intervention.

The findings of the 1987 Cleveland report (Butler-Sloss, 1988) which over a six-month period investigated 121 children considered to have been sexually abused and diagnosed using a physical test (reflex anal dilatation test), resulted in parental uproar and public disquiet. It had a direct impact on the amendments made to the Children Act 1989 prior to its implementation, particularly around empowering children to refuse medical assessments if they wished (Section 44(7)) and providing accommodation for potential abusers so that children could stay at home (Schedule 2, Para 5), rather than being placed in care or in hospital wards. The main findings of the report confirmed that child sexual abuse was more widespread than had previously been acknowledged. This was also supported by accounts from adult survivors of child sexual abuse in the United States (Brady, 1979). The inquiry was highly influential in terms of amendments being made to the first draft of the 1986 Working Together to Safeguard Children guidelines (DHSS, 1988), that were updated in 1991 and 1996 reinforcing that social workers and police should conduct joint investigations This important and often overlooked piece of policy guidance was further amended to the current version in 2010 (Department for Children, Schools and Families, 2010).

Learning activity

Read Chapter 2 of the 'Working Together to Safeguard Children' government guidance (Department for Children, Schools and Families, 2010). See if you can identify the roles and responsibilities of your (intended) profession and compare this to other professional groups you work with. A copy can be downloaded from the Department for Education website (www.education.gov.uk).

During the 1980s, allegations and publications into ritual/satanic abuse became a focus in the United States (Spencer, 1989), followed by the Orkney case in 1991 (Clyde, 1992) in the United Kingdom. Allegations of ritualistic sexual abuse of nine children from four families were made against a church minister and the parents of the children. Jean La Fontaine conducted research between 1987 and 1992 commissioned by the Department of Health, confirming that from the analysis of 84 cases there was no hard evidence to support the ritualistic/satanic abuse of children resulting in torture and killing. The research did, however, confirm abuse from one or more perpetrators through extended family networks and in a few cases through organised paedophile rings (La Fontaine, 1994). During the same period, the Pindown Inquiry (Levy and Kahan, 1991) highlighted system abuse in residential settings, through the use of controlling children in care that were deemed to be challenging. This abusive regime led to concerns that it was occurring in other counties, although inquiries found that it was isolated to Staffordshire at the same time as uncovering sexual abuse in residential care settings. While the Utting Report (1991) was commissioned to examine the strengths and weaknesses within the care system generally, reaffirming the low status given to this type of care, in North Wales allegations were emerging of widespread sexual abuse in children's homes involving powerful figures of the community (Waterhouse, 2000).

In-between this period *Child Protection: Messages from Research* (Department of Health, 1995) examined the implications for child protection policy and practice, concluding that child protection work had become enveloped in bureaucratic procedures focusing too much on incidents of physical and sexual abuse at the expense of not considering neglect and family support. Resources being ploughed into child protection cases meant that 'children in need' cases that required early intervention and support were being overlooked, increasing their likelihood of becoming child protection cases. There was a refocus from child protection to family support between 1995 and 2000 and arguably to the present day so that new guidelines for safeguarding children emerged (Department of Health, 1999) and the Quality Protects programme was launched (Department of Health, 1998).

In February 2000, the death of eight-year-old Victoria Climbié marked a major turning point in multi-agency child protection work. Following years of maltreatment and abuse by her great-aunt, Marie-Therese Kouao, and her partner Carl Manning, she spent most of the winter that preceded her death living and sleeping in a bath in an unheated bathroom, bound hand and foot inside a bin bag, lying in her own urine and faeces. At the end, young Victoria's heart, lungs and kidneys all failed and she was reported to have no less that 128 separate injuries to her body (Laming, 2003). Unlike other child death inquiries, there was a strong focus on the failure of health, social care and police agencies and professionals that maintained no ongoing consistent involvement with Victoria and her family. Laming reported a gross failure of the system, widespread organisational malaise across the professions and management issues resulting in 128 recommendations.

The Victoria Climbié Inquiry (Laming, 2003) reported that early intervention was vital if children were to be protected from risk of serious harm. This led to the emergence of 'Every Child Matters' (Department for Education, 2004a), which sets out a number of legislative commitments, some of which have been taken forward in the Children Act 2004. The Children Act 2004 builds on the Children Act 1989 through covering universal services which every child accesses, as well as more targeted services for those with additional needs. Its overall aim is to encourage greater integration of services and to improve multidisciplinary working. It also places a new duty on local authorities to promote the educational achievement of looked-after children. In September 2004, the Department for Education also published 'Safeguarding Children in Education', (2004b) setting out guidance on the arrangements that local education authorities, school governing bodies and head teachers should have in place to protect children. Standard 5 of the 2004 National Service Framework for Children, Young People and Maternity Services also highlighted the need to focus on safeguarding and promoting the welfare of children and young people. During this same period, the Bichard Inquiry (2004) investigated child protection measures, record keeping, vetting and information sharing, following the conviction of Ian Huntley for the murder of Soham schoolgirls, Holly Wells and Jessica Chapman.

Learning activity

Read the National Service Framework (NSF) for Children, Young People and Maternity Services, Core Standard 5 (Safeguarding and Promoting the Welfare of Children and Young People) as a guide and identify the local policies and protocols in place in the locality where you are working as a student or professional to protect children. Analyse these policies to see if they meet the requirements set out in the NSF.

Following this, the Department for Children Schools and Families Children's Plan (2007), Building Brighter Futures, was published, highlighting the strengthening of support for all families during the formative early years of their children. It also heralded a new leadership role for Children's Trusts, a new role for schools as the centre of their communities, and more effective links between schools, the NHS and other children's services so that together they can engage parents and tackle the barriers to the learning, health and happiness of every child through an integrated children's system.

Integrated services and the Common Assessment Framework

Integrated services for children and young people were to be based on the local implementation of centrally driven processes that are common to all disciplines in the children's workforce (Hoyle, 2008: 1). The system is now fully in force across the country and has involved statutory social service departments undergoing extensive restructuring and the setting up of multi-agency teams, heralding team around the child provision (Siraj-Blatchford *et al.*, 2007; Gasper, 2010) or tiered systems that aim to target early years children through working preventatively in a move to minimise the likelihood of them moving up to comprehensive assessment and/or child protection teams. Models for early intervention were also developed nationally and delivered locally through extended schools and SureStart Children's Centres with *Working Together to Safeguard Children* inter-agency guidance (Department for Children, Schools and Families, 2010) being further promoted as the framework from which to protect children and promote their welfare.

Learning activity

Think of a child you have observed or worked with where you have been concerned that they may be a 'child in need' (Section 17) or a 'child at risk of significant harm' (Section 47) CA1989. Use the charts in Chapter 5 of *Working Together to Safeguard Children* to trace the procedures that would need to be followed. This will familiarise you with child protection procedures.

These structures were to be supported by the *Common Assessment Framework* (Department for Education and Skills, 2005), a multi-agency assessment tool that can be used by all professionals who have a duty to safeguard and promote the welfare of children and young people. There are, however, criticisms of the *Every Child Matters* reform agenda as it only incorporates children and young people living in England and does not reach diverse groups of children, such as those seeking asylum or carrying refugee status. Equally, there is a compounding issue around it intruding on the rights of children and their families (Article 8, of the European Convention on Human Rights) and compromising their privacy. Hoyle (2008: 1) provides a useful critique of the system stating that:

> *Every Child Matters effectively enables politicians and civil servants to centralise credit to themselves for driving forward a grand vision, whilst simultaneously diverting any blame for failures in the delivery of that programme onto local Council services, their partners and other local bodies.*

Equally, for any integrated system to be successful it requires a commitment to 'information sharing' (Department for Children, Schools and Families, 2008) and the ability to use a common language and adopt a common core of knowledge and skills throughout the children's workforce (Children's Workforce Development Council, 2010). These issues have formed part of the government's drive and commitment to produce policy that supports the promotion of inter-agency collaboration.

Despite the plethora of policy that followed the Laming Inquiry (2003) that informed practice in August 2007, Peter Connelly (aged 17 months) died after suffering more than 50 injuries during which time he was repeatedly seen by the London Borough of Haringey Children's Services and NHS health professionals and was subject to a child protection plan. The Serious Case Review conducted by Haringey's Local Safeguarding Children's Board (Department for Education, 2010), highlighted the need for authoritative child protection practice, improved inter-agency communication and an over-reliance on medical and criminal evidence. Laming (2009: 4) was requested to conduct the Protection of Children in England Progress Report stating that:

> One of the main challenges is to ensure that leaders of local services effectively translate policy, legislation and guidance into day-to-day practice on the frontline of every service.

The report recommended the 'remodelling of social work', particularly in light of recruitment and retention issues and high case loads. The Department of Health was to prioritise its commitment to promote the recruitment of health visitors, reviewing the healthy programme for 0–5 year olds, as well as ensuring the statutory duty placed on GP providers to comply with child protection legislation. The provision of a national training programme for children's health workers, midwives, health visitors, GPs and school nurses was also heralded, alongside the need for child protection police to be well resourced. More recently, Graham Allen MP (2011) reported on 'the next steps in early intervention, stating that the culture of late intervention is both expensive and ineffective and that all parties should commit to the central objective of early intervention. The Statutory Framework for the Early Years Foundation Stage (EYFS) (Department of Health, 2012), also advocates for all early years providers to ensure that children learn and develop well and are kept healthy and safe with Section 3 of the standards highlighting safeguarding and welfare requirements mandated by the Childcare Act 2006 S39 (1)(b).

In Munro's (Department for Education, 2011) review of child protection report entitled *A Child-Centred System*, she stated that the system had become too focused on compliance with rules and procedures and had lost its focus on the needs and experiences of children and young people. She recommended more direct work, less of a focus on bureaucracy and time-frames and the measuring of outcomes to see if children are receiving effective services. This was underpinned with the key message that uncertainty and risk are features of child protection work and early help is better for children. The government are taking steps to respond to these latest recommendations (NSPCC, 2011), but we are yet to see during a time of ongoing recession and depleting resources whether legislation, policy and funding will be reconfigured to create a robust but flexible system that truly can safeguard and protect vulnerable children and young people.

Recognising abuse: signs and symptoms

There is no universally agreed definition of child abuse. At its simplest, child abuse can be defined as ways of treating a child that are harmful and morally wrong. There is, however, considerable variation over time and between cultures in what is deemed abusive (Munro, 2002). At an international level, Article 19 of the 1989 United Nations Convention on the Rights of the Child defines child abuse as 'all forms of physical or mental violence, injury or abuse, negligent treatment, maltreatment or exploitation, including sexual abuse'. The national level definition is incorporated into the Children Act 1989, specifically Section 47 (the child is suffering or likely to suffer significant harm) and Section 31 (the harm or likelihood of harm is attributable to a lack of adequate parental care or control).

There are many child protection organisations that have their own definitions of child abuse, but for the purpose of this chapter we will refer to the *Working Together to Safeguard Children* (Department for Children, Schools and Families, 2010: 37) government guidance on inter-agency working that defines abuse and neglect as:

> *Forms of maltreatment of a child. Somebody may abuse or neglect a child by inflicting harm, or by failing to act to prevent harm. Children may be abused in a family or in an institutional or community setting, by those known to them or more rarely, by a stranger, for example, via the internet. They may be abused by an adult or adults, or another child or children.*

Child abuse can be very difficult to detect as it usually takes place behind closed doors and can take the form of a 'one-off' event or a series of events that can span a long period of time. It is not always detected during early childhood and can come to light or be disclosed some considerable time after it occurred. The impact on children regardless of the degree, extent, duration, frequency or whether it was premeditated can be traumatising and lifelong. Child abuse presents an unwelcome and direct challenge to the values and beliefs enshrined in society about the care and safety of children, family life and the nature of parenthood (Parton, 1985).

Beliefs about acceptable and unacceptable ways of treating children and the threshold at which to intervene in the face of assessing need and risk against intrusion into family life can pose difficult decisions for professionals to make. For these reasons, the private act of child abuse becomes a matter of public interest and concern that can lead to moral outrage and anger. Social workers have long been criticised by the media for failing to protect children, receiving a negative public perception, however, media coverage of the Victoria Climbié Inquiry (Laming, 2003) and the Peter Connelly serious case review (Department for Education, 2010), also began to highlight problems within other professional groups. While the media is responsible for publishing damning reports on the failure of professionals, they also have a duty to inform the public of social care issues and to promote public awareness and can play a key role in influencing policy on child death cases, abuse and neglect (Elsley, 2010). This 'blame culture' that exists within child protection work when children are abused or die can lead to child protection professionals and services feeling undermined and devalued, despite incompetencies and failure being highlighted in a minority of cases compared to the vast number that lead to successful outcomes for children and their families.

Types of abuse

There are four categories of abuse in use in the UK child protection system: physical abuse, emotional abuse, sexual abuse and neglect. Table 10.1 provides an adapted overview of how the categories are interpreted (Department for Children, Schools and Families, 2010: 38–39).

In general, when a child has been abused, more than one type of abuse or neglect can be present. For example, if a child has been a victim of physical or sexual abuse, it is also important to consider the emotional effect on the child's intellectual development and behaviour. When trying to recognise all forms of abuse, it is important to consider any kind of abuse within the context of the different cultural approaches to discipline. Aronson Fontes (2005) provides a detailed overview of working with diverse families and recognising child abuse within the context of culture.

Table 10.1 Categories of abuse

Physical abuse	Hitting, shaking, throwing, poisoning, burning or scalding, drowning, suffocating, or fabricating the symptoms of, or deliberately inducing illness in a child
Emotional abuse	Persistent emotional maltreatment of a child, such as to cause severe and adverse effects on the child's emotional development. Conveying to children they are worthless and unloved, inadequate or valued only insofar as they meet the needs of another person. Not giving the child opportunities to express their views, deliberately silencing them or 'making fun' of what they say or how they communicate. It may feature age or developmentally inappropriate expectations being imposed on children or interactions beyond the child's developmental capability. Over-protection and limitation of exploration and learning or preventing the child participating in normal social interactions. Seeing or hearing the ill-treatment of another. Serious bullying (including cyber-bullying), causing children to frequently feel frightened or in danger or the exploitation or corruption of children
Sexual abuse	Forcing or enticing a child or young person to take part in sexual activities, whether or not the child is aware of what is happening. Physical contact including assault or penetration (for example, rape or oral sex) or non-penetrative acts, such as masturbation, kissing, rubbing and touching outside of clothing. Involving children in looking at, or in the production of sexual images, watching sexual activities, encouraging children to behave in sexually inappropriate ways, or grooming a child in preparation for abuse (including via the internet)
Neglect	The persistent failure to meet a child's basic physical and/or psychological needs, likely to result in the serious impairment of the child's health or development. Failing to provide adequate food, clothing and shelter or protecting a child from physical and emotional harm or danger. Ensuring adequate supervision and access to appropriate medical care or treatment or not responding to a child's basic emotional needs. It may occur during pregnancy as a result of maternal substance abuse

Physical abuse

Physical abuse can include fingertip bruising on the body, arms and legs, bruising to the cheeks, particularly in babies, sometimes accompanied by a torn fraenulum, which may indicate that the child has been gripped by the face during force-feeding, bruising that shows the shape of a hand or other object with which the child may have been hit or bruises of different ages defined by their colour, small round burns, which may be caused by a cigarette, and burns and scalds in unusual places, or with a neatly defined shape or bite marks. Internal injuries are difficult to detect but can result in pain, fever, vomiting, restlessness and difficulty in breathing. Physical abuse also includes broken bones, head injuries or unlikely or inconsistent explanations for injuries and those that go untreated. It may cause a change in behaviour in the abused child and a pattern of behaviour in the perpetrator. The behaviour in the child will vary a great deal with the age of the child (Hobart and Frankel, 2001)

Generally, physical injuries are easier to detect due to their visibility. It is not, however, straightforward in terms of determining those which are accidental and those that have been inflicted. We would expect a medical professional to examine and determine the cause of injuries, although other professionals working with children do need to be able to recognise signs and symptoms in order to make a judgement about suspicious injuries and to seek the opinion of a medical practitioner (Beckett, 2007). Parents are also not the only perpetrators of physical abuse. Older siblings, relatives or others taking care of the child can also be responsible. Living in large families, in deprivation and poverty can also increase the risk to children, particularly younger children who are more vulnerable and dependent on their caregivers. Children with disabilities can also be at heightened risk as a result of the level of physical care needed, often by a number of different carers, and in some cases as a result of not having the mental capacity to recognise abuse or the ability to communicate abuse that is taking place. Howe (2005: 69) also reminds us that:

All aggression by others causes those who are attacked to feel threatened, aroused and distressed. The younger and therefore the more helpless the child, the more fear and agitation are suffered. This is a reminder that physical abuse is not just a body blow; it is also an assault on one's psychological integrity.

Emotional abuse and neglect

Emotional abuse and neglect are not as easy to detect as specific incidents, such as physical and sexual assault that can be medically examined, although it could also be argued that you are more likely to witness incidents of emotional abuse and neglect taking place in day-to-day encounters between children and their parents and carers. However, what constitutes emotional abuse and neglect can often be enshrined in the witness' own experiences and perceptions, making it an area of potential disagreement between professionals.

Neglect is the failure to provide minimum standards of care to meet the basic needs of the child. It needs to be considered in relation to physical neglect, educational neglect and emotional neglect (see Hobart and Frankel, 2001: 67–69 for a detailed list). Generally, you would look for:

- poor levels of physical development, being underweight and short in stature for the child's age or the child appearing thin and looking unhealthy
- poor hygiene, e.g. dirty, smelly clothes, unwashed body and hair, persistent nappy rash, inadequate clothing, hunger or overeating
- tiredness
- lack of interest, difficult to stimulate

- persistent minor illnesses, e.g. colds, coughs, diarrhoea or injuries that have not been attended to
- the child may be persistently late to school or frequently miss school, although older children may hang around before and after school
- unresponsive to adults or indiscriminate in seeking attention from adults
- sudden and noticeable improvements in all aspects of the child's behaviour and appearance when there is a change in the care situation.

A child who is brought up in a home where he or she is unloved, unwanted, made to feel worthless or inconvenient or who is rejected, bullied, ridiculed, shouted at, undermined or made to feel a failure is likely to find it difficult to respond appropriately to his or her own or other people's emotional needs. This can have a direct impact on their development, causing delay, comfort-seeking behaviour, fear of new situations and low self-esteem and a lack of confidence. Children can swing between being passive or aggressive, withdraw or may inappropriately seek attention through telling lies, stealing or throwing temper tantrums. Some children will have poor concentration, may wet the bed, find it difficult to maintain social relationships or to enjoy themselves and have fun. In extreme cases, it can lead to self-mutilation.

Parents and carers who emotionally abuse a child, may have a history of being abused or neglected themselves, and may not have had a strong attachment to a caregiver. Equally, they may have a mental illness or personality disorder, or have a drug or alcohol addiction or may be in a difficult situation or relationship that prevents them from having the capacity to notice their abuse or neglect of a child (Hobart and Frankel, 2001). Howe (2005: 90) refers to this as 'psychological maltreatment', in terms of parents and carers failing either wilfully or defensively to respond to distress presented by their child. Beckett (2007: 70) refers to negative verbal and non-verbal 'messages' being given to the child. Recognising that even the most caring parents at times can emotionally abuse their child if they are tired or pre-occupied, leading to them doing or saying hurtful things in anger or frustration, most parents however will recognise this behaviour and feel remorse, regret, even guilt and can convey this to the child who is likely to have some level of resilience, as all children do, to overcome it. It is when negative messages become persistent and predominant with a lack of insight from the parent or carer that the emotional abuse to the child can become serious and damaging.

It is fair to say that children who experience other types of abuse are also likely to feel the effects of emotional abuse, so these indicators may be apparent alongside the signs of physical or sexual abuse or neglect. For a detailed discussion on issues that surround identifying emotional and psychological abuse, see O'Hagan (2006).

Sexual abuse
Sexual abuse is an abuse of power and a violation of a child's right to a safe and caring and trusting relationship. It is often undertaken without physical force as a result of children loving and being dependent on their caregivers. Younger children may not even be aware they are being sexually abused, believing it happens to everyone. Children may become aware that it is wrong but may have limited understanding, knowledge or experiences to compare it with. Sexual abuse can happen to boys and girls and is perpetrated by men and women and other children. It is not class related or culturally distinct and can occur in all types of families, and across all religious groups. The majority of children who are abused

know the perpetrator. Acts committed by a stranger, which are rarer, would be considered to be sexual assault rather than sexual abuse and would be investigated by the police and criminal courts. In general, you would look for:

- soreness, redness, bruising and cuts around the genitals or anus
- pain or discomfort around the vagina or penis, or the anus
- discomfort or difficulty in walking and sitting
- discharge or bleeding from the vagina or penis
- pain during urination
- sexual knowledge and/or behaviour that seem inappropriate to a child's age and maturity. Sexual play with other children that demonstrates sophisticated knowledge
- running away, anxiety, despair. Fear of certain adults, withdrawal from children
- acting out sexual scenes through play or drawing
- regressive behaviour, for example thumb-sucking, wetting the bed, fear of the dark
- anger, hostility, aggression towards adults and other children
- behaviour and achievements in nursery or school deteriorate
- sleep and eating disturbances
- telling lies
- unexplained or psychosomatic illnesses
- persistent masturbation
- self-dramatising behaviour, for example tantrums, attention-seeking behaviour, elaborate fantasies, hysterical attacks, weeping fits
- promiscuity, and in older girls, pregnancy, sexually transmitted diseases

(Hobart and Frankel, 2001: 71–710).

In more recent times, the discourses surrounding child sexual abuse have taken on new dimensions, largely as a result of the feminist movement and adult survivors of child sexual abuse speaking out. Children are being encouraged to come forward, backed by national projects such as the NSPCC and Childline. There has been a growth in research and literature that consider the long-term effects of child sexual abuse and therapeutic approaches to working with children and adult survivors. Research around the effectiveness and outcomes of different approaches remains, however, underactive and today we recognise child sexual abuse as a long-standing problem that needs to be adequately addressed. While the scale of the problem of sexual abuse is beginning to be recognised and to receive considerable media attention, there are still many individuals and childcare professionals who continue to minimise or deny the scope and severity of the problem (Wickham and West, 2002: 1). The emotional and psychological impact of both physical and sexual abuse can last a lifetime, with consequences for adult relationships and for the next generation when adult survivors of abuse become parents themselves.

The long-term effects of sexual abuse include self-destructive behaviour, anxiety, feelings of isolation and stigma, poor self-esteem, substance abuse, sexual problems and psychological problems. Survivors of child sexual abuse are more likely to become mentally ill and/or develop obsessive-compulsive behaviour (Wyatt and Powell, 1988). Indeed, all forms of child abuse and neglect do not only pose a considerable amount of harm and danger to the child or young person when the abuse is taking place, but can also cause a considerable amount of distress and trauma throughout the course of a person's life.

Prevalence

In the United Kingdom, national statistics of the extent of child abuse were not recorded until 1988. Since this time, the Department of Health has collated the numbers of children on child protection registers in England on an annual basis, and more recently, since the abolishment of registers, the number of children who are subject to child protection plans. In 2010, figures were then taken from the children in need census. It is important to remember, however, that any statistics will only measure the extent of abuse in cases that become known to local authorities; there will always be cases of child abuse that are not reported or go undetected. Table 10.2 provides an overview of the numbers of children on child protection plans from the period 2007 to 2011 and Table 10.3 shows the number of children on a child protection plan by age and gender (Department for Education, 2011a).

Table 10.2 shows that figures have consistently risen across the five-year period with emotional abuse and neglect accounting for 72 per cent of cases, although it is also these two categories of abuse, alongside others, that are more likely to also account for the majority of the 5000 children recorded as experiencing multiple forms of abuse. Table 10.3 demonstrates there is little variation between boys and girls and that there are fewer recorded cases of children under one, who may be much more difficult to detect if they are not accessing health or social care services. Children over the age of 16 years, where there are even fewer

Table 10.2 Numbers of children on child protection plans from 2007 to 2011

	2007	2008	2009	2010	2011
Neglect	12 500	13 400	15 800	17 200	18 700
Physical abuse	3500	3400	4400	4700	4500
Sexual abuse	2000	2000	2000	2200	2300
Emotional abuse	7100	7900	9100	11 400	12 100
Multiple	2700	2500	2900	3400	5000
Total	27 900	29 200	34 100	39 100	42 700

Table 10.3 Number of children on child protection plans by age and gender at the end of March 2011

	Boys	Girls	All children
Unborn			738
Under 1 year	2360	2190	4630
1–4 years	6980	6430	13 420
5–9 years	6110	5840	11 970
10–15 years	5520	5360	10 890
16 years and over	430	580	1010
Unknown age	10	10	30
Total	21 420	20 420	42 960

recorded cases, are more likely to be able to manage the abuse, minimise it through avoiding abusive situations and not report it through fear of losing a parent or care-giver or being moved into the child care system. Children aged between 2 and 15 years are more likely to be attending nursery, a children's centre or school, where frequent contact with health care and teaching professionals makes abuse easier to detect. Equally, as the child grows older and becomes more aware and knowledgeable of abuse taking place, the chances of it being reported are increased.

Documentation of the scale of child abuse is generally categorised into two types: 'incidence studies' that attempt to estimate the number of new cases usually within a year and 'prevalence studies' that attempt to estimate the proportion of a population that have been abused in the course of their childhood. Research studies can, however, be fraught with problems, largely as a result of the many definitions of what constitutes child abuse. Studies can also vary according to what ages, facts and types of relationships are being examined and measured. This makes comparisons difficult (Finkelhor, 1986). Prevalence and incidence studies of child abuse may be marred by definition and methodological problems, but can, if carefully interpreted, add to our understanding of the problem (Corby, 2006).

The prevalence of child abuse is also related to the situations and people that can cause child abuse to occur. Although both mothers and fathers and others known to the child can and do abuse children, it is generally thought that mothers are mainly responsible for abusing children in cases of neglect and physical abuse, especially younger children, and that fathers or father substitutes are more likely to be responsible for acts of intra-familial sexual abuse of children (Corby, 2006). Masson and Erooga (1999) have also focused on the abuse of children by adolescents.

With an increasing divorce rate, a rise in single parent families, young mothers and step-families, children are more likely to be exposed to abuse (Fox-Harding, 1996). The vast majority of children do live healthy and fulfilling lives in all sorts of family situations, however living with an older sibling or parent or carer that is not related to the child can increase the chances of abuse taking place. This is largely as a result of problems developing in the forming of new relationships and, in the case of older children, through developing physical relationships based on familiarity and a lack of kinship that can be used as an excuse for sexual contact, with or without consent, and with no consideration for the young person's age.

Inexperienced young mothers and fathers who may have been abused themselves and/or have not been exposed to 'adequate and safe parenting practices', may find the pressure of parenting difficult to manage, resulting in the abuse and neglect of their children (Baldwin and Oliver 1975; Greenland 1987). Equally, children living in poverty are more likely to be exposed to parents and carers who have mental health problems or drug and alcohol addiction. Compounded with unemployment and limited funds, this can exacerbate their ability to safely parent their children. The Department of Health's 1995 'Messages from Research' showed that 95 per cent of children who were on child protection registers at the time, were from poor families.

Domestic violence is another area that can expose children to abuse. One in four women will experience domestic violence in their lifetime and two women per week are killed by current or ex partners (Women's Aid, 2012). The Department of Health (2002) also estimated that 750 000 children a year witness domestic violence and in some cases will suffer physical or sexual abuse from the same perpetrator. Children can get caught up in domestic violence incidents, can witness it directly or hear it behind closed doors. Section 120 of the Children and Adoption Act 2002 now recognises that all children witnessing domestic violence are being emotionally abused and can be subjected to 'significant harm'. Mullender *et al.* (2003) have raised awareness and conducted research around the importance of listening to the experiences of children living with domestic violence.

The majority of children now also have access to computers in their homes and learning environments increasing the likelihood of online abuse. This can be in the form of cyber-bullying, whereby children can receive an upsetting or abusive message that can pose a risk to the child on its own or escalate or be part of an ongoing wider bullying campaign (Bond, 2010; Bond and Carter, 2011). With the growth in social networking sites, such as Facebook and Twitter, and the wide use of email, chat and instant messaging, it can be easy for children to find themselves communicating online with potential abusers, and vulnerable children can be groomed into meeting up, can lose their privacy or be exposed to inappropriate material.

In 2009, the NSPCC launched its 'Keeping Children Safe Online Campaign', calling for a clamp down on individuals that view and share indecent images online. Despite this, the Child Exploitation and Online Protection Centre reported in their 2012 study on threats to children that 'images are becoming more extreme, sadistic and violent' with children in the images getting younger and the offences committed against them more extreme. Although the internet is fundamentally a great place for children to learn and enjoy activities, it has nonetheless increased opportunities for children to be abused.

While we need to remain acutely aware of the situations and people that can abuse and cause harm to children, this needs to be balanced with the recognition that all children manage situations differently; their support structures, coping mechanisms, personalities and factors surrounding the abuse will impact on the level of resilience a child will display in the face of adversity (Corby, 2006).

The child protection system and safeguarding

The child protection system in the UK is characterised by an elaborate set of organisational arrangements, designed to secure 'joint working' among the many agencies and professionals involved. *Working Together to Safeguard Children* (Department for Children, Schools and Families, 2010: 7) sets out 'how organisations and individuals should work together to safeguard and promote the welfare of children and young people in accordance with the Children Act 1989 and Children Act 2004'. It is therefore of vital importance that all professionals working to safeguard children and young people understand fully their responsibilities and duties as set out in primary legislation and associated regulations and guidance. Chapter 2 of the *Working Together to Safeguard Children* guidance details the roles and responsibilities of all the key professionals and agencies. Chapter 5 details the managing of individual cases where there are concerns about a child's safety and welfare, including five flow charts that explore what happens through the various stages (Department for Children, Schools and Families, 2010: 87–190).

When a referral is received that highlights that a child 'may be at risk of significant harm', urgent action is taken to safeguard the welfare of the child. A strategy discussion will take place between the local authority, police and other agencies as required to clarify the concerns and the 'risk'. If confirmed, a Section 47 (Children Act, 1989, S. 47) enquiry is initiated. A social worker will lead the completion of a core assessment (Department of Health, 2000), which will include input from other professionals and at the same time a police investigation will begin if a suspected crime has been committed. If the concerns are substantiated, a child protection conference is convened within 15 days of the initial strategy discussion and will include all the relevant professionals that work with and/or have contact with the child. If the child is considered to be at risk, the child becomes subject to a child protection plan, which is outlined and a core group of professionals are established.

The core group will meet within 10 days of the child protection conference, to develop the plan and commission further specialist assessments as necessary. A review conference is held within three months and every six months thereafter for as long as the child is subject to a child protection plan. The core group of professionals will continue to meet 'sufficiently regularly' to implement and review the plan until a conference decides it can be discontinued. The child protection plan should be explained to and agreed with the child in a manner which is in accordance with their age and understanding and parents should be clear about the evidence of significant harm (Department for Children, Schools and Families, 2010: 93–93). Children in accordance with age and understanding and parents/carers will be invited to attend conferences and core group meetings, if this is not likely to put the child at further 'risk of harm'.

The child protection system is underpinned by Local Safeguarding Children's Boards mandated through the Children Act 2004, which are responsible for developing thresholds, policy and procedure, communicating to relevant bodies and raising awareness and monitoring and evaluating the effectiveness of the system. They undertake serious case reviews in the event of a child's death and arrange and identify multi-agency training. They also have joint responsibility with Children's Trusts Boards to 'promote co-operation to improve the well-being of children in the local area across the *Every Child Matters* outcomes' (Department for Children, Schools and Families, 2010: 99). This includes ensuring workforce strategies are developed and making sure training opportunities are available. Despite these robust systems being put in place, inter-agency collaboration, as we have seen, remains problematic.

Inter-agency collaboration and working in partnership

It is clear from the numerous serious case reviews and revisions of the *Working Together to Safeguard Children* guidance (Department for Children, Schools and Families, 2010) that we are still not functioning at a level that would suggest that inter-agency collaboration is effective enough to fully safeguard and promote the welfare of children. This is further supported by the current consultation that is taking place to make further changes to the *Working Together to Safeguard Children* guidance at the end of this year (Loughton, 2012) in line with supporting Munro's (Department for Education, 2011b) recommendations to remove time-frames from assessment processes so that more time can be gained working directly with families to promote further engagement and stronger partnership working with children and their families. The trend across the last 20 years to increase recognition of the need for professionals to work more effectively together is therefore one that is set to continue. Gasper (2010: 9) explains:

> There has been a growing understanding that service structures and relationships are no longer adequate to meet changing needs, and that this combined with the growing understanding of the consequences of poverty in terms of health, social and educational deprivation ... has required effective lobbying from early years, health and social care professionals to break cycles of deprivation by developing shared understanding and more coherent and joined up practice.

Developing effective partnership working among professionals also requires the same process to be applied to work with children and families deemed to be 'at risk'.

The majority of families will experience high levels of stress during child protection procedures that can lead to intrusion into family life. They can feel they are being treated 'like a criminal', that they have 'limited influences on decision making', and that participation in conferences and professional meetings can feel 'daunting and intimidating' (Ghaffar *et al.*, 2011: 2–8). This clearly impacts on the ability of professionals to build effective working relationships with children and families which require empathic professionals who have the skills to engage, as well as the ability to empower families taking a strengths perspective that is underpinned with a commitment to be transparent, honest, trustworthy and supportive.

Brandon *et al.* (2006) examined what could help or hinder practitioners implementing the multi-agency common assessment framework, stating that professionals can feel hindered by the emotional impact of the work, generating fear and anxiety and a lack of confidence around using new skills. Confusion about processes was highlighted as having a tendency to cause bickering and professional mistrust. Power, status and trust have long been recognised as having an impact on the ability of professionals to collaborate and work in partnership with families. Professionals can become preoccupied with status, centred on self-interest and concern about threats to their autonomy. Health professionals adopting a medical model approach based on facts that can be evidenced can often lead to assumed authority. However, the social model adopted by social care professionals that supports parameters shifting and changing situations and relationships, and works on the notion that it is not always possible to verify information that is shared or investigated, makes it easier for social care assessments and judgements to be mistrusted or criticised. We can therefore assume that although social care professionals may seem to hold the power in their position of having to take on the role of 'lead professional' in child protection cases, this is not what is necessarily perceived or experienced by them within inter-agency forums.

Developing a greater understanding of professional roles and responsibility can lead to clarity and mutual expectations. An entire chapter is devoted to this in the *Working Together to Safeguard Children* guidance (Department for Children, Schools and Families, 2010: 40–86). A diffusion of roles or an overlap of roles, if not understood, can lead to professionals repeating work with children and families and causing frustration and confusion. A clear illustration of this can be found if, for example, social workers and health visitors do not communicate about the support and intervention they are putting in place around 'healthy eating' and 'keeping safe' work. Collaboration and communication, if effective, would ensure that the professionals better equipped with a stronger connection to the family and access to resources would undertake the direct work or that a clear understanding is conveyed to all parties if the work is to be shared (Hallet, 1995). Indeed, the aggregation of skills and resources from different professionals has been emphasised since the late 1960s (Helfer and Kempe, 1968). Mouzakitis and Goldstein (1985: 218) in a discussion of multidisciplinary practice stated that 'no one discipline could understand and handle such a complex problem. Various disciplines make distinct contributions to a comprehensive diagnosis of the abusive family and the abused or neglected child.' This clear message is one that still needs to be reinforced today alongside the need to communicate and share information to prevent further abuse and neglect of children who are subject to child protection plans.

Professional networks ultimately provide the basis for information to be transmitted. As well as verbal exchanges of information, opinion and judgement during child protection case conferences and core group meetings, both verbal and written communication should remain at an optimum level in-between such meetings. Shared information should be accurate, up to date and necessary for the purpose for which it is being shared and clear records need to be kept. Equally, children and families should give consent and be informed about information sharing, unless a court order is in place, and even in these cases it is good practice to seek consent. This links to the importance of building relationships based on honesty and openness (Spray and Jowett, 2012: 53).

One of the key issues around communication and information sharing is the problems encountered with professional organisations using different IT systems. In support of the integrated children's system, a computer database called ContactPoint was launched in 2008 to hold information about every child in England and designed to enable information sharing between agencies. This was disbanded in 2010 due to concerns around security and to date has not been replaced. The government will instead be trying to capitalise on opportunities for existing IT systems to be used to improve information sharing in child protection practice.

Inter-agency collaboration and partnership working requires us to be mindful of the implications that can impact on children and their families. If we become too focused on power, status and mistrust or if we ineffectively communicate and share information without using a common language, if we are not clear about our roles and responsibilities and do not participate in joint training and learn from changing policy and procedure, research and serious case reviews, then we are not able to maximise the resources that can be 'pooled' from the expertise and experience of our different professions. Equally, parents and carers are more likely to conceal information and maintain negative views of professional involvement if we do not ensure they have an understanding of the safeguarding responsibilities of professionals working with them and their children. As early years professionals, we need to be taking a 'family-orientated' approach to intervention, that remains child-centred and values the wishes and feelings of children, upholding their rights to be included in decisions made about their welfare (Children's Rights Alliance, 2012). This needs to be supported with a consistent response from professionals to effectively 'work together' and identify available resources.

Throughout this chapter, we have been able to identify that multi-agency working and working in partnership is not a rhetorical notion. It does happen and is widely accepted as a central component of the child protection system. It is not, however, functioning at a level that could give cause to celebrate. While it is impossible to completely eradicate the abuse and neglect, and in some cases the death of children, we need to continue to strive to detect and safeguard the welfare of all vulnerable children who find themselves entrusted to our care.

Learning activity

As we have seen throughout this chapter, law and policy guidance is always undergoing change and development and this is set to continue. Keep yourself up to date with these changes by regularly visiting government websites relevant to your area of work.

Conclusion

This chapter has provided you with a brief overview of the history of legislation, policy and procedure that has led to the current laws and policy that support the child protection system in force today. It has identified key child death inquiries and serious case reviews raising concerns around the complex issues facing professionals working in a multidisciplinary setting, as well as highlighting what we need to learn from them. We have explored the signs and symptoms of abuse, and considered prevalence, making links to key areas where children may be more exposed to 'risk' and 'harm'. We have briefly journeyed through the process that exists in the child protection system, exploring issues that can arise through the process of working together and building effective partnerships, linking in signposts for further reading and research. Ultimately, we have learned that the multidisciplinary child protection system has not evolved without presenting some problems. If, however, it is embraced by all professionals working with children and families subjected to child protection investigations and plans, with a clear commitment to co-operate with each other, while truly engaging families and maintaining a focus on the child, it can potentially be effective.

Evaluate your learning

- Detecting child abuse is not an exact science, but the number of children on child protection plans have risen year on year. What do you think are the contributing factors and to what extent do you feel government statistics reflect the true nature of child abuse in the UK?
- How can our very robust and risk-focused child protection system in the UK maintain its processes at the same time as taking a more family-orientated approach that promotes partnership working?
- Professional core groups are a fundamental aspect of ensuring a child protection plan is monitored and progressed. How can professionals make effective use of core group meetings, both in terms of taking an inclusive approach with children and families and ensuring inter-agency collaboration is being upheld?

References

Allen, G (2011): *Early Intervention: The Next Steps*: An Independent Report to Her Majesty's Government. London: HM Government.

Aronson Fontes, L (2005): *Child Abuse and Culture: Working with Diverse Families*. New York: The Guilford Press.

Baldwin, JA and Oliver, JE (1975): Epidemiology and family characteristics of severely abused children. *British Journal of Preventive and Social Medicine* **29**, 205.

Beckett, C (2007): *Child Protection. An Introduction*, 2nd edn. London: Sage.

Bichard, M (2004): *The Bichard Inquiry Report*. London: The Stationery Office.

Bond, E (2010): Managing mobile relationships: Children's perceptions of the impact of the mobile phone on relationships in their everyday lives. *Childhood* **17**(4), 514–29.

Bond, E and Carter, P (2011): The Suffolk Cybersurvey. Ipswich: University Campus Suffolk. (Online). Available from: www.ucs.ac.uk.

Bowlby, J (1951): Maternal Care and Mental Health: A Report Prepared on Behalf of the World Health Organisation as a Contribution to the United Nations Programme for the Welfare of Homeless Children. Geneva: World Health Organisation.

Brady, K (1979): *Father's Days: A True Story of Incest*. New York: Dell.

Brandon, M, Howe, A, Dagley, V, Slater, C and Warren, C (2006): What appears to be helping or hindering practitioners in implementing the common assessment framework and lead professional working? *Child Abuse Review* **15**, 396–413.

Butler-Sloss Lord Justice E (1988): Report of the Inquiry into Child Abuse in Cleveland, Cmnd 412, London: HMSO.

Children Act (1989) London. Stationery Office.

Caffey, J (1946): Multiple fractures in the long bones of infants suffering from chronic subdural hematoma. *American Journal of Roentgenology* **56**, 163–73.

Child Exploitation and Online Protection Centre (2012): Threat Assessment of Child Sexual Exploitation and Abuse. (Online). Last accessed July 2012. Available from: http://ceop.police.uk/Documents/ceopdocs/ CEOPThreatA2012_190612_web.pdf.

Children's Rights Alliance (2012): Ready, Steady, Change. (Online). Last accessed July 2012. Available from: www.crae.org.uk/networks/rsc.html.

Children's Workforce Development Council (2010): Common Core of Skills and Knowledge for the Children's Workforce, Supported by the Department for Children, Schools and Families. London: HMSO.

Clyde, Lord (1992): Report of the Inquiry into the Removal of Children from Orkney in February 1991, HoC 195. London: HMSO.

Corby, B (2006): *Child Abuse: Towards a Knowledge Base*, 3rd edn. Buckingham: Open University Press.

Corby, B, Doig, A and Roberts, V (2001) *Public Inquiries into the Abuse of Children in Residential Care*. London. Jessica Kingsley

Curtis Committee (1946): Report of the Care of Children Committee (Training in Child Care), paper number cmd. 6922. House of Commons Parliamentary Papers.

Department for Children, Schools and Families (2007): *The Children's Plan: Building brighter futures – Summary.* London: HMSO.

Department for Children, Schools and Families (2008): *Information Sharing: Guidance for Practitioners and Managers.* Nottingham: DSCF Publications.

Department for Children, Schools and Families (2010): *Working Together to Safeguard Children: A Guide to Inter-agency Working to Safeguard and Promote the Welfare of Children.* London: HM Government.

Department for Education (2004a): *Every Child Matters.* London: HMSO.

Department for Education (2004b): *Safeguarding Children in Education.* London: HMSO.

Department for Education (2010): *Haringey Local Safeguarding Children's Board: Serious Case Review 'Child A' relating to Peter Connelly.* London: HMSO.

Department for Education (2011a): Characteristics of Children in Need in England, 2010–11. (Online). Last accessed July 2012. Available from: www.education.gov.uk/rsgateway/DB/STR/d001041/index.shtml.

Department for Education (2011b): *The Munro Review of Child Protection: Final Report – A Child Centered System.* London: HMSO.

Department for Education and Skills (2005): *Common Assessment Framework.* London: HMSO.

Department of Health (1995): *Child Protection: Messages from Research.* London: HMSO.

Department of Health (1998): *The Quality Protects Programme: Transforming Children's Services*, LAC(98)26. London: HMSO.

Department of Health (1999): *Working Together to Safeguard Children: A Guide to Inter-agency Working to Safeguard and Promote the Welfare of Children.* London: HMSO.

Department of Health (2000): *Framework for the Assessment of Children in Need and their Families.* London: The Stationery Office.

Department of Health (2002): *Women's Mental Health: Into the Mainstream: Strategic Development of Mental Health Care for Women.* London: HMSO.

Department of Health (2004): *National Service Framework for Children, Young People and Maternity Services.* London: HMSO.

Department of Health (2012): *Statutory Framework for the Early Years Foundation Stage.* London: The Stationery Office.

Department of Health and Social Security (1974): *Report of the Committee of Inquiry into the Care and Supervision Provided in Relation to Maria Colwell.* London: HMSO.

Department of Health and Social Security (1985): *Social Work Decisions in Child Care. Recent Research Findings and their Implications.* London. HMSO.

Department of Health and Social Security (1988): *Working Together: A Guide to Inter-agency Cooperation for the Protection of Children from Abuse.* London. HMSO.

Elsey, S (2010): *Media Coverage of Child Deaths in the UK: The impact of Baby P: A Case for Influence?* London: NSPCC: Briefing No.8.

Finkelhor, D (1986): *A Sourcebook on Child Sexual Abuse.* London: Sage.

Fox-Harding, L (1996): *Family, State and Social Policy.* Basingstoke: Macmillan.

Gasper, M (2010): *Multi-agency Working in the Early Years: Challenges and Opportunities.* London: Sage.

Ghaffar, W, Manby, M and Race, T (2011): Exploring the experiences of parents and carers whose children have been subject to child protection plans. *British Journal of Social Work* **10**, 1–8. (Online). Available from: http://bjswoxfordjournals.org/content/early/2011/09/13/ bjsw. bcr132.full.

Greenland, C (1987) *Preventing CAN Deaths: An International Study of Deaths due to Child Abuse and Neglect.* London: Tavistock Publications.

Hallett, C (1995): *Inter-agency Co-ordination in Child Protection.* London. HMSO.

Helfer, RE and Kempe, CH (eds) (1968): *The Battered Child.* Chicago: University Press.

Hobart, C and Frankel, J (2001): *Good Practice in Child Protection.* Cheltenham: Nelson Thornes Ltd.

Home Office (1945): *Report by Sir Walter Monckton on the Circumstances that Led to the Boarding-out of Dennis and Terrance O'Neil at Bank Farm, Minsterley and the Steps Taken to Supervise their Welfare.* Cmd. 6636. London: HMSO.

Howe, D (2005): *Child Abuse and Neglect: Attachment, Development and Intervention.* Basingstoke: Palgrave Macmillan.

Hoyle, D (2008): Problematizing Every Child Matters, (Online). Last accessed July 2012. Available from: www.infed.org/socialwork/every_child_matters_a_critique.htm.

Kempe, C, Silverman, F, Steele, B, Droegemueller, W and Silver, H (1962): The battered child syndrome. *Journal of the American Medical Association* **181**, 17–24.

La Fontaine, J (1994): *The Extent and Nature of Organised and Ritual Abuse: Research Findings.* London: HMSO.

Laming, Lord (2003): *Victoria Climbié Inquiry.* London: HMSO.

Laming, Lord (2009): *The Protection of Children in England: A Progress Report.* London: The Stationery Office.

Levy, A and Kahan, B (1991): *The Pindown Experience and the Protection of Children.* Stafford: Staffordshire County Council.

London Borough of Brent (1985): *A Child in Trust: The Report of the Panel of Inquiry into the Circumstances Surrounding the Death of Jasmine Beckford.* London: London Borough of Brent.

Loughton, T (2012): Speech: Tim Loughton Addressed Community Care Live. (Online). Last accessed July 2012. Available from: www.education.gov.uk/childrenandyoungpeople/social/a00209139/community-care-live.

Masson, H and Erooga, M (1999): Children and young people who sexually abuse others: incidence characteristics, causation. In Erooga, M and Masson, H (eds), *Children and Young People who Sexually Abuse Others: Challenges and Responses.* London: Routledge.

Mouzakitis, CM and Goldstein, SC (eds) (1985): A multidisciplinary approach to treading child neglect. *Social Casework* **4**(66), 218–24.

Mullender, A, Hague, G, Iman, U, Kelly, L, Malos, E and Regan, L (2003): *Children's Perspectives on Domestic Violence.* London: Sage.

Munro E (2002): *Effective Child Protection.* London: Sage Publications.

National Society of the Prevention of Cruelty to Children (NSPCC) (2009): Keeping Children Safe Online Campaign. Press release. (Online). Available from: www.nspcc.org.uk/news-and-views/media-centre/press-releases/2009/09-06-15-campaign-to-keep-children-safe-online/09-06 15_NSPCC_launches_campaign_to_keep_children_safe_online_wdn75029 .html.

National Society of the Prevention of Cruelty to Children (NSPCC) (2011): A Survey of the Government's Response to the Munro Report. (Online). Last accessed July 2012. Available from: www.nspcc.org.uk/inform/research/briefings/government_response_to_munro_wda83247.html.

O'Hagan, K (2006): *Identifying Emotional and Psychological Abuse: A guide for Childcare Professionals.* Berkshire: Open University Press.

Parton, N (1979): The natural history of child abuse: a study in social problem definition. *British Journal of Social Work* **9**, 431–51.

Parton, N (1985): *The Politics of Child Abuse.* London: Macmillan.

Polnay, J and Polnay, L (2007): *Child Protection Reader: Recognition and Response in Child Protection.* London: Royal College of Paediatrics and Child Health.

Reder, P, Duncan, S and Gray, M (1993): *Beyond Blame: Child Abuse Tragedies Revisited.* London: Routledge.

Seebohm, F (1968): *Report of the Committee on Local Authority and Allied Personal Social Services,* Cmnd 3703. London: HMSO.

Siraj-Blatchford, I, Clarke, K and Needham, M (2007): *The Team Around the Child: Multi-agency Working in the Early Years.* London: Trentham Books Limited.

Spencer, J (1989): *Suffer the Child.* New York: Simon and Schuster.

Spray, C and Jowett, B (2012): *Social Work Practice with Children and Families.* London: Sage.

Utting, Sir W (1991): *Children in the Public Care: A Review of Residential Child Care.* London: HMSO.

Waterhouse, Sir R (2000): *Lost in Care: The Report of the Tribunal of Inquiry into the Abuse of Children in Care in the Former County Council Areas of Gwynedd and Clwyd since 1974,* HC 201. London: The Stationery Office.

Wickham, RE and West, J (2002): *Therapeutic Work with Sexually Abused Children.* London: Sage Publications.

Women's Aid (2012): Statistics. (Online). Last accessed July 2012. Available from: www.womensaid.org.uk/ domestic violence topic.asp.

Wyatt GE and Powell, GJ (eds) (1988): *Lasting Effects of Child Sexual Abuse.* Newbury Park, CA: Sage.

Further reading

Aldgate, J, Jones, D, Rose, W and Jeffrey, C (2004) *The Developing World of the Child.* London. Jessica Kingsley.

Davis, JM and Smith, M (2012) *Working in Multi-Professional Contexts: A Guide for Professionals in Children's Services.* London: Sage.

Ferguson, H (2011) *Child Protection Practice.* Basingstoke: Palgrave Macmillan.

Trotter, C (2004) *Helping Abused Children and their Families.* London: Sage.

11 Child health

Jayne Taylor and Helen Donovan

This chapter aims to:
- explore the origins of child health practice from an historical perspective
- discuss the current situation and the changes to commissioning of children's healthcare and public health
- highlight key issues in working with ill children and in particular the need for partnership working as a way of minimising the impact of illness.

Introduction

This chapter explores child health and the importance of understanding our responsibilities for promoting good health and how we can better work with children during episodes of acute and longer-term ill health. It is not intended to be a manual of childhood illness, but recognises that when working in early years settings there will be frequent occasions when workers are faced with acute childhood illness and when workers will be involved with children who have longer-term conditions, such as asthma or diabetes. The chapter includes a very brief synopsis of the key historic milestones in health services for children and current policy as it relates to the organisation of health and well-being services for young children. The chapter will then move on to explore key issues in child health, including the state of children's health; childhood obesity, physical exercise, immunisation; and childhood illness including acute ill-health and long-term conditions. It will particularly emphasise the need for partnership working between different parts of the health services system, schools and social care.

Child health: a national concern?

The 2012 Children and Young People's Health Outcomes Forum report (Department of Health, 2012a) highlighted the need to improve healthcare services for children and the need for coordinated services to be available for children. The report identifies the need for adequate training in child health for all healthcare professionals and particularly those in primary care who will be the first contact for most children. These are noble sentiments but perhaps ones which most people would consider to be obvious for the 21st century and yet fewer than half of all general practitioners in this country have been formally trained in child health (Department of Health, 2012b). As the forum states, there is a sense from the general public that healthcare for children is good. Yet in comparison with our European neighbours, the outcomes for children and young people in the UK are poor, with the UK ranked at the bottom of 21 counties comparing a range of indicators measuring children's health (UNICEF, 2007). The Kennedy review (2010) argues that for decades children's healthcare has been described as a priority and yet also as the 'Cinderella service'. The consequences of the Cinderella service are significant and there needs to be long-term political will to fund and improve services.

A historical view

Our nation's concern with child health is an interesting phenomenon and it is useful to reflect for a moment upon the origin of this concern, so that we may be able to understand it more clearly and perhaps utilise it in a positive way. First, we consider if this concern is new. Certainly in the pre-Victorian era, and to some extent during the Victorian age, the value placed on the lives of children by the nation appeared to be less significant than it is today. That is not to say that parents did not love their children as much as we do now, but rather it reflects the treatment of children by society – particularly the children of the poor and the orphaned. According to Cox (1983), many of these children grew up in the workhouses or, worse, ended up on the streets of the major cities. Kosky (1992), in an account of the founding of the Queen Elizabeth Hospital in Hackney Road, cites an account in the *Daily News* from 1870, which vividly describes the plight of such children:

> In this district of Bethnal Green, in the centre of which the new child's hospital stands, we know of hundreds of tiny breadwinners of two and a half years upwards. It is here that the trade of Lucifer boxes absorbs the energies of infants long before they can speak, and where street after street can be shown full of little workers who pass from infancy to childhood and from childhood to maturity without ever seeing a toy or gazing upon a green field.

Concern over children's heath has had interesting discrepancies over the years. From sentimental stories about children suffering from terrible diseases like polio to more recent news reports and concern for children living with terrible disability. The BBC's Children in Need fund-raising success focuses on the plight of sick and needy children to tug at the public's heartstrings and as such raises phenomenal amounts of money, and yet sick children in history and now do not always receive adequate medical care or protection. Surprisingly, many attempts to help the plight of children have met with marked opposition over the years. This is probably mainly due to their ability to provide cheap labour for the powerful industrialists and at least some income (albeit meagre) for the family (Kosky, 1992). While various Education Acts (e.g. those passed in 1887 and 1906) introduced social reforms which made education both compulsory and free, and the Coal Mines Act (1845) and various pieces of legislation relating to factories, including the Ten Hours Act of 1847 and the Factory Act of 1901, had limited the legal number of working hours and improved the social conditions of children working in the factories, mines and mills, many children still worked long hours in appalling conditions, and had little or no schooling.

However, even during these seemingly 'dark ages' for children, there were glimmers of the concerns with which we are familiar today. The public health movement of the mid-19th century, for example, which developed following two cholera outbreaks in England, was a prime example of middle-class concern for the children of the poor (and marked the beginning of the health visiting service). Voluntary organisations, such as Barnardos and the National Children's Home, helped many, many homeless and orphaned children, and philanthropists, such as Thomas Coram and Charles West, campaigned tirelessly to open the Foundling Hospital in Coram Fields and the Hospital for Sick Children in London (more commonly known as Great Ormond Street Hospital).

Another development which influenced the nation's view of child health at the beginning of the last century resulted from the 1904 Interdepartmental Committee on Physical Deterioration. The knowledge that over half of the young men who had volunteered for the Boer War were unfit for service had prompted the instigation of the committee which recommended, among other reforms, the setting up of a school health service (Meredith Davies, 1975).

At this time, there was also a growing interest in the infant welfare movement, which led to the establishment of the first milk depots, improved medical and nursing care, developments in pharmaceutics and better sanitation. These measures undoubtedly made a contribution to the fall in the infant mortality rate, which decreased from 163 per 1000 live births in 1899 to less than 100 per 1000 live births in 1915 (Clark, 1973).

Epidemiology and the relationship between the social conditions in which people live and disease is now more clearly understood, starting with the work of John Snow and others in the early 19th century. The epidemiology of diseases and how they affect particular populations is the cornerstone of public health and informs policy on preventative health and social care. Many 'killer' diseases, such as cholera and typhoid, gradually became rarer throughout the 20th century, although scarlet fever, tuberculosis, diphtheria and poliomyelitis were still widely prevalent (Department of Health and Social Security, 1976). In 1947, for example, 7984 cases of poliomyelitis were recorded, and almost 10 per cent of sufferers died. A second major epidemic between 1952 and 1954 saw 845 deaths in the UK (Department of Health and Social Security, 1976). The number of cases of tuberculosis gradually decreased with improved social conditions and diet and with the introduction of mass screening and improved drugs, as well as the introduction of the BCG vaccination in the early 1950s. Diphtheria continued to kill many children a year until the early 1940s. In 1940, when immunisation against diphtheria was introduced, there were more than 61 000 cases with 3283 deaths notified in the UK. By 1957, this had reduced to 38 cases and six deaths in that year (Department of Health, 2012c).

Following the Second World War, and the decline of infectious and nutritional disorders, attention moved away from these childhood problems and tended to focus on children with chronic illness and disability (Hall, 1992). It was recognised that most childhood disability could be traced back to the perinatal period and that 'early intervention might lead to cure or at least substantial improvement' (Hall, 1992: 649). The conviction that if intervention occurred quickly enough, disability would be minimised, led to one of the most dramatic changes in the child health services during the 20th century. No longer were health professionals to wait for parents to notice anomalies in their child's development and then to seek help. Instead, health professionals needed to go out and assess development in a proactive way so that intervention could be instigated as soon as possible. Nor, according to Hall (1992), was it thought sufficient only to focus upon those children who were thought to be at risk. All children should be brought into the assessment process, and routine developmental screening should be a universal activity.

As a result of these convictions our child health services developed along two almost mutually exclusive pathways during the last decades of the 20th century. First, we had the preventative child health services – community-based healthcare professionals, including health visitors and school nurses – who spent significant amounts of their time undertaking mass screening of the childhood population. The preoccupation with screening was however, according to Hall and Elliman (2003), not only wasteful in terms of resource allocation, but also doubtful in terms of its efficacy, given that many of the screening tests being utilised were not based on sound evidence. The revised *Health for All Children* (Hall and Elliman, 2006) guidance advocated the need for universal services and the development of the *Healthy Child Programme* (HCP) (Department of Health, 2009a, 2009b). The HCP has a key role in ensuring that there is an effective early intervention prevention and public health programme offered to all children. It is noted, however, that the priority given to the HCP across the country is variable and services for children as a result are far from universal.

The second pathway has been the development of acute hospital services which have undergone radical change, partially as a result of the implementation of the *National Service Framework (NSF) for Children, Young People and Maternity Services Part 1: Standards for Hospital Services* (DH/DfES, 2004). The problem for the child and the family is that the preventative and therapeutic services have tended to function in separate silos, with little common ground between the two. Add to this picture the input of social services who work in yet a third silo and we can start to see that it is possible for some families to be caught up in at least three bureaucratic systems. This is indeed the story we hear time and time again in our work with children – particularly those with ongoing health needs who have contact with multiple services. Families frequently report having to cope with multiple appointments for children in different locations and on different days (Wolfe, 2011). There is, however, still a growing awareness of the need for properly thought out care pathways linking community and acute services and improved liaison between generalists and specialists (Royal College of General Practitioners, 2012). The Royal College of Paediatrics and Child Health advocate a 'whole system' approach with better networks to support teams working together to support children. The report cites examples of where a whole system approach has been implemented effectively. Acknowledging the effect social factors have on children with particular health problems, such as asthma or complex disability, is probably obvious but all too often does not happen. It is, however, essential to look at the whole child and the whole system if we are to improve the outcomes for children's health (Kenyon *et al.*, 2007).

The situation today

Healthcare over the last 30 years has gradually been moving away from hospital services towards primary care, the aim being to keep children out of hospital wherever possible (Department of Health, 2012b, see www.dh.gov.uk/health/files/2012/07/CYP-Acutely-Ill.pdf).

The emphasis has been to ensure social care is integrated with healthcare and services for children are aligned. The previous version of this book highlighted that 'the situation at the beginning of the 21st century was one of variability'. This is still the same today as highlighted by the HCP (Department of Health, 2009a, 2009b), the Kennedy Report (2010) and the *Children and Young People's Health Outcomes Forum: Report by the Acutely Ill Themes Group* (Department of Health, 2012b). There are examples of excellent care for children, but these are not consistent across the country. The implementation of the Health and Social Care Act (2012) will further affect service delivery for children's healthcare. The act imposes extensive changes to the commissioning of children's services from April 2013 and will have considerable impact on child health services in the next few years.

From April 2013, the Clinical Commissioning Groups (CCGs) and NHS Commissioning Boards (NHS-CB) will broadly take over the commissioning role previously delivered by Primary Care Trusts (PCTs). In addition, public health (PH) teams will move to the local authority (LA) and take over specific PH commissioning. Public Health England (PHE) will take over the roles currently provided by the Health Protection Agency.

The arrangements are complex, but in summary the commissioning of services for children are outlined below:

- Clinical Commissioning Groups will be responsible broadly for commissioning health services to meet the needs of their patients. For children, this will mean children's healthcare, including both physical and mental health, community and acute services.
- NHS Commissioning Boards will be responsible for commissioning more specialist services. This will include the public health services for children to deliver the HCP and health visiting and family nurse partnership. (The intention is that the commissioning for these will move to the local authority public health teams to commission from 2015.) The NHS-CB will also commission newborn screening and maternity services. Immunisation and screening generally will also be the responsibility of the NHS-CB alongside PHE.
- Local authorities will take over the majority of public health functions and be responsible for commissioning the HCP for school-aged children, the national child measurement programme focused on reducing child obesity, and sexual health.

Reducing inequalities

The intention is that services are designed and implemented to meet the needs of the population. However, there needs to be careful work to ensure the changes do not lead to even more patchy care delivery and variable services, what has colloquially been termed the 'postcode lottery of care'. In order to achieve maximum effectiveness, health, education and social services departments will need to work together. The RCPCH Report (2012) and Kennedy Report (2010) cite excellent examples of good partnership working between community child health and social services, and between acute and community-based services. It is perhaps an opportune time to develop further these good practices. Law *et al.* (2012) discuss why policies to reduce inequalities in child health have failed over the years and one of the issues they consider is that more time needs to be given to see the effects of policies which need to be embedded into practice. It is therefore important that, during the changes, where there are examples of good collaborative working these are further developed. Evidence from other countries shows that having all staff trained to a level to be able to support children and families, being able to diagnose and treat problems earlier, would have a significant impact on child mortality and morbidity (Wolfe, 2011). It is also fundamental that the way the effect of policies and child health overall are measured needs to be meaningful and relevant. It is essential that preventative child health services and public health work together to actually reduce inequalities.

In terms of reducing health inequalities across all sectors of children's health services, the *National Service Framework (NSF) for Child Health and Maternity* was published in 2004 (DH/DfES, 2004) as a ten-year programme to support long-term and sustained improvement in children's health. The framework set standards covering services applicable to all children and those relating to specific groups of children: the ill child, the child in hospital, disabled children, children with mental health problems and medicines for children. It also set standards for pregnant women, with the aim to ensure fair, high quality and integrated health and social care, from pregnancy right through to adulthood. It remains a useful guide for child health. The *Healthy Child Programme* (HCP) (Department of Health, 2009a, 2009b) gives more detail to the NSF and provides a framework for care of children starting before birth, in the antenatal period and follows through early childhood to 19 years of age. The programme comprises screening tests, immunisations, developmental reviews, as well as the provision of information, parenting support and guidance on health choices. In addition, it is the mechanism to identify children with particular needs relating to social, physical or mental health to make sure services are available to provide additional help.

More recently, the *Children and Young People's Health Outcome Forum* (Department of Health, 2012b) sets out a programme for change and specifically looks at different themes: mental health, public health and prevention, acute illness, long-term conditions, disability and palliative care and inequalities in health. This will provide a framework for development which aligns with the radical reorganisation of the health services, as described above.

So why do we need to consistently set out frameworks for reducing inequalities when we know that we should all be addressing inconsistent service provision? The answer is of course that, in spite of years of initiatives, inequalities remain. Law *et al.* (2012) argue that one reason for the failures to reduce health inequalities may be that we are measuring the wrong things. An attempt to set meaningful public health outcome measures has been articulated in *The Public Health Outcomes Framework* (PHOF) (Department of Health, 2012d). It includes several indicators for children, including child development milestones at age 2–2.5 years. How best to measure the impact of changes is under consideration (Bedford *et al.*, 2012). Since the publication of the White Paper in 2010 and other reports, such as *A Strategy for Social Mobility* (HM Government, 2011) and the Marmott Report, *Fair Society, Healthy Lives* (Marmott *et al.*, 2010), there has been reinforcement of the need for prevention through early intervention, and measurement of this is challenging without doubt. Field (2010) and Allen (2011) called for the creation of an outcome measure of children's health and development between the ages of two and three years. Tickell (2011) recommends that early years practitioners should provide parents and carers with a short summary of their children's communication and language, personal, social and emotional and physical development between 24–36 months so that they can assess progress of their own child. The possibilities are being considered too for bringing this early years summary together with the HCP two-year review into a single integrated review from 2015, when the expanded health visiting service will allow it (Bedford *et al.*, 2012).

In summary, public health in its widest sense seeks to improve health and tackle inequalities by working with individuals, communities and government. In terms of young children, this might be realised through the design and implementation of programmes designed to encourage for example, physical activity, promote a positive diet and reduce stress. It is not a case of health workers alone undertaking these programmes, rather an integrated approach with health, education, parents and children themselves, as well as the local community addressing the issues together (NICE, 2012).

Promoting public health has much to do with reducing inequalities and addressing poverty. The Acheson Report (Acheson, 1998) highlighted a multitude of health inequalities, many of which have since been taken up as government initiatives. In 1996/97, 26 per cent of children in the UK lived in a household in relative poverty, this is with an income below 50 per cent of the contemporaneous average income after housing costs. However, despite a decade of activity aimed at reducing inequalities, there are still considerable numbers living in poverty in the UK and above the rates in other European countries (UNICEF, 2007). Those working with young children continue to work to promote healthier life-styles for children, for example encouraging cycling and walking, addressing nutrition and supporting children's emotional well-being by creating an accepting environment where they feel secure and can express their hopes, fears and concerns. The Acheson Report (Acheson, 1998) further advises the need to identify additional resources for children from less well-off groups, improving nutrition within schools, adding fluoride to water and developing health-promoting schools.

Increasing capacity to reduce inequalities

The 2011 health visitor implementation plan *A Call for Action* (Department of Health, 2011) clearly identifies the government's commitment to supporting child health. The plan sets out the process to increase health visitor numbers and clearly acknowledges that professionals working with children and families are ideally placed to improve the health of children and that support during the early years of a child's life are crucial. The introduction of the Family Nurse Partnership (FNP) in many parts of the country has also been a significant initiative. The FNP programme targets resources on young teenage mothers, with the aim to provide intensive support and guidance to families where there is unlikely to be any family support. The programme has shown significant improvements in the outcomes for the children. There is a clear evidence base behind the programme going back for 30 years in the United States which shows that when these children grow up they are more likely to achieve educationally and obtain secure employment and are less likely to be involved in criminal activity (Olds, 2006). The early evaluation of the schemes running in the UK show that the women involved have improved their overall health behaviours, such as reduction in smoking and making improvements to their diet, and they are more likely to breast-feed. They also report improved overall satisfaction and reported to have better parenting attitudes (Department of Health, 2012e).

The public health approach

Health, in its widest sense, is central to child and human development. The promotion of health, taking account of physical, mental, emotional and social well-being, will ensure that children can take advantage of their opportunities during their time of greatest growth and development, as well as reducing health problems in later life. To do this necessitates a wide or public health approach facilitating the well-being of children in the context of the family, school and community. This approach is clarified within the recommendations in the NICE guidance, *Social and emotional wellbeing: early years* (NICE, 2012). This will require the assessment of health needs both on an individual and group basis. Such needs may be problem-orientated – looking at the causes of diseases or pathogenesis or using the 'salutogenic model' which is concerned with the relationship between health, stress and coping, exploring factors that contribute to healing or a resistance to breakdown, physical or psychological (Antonovsky, 1996). Activities and structures that build and create health should be developed by the children, parents and early years professionals concerned, so that all children develop to the highest possible level in terms of health and then, probably as a result, academic achievement.

Empowering families to reduce inequalities

Another significant change over the last few years has been the growing need to acknowledge the importance of working with families and the relationship between professionals, children and their parents to deliver the public health agenda. 'Empowerment' of patients/ clients and 'patient and public involvement' are popular buzz words to describe enabling of better decision-making through the acquisition of knowledge. Empowerment is seen as crucial in eliciting the change in behaviours necessary for health improvement. Health is big business, with newspapers, the television and radio news liberally allocating their columns and time-slots to issues on child health and well-being. Usually, such news reports adversity, but it nevertheless serves an educative function and helps to empower through the acquisition of knowledge. Take a look also along the shelves in any large newsagent, and there will be a vast array of magazines devoted solely (or largely) to health. Many of these relate specifically to child health matters and play an important role in informing parents about current child health practices and child care issues, including prevention of ill health as well as health promotion. The internet too provides a multiplicity of sites and information about child health – it is possible to find information on almost any topic. This can have significant adverse effects, as well as positive benefits, as seen in the coverage of the discredited concerns over the MMR vaccine and the significant increases in cases of measles which we are still facing. Parents and health professionals can often find it difficult to discriminate between credible and well-researched information and information with significant bias (Scullard *et al.*, 2010). Brecht *et al.* (2011) found that repeated exposure to misinformation adversely affected parents' perception of the risks versus benefits of vaccination, for example. Although vaccination rates have increased significantly in the last few years, it is essential that we are not complacent. 'Scare stories' on the safety of vaccination have been shown to skew the balance of perceived risk versus benefit in parents' minds and as such require careful and informed conversations with parents to advise on the evidence of the benefits of vaccination.

Current challenges

The previous edition of this book commented on the emergence of new and different health issues affecting our children. These issues require systematic and strong health promotion work with families and children to ensure the messages on, for example, healthy eating and lifestyles are understood and taken on board. They also require close networks with the wider community, such as schools and local authorities. Child obesity is an increasing national concern and the prevalence has dramatically increased over recent years. In 2010, around three in ten boys (31 per cent) and girls (29 per cent) aged 2–15 years were classed as either overweight or obese (NHS Information Centre 2012). This is a significant increase from 1995. The NHS Information Centre (2012) highlights that there has been a reduction in physical activity and an increase in spend on high fat foods, as well as a reduction in consumption of fruits and vegetables in children. There is, however, a sense that the rates have stabilised and the trend, albeit small, is that physical activity is increasing and there is a slight decrease in food consumption as measured by calorie intake. There is a growing awareness that being overweight has significant impact on a child's health and well-being (Reilly *et al.*, 2003). Obesity has physical and mental health effects in the short and long term and is very difficult to treat, so that the chances are that if a child is overweight or obese they will remain so into adulthood (Cornette, 2008). Current research (see Caird *et al.*, 2011) indicates that there may be a relationship between obesity and poor school performance which in turn lead to less favourable life chances. Clearly, the link is not a simple correlation, but we are undoubtedly facing a major public health challenge. Obesity contributes to the risk of heart disease and diabetes in later life, and to more immediate negative feelings of self worth and poor mental health. Children are exposed to temptations away from more healthy options, from more access to sedentary games rather than physical activity to unhealthy food choices which are seen to be increasingly available near where children are, such as outside schools. This trend is worryingly more prevalent in more deprived areas (Patterson *et al.*, 2012). Initiatives to support healthy eating in schools and to reduce the access to sugary drinks for children need to be extended, as well as the work with individuals to motivate a change in family and children's behaviour.

Another key current issue is vitamin D deficiency which is seen as a worldwide problem. The cause is complex, but is linked to lack of exposure to sunlight. This might be because of covering exposed skin for cultural reasons, or because of darker skin pigmentation, resulting in less absorption of vitamin D. It is also increasingly due to the use of high factor sun creams advocated to prevent skin cancers, but which limit the absorption of vitamin D (Holick and Chen, 2008). The effects of vitamin D deficiency are linked not just to bone deformity, but also to autoimmune problems and asthma (Bener, *et al.*, 2012). Some autistic children have also been shown to have a lower concentration of vitamin D in comparison to others (Mostafa and Al-Ayadhi, 2012). The Department of Health (2012f) has advocated supplements for those at particular risk, such as pregnant women and children, and that the vitamin supplements must be available to them. Those working with children should be aware of where to advise women to go and what arrangements are in place locally. As formula milk is already fortified, further supplements are not needed, but it is essential that women do not then perceive in any way that formula feeding is better than breast-feeding because it is supplemented. The evidence of the positive effects of breast-feeding are clear and the UNICEF baby-friendly initiative has clearly demonstrated the impact breast-feeding has in preventing disease and saving resources (UNICEF, 2012). Health professionals and others working with mothers and babies have been shown to have a positive impact in not only promoting breast-feeding in the first place, but in supporting women to continue (NICE, 2008).

Professionals working with children, as well as more generally in health promotion, are increasingly aware of the need for good listening and counselling skills in their conversations and consultations with parents in order to motivate a positive change in behaviour. Motivational interviewing is becoming increasingly important in many aspects of health promotion and has been shown to support patients to adopt changes to their behaviours and improve health (Levensky *et al.*, 2007). It is a patient-centred method of counselling which is designed to promote a change in behaviour and/or encourage people to understand and resolve their ambivalence to such change. As with any health promotion activity with children, a complex relationship between the child, their parents and carers, alongside the health professionals involved needs to develop. The motivational interviewing approach which engages the issues for the individual concerned can effectively enable this to happen and prompt positive changes in behaviour (Erickson *et al.*, 2005; Schwartz *et al.*, 2007).

Obesity and vitamin D deficiency are just two of the major public health issues facing the current generation of children in this country. Linked to the obesity epidemic is the lack of physical exercise undertaken by children (and their families). The new health landscape is attempting to tackle obesity and other major public health issues through the newly established Health and Well-Being Boards which will lead local multi-agency approaches to significant local issues.

The shift from hospital services

A significant number of children experience episodes of acute ill health and others are living with long-term (often complex) health needs. In the remainder of this chapter, we will focus on these children and how early years workers can best minimise the effects of illness on the chid.

Standard 6 of the NSF for children, young people and maternity services (Department of Health/Department for Education and Skills, 2004) is concerned with children and young people who have an acute illness or injury and children who have (or are at risk of having) a long-term condition, which is not disabling. Standard 6 states that:

All children and young people who are ill, or thought to be ill, or injured will have timely access to appropriate advice and to effective services which address their health, social, educational and emotional needs throughout the period of their illness.

When a child becomes ill – even if it is a relatively minor, self-limiting illness – the equilibrium of normal family life becomes upset. The degree to which this happens will vary according to the nature of the illness and the context of the family. An illness that might seem devastating to one family might be played down or even ignored by another. A parent or carer may well adopt a 'wait-and-see' approach, use over-the-counter medication and check their perception of the child's illness with significant others, such as grandparents or friends, in what is often termed the 'lay referral system' which was first defined by Freidson (1960). What is evident in 21st-century healthcare for children is that health professionals do not have the monopoly in caring for, or making decisions about, the ill child. Parents are likely to be the most significant role players. When we consider everyday self-limiting illness, they may well be the only health carers involved. In the NSF, it is estimated that in 80 per cent of all childhood episodes of illness, parents do not involve the professional healthcare system at all (DH/DfES, 2004; NHS Institute for Innovation and Improvement 2011).

Although a significant amount of caring for ill children takes place within the family, children are actually avid users of the professional health services. The NHS Institute for Innovation and Improvement (2011) found that 28 per cent of all attendees at Accident and Emergency (A&E) departments were children and 40 per cent of activity at GP practices concerned children. A preschool child will, in a typical year, see a GP about six times, while a school-aged child will see the GP two to three times. Up to half of all children under one year old, and a quarter of older children, will visit A&E, almost 10 per cent will attend hospital as an out-patient, and 7–10 per cent will be admitted to hospital (Cooke and Alberti, 2007).

This latter statistic represents a marked reduction in hospital in-patient admissions over the latter half of the 20th century. Consider for a moment the findings of the Platt report from 1959 which highlighted that one-third of all children were admitted to hospital to have their tonsils removed, without counting admissions for other ailments. The Platt report, which paid deference to the work of psychologists such as Bowlby and Robertson who had vividly displayed on film the despair and misery that children experienced in hospital, was instrumental in bringing about the reduction in hospital admissions. The report recommended that children should only be admitted to hospital as a last resort and that care should be available to children in their own homes – an aspiration which is as pertinent today as it was then.

Keeping children out of hospital and providing community-based services to support children who are ill and their families is an admirable aspiration, but does nevertheless bring with it a different set of issues that need to be addressed. Not least is the very ad hoc way that the shift from hospital- to community-based child care has taken place. The lack of trained community-based children's nurses, for example, has placed the burden of professional care with health visitors, GPs, practice nurses, parents and generic district nurses, many of whom will have had little or no training in the specific needs of ill children and their families. Where community children's nursing services do exist, they often comprise a very small team who cannot provide continuous cover to support families. What seems to be evident is that care has shifted from hospitals to communities in some areas, regardless of whether tangible support services exist or not. This was highlighted in the NSF for children (DH/DfES, 2004). The NSF outlines a training strategy so that practitioners without child-specific qualifications, but who are working with ill children, can gain the skills and knowledge they need to work effectively and safely. They do not suggest that service delivery stops, but that service developers view the next few years as a transitional period during which time sufficient numbers of qualified children's practitioners should be fully trained, while in the interim GPs receive training in certain core aspects of working with children. As with all major change, there is a time lag between planning and implementation. The Royal College of General Practitioners has accepted the move to extend GP training for a further year and to enhance the child health content of that training (Royal College of General Practitioners, 2012), although it will be some time before the impact of the extension is seen.

The provision of qualified children's practitioners is not going to be a case of replacing generic workers with children's workers. What is evident is that the number of ill children in the community is ever increasing for a number of reasons and that this will lead to a demand for more and more workers competent in the care of ill children (RCGP, 2012). First, improved surgical and anaesthetic procedures allow children to be discharged more quickly from hospital; indeed, in some cases they no longer need to spend the night as an increasing number of procedures are carried out on a day-case basis or in an outpatient setting. Second, the number of very premature babies who now survive has increased, and some of these tiny infants who would previously have spent many months in hospital are discharged into the community, so that separation of the family is minimised. A number of these babies do, however, come home with significant health needs, with some requiring 24-hour care. Third, there are those children with a long-term illness, such as cystic fibrosis, diabetes, cerebral palsy, epilepsy or leukaemia, which may previously have necessitated frequent admissions to hospital for pharmaceutical and other interventions. These children are more usually being cared for in the community because frequent admissions have been shown to have adverse effects on the child's well-being (Taylor et al., 1999).

Developing local and strategic children's clinical networks

When children and their families do come into contact with the professional health services, it is often a traumatic time. Children tend to become ill very quickly, and it is often difficult to separate what might be a relatively trivial ailment from a more serious condition that may require the child to be admitted to hospital. It is important, therefore, that children and their families have access to healthcare systems that are designed to maximise timely assessment and diagnosis so that they receive appropriate care in the appropriate setting. It is also important that those who work with children in any early years setting are able to quickly differentiate between simple ailments and more serious potentially life-threatening conditions so that they can refer children to the appropriate healthcare setting if required.

The NSF supported the development of local children's clinical networks, which would provide an integrated, safe and comprehensive service to support children and their families during illness (Department of Health/Department for Education and Skills 2004). The aim was that a local children's clinical network should operate effectively at all points in the child's illness experience. The idea was that everyone within the network – and particularly the child and the family – should be aware of where and to whom they should go for support in the event of a specific need arising. There should be clear clinical and managerial leadership and accountability for the clinical network, common and agreed protocols for careful management of resources, trust and collaboration between the respective parts of the network and robust audit and governance arrangements (DH/DfES, 2004). The aim was to develop pathways of care through the system, with easy and known access to services that are required at a particular point in time.

Building on the successes of local networks in some parts of the country, the NHS Commissioning Board has proposed strategic networks including a network covering children's and maternity services. They want to ensure that there is 'access to a broad range of expert clinical input to support and inform their decisions about the way care for local populations is planned and delivered' (NHS Commissioning Board, 2012: 4).

The important aspect of the clinical network is that there is a robust system to support children, not only when needs arise due to acute episodes of illness, but also for those with a specific long-term illness. Parts of the clinical network that are in place to support the child at the beginning of the illness and around the time of diagnosis, such as the specialist paediatric team and NHS 111, become less important and significant to the child and family over time, when other parts of the network take over. It is possible to plan this to some extent. For example, we know that starting school can be a particularly traumatic time for children and parents, and a different part of the network such as the school nursing service will have an important role during this time.

Developing family-centred care

Developing a local children's clinical network relies heavily on parents being empowered to make decisions and knowing who they need to contact in any given situation, mainly because they are the family and the constant in the child's life. As noted above, while various parts of the network play differing parts in the child's care pathway, the family will be there at all times. Developing family-centred care means embracing the child and family as a unit and actively encouraging the inclusion of the family in the planning and provision of the child's care in the health-care setting (Murphy and Fealy, 2007).

In order to empower parents and promote and support family-centred care, parents need to be fully informed about the child's illness, the choices available to them, sources of support and intervention and any other information that will help the parents to become 'expert' in their understanding of their child's illness. In many instances, parents will become more knowledgeable about a particular illness than the professionals involved (remember that the parent is learning about one illness trajectory, whereas most professionals have to be knowledgeable about many), and some professionals find this unsettling. True partnership is about sharing and this must be a two-way process. Remember that the aim is to empower parents so if they know more than you do, you have achieved your aim! Parents and children – if and when they are able – should be encouraged to become 'experts' and should be supported to develop self-confidence and self-management skills. We do, however, emphasise the 'if' as we should recognise that parents and children may vary in terms of the amount of involvement they want to have in the care of themselves or in the case of parents, with their child's illness (Coleman, 2009). Not every parent will be willing or able to spend hours scouring the internet or searching for information in the library, nor will they wish to become 'experts' in the care of their child. Many will rely on the relevant professionals to help them gain knowledge. Unbiased and complete information should be shared with parents, and pathways of care should be developed that meet the family's needs, socially, emotionally and financially. They need to be fully informed and the information must be provided in an appropriate way that is sensitive to developmental, cultural, social and language differences. This includes copies of relevant reports, letters and other communications about the child, which should be shared with the family according to current government policy.

Early years workers should be aware that information needs will vary between families and at various times during the child's illness. For example, at the time of diagnosis, parents will need a great deal of information, but this should be given at a pace determined by the parents. Some will want to know everything there is to know, whereas others will need time to assimilate the diagnosis and will want information in more of a 'drip-feed' fashion. Professionals should be aware too that information imparted at the time of diagnosis is not sufficient and their responsibility does not end at that point. When new information is discovered (e.g. through research), it is helpful if the professional can explain what this means, rather than leaving it to parents to guess when they hear a news story on the radio or read it in the newspaper.

The overall aim is to empower parents so that they are better able to cope with their child's illness. This is not a hollow aspiration but one which is based on sound evidence that coping behaviour will influence positively or negatively the outcomes of the illness for the child and for the family (Blake, 2006), particularly when the child has a long-term illness. Effective coping results in relevant adaptation to the child's illness, whereas ineffective coping can have harmful consequences and lead to maladaptation. One of the purposes of professional intervention must therefore be to maximise and facilitate coping skills which will lead to greater independence and competence.

The child too, if he or she is able, should be empowered so that he or she can exercise the right to be included in decision-making processes (Coulter and Collins, 2011). For many children – and particularly those with long-term conditions – their role includes taking on significant aspects of self-care as they move towards adulthood (Department of Health,

2008). This may mean taking on responsibility for self-medication, exercise regimes, avoidance of certain activities that will exacerbate a particular condition or undertaking other therapeutic interventions that might once have been performed only by health professionals but which mean a greater degree of independence if the child can carry out the intervention alone.

Professionals need to be aware that where a child has a long-term illness (and this may be right at the start, depending on the age and stage of development of the child), they will become increasingly autonomous and parental advocacy will usually diminish. This requires professionals to make judgements about when it is appropriate rhetorically to put the child in the 'driving seat' and allow them to make judgements about what information is given to the parents. For example, an adolescent may no longer wish parents to be involved in routine physical examinations and may wish to be given information without parents being present. Professionals need to be cautious to maintain the patient's confidentiality (in this case, the child), while balancing the parents' need for information (DH/DfES, 2004). It can sometimes be a tricky job to balance the demands and needs of the child and parents.

Minimising the impact of illness

We have discussed above the need to empower parents and children through information and encouraging them to become experts in their illness trajectories. Illness – particularly if it is long term – can, however, have a devastating effect on all aspects of the child and family's life and early years workers will need to work with families to minimise the impact of illness to allow the child to lead as normal a life as possible. This applies to children with non-life-threatening illness, as well as to those who may eventually die as a result of their illness.

One of the most tangible difficulties is the impact of illness on educational opportunities. Episodes in hospital, for example, can mean children missing vital time at school, and it also impacts on normal friendships and other extracurricular activities. Guidelines have been published to support children missing school for medical reasons (Department of Children, Schools and Families, 2012) and these should be considered carefully. Hospital staff will need to develop good communication channels with the child's school to help the child develop and achieve full educational potential. The NSF discusses the need for health and education services to develop joint protocols to ensure the smooth transition from school to hospital and hospital back to school, where an admission is planned (DH/DfES, 2004). The named teacher and named health contact in consultation with the child and family should develop, monitor and review healthcare plans which detail respective support requirements. When a child's needs change – for example, if medication or treatment is revised – the care plans should be altered accordingly and all parties informed.

Learning activity

Identify a school-aged child with complex health needs. With the cooperation of the child and his or her parents, identify the different health, education and social care services with which the child/family has had contact, both currently and in the past.

- For each service, identify the key aims of the services provided. Pay particular attention to any areas of overlap.
- Consider ways in which the number of contacts the child and family have with different services might be reduced.

It is not only hospital admissions that can have an adverse impact on education. Children who need frequently to attend out-patient departments or assessment centres can be helped by sensitive scheduling of appointments; for example, at the start or end of the list so that they spend a minimum time away from school. Schools should also encourage children and parents to attend school for part-days if, for example, the child is unwell in the morning, but feels better later in the day. For example, some parents – if a child has a fit first thing in the morning – will keep them away from school for the whole day, yet the child may be feeling fine within an hour or two and be quite well enough to attend.

Encouraging children to participate in other normal childhood activities and in friendship groups is also an important way of minimising the impact of illness (Venning *et al.*, 2008). Parents may be reluctant for their children to participate in activities that cannot be overseen by themselves or a trusted teacher and they can develop an over-protective attitude to the ill child. Other parents and friends may likewise have fears about a child with a particular health need being entrusted to them. Helping parents and children to find a healthy balance that enables the ill child to participate in activities safely can be achieved through simple suggestions. Examples include encouraging a friend and parent to visit the ill child at home first and giving a range of emergency contact numbers. Likewise, encouraging the parent of the ill child to write down a few facts about the illness or provide leaflets about an illness can all be useful.

Partnership working

A significant number of children are living with long-term (often complex) health needs. Health, social services and education will need to work closely together to support improving child health. The changes to the NHS with the implementation of the 2012 Health and Social Care Act will mean that partnerships will be increasingly important, but they also provide an opportunity to develop these relationships by aligning services and moving public health teams to local authorities which will potentially enable far closer working between health and other services. For children, it will be essential for services to develop links around them and this will be helped by the Strategic Clinical Networks (NHS Commissioning Board, 2012). This will also be helped with the development of Health and Wellbeing Boards.

There is a move to develop specific programmes for the individual child rather than delivering a universal message. All those working with the child need to understand the wider social impacts in the child's life and understand and embrace their role in promoting child health (Blair, 2010). The Royal College of Paediatrics and Child Health (2012) have launched a guide to implementing clinical networks which involve planning, commissioning and service performance management involving clinical experts to make sure the needs of the child are met. It is essential to acknowledge that a range of professionals are required to meet the needs of the child and no one person can have all the information (Kenyon *et al.*, 2007).

Conclusion

Since the last edition of this book, the evidence shows that the health of children remains an issue of national concern, and in this chapter we have discussed how the value placed upon children's health has developed over time and how children's health services have developed to respond to the needs of children and families. The health of children has to be the responsibility of all early years professionals who must take, and seek out, opportunities to promote the health of children and to prevent ill health. As the body of evidence increases, there is a growing need to work together and utilise the different skills in a network approach. This is particularly necessary to meet the needs of children and their families with complex needs. There is still a long way to go and still a need for greater integration of services. The Health and Social Care Act (2012) provides some opportunities with this but also challenges with the change to NHS and social care services. What is essential is training and education with enhanced understanding of inter-professional roles and responsibilities. Professional barriers must never be allowed to overshadow the need to provide excellent, integrated, child-focused services.

Evaluate your learning

- What are the key changes to the NHS that will impact on children's health?
- What are the advantages of public health working more closely with local authorities?
- Why is it important that children and parents with chronic illnesses are informed about the condition they have?

References

Acheson, D (1998): *Independent Inquiry into Inequalities in Health.* London: The Stationery Office.

Allen, G (2011): *Early Intervention: The Next Steps.* London: HM Government.

Antonovsky, A (1996): The salutogenic model as a theory to guide health promotion. *Health Promotion International* 11(1), 11–8.

Bedford, H, Walton, S and Ahn, J (2012): *Measures of Child Development: A Review.* Policy Research Unit in the Health of Children and Young People and Families. Centre for Paediatric Epidemiology and Biostatistics UCL Institute of Child Health.

Bener, A, Ehlayel, M, Tulic, M and Hamid, Q (2012): Vitamin D deficiency as a strong predictor of asthma in children. *International Archives of Allergy and Immunology* 157(2), 168–75.

Betsch, C, Renkewitz, F, Betsch, T and Ulshöfer, C (2010): The influence of vaccine-critical websites on perceiving vaccination risks. *Journal of Health Psychology* 15(3), 446–55.

Blair, M (2010): Promoting children's health. *Paediatrics and Child Health* 20(4), 174–8.

Blake, J (2006): Supporting anxious parents in search of internet information. *Nursing Times* **102**(19), 24.

Caird, J, Kavanagh, J, Oliver, K, Oliver, S, O'Mara, A, Stansfield, C and Thomas, J (2011): *Childhood Obesity and Educational Attainment: A Systematic Review*. London: EPPI-Centre, Social Science Research Unit, Institute of Education, University of London.

Clark, J (1973): *A Family Visitor*. London: Royal College of Nursing.

Coleman, V (2009): The evolving concept of child and family centred health care. In Smith, L and Coleman, V (eds), *Child and Family-Centred Healthcare – Concept, Theory and Practice*, 2nd edn. Basingstoke: Palgrave Macmillan.

Cooke, MW and Alberti, KGGM (2007): Emergency care for children – the next steps. *Archives of Disease in Childhood* **92**(1), 6–7.

Cornette, R (2008): The emotional impact of obesity on children. *Worldviews on Evidence-Based Nursing* **5**(3), 136–41.

Coulter, A and Collins, A (2011): *Making Shared Decision Making a Reality*. London: Kings Fund.

Cox, C (1983): *Sociology: An Introduction for Nurses, Midwives and Health Visitors*. London: Butterworths.

Department of Children, Schools and Families (2012): *Illness (pupils missing school for medical reasons): Good Practice Guidance*. London: DCSF.

Department of Health (2008) *Transition: Moving on Well*. London: The Stationery Office.

Department of Health (2009a): *Healthy Child Programme, Pregnancy and the First Five Years of Life*. (Online). Last accessed: October 2012. Available from: www.dh.gov.uk/en/Publicationsandstatistics/Publications/PublicationsPolicyAndGuidance/DH_107563.

Department of Health (2009b): *Healthy Child Programme: The Two Year Review*. (Online). Last accessed: October 2012. Available from: www.dh.gov.uk/en/Publicationsandstatistics/Publications/PublicationsPolicyAndGuidance/DH_107565.

Department of Health (2011): *Health Visitor Implementation Plan 2011–15, A Call to Action*. London: The Stationery Office.

Department of Health (2012a): *Children and Young People's Health Outcomes Forum Report*. London: Department of Health.

Department of Health (2012b): *Children and Young People's Health Outcomes Forum – Report by the Acutely Ill Theme Group*. London: DH.

Department of Health (2012c): *Immunisation against Infectious Diseases (The Green Book)*, (Online). Last accessed: October 2012. Available from: http://immunisation.dh.gov.uk/category/the-green-book/.

Department of Health (2012d): *The Public Health Outcomes Framework for England 2013–2015*. London: DH, Gateway ref 16891.

Department of Health (2012e): *Summary of the Formative Evaluation of the First Phase of the Group-based Family Nurse Partnership Programme*. London: The Stationery Office.

Department of Health (2012f): *CMO letter Vitamin D Advice on Sipplements for at risk groups*. (Online). Last accessed: October 2012. Available from: www.dh.gov.uk/en/Publicationsandstatistics/Lettersandcirculars/Dearcolleagueletters/DH_132509.

Department of Health and Social Security (1976): *Prevention and Health: Everybody's Business*. London: HMSO.

Department of Health/Department for Education and Skills (2004): *The National Service Framework for Children, Young People and Maternity Services*. London: Department of Health.

Erickson, S, Gerstle, M and Feldstein, S (2005): Brief interventions and motivational interviewing with children, adolescents and their parents in pediatric health care settings. *Archives of Pediatric and Adolescent Medicine* **159**, 1173–80.

Field, F (2010): *The Foundation Years: Preventing Poor Children Becoming Poor Adults*. London: The Stationery Office.

Freidson, E (1960): Client control and medical practice. *American Journal of Sociology* **65**, 374–82.

Hall, DMB (1992): Child health promotion, screening and surveillance. *Journal of Child Psychology and Psychiatry* **34**, 649–58.

Hall, DMB and Elliman, D (eds) (2003) *Health for All Children*, 4th edn. Oxford: Oxford University Press.

Hall, DMB and Elliman, D (2006): *Health for All Children*, 4th edn. Oxford: Oxford University Press.

HM Government (2011): *Opening Doors, Breaking Barriers: A Strategy for Social Mobility*. (Online). Last accessed: October 2012. Available from: https://update.cabinetoffice.gov.uk/resource-library/opening-doors-breaking-barriers-strategy-social-mobility.

Holick, M and Chen, T (2008): Vitamen D deficiency: a worldwide problem with health consequences. *American Journal of Clinical Nutrition* **87**, 1080–6.

Kennedy, Professor Sir I (2010): *Getting it Right for Children and Young People: Overcoming Cultural Barriers in the NHS so as to Meet their Needs*. (Online). Last accessed: October 2012. Available from: www.dh.gov.uk/prod_consum_dh/groups/dh_digitalassets/@dh/@en/@ps/documents/digitalasset/dh_119446.pdf.

Kenyon, C, Sandal, M, Silverstein, M, Sakir, A and Zuckerman, B (2007) Revisiting the social history for child health. *American Academy of Pediatrics* **120**(3), 734–8.

Kosky, J (ed) (1992): *Queen Elizabeth Hospital for Sick Children: 125 Years of Achievement*. London: Queen Elizabeth Hospital.

Law, C, Parkin, C and Lewis, H (2012): Policies to tackle inequalities in child health: why haven't they worked (better)? *Archives of Disease in Childhood* **97**(4), 301–3.

Levensky, R, Forcehimes, A, O'Donohue, W and Beitz, K (2007): Motivational interviewing: An evidence-based approach to counselling helps patients follow treatment recommendations. *Advanced Journal of Nursing* **107**(10), 58–66.

Marmott, M, Allen, J, Goldblatt, P, Boyce, T, McNeish, D and Grady, M (2010): *Fair Society, Healthy Lives: Strategic Review of Health Inequalities in England post-2010*. (Online). Last accessed: October 2012. Available from: www.ucl.ac.uk/gheg/marmotreview.

Meredith Davies, JB (1975): *Preventive Medicine, Community Health and Social Services*, 3rd edn. London: Ballière Tindall.

Mostafa, G and Al-Ayadhi, L (2012): Reduced serum concentrations of 25-hydroxy vitamin D in children with autism: relation to autoimmunity. *Journal of Neuroinflammation* **17**(9), 201.

Murphy, M and Fealy, G (2007): Practices and perceptions of family centred care among children's nurses in Ireland. *Journal of Children's and Young People's Nursing* **1**(7), 312–9.

NHS Commissioning Board (2012): *The Way Forward: Strategic Clinical Networks.* London: NHS CB.

NHS England (2012): *The Health and Social Care Act 2012.* London: The Stationery Office.

NHS Information Centre (2012): *Statistics on Obesity, Physical Activity and Diet: England, 2012.* London: NHS IC.

NHS Institute for Innovation and Improvement (2011): *A Whole System Approach to Improving Emergency and Urgent Care for Children and Young People: A Practical Step-by-step Guide and Resources Pack.* Coventry: NHSI.

NICE (2008): *Guidance for Midwives, Health Visitors, Pharmacists and Other Primary Care Services to Improve the Nutrition of Pregnant and Breastfeeding Mothers and Children in Low Income Households.* (Online). Available from: http://guidance.nice.org.uk/PH11.

NICE (2012): *Social and Emotional Wellbeing: Early Years NOCE Public Health Guidance 40.* (Online). Available from: http://guidance.nice.org.uk/PH40.

Olds, D (2006): The Nurse-family partnership: An evidence based preventative intervention. *Infant Mental Health Journal* **27**(1), 5–25.

Patterson, R, Risby, A and Chen, M (2012): Consumption of takeaway and fast food in a deprived inner London Borough: are they associated with childhood obesity? *British Medical Journal* **2**, e000402.

Reilly, J, Methven, E McDowell, Z, Hacking, B, Alexander, D, Stewart, L and Kelnar C (2003): Health consequences of obesity. *Archives of Disease and Childhood* **88**(7), 748–52.

Royal College of General Practitioners (RCGP) (2012): *Preparing the Future GP: The Evidence for Enhancing Clinical Skills.* London: RCGP.

Royal College of Paediatrics and Child Health (RCPCH) (2012) *Bringing Networks to Life – An RCPCH guide to Implementing Clinical Networks.* (Online). Available from: www.rcpch.ac.uk/networks.

Schwartz, R, Hamre, R, Dietz, W, Wasserman, R, Slora, E, Myers, E, Sullivan, S, Rockett, H, Thoma, J, Dumitru, G and Resnicow K (2007): Office-based motivational interviewing to prevent childhood obesity. *Archives of Pediatric and Adolescent Medicine* **161**, 495–501.

Scullard, P, Peacock, C and Davies P (2010): Googling children's health: reliability of medical advice on the internet. *Archives of Disease in Childhood* **95**(8), 580–2.

Taylor, J, Muller, D, Harris, P and Wattley, L (1999): *Nursing Children: Psychology, Research and Practice,* 2nd edn. London: Stanley Thornes.

Tickell, C (2011): *The Early Years: Foundations for Life, Health and Learning – An Independent Report on the Early Years Foundation Stage to Her Majesty's Government.* London: Department for Education.

UNICEF (2012): *Preventing Disease and Saving Resources: The Potential Contribution of Increasing Breastfeeding Rates in the UK.* Unicef baby friendly initiative. (Online). Last accessed: October 2012. Available from: www.unicef.org.uk/Documents/Baby_Friendly/Research/Preventing_disease_saving_resources.pdf.

UNICEF (2007): *Child poverty in perspective: An Overview of child well-being in rich countries. UNICEF report.* (Online). Last accessed: October 2012. Available from: www.unicef.org/media/files/ChildPovertyReport.pdf.

Venning, A, Eliott, J, Wilson, A and Kettler, L (2008): Understanding young peoples' experience of chronic illness: a systematic review. *International Journal of Evidence-Based Healthcare* **6**, 321–36

Wolfe I (2011): Improving child health services in the UK: insights from Europe and their implications for the NHS reforms. *British Medical Journal* **342**, 901–4.

Further reading

Department of Health (2009): *Healthy Child Programme: pregnancy and the first five years of life*. London: Department of Health.

O'Dea, JM (2010): Considerations in the prevention of obesity among children and adolescents 'First do no harm'. In Douglas, J, Eale, S, Handsley, S, Jones, L, Lloyd, CE and Spurr, S (eds) *A reader in promoting public health: challenge and controversy*, 2nd edn. London: Sage publications Ltd., pp. 143–150.

Rudolf, M, Lee, T and Levine, M (2011): *Paediatrics and Child Health*, 3rd edn. Massachusetts: Wiley-Blackwell.

12 Young children with disabilities

Sue Hollinrake

This chapter aims to:
- explore the experiences of disabled children and their families
- consider key changes in policy and practice developments in recent years in relation to disabled children and their families
- discuss some of the challenges currently presented to professionals working with disabled children and their families.

Introduction

It may now seem as though we are stating the obvious that children with disabilities, while having additional specialist needs resulting from specific impairments, otherwise have the same needs as all children – a need for food and warmth, for love and affection, praise and recognition, stability and stimulating activities and new experiences through play and education. However, it is not that long ago that in this country a child's disability was often seen as the barrier to meeting many of these needs.

Institutionalisation and exclusion from educational provision in the past meant that some children with disabilities often faced a bleak future (Oswin, 1971, 1978) or their parents battled for better provision and support in the face of many difficulties. Much has improved since the days when professionals might have encouraged parents to give up their profoundly disabled child to an institution, but real inclusion in mainstream society for children with disabilities still entails the overcoming of significant disabling barriers (Audit Commission, 2003). Segregated provision still exists within social care and debates continue in education as to whether full inclusion is achievable or indeed desirable (Croll and Moses, 2000; Norwich, 2007; Runswick-Cole, 2008; Schaeffer, 2010).

Currently, one in 20 children in the United Kingdom is known to have a disability and there are approximately 770 000 disabled children under the age of 16 years (Contact a Family, 2012a). Impairments can occur from limitations to sensory, motor or cognition functioning, or a combination of these. The complexity of the additional needs that can arise from these young children's attempts to interact with the world around them can impact on their development and capabilities, as well as on family functioning, well beyond their early years. So, the importance of getting it 'right from the start' (Scope, 1994) is, as ever, crucial to maximise well-being.

This chapter begins by identifying some of the key changes in policy and legislation which have affected the lives of young disabled children and their families in recent decades, highlighting the shift in values underpinning these policies. Due to the constraints imposed by covering such a broad area in a single chapter, the focus of the discussion will be mainly on impairments and disability generally rather than specific conditions, and the discussion on policy and legislation refers mainly to England, unless otherwise stated. The experiences of families are considered and challenges for practitioners working in this area are identified.

Changing values: the move towards inclusion

An examination of social policy and legislation provides an appreciation of the crucial role of values, ideology and discourse in the field of disability generally, highlighting such issues as the allocation of value and worth, affecting life chances and quality of life for disabled people. Maureen Oswin (1971 and 1978) wrote powerful, seminal accounts of the neglectful treatment of children with multiple disabilities living in long-stay hospitals, which in those days offered a totally institutionalised way of living for them, excluded from the rest of society. At that time, there were about 12 000 children living in long-stay hospitals in this country, many in children's wards attached to the large mental handicap hospitals, each housing about 20 or 30 children with severe physical and learning disabilities (Oswin, 2000).

Despite a move away from the policies and practices of segregation towards inclusion, the 'out of sight, out of mind' approach has left a legacy of oppressive attitudes in the public mind with which disabled children and adults and their families still wrestle (Stocks, 2012). There continues to be a struggle in confronting issues of human difference and a tendency to manage these issues in ways that have usually reinforced the differences through negative stereotypes rather than valuing them or even perceiving them neutrally. For disabled people this has given rise to a continuum of hurt and harm from negative media images emphasising dependency, to name-calling and bullying (Mencap, 1999) and to disability hate crime (Section 146 of the Criminal Justice Act 2003), for example, The Office of the Children's Commissioner (2006) found that children with disabilities are twice as likely to be subject to bullying than their non-disabled peers.

Concepts of normality often lie behind definitions of disability and these have been the subject of some debate. For physically disabled people, an inability to negotiate access to the physical environment such as buildings, transport and leisure activities has been viewed in terms of individual limitations rather than a collective lack of regard to their particular needs. In relation to learning disabilities, for example, the medical profession has defined it in terms of a physical, organic abnormality, while educationalists have defined it as a statistical deviation from the norm and psychologists as a deviation from socially acceptable behaviours. Such concepts identify the individual as 'different' or 'abnormal', producing an individual 'personal tragedy' and 'deficit' model of disability, or 'medical model' implying a cure. In contrast, the social model, with its emphasis on materially or socially constructed meanings, was developed (Finkelstein, 1980; Oliver, 1990) which now has a significant impact on policy and professional practice.

The disability and self-advocacy movements organised by people with both physical and learning disabilities have contributed significantly through their campaigning to a reclaiming of this territory and definition of the experience of people with disabilities. This has produced a climate of challenge to policy makers and a more enlightened professional approach. These activities have had a major influence on the development of the linked policies of de-institutionalisation and care in the community for children and adults with disabilities, and have been a force for change in the organisation and delivery of health and social services for people with disabilities since the 1980s. The idea of normalisation (Wolfensberger, 1983) permeated the philosophy behind community care and developed more generally into an approach to care and support that should empower recipients of services as active participants in the assessment of their needs and in the choice of interventions which is in marked contrast to the traditional medical model of the powerful expert professional and the passive patient.

Public consciousness of the needs of disabled children was increased due to media exposure in the late 1960s over the thalidomide drug and birth defects caused by its use by pregnant women and since then, campaigning organisations for children with disabilities such as Contact a Family, the Council for Disabled Children and Mencap have had a significant influence on public attitudes and government policy. The emphasis on ordinary lives with access to the same rights as non-disabled children, continues in policy development for children with disabilities (see below) through human rights, civil rights and entitlements as expressed in the UN Convention on the Rights of the Child, the Human Rights Act 1998, the Equality Act 2010, the Children Act 1989 and the Chronically Sick and Disabled Person's Act 1970.

Learning activity

Think about your own values and attitudes towards disability. How were these values and attitudes formed? What significant influences and experiences can you identify that have shaped your attitudes towards disabled people? Have you had experiences that have changed or challenged any of your attitudes about and perceptions of disability? Do you think your attitudes and perceptions differ in relation to disabled children and disabled adults? If so, why do you think this is? Try to be honest with yourself and recognise how we can all be influenced by negative labelling, stereotypes, discriminatory and oppressive attitudes and behaviours from a range of sources *and* be open to experiences that challenge these throughout our lives.

Main themes in contemporary policy and practice

In the field of child care, the Children Act 1989 was a major turning point in the inclusion of disabled children in mainstream child welfare legislation and service provision. It was the first piece of legislation in which disabled children were recognised as a group with special needs that had to be met by local authorities. It imposed a duty on local authorities to maintain a register of disabled children in their area and provided a definition of disability:

> A child is disabled if he is: deaf, blind or dumb or suffering from a mental disorder or is substantially and permanently handicapped by illness, injury, congenital or other disability.

(Children Act 1989, Section 17, para. 11)

Unfortunately, the medical model of disability underpins this definition and the Act's approach to disabled children, who are constructed as a problem, with 'special needs', in contrast to the norm of able-bodied children. In this respect, the Children Act 1989 failed to take on board the gains of the disability movement in contesting definitions of disability. The Act also states that the aims of services for disabled children are:

> (a) to minimise the effect on disabled children within their area of their disabilities; and (b) to give such children the opportunity to lead lives which are as normal as possible.

(Children Act 1989, Schedule 2, para. 6)

Again, the assumption is that it is the disability (or rather the impairment) which requires attention and not society, and the notion of normality here, when linked to the concept of 'special needs', seems to avoid the debate about who should be 'normalised' and continues with the construction of disabled children as different and 'other' because they are not able-bodied.

On a more positive note, the Children Act 1989 drew together and simplified the pre-existing legislative framework in relation to children and families and imposed new duties on local authorities, such as the identification and assessment of 'children in need'. The local authority has a duty to respond to children in need in its area in a number of ways, through the provision of preventative services, aimed at avoiding deterioration in family circumstances and at improving a child's health and development.

Children with disabilities are automatically regarded as 'children in need' within the terms of the Act. Aldgate and Tunstill (1995) found that in the years immediately following its implementation, services and budgets within local authorities for disabled children had expanded, with specialist teams of social workers and allied professionals being created to respond to need. However, local authorities can use the gate-keeping effect of definitions of thresholds of need and use severity of disability as a means of rationing services by targeting the more severely disabled children and leaving those with less severe or less definable disabilities to compete for priority within the non-specialist child support services.

Decisions about which services to provide should be based on an assessment of need. The concepts of need and needs assessments have in recent years become central to health and social care professional practice as a result of both child care and community care legislation, guidance and policy. In relation to children, including children with disabilities, the *Framework for the Assessment of Children in Need and their Families* (Department of Health/ Department for Education and Employment/Home Office, 2000) and Standard 8 of the *National Service Framework for Children, Young People and Maternity Services* (Department of Health/Department for Education and Skills, 2004) provide in-depth guidance and advice to professionals. The Coalition Government has recently produced new draft guidance (June 2012) for consultation to revise aspects of the *Framework for Assessment*, proposing to replace nationally prescribed time-scales for assessment with a more flexible approach focusing on the needs of the child. The *National Service Framework* (DH/DfES, 2004) describes what effective health and social care services should look like in practice. These services should be designed and delivered around the needs of children and families, in line with the *Every Child Matters* outcomes (see below). There is a standard specifically for disabled children that works alongside the framework's core standards (applicable to all children), and which states:

> *Children and young people who are disabled or who have complex health needs receive coordinated, high-quality and family-centred services which are based on assessed needs, which promote social inclusion and, where possible, which enable them and their families to live ordinary lives.*

Launched in 2002, *Every Child Matters: Change for Children* (DfES, 2004a) was a government initiative for England and Wales (*Getting it Right for Every Child* is the equivalent for Scotland), designed, in part, in response to the death of Victoria Climbié (see Chapter 10, for a more detailed discussion). It was an important and aspirational policy initiative intended to promote radical reform of services for children, and was also the title of the Green Paper published in September 2003.

Every Child Matters (ECM) continues to apply to children and young adults up to the age of 19, or 24 for those with disabilities, and aims to improve outcomes for all children, requiring multi-agency partnerships and integrated services to support parents and their children to achieve the five named outcomes (be healthy, stay safe, enjoy and achieve, make a positive contribution and achieve economic well-being). It was followed by a series of government publications between 2004 and 2007 to underpin the implementation of the Children Act 2004 in each local authority area in England. However, while focusing on other groups of children in need, none of these papers addressed specifically the needs of children with disabilities. Research has highlighted that while the ECM outcomes framework is relevant for disabled children, there are different priorities and different aspirations for disabled children and their parents due to the different developmental trajectories when children's abilities may be decreasing and their needs and dependencies increasing because of their particular condition (Sloper *et al.*, 2009).

Following on from the ECM initiative, a national campaign was set up in 2006 by four national organisations working with disabled children and their families (Contact a Family, the Council for Disabled Children, Mencap and the Special Educational Consortium) in order to raise the profile of disabled children in a political context with local and central government. The campaign continues to fight for the rights of disabled children and for justice, through lobbying government to ensure that services and support are available to enable them and their families to lead ordinary lives. It demands new and improved support for families and tries to raise the priority given to them by government. Its campaigns cover areas such as health, social care, education and housing and it has been involved in lobbying government in relation to the forthcoming Children and Families Bill, planned for introduction in 2013 (see below).

The last Labour Government (2005–10) introduced a programme which specifically targeted disabled children and their families and which built on their *Children's Plan*

(Department for Children, Schools and Families, 2007). They called it *Aiming High for Disabled Children: Better Support for Families* (AHDC), introduced in 2007 to transform services for disabled children, young people and their families, in order to help them get the support and chances they need to make a difference and to enable them to live ordinary lives. It built on the *National Service Framework for Children, Young People and Maternity Services* (DH/DfES, 2004) and aimed to improve service provision generally for disabled children and their families, enhancing equality and opportunity for them. Particular areas of focus affecting young children with disabilities were the availability of short breaks, child care to improve opportunities for parents to work should they wish to and improved specialist support for children with life-limiting conditions. Currently, the Coalition Government has shown a commitment to many of the principles of *Aiming High for Disabled Children*, such as short breaks, information and transparency for parents, and Early Support (see below).

In the arena of education, the Special Educational Needs and Disability Act 2001 (implemented in 2002 with its accompanying code of practice (Disability Rights Commission, 2002)) imposed a mandate on schools (previously exempted) that they are not allowed to treat pupils with disabilities 'less favourably' than non-disabled pupils without being able to justify such treatment. They are also required to make reasonable adjustments so that pupils with disabilities are not substantially disadvantaged compared with non-disabled pupils, and plan strategically and make progress in increasing physical accessibility to schools and the curriculum. For parents of young disabled children seeking inclusive education provision, should local negotiations prove unhelpful, this Act may be used to challenge a school's inclusion practices if it is considered that reasonable steps have not been taken to ensure a child is properly included in mainstream activities.

In relation to parents, the Carers (Recognition and Services) Act 1995 and the Carers and Disabled Children Act 2000 entitle carers to have their needs assessed, to be informed about their entitlement and to receive services through the local authority directly in order to help support them in their caring role and to help maintain their health and well-being. The Carers and Disabled Children Act introduced direct payments for parents with a disabled child, giving local authorities the power to make payments to them to directly secure the provision of services for their child, instead of services being provided under Section 17 of the Children Act 1989 for a child in need (see below) and to secure services to meet their own assessed needs (e.g. for a break from caring). This helps parents and their children to choose more inclusive provision and to tailor more flexible patterns of care to the child's individual needs. Also, the Carers' Equal Opportunities Act 2004 states that carers' assessments should always consider a carer's (or parent carer's) outside interests, such as work, leisure or study when carrying out an assessment.

While much progress has been made in this country in terms of service provision and its underlying principles, though still having some way to go, this is sadly not reflected everywhere in the world (Jones, 2001) and in war zones, children can become disabled as long-term victims of the indiscriminate effects of modern weaponry. The needs and rights of disabled children are frequently overlooked because they experience the double invisibility of being a child and being disabled. Lack of commitment and awareness means that disabled children can become easily marginalised within the general children's agenda despite the United Nations Convention on the Rights of the Child (UNCRC) which came into force in 1990 and was ratified by the British Government in 1991. It proclaimed a number of rights for all children such as the right to life, to care and protection, to freedom of expression and thought. Article 23 also has specific things to say about disabled children as follows:

> *... that a mentally or physically disabled child should enjoy a full and decent life, in conditions which ensure dignity, promote self-reliance and facilitate the child's active participation in the community ...*

and also that disabled children have:

> *... the right to special care ...*

(United Nations, 1990)

The four guiding principles of the Convention as criteria of good practice are as follows:

1. Non-discrimination
2. Survival and development
3. The best interests of the child
4. The child's right to have her/his opinion heard.

Diagnosis and disclosure

I have met many parents of children with disabilities over the past 30 years of working in this area and very few have reported satisfaction with the way in which they learned the news of their son's or daughter's newly diagnosed disability. This can happen at the time of birth or later as the child develops and does not attain expected milestones. I have often been struck too by how readily parents will discuss their recollections in later years, which I have taken as an indicator of how alive the issues remain for them and how vivid their memories are of such a significant turning point in their lives. It can be a very traumatic time for parents and a period of great crisis (Audit Commission, 1994; Scope, 1994). Criticism of professional behaviour and support during this time is often high.

In some ways, this is not surprising, since 'the bearer of bad news' is rarely praised or appreciated for his or her efforts. However, in my experience, parents' vivid and clear memories of the way in which they were told often revealed insensitive and neglectful practice. Parents' complaints encompassed such approaches as one parent being told on their own and then left to share the news with the other parent; professionals avoiding or ignoring parents' anxieties about their child's development who were left feeling that they were over-anxious or 'fussy' parents; being given very bleak scenarios about their child's future in which negative projections about the impact of the disability on themselves as parents and on their child's future life chances were emphasised; parents being told in an abrupt and insensitive manner and then left to struggle on their own with the impact and to search by themselves for information and advice. Parents have a great deal to cope with at this time, facing new challenges and a range of possible emotions that these realisations will bring. Receiving a great deal of information at once may be too much for them to take in, though they will need to digest a new body of knowledge about specific diagnoses and support systems and they will need support in managing and adjusting their expectations over time.

The tasks of diagnosing and then disclosing such information to parents often fall to medical professionals, such as doctors and nurses. These are clearly difficult tasks, requiring skilled interventions. They are particularly difficult within a professional culture which still predominantly embraces a medical model, emphasising cure and treatment – approaches that may not have anything to offer to parents of disabled children. Additionally, wider cultural views that still marginalise disability and see disabled people as less valuable than non-disabled people can also have their influence on professional attitudes and approaches.

It is therefore vital that professionals undertaking these tasks are aware of their own values and beliefs about disability and have had the opportunity to examine, question and reflect on the discriminatory attitudes and stereotypes that will have been part of their own socialisation. Valuing the child and respecting the parents are fundamental to good professional practice (Scope, 1994; DH/DfES, 2004).

Almost 20 years ago, the national charity, Scope, published research that focused on the experiences of parents at the time of diagnosis of disability or special needs called *Right From the Start* (Scope, 1994). The research highlighted good and bad practice in diagnosis and disclosure and promoted the notion of partnership with parents and recommended that guidelines should be adopted by all health authorities and maternity hospitals and units, building on the good practice identified as already existing in some areas of the country. The need to get this right was reinforced in the *National Service Framework* (DH/DfES, 2004), and materials now exist deriving from the *Early Support Programme* (see below) giving guidance to professionals on how to break the news, emphasising a positive approach that values the child and respects the parents, conveying information in an open, honest, direct and sensitive way, and showing understanding for parental concerns and feelings.

Good practice demands that professionals working in this area have effective communication skills. They need to be able to impart information in non-specialist and non-jargonised language that can be understood and remembered by parents who are under stress. Sensitivity has to be used in gauging the amount of information a parent can digest at a particular time, along with their need for space and time to process information during a period of crisis and adjustment. Parents may need also to revisit issues at their own pace. For this reason, highly tuned interpersonal skills are needed not just in the initial phase of diagnosis and disclosure but in the weeks, months and even years which follow, since future transitions may cause parents to re-examine their beliefs, views and attitudes about their son or daughter as they grow up and re-awaken earlier experiences. Other professionals who work with parents at later stages need to be aware of how the parents they are working with have managed their adjustment and be sensitive and responsive to their understanding of and adaptation to their child's disability with the passage of time. Working with parents from minority ethnic groups requires consideration of additional communication issues, such as the use of interpreters and some knowledge of the family's culture, religion and beliefs, as misunderstandings and disagreements can arise more readily when language, cultural values and understandings are different.

Understanding parents' perspectives

The psychological models that have been used to aid understanding of the impact on parents of having a disabled child derive from those concerning human reactions to bereavement and loss. The relevance of such models is based on the notion that parents are grieving the loss of the normal child they were expecting. Behind this lie culturally determined notions that disabled people are less valuable than non-disabled people. In these models, most notably described by Lindemann (1944), Kubler Ross (1969), Bowlby (1979) and Worden (1991), certain stages or phases of grief (including tasks which are to be completed in each stage (Worden, 1991)) are proposed, and though each of the above writers may vary in terms of the number and names of the phases, they broadly cover the following:

- shock and numbness
- yearning and longing
- denial
- anger
- bargaining
- sadness and depression
- acceptance and re-organisation.

These models have, however, been criticised for being prescriptive and fostering judgements about what is normal or abnormal, thus denying individual difference and diversity in the grieving process, and other models have emerged which refine the earlier models and emphasise the individual context of grief and social, behavioural and spiritual dimensions, as well as the emotional and physical ones (Payne, 1999).

Olshansky (1962) developed the concept of 'chronic sorrow', later supported by the research of Wikler *et al.* (1981), which he applied to parents of disabled children, suggesting that the grieving process was ongoing and that later life cycle events and transitions often serve as a reminder of the original loss and re-awaken the process of grieving. This was not seen as an indication of poor adjustment to the loss, but as a normal coping reaction.

While in the context of a world which discriminates against and devalues disabled people, these models and stages may be useful in understanding the reactions of some parents of newly diagnosed children, there may be other emotional responses which should also not be overlooked, such as relief that a diagnosis has been made after a long period of suspicion that the child was not developing as expected. Other parents may adopt a determination to overcome negative perceptions and view their child in a very positive and hopeful way. Parents will react in different ways, and generalisations and assumptions should not be made about how they are likely to think and feel.

While there is a range of potential reactions and coping strategies for parents, some parents indicate understandably strong protective feelings towards their children and develop an intense bond, especially with those who remain highly dependent. Early intervention and emotional support for parents is crucial to enable them to manage family relationships, balance different needs and enhance the amount of pleasurable interactions between the baby/young child and family members. Talking to other parents in similar situations can be a great help for parents of a newly diagnosed child, so that they can learn from the experience of others and share their thoughts and feelings with others who have been through similar experiences.

Preschool years

Advances in health technology have made it easier to detect impairments at an earlier age in some instances (see Chapter 2) – the National Newborn Hearing Screening Programme, for example – and government policy in the last decade has emphasised the need to improve the provision of both practical and emotional support for parents and their children in the early years following diagnosis with the emphasis on multi-professional service provision. The Department for Education and Skills (now Department for Education) developed the *Early Support Programme* in England (DfES, 2004b), a pan-disability initiative to improve services for disabled children from birth to three years, and their families, funded as a pilot for four years between 2002 and 2006, and then a key component of the wider AHDC programme. It aims to make a positive impact on a child's development and to challenge the possibility, where relevant, of early decline or regression, through effective multi-agency family support and the involvement of parents in the planning and delivery of services through the use of family-held records (The Family File and Family Service Plan). Good quality information should be available for parents so that they are aware of the range of support services and their statutory entitlement. Improved professional knowledge and skills have also been emphasised. The programme initially produced policy and practice guidance entitled *Together from the Start* (DfES, 2003) for professionals working with disabled children, aimed at achieving a family and child-centred response from professionals. Also, the policy guidance entitled *Developing Early Intervention? Support Services for Deaf Children and Their Families* (DH/DfES, 2003) reflected the same aim.

Intrinsic within this is the development of care coordination through the role of key workers which seeks to minimise the difficulties parents can experience in having to negotiate a range of services to access support, often having to tell their story repeatedly to a trail of different professionals in order to get their needs met. A single point of contact is provided and continuity through key working. Service delivery should be child- and family centred and partnership focused. The scheme responded to messages from research (Beresford *et al.*, 1996; Britton, 2001) which had presented parents' dissatisfaction with service quality and arrangements. Families who have someone who acts as a coordinator or 'key worker' tend to have better relationships with services, higher morale, fewer unmet needs and are better informed (Beresford, 1995; Sloper and Turner, 1992). Evaluation is also a key component of this approach carried out through the Early Support multi-agency planning tool which can be used as a cross-agency audit tool to plan for improvements in outcomes for families.

In recent years, integrated services have become a key aspect of children's services. This began under the last Labour Government. In an attempt to promote social inclusion and raise standards in early years provision generally for children with disabilities, as well as children and families with other social and educational needs, the Early Excellence Programme pilots were established by the New Labour Government in 1997 following the White Paper *Excellence in Schools* (DfES, 1997) and embracing other government initiatives and projects, such as SureStart. The aim was to provide good quality integrated services for children and their parents needing the support of centre-based provision. Another aim which is consistent with much other current social policy is to promote effective multi-agency cooperation between education, social services, health and other agencies. The previous Labour Government under the Children Act 2004 established a legal basis for integrating education and social services united into one children's department. They also set up Children's Trusts to develop wider integration but the current Coalition Government has been less enthusiastic about these and has sought to minimise bureaucracy in promoting multi-agency cooperation. Integrated services though are now a key feature of provision for children, including children with disabilities, who may have their needs met through universal provision, as well as through specialist, targeted provision.

All children need to play and have fun. However, there is a danger that when a child has additional needs due to a disability, this important developmental experience can be lost due to a lack of opportunity. Play is essential to the development of communication, language and early numeracy and the acquisition of basic skills in these areas. Opportunities for inclusive play activities with non-disabled children are very important to the development of disabled children. The support of home learning specialists for preschool children and their parents (National Portage Association, www.portage.org.uk) can also help with play and a range of other important developmental issues, offering stability, encouragement and support for parents in what can be an uncertain time for them.

Early school years

Children with disabilities currently access a range of educational provision across mainstream and special schools and units (i.e. just for children with statements of special educational needs) offering both separate and integrated opportunities. Local authorities and schools do not at the moment provide statistics on disabled children in schools (mainstream or special), just those with special educational needs (which may be with or without a specific disability), so it is not possible to provide clear information on numbers of children with disabilities in schools, though the Department for Education is seeking to rectify this. In January 2012, some 226 125 pupils (2.8 per cent) across all schools in England had statements of SEN (DfE, 2012b). This percentage has remained unchanged in recent years.

The term 'special educational needs' was introduced in the 1981 Education Act and replaced the categories of handicap used in the 1944 Education Act. Inclusion in the education system is a fairly recent development for children with severe learning difficulties with the implementation in 1971 of the Education of Handicapped Children Act 1970. Prior to this, doctors had reserved for themselves the right to decide whether a child was 'educable' or 'ineducable', the latter being sent to junior training centres run by local health authorities.

The 1993 and 1996 Education Acts continued to employ the term 'special educational needs', and a system of statutory assessment for children leading to provision has developed around this concept which is currently maintained through the Revised SEN Code of Practice (DfES, 2001). This is a guide for early education settings, state schools and local education authorities, detailing the help they should give to children who have, or are thought to have, special educational needs. Schools and local education authorities must take account of the code when they deal with a child with special educational needs. A Statement of Special Educational Needs resulting from an assessment is designed to ensure that the support needed by an individual child to progress educationally is available to him/her either in a mainstream or special school setting.

The educational framework in England is based on the notion of the identification of children's differences in learning needs which can be a useful process to ensure that children's individual characteristics and needs are recognised and met, but can also be seen as a process of labelling through a deficit model which devalues children's differences from the 'norm'. Within current debates, special schools can be seen either as protective enclaves or as a useful facility to address individual needs and differences within a broad inclusion strategy, as part of a wider project that aims towards a more inclusive society generally (Cigman, 2007). As Mittler (2000) has pointed out, schools generally are society's agents for socialising children and young people and, as such, have a duty to promote inclusion effectively in order to challenge negative attitudes and promote by example the respect for, and valuing of, diversity and difference. There is, however, evidence that there is some way to go in challenging negative attitudes as children with disabilities are at higher risk of being bullied in mainstream schools as they advance within the school system, than their non-disabled peers (McLaughlin *et al.*, 2012).

Formal assessment can provoke considerable concern for some parents who may be anxious about their child acquiring a label. The process can be very stressful and even intimidating for parents only just coming to terms with their child's disability. On the other hand, for some parents it can come as a relief to have their child's needs assessed to provide a detailed picture of their needs and thereby help them to secure the right kind of educational support and provision for their child.

Statemented children can have a wide variety of needs related to a wide range of disabilities or difficulties from learning disability or physical disability, hearing or visual impairment to autism and Asperger's syndrome and emotional and behavioural difficulties – or a combination of these. The code of practice states that 'Statements will be rare for children under two …' (SEN Code of Practice, 2001, Section 4.48).

For very young children who are screened and found to be deaf, then early intervention may be extremely important to facilitate communication between these children and their families and the development of linguistic skills, providing the parents have come to terms with the news of their child's deafness and are ready to make informed decisions. If the child has other disabilities in addition to deafness, such as visual impairment or physical disability, then it will be very important that a multi-professional assessment is undertaken as soon as possible to determine an appropriate support programme for the child.

The debate about integration versus segregation remains a contentious one as highlighted earlier. Opinions are still divided between those who promote inclusion for all pupils regardless of their disabilities and difficulties and those who see a continuing role for special schools to cater for those with the most complex needs. Mainstream schools now take many children who would have previously been sent to special schools and the severity of disabilities and difficulties has thereby now increased in special schools – particularly as those children with profound and multiple disabilities are surviving much longer because of improvements in medical interventions.

Different models of inclusive practice have been developed across the country by individual schools and local education authorities responding to local needs, including special schools or units linking with mainstream schools and working together; generic special schools which range across, for example, MLD (moderate learning difficulties), SLD (severe learning difficulties) and autistic units all in the same building; regional centres for low-incidence disabilities, such as visual or hearing impairments; the relocation of special schools and units on mainstream sites with dual registration for children in mainstream and special schools (for example with children with severe learning difficulties to help them to be a part of the school community and not an occasional addition). Resistance can be found in mainstream schools to inclusion, when it is seen as detrimental to other children and a change in attitude here through countering ignorance and fear is fundamental to pursuing this important shift in policy and practice.

Many parents find the experience of the school years positive and supportive. The school environment can act as a fairly easy contact point for other services, such as health and social care, where a multi-professional approach is fostered. Contact with other parents informally or through support groups contributes to a sense for parents of accessible sources of support, information and advice.

The current Coalition Government wants to reform education and health support for children with special educational needs (SEN) and disabilities. It is heralded as the biggest programme of reform in this area for 30 years, seeking to address deficiencies in the current system and eliminate delays for parents in accessing the right provision, support and equipment for their child and a Green Paper (for consultation) was published in 2011 entitled *Support and Aspiration* (DfE, 2011). The Department for Education wanted to set up test areas known as 'pathfinders' (20 were identified in September 2011) to test out some core elements of their proposed policy, including, importantly:

- a single education, health and care plan from birth to 25 years old
- personal budgets for parents of disabled children and children with SEN
- the role of voluntary and community sector organisations and parents in a new system.

The government has also published the SEN and Disability (SEND) Green paper *Progress and Next Steps* (DfE, 2012a) which reveals key aspects of the Children and Families Bill and reports on the government's next steps in relation to other SEN reforms. In May 2012, it was announced in the Queen's Speech that the Children and Families Bill would be introduced to Parliament in Spring 2013. The government proposes to introduce the new single assessment process and 'Education, Health and Care Plan', to replace statements of SEN, reduce the time currently taken for the statutory assessment process and tackle delays in the provision of advice for the statutory assessment. The single assessment process will combine education, health and care plans so that health and social services are included in the package of support, along with education, and ensure assessment and plans run from birth to 25 years old, giving families one single package of support, tailored to their individual needs. This will include a health and development review for children aged between 2 and 2½ years, as well as effective integrated support for children with the most complex needs.

Communication

For professionals working with young disabled children, ascertaining their wishes and feelings is an important aspect of any direct work. Just like all children, disabled children have the right to express their views, wishes and feelings and for these to be taken into account in decision making on issues affecting them. This right finds expression in Article 12 of the UN Convention on the Rights of the Child and underpins the Children Act 1989. Young children with disabilities may be delayed in learning conventional modes of communication and may require specialised interventions in order to develop their communication skills. Augmentative and alternative communications can be used to supplement or replace verbal communication through the use of computerised approaches, photographs, symbols, gestures and signs. Some disabled children do not develop verbal communication at all, so familiarity with signing systems such as Bliss, Makaton and British Sign Language will be extremely important for anyone interacting with these children as they grow and develop.

For some children, the severity of their impairment may appear to prevent them from communicating. There is an increased awareness of communication techniques in work with children and adults with profound and multiple learning disabilities (e.g. Caldwell, 1996; Grove *et al.*, 2000; Porter *et al.*, 2001; Lawton, 2006; Goldbart and Caton 2010; The Communication Trust, 2011) where intellectual and physical communication difficulties may limit the articulation of wishes, preferences and choices. However, a particularly concerning issue and evidence of persisting disabling attitudes would be the assumption that because they do not communicate verbally, then they do not have a view to express or another way of expressing it. In these instances, it is necessary to tune in to non-verbal communication. Observation skills are very important to pick up facial expressions (the 'language of the eyes'), body language and the meaning of specific sounds. Professionals need to ensure they make the time and effort to appreciate such sounds and signs. Communication by health professionals is identified as problematic in research that informed Mencap's 2010 guide to communication with people with the most complex needs (Goldbart and Caton, 2010).

In fact, the Children Act 1989, under which services may be accessed for disabled children (e.g. respite care), requires that the Social Services Department 'ascertain [their] wishes and feelings' and take these into account when making decisions (Children Act, Sections 20 (6), 22 (4) and (5)). Additionally, Children Act Guidance and Regulations (Department of Health, 1997) state that, 'No assumption should be made about "categories" of children with disabilities who cannot share in decision-making or give consent to or refuse examination, assessment or treatment'. Choice is a crucial aspect of growing personal autonomy and those who work directly with children with profound and complex disabilities know that, like everyone else, they make choices all the time – for example, showing preferences in relationships by gravitating repeatedly towards a particular individual or avoiding another. There is a need therefore to develop finely tuned communication skills, such as listening and observation, to pick up changes in expression or demeanour – what Beamer and Brookes (2001: 29) refer to as 'choice-making behaviour'. Close working with family members who usually know the child best, wider networks and an internal dialogue and reflexive approach on the part of the professional worker are all necessary to ensure as accurate an interpretation of meaning as possible. Inclusion of the whole network of people who know the child will be important as a means of accessing a detailed knowledge and understanding of the child's communication patterns and ways of expressing feelings and preferences.

Disabled children: vulnerability and protection

Child protection policy and practice are discussed in Chapter 10. While it is not possible to explore this in any depth here, it is important briefly to outline issues about vulnerability and protection which are of particular significance for disabled children and their parents/carers.

Over the last 20 years or more, individuals and organisations have struggled to bring to the attention of government, local authorities and major children's organisations that disabled children are more vulnerable to neglect and abuse (physical, sexual and emotional) than non-disabled children (Westcott, 1991; Kennedy, 1992; Westcott and Cross, 1996; Morris 1999; DH/DfES, 2004). The NSPCC has acknowledged that:

all the evidence that we have about disabled children's experiences suggests that they are more vulnerable to abuse than non-disabled children.

(NSPCC, 2003: 9)

There are a number of reasons for this which the above document explores very comprehensively (NSPCC, 2003: 21–23). For many years, the social context which made disabled children invisible led to professional inertia and indifference towards their vulnerability. There was a mistaken belief that disability protected disabled children from abuse or that they were less likely to be damaged than other children by abuse. The climate has changed, but prejudice, discrimination and oppression still remain factors to be challenged within organisations and within individual professional workers (Westcott and Cross, 1996; Colton, 2002). Disabled children often have a continuing physical and social dependency on carers as a result of their impairments and may be unable to communicate that abuse is happening, may lack appropriate vocabulary or carers may be reluctant to hear what is being communicated. There may also be multiple caregivers involved with a particular child's care due to respite care or residential schooling, which may expose that child to increased risk. At home, pressure on families when a child has challenging behaviours or very demanding physical needs can also be a contributing factor to stress levels within a family and in such instances regular support and breaks for parents are important in the protection of children through ensuring that parents are adequately supported themselves.

In 2009, specialist advice entitled *Safeguarding Disabled Children* was published by the then Department for Children, Schools and Families, and the *Staying Safe: Action Plan* (Department for Children, Schools and Families, 2008) made a commitment to target policies to protect disabled children and to promote their welfare. A key practice requirement across all professions involved is effective information sharing. In a general review of safeguarding, the findings of Holmes *et al.* (2010) suggested that agencies are continuing to develop and improve this. However, a report published by Ofsted in August 2012 suggests that disabled children are still less likely to be subject to child protection, as concerns were less likely to be recognised and dealt with early enough (Ofsted, 2012).

Family matters

There is a range of literature that has emerged during the past 40 years or so, highlighting the experiences of parents caring at home for a disabled child, and the stresses and difficulties commonly faced (e.g. Gath, 1978; Baldwin, 1985; Read, 1991; Shah, 1992; Beresford, 1994; Burke and Cigno, 1996; Read, 2000; Redmond and Richardson, 2003; Evans, 2004).

What is clear from surveying the research is that the relevant themes that emerge have not changed significantly over the years in key areas. The stresses which parents experience (financial, practical and emotional) continue to be highlighted (Zijlstra and Vlascamp, 2005; Oelofsen and Richardson, 2006; Contact a Family, 2003, 2011, 2012a; The Children's Society, 2011), as do the difficulties for siblings (Atkinson and Crawford, 1995; Dodd, 2004).

Some research has highlighted the rewards of family caregiving (Clifford, 1990; Beresford, 1994), while other studies have focused on the impact on the parental relationship (Contact a Family, 2003) with stress, depression and lack of sleep being commonly experienced problems for parents, with unhelpful professional attitudes and approaches (Beresford *et al.*, 1996) and ways of improving these (Davies and Gavidia-Payne, 2009).

The needs of families have long been documented in academic literature. Glendinning (1983) highlighted several important areas of support for families from social workers – someone to talk to, the provision of practical help and sensitive responses to ambivalent feelings. Anderson (1982) also stressed the relevance of both emotional and practical support and the importance of focusing on both in order to achieve meaningful interventions. In 2003, the Audit Commission produced an important report on services for disabled children (Audit Commission, 2003). The researchers interviewed 240 disabled children, young people and their families about their experiences. The study found that it is harder for disabled children and their families to contribute to everyday life in the way that others take for granted. At worst, this can result in the social exclusion of the whole family. Key issues for parents were barriers to economic participation and concerns about housing, limited child care options and inaccessible benefits information. Play and leisure services were critical for children. Where there was flexibility and sensitivity to a child's needs, the opportunity to play with disabled and non-disabled peers was highly valued. Restricted access, service gaps or bullying cultures put pressure on the whole family. Parents and children said that their successful access to services, social activities, education and employment depended crucially on the accessibility of transport. The research confirmed the impact of the so-called 'postcode lottery of care' on access to services. It also found that often too little was being provided, too late, with long waits for information, equipment and treatment, and that families have to negotiate a maze of services which is frustrating and confusing.

Subsequently, governments have attempted to address these issues as outlined above (AHDC programme), but research carried out by Contact a Family (CAF) in 2011 and 2012 (cited above) confirms many of these issues are still affecting families through the financial, practical and emotional pressures arising from insufficient support services, inadequate incomes, isolation, bullying, discrimination and unmet psychological needs. Lack of support from statutory services, low income levels and stigma are the main causes of isolation. On the financial front, research statistics from the CAF website (Contact a Family, 2012b) reveal that 99.1 per cent of disabled children live at home and are supported by their families, and it costs up to three times as much to raise a disabled child as it does to raise a child without disabilities, so that 52 per cent of families with a disabled child are at risk of living in poverty. While in many families both parents now work, only 16 per cent of mothers with a disabled child work, compared to 61 per cent of other mothers. Currently, families with a disabled child may be entitled to receive support through the disability elements of child tax credit. Under the proposed 'universal credit', this support is to be provided through 'disability additions' within household benefit entitlements. Some believe that the policy intention of the current Coalition Government to halve the maximum level of support provided through these disability additions will push some families with disabled children below the poverty line (The Children's Society, 2011: 14).

One positive area of development under the previous Labour Government was the emphasis on increasing the availability of positive short break opportunities for children with disabilities. These were developed through the AHDC programme (see above) and more recently the Coalition Government has announced its support. However, in a time of austerity, there is concern that the need for families to access a range of specialist and universal services and have a voice in how they are provided, may be compromised by cuts to local authority budgets.

Learning activity

Thinking about the needs of families, can you list some of the areas of practical and emotional support that you think would be important to encourage integration and enable disabled children, their parents and siblings to lead lives that they would consider 'normal'? You could include in your list support groups, leisure and recreational activities, transport needs, practical help within the home and therapeutic interventions. Who would be responsible for providing this support? Can you think of services and opportunities local to you that would provide such support?

Partnership

Working in partnership has become an important aspect of professional interaction with parents who use formal services. It has been part of a wider policy development towards more consumer power generally as the public sector became increasingly subjected to a market-style approach. The Children Act 1989 recognised the crucial role of families as the most appropriate place for children to be brought up. Supporting parents in doing this effectively, in partnership with professionals, is seen, in the majority of cases, as the most efficient use of public resources.

Research over the years has consistently demonstrated that professional support for parents of disabled children is beneficial (Younghusband *et al.*, 1970; Glendinning, 1983; Young *et al.*, 2008) and also that parents' unique knowledge and expertise about their child must be recognised (Beresford, 1995).

However, 'partnership' is not an easy concept in practice. With the highlighting of the importance of working in partnership with parents in the Children Act (Department of Health, 1997: 9), social work literature in the 1990s paid much attention to trying to tease out its meaning and usefulness for practitioners. As Stevenson and Parsloe (1993) comment, 'Partnership is very vague since it suggests an equality which is rarely possible' (Stevenson and Parsloe, 1993: 6).

Handy (1985) attempted to analyse the operation of power in organisations and described five aspects of 'social' power which could be used to exert influence over another person:

- physical power
- resource power
- position power
- expert power
- personal power.

Professionals can be seen to have resource power, position power (conferred via their perceived status and role) and expert power (knowledge gained through training that is ascribed to their particular role) and may be able to use personal power through the force of their own personality. Physical power in extreme cases may be wielded with the support of the organisation by invoking state power through legislation to remove children from their families to prevent harm. Against this weighty armour, parents and service users may have less overall power, though policy and practice in recent years have attempted to shift the balance towards them by ensuring consultation and consideration of their views and making professional decision-making more transparent. Within the professional–parent relationship, an explicit exploration of the expertise that each brings to the situation, and an honest explanation of professional power (its extent and limitations), is a helpful way forward.

Solomon (1976), in a seminal work on black service users' interactions with formal welfare service provision in America, identified three potential sources of powerlessness which can be usefully generalised, covering negative self-images, negative experiences in engaging with external systems and systems which consistently block and deny powerless groups the opportunity to take effective action. Solomon made a direct link between empowerment and the service delivery system, 'The success or failure of empowerment is directly related to the degree to which [the] service delivery system itself is an obstacle course or an opportunity system' (Solomon, 1976: 29).

Service delivery systems can indeed be hard for parents to negotiate and there is research literature that supports this. The national report, *Services for Disabled Children* (Audit Commission, 2003) found a jigsaw puzzle of services with families struggling through a maze of services to track down essential information. Research by Davies and Gavidia-Payne (2009) demonstrates that parental perceptions and experiences of family-centred professional support is one of the strongest predictors of family quality of life. Their findings provide evidence of the significance of a family-focused approach to support and of intervention that acknowledges the unique needs of individual families. This is best achieved through a relationship-based and partnership-based approach from professionals.

Partnership between agencies has also been a policy aim of government for some time, both at strategic and operational levels, with limited success. Professional teams working in different organisations, with different management structures, different cultures, values, pressures and priorities can work against meeting the needs of children and families effectively and efficiently and in an holistic way. Developments within the Children Act (2004) have emphasised a need for a change in culture with greater emphasis on partnership and more joint working between agencies. Ways forward included the development of a common assessment framework between agencies; more integrated services and organisational structures; improved information sharing; and more clearly defined accountability through the introduction of lead professionals where several different professionals are involved with a family. The lead professional will be responsible for ensuring a coherent and coordinated package of services for an individual child and family. There is a real need for what the *National Service Framework* (Department of Health/Department for Education and Skills, 2004: 24) calls 'seamless integrated working'.

Conclusion

Changes in culture can take time to manifest, but there have been a number of government initiatives over the last 20–30 years that have worked to improve services and to develop an integrated and inclusive approach for disabled children and their families. The New Labour governments prior to 2010 were actively driving policy changes on this front and the current government seems to be continuing this trend.

This chapter has looked very broadly at policy and practice issues and developments for disabled children and their families. While progress remains ongoing, with hard-pressed statutory agencies often struggling to provide an adequate service for an increasingly complex population of disabled children, it can be seen from the limited scope of this discussion that significant steps forward are being taken in the drive to provide a more inclusive experience for young disabled children and support for their families.

Evaluate your learning

- What do you see as the most significant changes for disabled children and their families in the last 50 years?
- What supports do you think are most important for families during the early years of a disabled child's life?
- How can disabled children be supported to be further integrated into their local communities?

References

Aldgate, J and Tunstill, J (1995): *Making Sense of Section 17. A Study for the Department of Health: Implementing Services for Children in Need within the 1989 Children Act.* London: HMSO.

Anderson, D (1982): *Social Work and Mental Handicap.* London: Macmillan.

Atkinson, N and Crawford, M (1995): *All in the Family: Siblings and Disability.* London: NCH Action for Children.

Audit Commission (1994): *Seen But Not Heard: Coordinating Community Child Health and Social Services for Children in Need.* London: HMSO.

Audit Commission (2003): *National Report on Services for Disabled Children.* London: HMSO. (Online). Last accessed: 29 April 2004. Available from: www.audit-commission. gov.uk/reports.

Baldwin, S (1985): *The Costs of Caring: Families with Disabled Children.* London: Routledge and Kegan Paul.

Beamer, S and Brookes, M (2001): *Making Decisions. Best Practice and New Ideas for Supporting People with High Support Needs to Make Decisions.* London: Values into Action.

Beresford, B (1994): *Positively Parents: Caring for a Severely Disabled Child.* London: HMSO.

Beresford, B (1995): *Expert Opinions: A Survey of Parents Caring for a Severely Disabled Child.* Bristol: Policy Press.

Beresford, B, Sloper, P, Baldwin, S and Newman, T (1996): *What Works in Services for Families with a Disabled Child?* Barkingside: Barnados.

Bowlby, J (1979): *The Making and Breaking of Affectional Bonds.* London: Tavistock.

Britton, C (2001): *Telling It How It Is: Researching the Family's Perspective – What Is It Really Like for Families Managing Their Child's Serious Condition at Home?* Birmingham: Handsel Trust.

Burke, P and Cigno, K (1996): *Support for Families. Helping Children with Learning Disabilities.* Aldershot: Avebury.

Caldwell, P (1996) *Getting in Touch.* Brighton: Pavilion.

Cigman, R (2007): *Included or Excluded? The Challenge of the Mainstream for Some SEN Children.* Oxford: Routledge.

Clifford, D (1990): *The Social Costs and Rewards of Care.* Aldershot: Avebury.

Colton, M (2002): Factors associated with abuse in residential child care institutions. *Children and Society* **16**(1), 33–44.

Contact a Family (2003): No Time for Us. Relationships Between Parents Who Have a Disabled Child. [Online]. Last accessed 18: August 2012. Available from: www.cafamily.org.uk/professionals/research/statistics.html.

Contact a Family (2011): *Forgotten Families. The Impact of Isolation on Families With Disabled Children Across the UK.* London: Contact a Family.

Contact a Family (2012a): *Counting the Costs. The Financial Reality for Families With Disabled Children across the UK.* London: Contact a Family.

Contact a Family (2012b): *Statistics and Research for Professionals.* (Online). Last accessed: 21 August 2012. Available from: www.cafamily.org.uk/professionals/research/statistics.html.

Croll, P and Moses, D (2000): Ideologies and utopias: education professionals' views of inclusion. *European Journal of Special Needs Education* **15**(1), 1–12.

Davies, K and Gavidia-Payne, S (2009): The impact of child, family, and professional support characteristics on the quality of life in families of young children with disabilities. *Journal of Intellectual and Developmental Disability* **34**(2), 153–62.

Department for Children, Schools and Families (2007): *The Children's Plan: Building Brighter Futures.* London: Department for Children, Schools and Families.

Department for Children, Schools and Families (2008): *Staying Safe: Action Plan.* London: Department for Children, Schools and Families.

Department for Education (2011): *Support and Aspiration: A New Approach to Special Educational Needs and Disability.* London: Department for Education.

Department for Education (2012a): *Support and Aspiration: Progress and Next Steps.* London: Department for Education.

Department for Education (2012b): Special Educational Needs in England, January 2012 National Statistics. (Online). Last accessed 21 August 2012. Available from: www.education.gov.uk/rsgateway/DB/SFR/s001075/index.shtml.

Department for Education and Skills (1997): *White Paper, Excellence in Schools*. London: HMSO.

Department for Education and Skills (2001): *Revised Code of Practice for Special Educational Needs*. London: HMSO.

Department for Education and Skills (2003): *Developing Early Intervention? Support Services for Deaf Children and Their Families*. London: HMSO.

Department for Education and Skills (2004a): *Every Child Matters: Change for Children*. London: HMSO.

Department for Education and Skills (2004b): *Early Support. Helping Every Child Succeed. Professional Guidance*. London: HMSO.

Department of Health (1997): *The Children Act 1989 Guidance and Regulations*. London: Department of Health.

Department of Health, Department for Education and Employment and the Home Office (2000): *Framework for Assessing Children in Need and their Families*. London: The Stationery Office.

Department of Health/Department for Education and Skills (2003): *Together from the Start. Practical Guidance for Professionals Working With Disabled Children (Birth to Third Birthday) and Their Families*. London: HMSO.

Department of Health and the Department for Education and Skills (2004): *The National Service Framework for Children, Young People and Maternity Services: Standard 8*. London: DH.

Disability Rights Commission (2002): *Code of Practice for Schools – Disability Discrimination Act 1995: Part 4*. London: TSO.

Dodd, LW (2004): Supporting the siblings of young children with disabilities. *British Journal of Special Education* **31**(1), 41–9.

Evans, K (2004): One family's fight. *Community Care* **1522**, 42–3.

Finkelstein, V (1997): Emancipating disabling studies. In Shakespeare, T (ed), *The Disability Reader: Social Sciences Perspectives*. London: Cassell.

Gath, A (1978): *Down's Syndrome and the Family – The Early Years*. London: Academic Press.

Glendinning, C (1983): *Parents and their Disabled Children*. London: Routledge and Kegan Paul.

Goldbart, J and Caton, S (2010): *Communication and People With the Most Complex Needs: What Works and Why This Is Essential*. London: Mencap.

Grove, N, Bunning, K, Porter, J and Morgan, M (2000): *See what I Mean: Guidelines to Aid Understanding of Communication by People with Severe and Profound Learning Disabilities*. Kidderminster: BILD/Mencap.

Handy, C (1985): *Understanding Organisations*. Harmondsworth: Penguin.

Holmes, L, Munro, ER and Soper, J (2010): *Calculating the Cost and Capacity Implications for Local Authorities Implementing the Laming (2009) Recommendations*. London: LGA. (Online). Last accessed: 20 August 2012. Available from: www.lga.gov.uk/lga/aio/9387423.

Jones, H (2001): *Disabled Children's Rights: A Practical Guide, International Save the Children Alliance*. Sweden: Save the Children.

Kennedy, M (1992): Children with severe disabilities: too many assumptions. *Child Abuse Review* **1**, 85–7.

Kubler Ross, E (1969): *On Death and Dying.* London: Tavistock/Routledge.

Lawton, A (2006): *A Voice of Their Own – A Toolbox of Ideas and Information for Non-instructed Advocacy.* Kidderminster: BILD.

Lindemann, E (1944): The symptomatology and management of acute grief. *American Journal of Psychiatry* **101**, 141.

McLaughlin, C, Byers, R and Oliver, C (2012): *Perspectives on Bullying and Difference: Supporting Young People with Special Educational Needs and/or Disabilities in School.* London: National Children's Bureau.

Mencap (1999): *Living in Fear.* London: Mencap.

Mittler, P (2000): *Working Towards Inclusive Education: Social Contexts.* London: Fulton.

Morris, J (1999): Disabled children, child protection systems and the Children Act 1989. *Child Abuse Review* **8**, 91–108.

Norwich, B (2007): *Dilemmas of Difference, Inclusion and Disability: International Perspectives and Future Directions.* Oxon: Routledge.

NSPCC (2003): *'It doesn't happen to disabled children'. Child protection and disabled children. Report of the National Working Group on Child Protection and Disability.* London: NSPCC.

Oelofsen, N and Richardson, P (2006): Sense of coherence and parenting stress in mothers and fathers of preschool children with developmental disability. *Journal of Intellectual and Developmental Disability* **31**(1), 1–12.

Office of the Children's Commissioner (2006): *Bullying Today: A Report by the Office of the Children's Commissioner.* London: OCC.

Ofsted (2012): *Protecting Disabled Children: Thematic Inspection Report.* (Online). Last accessed: 22 September 2012. Available from: www.ofsted.gov.uk.

Oliver, M (1990): *The Politics of Disablement.* London: Macmillan.

Olshansky, S (1962): Chronic sorrow, a response to having a mentally defective child. *Social Casework* **43**, 190–3.

Oswin, M (1971): *The Empty Hours. A Study of the Weekend Life of Handicapped Children in Institutions.* Harmondsworth: Penguin.

Oswin, M (1978): *Children Living in Long-Stay Hospitals. Spastics International Medical Publications Research Monograph No. 5.* London: Heinemann Medical.

Oswin, M (2000): *Revisiting the empty hours.* In Brigham, L, Atkinson, D, Jackson, M *et al.* (eds). *Crossing Boundaries. Change and Continuity in the History of Learning Disability.* Kidderminster: Bild.

Payne, S (1999): *Loss and Bereavement.* Buckingham: Open University Press.

Porter, J, Ouvry, C, Morgan, M and Downs, C (2001): Interpreting the communication of people with profound and multiple learning difficulties. *British Journal of Learning Disabilities* **29**, 12–6.

Read, J (1991): There was never really any choice: the experience of mothers of disabled children in the United Kingdom. *Women's Studies International Forum* **14**(6), 561–71.

Read, J (2000): *Disability, the Family and Society: Listening to Mothers.* Buckingham: Open University Press.

Redmond, B and Richardson, V (2003): Just getting on with it: exploring the service needs of mothers who care for young children with severe/profound and life-threatening intellectual disability. *Journal of Applied Research in Intellectual Disabilities* **16**, 205–18.

Runswick-Cole, K (2008): *Between a Rock and a Hard Place: Parents' Attitudes to the Inclusion of Children with Special Educational Needs in Mainstream and Special Schools.* Oxford: Blackwell Publishing.

Schaeffer, A (2010): *The Disadvantages of Placing Students in Special Schools.* (Online). Last accessed: 2 August 2012. Available from: www.ehow.com/list_6154608_disadvantages-placing-students-special-schools.html#ixzz!Njf5TDxg.

Scope (1994): *Right from the Start.* London: Scope.

Shah, R (1992): *The Silent Minority. Asian Children with Disabilities.* London: National Children's Bureau.

Sloper, P and Turner, S (1992): Service needs of families of children with severe physical disability. *Child: Care, Health and Development* **18**, 259–82.

Sloper, P, Beresford, B and Rabiee, P (2009) Every Child Matters Outcomes: what do they mean for disabled children and young people? *Children and Society* **23**, 265–78.

Solomon, BB (1976): *Black Empowerment: Social Work in Oppressed Communities.* New York: Columbia University Press.

Stevenson, O and Parsloe, P (1993): *Community Care and Empowerment.* York: Joseph Rowntree Foundation.

Stocks, J (2012): *The day we were told our children were disabled: It was the most shattering moment of these parents' lives. MailOnline/femail.* (Online). Last accessed: 2 August 2012. Available from: www.dailymail.co.uk/femail/article-2085377/The-day-told-children-disabled-It-shattering-moment-parents-lives.html.

The Children's Society (2011): *4 in every 10. Disabled Children Living in Poverty.* London: The Children's Society.

The Communication Trust (2011): *Other Ways of Speaking: Supporting Children and Young People Who Have No Speech or Whose Speech is Difficult to Understand.* London: The Communication Trust. (Online). Last accessed: 18 August 2012. Available from: http://bit.ly/etJFrN

United Nations (1990): United Nations Convention on the Rights of the Child. New York: United Nations.

Westcott, HL (1991): The abuse of disabled children: a review of the literature. *Child: Care, Health and Development* **17**(4), 243–58.

Westcott, HL and Cross, M (1996): *This Far and No Further: Towards Ending the Abuse of Disabled Children.* Birmingham: Venture Press.

Wikler, L, Wasow, M and Hatfield, E (1981): Chronic sorrow revisited: parents vs. professional depiction of the adjustment of parents of mentally retarded children. *American Journal of Orthopsychiatry* **5**(1), 63–70.

Wolfensberger, W (1983): Social role valorisation: a proposed new term for the principle of normalisation. *Mental Retardation* **21**(6), 234–39.

Worden, JW (1991): *Grief Counselling and Grief Therapy,* 2nd edn. New York: Springer Publishing.

Young, A, Temple, B, Davies, L, Parkinson, G and Bolton, J (2008): Disabled Children (0–3 years) and integrated services – the impact of Early Support. *Health and Social Care in the Community* **16**(3), 222–33.

Younghusband, E, Birchall, D, Davie, R and Pringle, MLK (eds) (1970): *Living with Handicap*. London: National Children's Bureau.

Zijlstra, HP and Vlaskamp, C (2005): The impact of medical conditions on the support of children with profound intellectual and multiple disabilities. *Journal of Applied Research in Intellectual Disabilities* **18**, 151–61.

Further reading

Burke, P and Cygno, K (2000): *Learning Disabilities in Children*. London: Blackwell.

Hewitt-Taylor, J (2008): *Providing Support at Home for Children and Young People who Have Complex Health Needs*. Chichester: Wiley.

McWilliam, RA (2010): *Working with Families of Young Children with Special Needs*. Guildford: Guildford Press.

13 Children's geographies

Jessica Clark

This chapter aims to:

- discuss the remit of young children's geography as being broadly focused on the role of space and place in children's lives and the spatial construction of early childhood
- define key concepts, such as spatiality and place, recognising the social and cultural constitution of such spaces
- evaluate the dichotomies of particular spaces, such as urban versus rural, local versus global, public versus private and adult versus child
- consider the importance of listening to and reflecting upon children's experiences of such environments and the potential implications for participation and early years practice.

Introduction: what is 'children's geographies'?

Geographical study goes beyond describing or recording physical landscapes such as river estuaries or tectonic plates and despite the (possibly, not so fond) memories of learning place names some of us may have from school lessons, geography is so much more than just this. The Greek origins of the phrase geography, when literally translated, mean 'to write the world' (Cloke *et al.*, 2005). The world is, of course, made up of physical spaces and terrain but individuals, social groups and cultures are integral parts of this world and they too are a focus of the geographer, as well as how these landscapes and their inhabitants are represented. The academic study of geography is generally divided between physical and human geography (although as this chapter discusses it is difficult, if not impossible, to divorce the two). The arena of children's geographies can be broadly situated within the 'camp' of human geography and as a distinct subdiscipline in its own right draws on work from the fields of anthropology, childhood studies, cultural geography and cultural studies, economics, feminist geographies and gender studies, politics and political geography, psychology and sociology.

Children's geographies, as it will be considered within this chapter, can be situated broadly within the social studies of childhood (see Chapter 8 for a full discussion of the new sociology of childhood) and emerged as a subdiscipline in its own right in the 1990s as work in this arena reached critical mass (Holloway and Valentine, 2000), with the *Children's Geographies* journal launching in 2003. Geography, then, concerns what spaces and places are, how they are used, by whom and who gets to decide. It is also concerned with the meaning we attach to particular spaces, as representations of ideals, communities or nations, as well as constructs of home. Broadly then, it is the role of space and place in children's lives with which this chapter is concerned.

Place, space and all that other stuff

In order to begin to deconstruct the role of space and place in children's lives, it is useful to turn first of all to the concept of spatiality. Spatiality refers to the social construction of space and the constitution of human life through space. To put this more clearly, all being, all existence, all life, has to happen somewhere and geographers argue that where these lives happen matters. The variety of terms that shall be drawn across this chapter, such as place, location or landscape, and indeed all work in the discipline of children's geographies, 'attempts to express something about the "whereness" of the things in the world ... all things – human and non-human – only exist in and through space' (Cloke *et al.*, 2005: xi).

As such, children's geographers are interested not just in physical terrain or built environments but also in the people who inhabit (or not) such spaces. Ingold (2000) uses the concept of the 'zone of entanglement' to argue that environment is not simply something we act in or on, but something we are part of; the argument is that 'there would be no places were it not for the comings and goings of ... organisms to and from them, from and to places elsewhere' (Ingold, 2008: 1808).

So, places are physical terrain, the beings that inhabit it and the relations within and between the two. Place in this context is an abstract concept constituted by physical place, understandings of a place – perhaps considered as a sense of place, and ways in which these meanings are created – processes of place making (Pink, 2012). This chapter follows the work of Pink (2012: 24) who argues that rather than dividing understandings we should instead think of place as both the 'empirical realities of actual experienced environments and the practices that form a part of these'.

In this way, we consider the spatiality of place, how particular places are imbued with meaning as a result of human action and interaction. Consider this final example, many children will live in houses and such physical spaces allow for the distinction within the wider social order between the private and public spheres (Cloke *et al.*, 2005: xi). Dominant ideas of the private realm as the most appropriate, ideal space for children are only made possible by the existence of particular places, homes, which children can inhabit where they are spatially separate from the wider public sphere.

Domestic geographies and the spaces of 'home'

Figure 13.1 Home

The separation of work from family life, a legacy of the Industrial Revolution, saw the home become the key site of private lives and the space of the family, the 'modern domestic ideal' (Allan and Crow, 1989). The family as a private institution of social life is tasked with the responsibility of appropriately raising children to be productive future citizens. Thus, family spaces are considered the proper and ideal place for children. However, a singularly rose-tinted view becomes problematic considering that accidents involving children frequently take place within the home (Pain, 2006) and family spaces can also be the site of abuse, neglect, violence and exclusion (Blunt and Varley, 2004).

Domestic spaces are important areas for children's geographers to critically explore and they offer an opportunity for us to consider here how rules are negotiated and agency is practised. Children's bedrooms, for example, can be places of personalisation (Leverett, 2011) where boundaries are marked out and identities are constructed and presented in the form of personal objects or decoration. They are also spaces in which tensions must be negotiated as they are subject to parental surveillance (Sibley, 1995) and shared with other family members, such as siblings. Research examining children's negotiation of domestic spaces highlights the importance of not viewing, even toddlers and young children, as just pre-social objects rather, as full participants in domestic life (see also Chapter 1), attaching meaning to, and demonstrating imaginative use of, space (Gallacher, 2005).

The communal spaces of the home are also important aspects of children lives, as McKendrick (2004) demonstrates in explorations of the family meal as a significant space for intergenerational and sibling relationships. A site of familial and social bonds, houses are transformed into homes (Christensen *et al.*, 2000) that spatially order the activities of family life, such as communal eating or domestic labour (Douglas, 1991). The house as a place, a set of spaces, symbolises and gives a material reality to the abstract concept of home characterised by the social relations which comprise the family (Christensen *et al.*, 2000).

Home is a place, but it is also a space inhabited by family, people, things and belongings – a familiar, if not comfortable space where particular activities and relationships are lived.

(Mallett, 2004: 63)

So far, the spaces within homes have been considered, but it is also important to critically evaluate the abstract concept of home. Much material exploring social identity has viewed the home as a key source of rootedness (Christensen *et al.*, 2000). Following the early work of Barth (1969), identity formation is tied to particular geographical or spatial localities – home is thus viewed as a placed identity locus in early childhood (Christensen *et al.*, 2000). As the wider social sciences developed in the late 20th century, the influences of post-structuralism and post-modernism encouraged a critique of fixities and certainty, emphasising change, fragmentation and fluidity in contemporary social lives. Notions of the home thus moved from fixed to rooted in movement and studies which explore migration, street children and diasporic communities explore the making of home away from home (Rapport and Dawson, 1998).

Street children

Existing outside traditional spaces of childhood or in ways not compatible with the socio-spatial order also has implications for the lives of street children. The United Nations definition of a street child is:

Any minor for whom the street (in the widest sense of the world, including unoccupied dwellings, wasteland, etc.) has become his or her habitual abode and who is without adequate protection.

(Agnelli, 1986: 32)

The processes by which children come to live 'on the streets' are varied and complex. Some children migrate to cities in the Global South, for example, to work on the streets and as such, structural causes, such as poverty, play a significant role (Alexandrescu, 1996). It is important not just to consider economic factors and Conticini and Hulme's (2007) research cites violence and abuse within the family as key reasons for children to move to the street. Children have, however, also been shown to exercise agency on the streets, suggesting they employ a variety of skills and capacities (van Blerk, 2006). Beazley (2002) notes the local knowledge and mobility of children as they navigate the street accessing the best potential opportunities for economic activity.

The images presented of street children should be subject to critical evaluation, indeed, Bauman (1998) states that professional categories reduce the variance of the social world by not facilitating a regard for social diversity. It can be argued that 'those with social power … define the reality of others by shaping and constraining the ways it is possible to talk and think (Glauser, 1997: 151) as such dominant images of childhood shape how we define and understand street children and vice versa (see Gigengack (2000) for a detailed discussion of discourses surrounding street children). The home, the school, the nursery, the playground are all constructed as appropriate, even ideal, spaces for children in dominant discourses of the Minority World (see Majority and Minority Worlds box later in this chapter). As such, children on the street and children on the move are thus considered as not only outside the spaces for children, but outside childhood itself.

Places of education and the institutionalisation of childhood

Since the introduction of compulsory schooling in the UK, children have spent increasing amounts of time in 'educational' environments from schools, nurseries, children's centres and institutional childcare. From a geographical perspective, schools can be considered as institutions where children's bodies are regulated through a series of socio-spatial strategies (Pike, 2008). The spatial-temporal ordering of school shapes children's everyday experiences (Christensen and James, 2001). Consider for example how the spaces of a school or early years setting interact with the timetable for a given day. Children are expected to engage in different activities, in different spaces, at different times, with decisions made frequently by adults. Children are asked to sit quietly at desks for individual work, line up in single file to enter buildings from the playground or sit cross-legged on the floor for group activities. Even during free play there are boundaries imposed on children's use of, for example, certain equipment like computers or paints or particular spaces, such as the outdoors (for further discussion of how children's bodies are regulated see Chapter 3, *Embodied childhoods*).

It is at this juncture that readers are reminded that issues of power and control are central to an analysis of childhood space (Smith and Barker, 2000) and schools are key organisations where children's lives are constructed by adults. In their analysis of primary school lunchtimes, both Daniel and Gustafsson (2010) and Pike (2008) draw on the work of Foucault (1980, 1991) to highlight how spaces and the individuals which inhabit them are shaped by wider social policy, interventions and discourses and how children seek to carve out spaces of their own within an adult-controlled school day.

Foucault's concept of governmentality illustrates how governmental power is practised and executed through a myriad of techniques and practices. Of interest here is how particular governments or regimes seek to shape the actions of individuals and populations in particular places. As Foucault stated in *Discipline and Punish* (1991: 41) 'discipline proceeds from the distribution of individuals in space'. Crucial to this for children's educational geographies are the spatial practices deployed which limit children's fields of action (Pike, 2008). In this sense, the organisation of the school dining room, for example, emerges as governmental practice shaping children within the setting (Pike, 2008).

Despite work such as that of McKendrick (2004) emphasising the social importance of a meal and the meal-space, the focus in the dining room is on what children put in their mouths rather than the social context of food and eating in these communal institutional spaces. Travel within such eating spaces is often restricted, allowed for the purposes of gaining nutrition, but not for social interaction (Pike, 2008).

In considering the way children are constructed in UK social policy, Moss and Petrie (2002) make a distinction between children's services and children's spaces. Children's services, they suggest, are constructed as instruments or technologies for producing adult-driven outputs, for example education as producing productive healthy future citizens. They argue that the resultant provision is joyless and pose an alternative discourse of children's spaces:

Figure 13.2 Are you sitting comfortably?

Physical environments certainly, but also social cultural and discursive ... they foreground the present, rather than the future; they are part of life, not just preparation for it. They are spaces for children's own agendas, where children are understood as fellow citizens with rights ... agents of their own lives but also interdependent with others.

(Moss and Petrie, 2002: 107)

The school dining room is illustrated, by both Pike (2008) and Daniel and Gustaffson (2010), as a site of significant intervention in children's lives, notably in relation to nutrition and to well-being. A raft of policies have been implemented in this arena which highlight children as a special group requiring guidance on healthy choices (notable examples include Department of Health (2004) and Food Standards Association, 2007). Pike evidences this in citing both the placement of a salad bar and healthy eating posters on the walls as unavoidable landmarks all children must navigate within the school dining space:

Through the aesthetics and organisation of space, children are encouraged to adopt eating behaviours which conform to specific nutritional rationalities ... and discouraged from pursuing social interactions with their peers. Thus, the dominance of nutritional discourse over the social discourse is maintained by spatial practice.

(Pike, 2008: 418)

The lack of emphasis on the importance of the social aspect of school mealtimes and dining spaces is in direct contrast to the emphasis on families eating together within the home; the decline of which is often viewed as emblematic of broader anxieties about the moral condition of childhood. It can be seen that school spaces should be critically considered, not just as environments for children, but as part of wider social structures where power is articulated and as places where meaning is negotiated. There is an emerging body of literature which considers how the use of various forms of childcare shapes and is shaped by wider expectations of what it means to be a good parent (McDowell *et al.*, 2005) demonstrating that structures exist within and across particular spaces which serve to reinforce dominant discourses or ideas about children, childhood and families.

Figure 13.3 Imaginative use of spaces

Children's spaces in late modernity

It is argued that children's use of space has significantly changed in modern times, processes of domestication show a relocation of children's spaces from the external to the 'protected' spaces of the private domain (Hengst, 2007). In dominant westernised discourses, children, particularly young children, are located firmly within the private sphere of the family. Greater imposition of boundaries and regulations of spaces for children has led some to state that there has been an institutionalisation of childhood whereby children's activities are not only predominantly confined to the home, but increasingly placed in organised spaces, for example, schools (see Mayall (2002) for a discussion of the scholarisation of childhood).

Since the Industrial Revolution throughout the 19th century, children have, through the separation of work from family life and the introduction of compulsory education, been progressively confined to special spaces of childhood (Ansell, 2009: 193). The concept of islanding refers to how children navigate the spaces in their lives. They are perceived to jump from one bounded 'child' space to another – from home, to school, to child care, escorted, transported and constantly under adults' supervision. This fragmented experience of place is argued to be the result of the increasing domestication and institutionalisation of childhood and a declining use of public spaces. 'Children spend much of their time within the confines of islands such as houses, day care and recreation centre buildings, sports fields and playgrounds' (Zeiher, 2003: 66). These restrictions can result in children becoming invisible within local communities and when they are present in such spaces they can be viewed as illegitimate occupiers of the places of adults and adulthood (Skelton, 2000; Young, 2004).

Children and public spaces

Attitudes towards children's use of public space can be broadly categorised into two arenas. First, they are, more so in the case of older children, viewed as threats to public order. For example, the increasing privatisation of public space, such as shopping centres, can create tensions between children and adults as children are designed out of particular spaces (Malone, 2002). Business owners and staff can view children as a threat to public order without the consumptive power to be economically valuable. Second, perhaps more relevant to explorations of early childhood and somewhat paradoxically, children are seen as vulnerable to the dangers inherent in the adult public domain. Central to both of these perspectives is fear. Valentine (1996) states that parents associate public space with potential dangers for their children, such as traffic levels or abduction. These fears equate types of behaviours with particular places, the street as a physical environment is not necessarily problematic, rather it is the population of deviant 'others' that inhabit public spaces which pose a threat. As a result, children are protected by segregation and restricted access to the dangerous places of the adult public realm. These adult fears do not go unnoticed by children and they can internalise expectations of danger and withdraw further from public spaces (Holloway, 2005).

> *Thus children contribute through their own performative acts, towards producing public space as an adult space where they are not able to participate freely.*

(Valentine, 1996: 211)

Paradoxically, definitions of public space often draw on notions of a sphere available to everyone (Ganetz, 1995), yet it is these spaces which are so often conceptualised by adults as inappropriate for children.

Experience of local neighbourhoods for children vary as a result of a number of individual factors, such as gender or disability. There are other social factors to take into account, for example disadvantaged neighbourhoods are experienced differently by children in comparison to more affluent localities (Hill *et al.*, 2006) and despite prevailing romantic ideals about rural landscapes providing safe and expansive spaces for children, geographical ranges have been shown not to differ greatly from those of children in urban spaces (Matthews *et al.*, 2000).

The urban jungle and the rural idyll

Many of the fears expressed around children as vulnerable users of public space are based on anxieties surrounding children and urban spaces. While more than half of the world's children live in cities (Horschelmann and van Blerk, 2012), traditional views of urban landscapes are negative, while we tend to associate rurality with community and traditional urban spaces are characterised as strange and highly individual (Knox and Pinch, 2006). While none of these attributes are universally bad or desired, by noting contemporary fears surrounding the loss of childhood, the positively constructed relationship between children and rural spaces, a feature of current discourses (Jones, 2002) can be seen.

Cities are also spaces of poverty, exclusion and environmental problems. This is not to say that these issues are not relevant to other landscapes, but cities provide a stark contrast of rich and poor condensed in space, and cities in both the Majority and Minority Worlds are unequal environments.

Majority and Minority Worlds

The terms 'Majority World' and 'Minority World' refer to parts of the globe traditionally known as the Third and First Worlds and more recently as the Global South and Global North. They are used deliberately within this chapter, as is the case in Punch and Tisdall (2012), to recognise that the majority of population, land mass and lifestyles are located in the Majority Worlds of Asia, Africa and Latin America, thus seeking to shift the balance and avoid privileging western or minority 'north' perspectives (Punch, 2003).

The physical infrastructure of city shanty towns and slums in the Majority World is a key concern for children living in these spaces with limited or no access to clean water, sanitation and shelter, which are key features of absolute poverty. Greater access to public spaces and local communities are positive influences on children's well-being, but there are significant health implications of living in poor neighbourhoods (Bartlett, 1999). Cities of the Minority World are not immune to poverty and low income areas are characterised by few playgrounds, a lack of affordable leisure facilities and high volumes of traffic (Horschelmann and van Blerk, 2012). High rates of crime can lead to derelict and boarded up buildings, barbed wire fences and CCTV monitoring, all of which contribute to feelings of isolation and exclusion for children inhabiting such spaces (see Horschelmann and van Blerk, 2012).

Despite the negative implications for children of living in cities, urban environments have been seen to offer a variety of opportunities for engaging in the social life of the city. The back streets of slum neighbourhoods in many cities in the Majority World are inherently social spaces where children combine daily chores with opportunities for play (Horschelmann and van Blerk, 2012). Gough (2008) and Dalsgaard et al. (2008) both demonstrate how the lives of children are embedded in high density socio-spatial networks, characterised for the former by tensions between adults and children over music in Zambia and for the latter by the impact of social class on how children negotiate, as either threatening (for middle class) or as sites of peer relations (working class), the streets of Recife, Brazil.

In contrast to the sometimes dark and somewhat negative images we are provided with of city life for children, rural landscapes are idealised as the natural spaces of childhood. Rurality can be viewed as itself a social construct (Mormont, 1990). Images of rural landscapes are not just references to physical spaces or landmarks, they are imbued with particular meanings where individuals live healthy lives close to nature with a kind of community and freedom not associated with urban life. Rural life is thus idyllised – 'the process by which dominant myths about places and spaces come to reflect circumstances of … harmonious living' (Cloke, 2005: 452). Despite traditional understandings of nature as somehow outside culture (Anderson, 2010), the natural world should be considered as shaped as powerfully by human imagination as it is by physical territory and materials (Whatmore, 2005). Places are imbued with emotional meaning, in this context, the rural idyll generates 'environmentally induced awe and love for a natural world felt worthy of protection and respect' (Smith, 2001). Raymond Williams (1985) argues that popular culture serves up a continuing flood of sentimental and selectively nostalgic versions of country life. Children's television, toys and literature like Postman Pat, The Herbs, Teletubbies and Sylvanian Families all present images of safe, nostalgic countryscapes.

Figure 13.4 Natural space?

However, such stereotypes are problematic and serve to mask the darker side of rural life: social problems which threaten to destabilise constructions of rurality as the safe natural space of children and childhood. Social issues related to unemployment, housing, transport, poverty and social exclusion are not just the remit of urban landscapes and are prevalent in rural areas. Myths of rural culture can also serve to marginalise a range of individuals and groups from a sense of belonging in or to the rural (Cloke, 2005). Furthermore, Milbourne (1997) emphasises the othering of rural individuals along intersections of gender, sexuality, ethnicity, social class and, notably, age. As scholars of early childhood, it is thus important to critically consider the dominant constructions of particular spaces and consider what 'realities' may lie beneath.

One of the key themes that has emerged through this chapter is that of opposites, dichotomies – spaces for adults versus spaces for children, public versus private, urban versus rural. As we have seen, such dichotomies are not always straightforward, divorcing public from private spheres, for example, is impossible; they are fluid spaces which are intricately connected and meanings surrounding family life are historically specific. The same is increasingly the case for rural and urban landscapes as social change and technology, such as the speed and range of personal travel, telecommunications and suburban developments, destabilise traditional understandings of such concepts (Cloke, 2005). Wilson's (1992) book *The Culture of Nature* demonstrates that land development in North America – theme parks and golf courses (parallels of which can be drawn to other regions such as the UK and Europe) – produce artificial natural landscapes, climatised, commodified spaces controlled by human beings and produced through human action. Traditional constructs are thus undermined by changes to technology and built environments, what appears as natural, free rural space can turn out to be as highly cultivated and controlled as urban landscapes (Cloke, 2005).

Global childhoods: migration and movement

All the world seems on the move. Asylum seekers, international students, terrorists, members of diasporas, holidaymakers, business people, sports stars, refugees, backpackers, commuters, the early retired, young mobile professionals, prostitutes, armed forces – these and many others fill the world's airports, buses, shops and trains. The scale of this travelling is immense. Internationally, there are over 700 million legal passenger arrivals each year … there are 4 million air passengers each day; 31 million refugees are displaced from their homes and there is one car for every 8.6 people'.

(Sheller and Urry, 2006: 207)

As the quote above suggests, the world is on the move. This section of the chapter explores how social change and the processes of globalisation have changed the way children experience place and space, evaluating the relationship between local and global childhoods and examining children's experiences of international movement.

'Globalisation' is a difficult term to define, despite receiving a significant amount of academic attention. It can be broadly considered as a feature of contemporary social life (albeit with a long and significant history) whereby places are increasingly interconnected through economic, social, cultural and political processes (Giddens, 1990). Massey and Jess (1995) describe the stretching out of social relations between people across space and, as Harvey (1989) succinctly argues, the compression of time and space means the world appears to be shrinking. Consider Hondagneu-Sotelo and Avila's (1997) research exploring how Latin American female domestic workers in the United States phone relatives in El Salvador to talk with, discipline and advise their children, engaging in a kind of transnational mothering. As a result of flows of movement, economic migrants can move across continents for the purposes of work and, despite being in geographically diverse spaces, families can maintain relationships using technologies which facilitate global communication.

Explorations of global childhoods are not a new phenomenon, indeed Margaret Mead's seminal work (1973) made cross-cultural comparisons in the early 20th century about the lives of girls in North America and Samoa. Despite this tradition from the field of anthropology, it can be argued that globalisation processes have reached unprecedented speeds and as such children's 21st century lives are considered to be increasingly global, in different ways to those experienced historically. The music that is listened to, the bicycles ridden, food eaten and clothing worn are the result of complex economic and social systems that span the planet and are just some examples of the interactions between global processes and local, individual, lives.

Local and global

Relations between the global and the local are complex and interdependent and as such Massey (1994) argues that the global should not be viewed as a threat to the local, rather we should consider instead a global sense of place. Viewing the global, rather than as all-encompassing, as a series of networks or flows, neither just a collection of 'locals' nor the encroaching of a singular overarching system (Crang, 2005). Global issues are after all lived out in the microgeographies of everyday life. Katz's (1994) research in New York and Sudan demonstrates the local manifestations of global change by exploring redundancy in a Sudanese village and failing American public school systems, both in the context of wide public spending cuts. Katz shows both the link between the global and local and how children negotiate this to co-construct local cultures, for example, in organising their day by routes to school or journeys to collect water.

> The predominant experience of everyday life in the modern global world is that locally situated life worlds are permeated by remote events, relationships and processes.

(Hengst, 2005: 24)

The interconnections of global phenomenon are illustrated well through examination of the concept of diaspora which recognises that ideas about culture and cultural identity are no longer bounded in particular geographical places. The origin of the term lies in the dispersal of particular cultural groups from a place of origin or abode, prominent examples include the forced movement of individuals as part of the slave trade, and colonisation and subsequent population movement across the British Empire. The concept can also act as a theoretical tool through which multi-locational place attachments can be understood (Dwyer, 2005). Recognising that processes of transnational movement, combined with wider social, political and economic forces, leads to individuals who share a culture and complex senses of belonging that exist across geographical boundaries; connections to a range of different places they may call home (Clifford, 1994).

Diaspora enables us to challenge fixed notions of home, such as those understandings considered in the domestic geographies section of this chapter. The activity below encourages readers to use the resources at your fingertips to explore these geographical concepts in everyday life.

Learning activity

Popular literature, just like film or art, can be a useful tool as you try to get to grips with complex ideas. Find and read a work of fiction which explores issues relating to home, community and identity on a global scale and consider how the concepts explored in this chapter come to life. Examples of good books include Monica Ali's *Brick Lane*, Zadie Smith's *White Teeth* and Peter Godwin's *Mukiwa*. In these works, families must get to grips with a sense of belonging that transcends the immediate physical environment and they must negotiate everyday life, constructing identities which are significantly impacted by their place in the world as economic migrants from Asia and White Rhodesians in a changing Zimbabwe.

Migration

Koser (2005: 510) provides a useful description of the key concepts needed within this discussion:

- **Migration.** A subcategory of a wider concept of movement, which embraces a whole range of forms of human mobility, from daily commuting to permanent emigration.
- **Asylum seeker.** Someone seeking protection under the terms of the 1951 United Nations Convention relating to the Status of Refugees.
- **Refugee.** Someone who 'owing to well-founded fear of being persecuted for reasons of race, religion, nationality, membership of a particular social group or political opinion, is outside the country of his or her origin' (as defined by the 1951 United Nations Convention relating to the Status of Refugees).
- **Illegal migrant.** There are at least three ways an individual might be classified as an illegal migrant:
  ➤ entering a country illegally, without passing through an immigration checkpoint
  ➤ entering a country legally, for example with a short-term visa, then stay illegally, after the expiry of the visa
  ➤ legally resident individuals, with appropriate immigration documentation, but owing to engagement in illegal activities has not adhered to the conditions of their stay/status.

Learning activity

Understanding key concepts

Try covering up the definitions of key terms discussed above and see if you can write down the meanings of these concepts without rereading this section. Techniques like this can help with memorising important ideas, so you might also like to try it with the concepts of spatiality and place explored at the beginning of this chapter.

It is estimated that approximately 2000 children are detained each year for the purposes of immigration control at the UK borders (Crawley and Lester, 2005). They are bought to the attention of authorities in a variety of ways, from being found to be living illegally with family, seeking international protection or being trafficked across international borders. Child trafficking can be defined as the recruitment, transportation, transfer, harbouring or receipt of a child, that is 0–18 years old, for the purpose of exploitation (United Nations, 2002). The scale of such trafficking ranges from a one-off act involving an individual child to highly organised global networks and can involve children in prostitution, exploitative labour, street crime and domestic servitude.

The migration experiences of children are, just like their reasons for transnational movement, diverse. Hopkins and Hill (2008), in their research with unaccompanied asylum-seeking children in Scotland, explored the processes behind children's decisions to leave their countries of origin. Despite the participation of children in decisions which affect their lives being enshrined into the United Nations Convention on the Rights of the Child (UNCRC), this research found children were passive in the decision-making process. Beyond the lack of engagement in choices, the experiences of both trafficking and detention for immigration purposes for children are documented as causing significant fear, anxiety and uncertainty, with the potential of damage to both psychological (and physical) well-being (Her Majesty's Inspectorate of Prisons, 2008).

These examples do not, however, mean that children are not agentic during their experiences of migration. Bhatti's (1999) research of the experiences of Asian children in Britain reveals how children would manage their parents desire to respect cultural heritage and educational expectations by switching between Hindi, Punjabi, Urdu or Malayalam and English depending on the spatial and relational context. This demonstrates how children negotiate a complex array of expectations and identities (Bhatti, 1999: 119) as they navigate the geographical and cultural spaces of their everyday lives. Children have an interactive relationship with the world around them:

> *The impact of external influences on them (children) is mirrored by their active role in making sense of these influences and drawing on them to reinvent their worlds, and at the same time to develop their self-perceptions and sense of place within the social order.*

(Smith, 2010: 55)

Considering children's role in co-constructing the places and spaces within which they live their lives leads us into the final section of this chapter where the participation of children in spatial design, planning and decision making will be considered in more detail.

Children, participation and planning

The development of academic conversations surrounding the importance of children's voices, highlighted in the *New Sociology of Childhood* (James and Prout, 1997) and the development of the UNCRC within which children's participation in decisions which affect them is enshrined, has resulted in increasing interest in listening to children's views about the spaces and places within their lives. Part of the rationale for this lies in the concept of positionality and arguments that the social roles, statuses and identities we occupy impact how we see the world around us, how different landscapes are interpreted and represented. Law (2005) poses a pertinent question, do those with the power to make the decisions see the world as others do? While not suggesting that children are a homogenous group, they do occupy a variety of vantage points within spaces and places and thus have a range of experiences, which have the potential to differ from those of adults. Dudek (2011) highlights this effectively in critiquing the development and building processes of nurseries, children's centres and other institutional spaces for children. He considers design processes with the example of schedules of accommodation which may stipulate the size of an entrance hall or classroom or safe exit routes, but it is unlikely to consider a children's window, whereby children can wave goodbye to parents and carers as they enter. As such, listening to and hearing children's voices is vital to ensuring spaces are inclusive.

There exist critiques of participation mechanisms as sometimes being tokenistic, whereby what is said is mediated by adults as the information is transported or that participation is only made available to children in select arenas where their voices are constructed as appropriate. Techniques of participation can be limited by adult imaginations (Foley, 2011) and disappointment and cynicism can result for children if promises of being heard are not always taken seriously (Prout, 2003). It is useful here to consider the distinction between participation as a means or as an end. In the case of the former, control and power remains in the hands of experts as Parnell and Patsarika (2011) demonstrated in their research on local authorities, developers and planners. However, when participation is viewed as an end itself, stakeholders are given voice and control over decision-making, promoting a sense of ownership (Cooke and Kothari, 2001). As Cairns (2001: 355) states, simply asking children their views is 'not enough ... many ... want to do more ... play an active role in creating change'. Parnell and Patsarika's (2011) research explored children's participation in England's Building Schools for the Future Programme (which has since been cancelled). They found that participation was framed in terms of learning rather than as a right as enshrined by the UNCRC and that school gatekeepers, adults who chose those children able to participate in such activities, significantly mediated the range of voices that could be heard. Participation in decision making surrounding the spaces and places in their lives is vital for children, but effectively ensuring these voices are heard should be considered as far from straightforward.

Conclusion

Geographies of early childhood are primarily interested in exploring the role of space and place in the lives of young children. These concepts should not be considered as limited to physical terrain and the concept of spatiality promotes the view of place as socially constructed. What readers should be taking away from this chapter, perhaps more importantly than anything else, is an understanding of early childhood spaces as constituted both by the physical material environment and the human action and interaction that takes place within and across them.

Dominant social and political discourses surrounding what cultures believe early childhood should look like inform the spaces young children are 'allowed' to inhabit. The separation of public and private spheres, as places of work and home became separated during the Industrial Revolution and the introduction of compulsory schooling, has resulted in the increasing domestication and scholarisation of childhood in western societies. As such, the home and school become significant sites within which children's lives are played out. The social relations of the family are bound up in the abstract concept of home, given material reality in the spaces of a house. As such, the home is a space where children exercise independence and participate in communal family life. When children's 'home lives' do not adhere to socio-spatial norms, as in the cases of traveller communities or street children, such children are not only considered outside appropriate spaces for children, but outside childhood itself.

Schools and early years' provision are also significant places in children's lives and act as sites of embodied social control where spaces, such as the lunchroom, are sites where policies and interventions shape children's lives. It is important to remember, however, that children do also exercise agency within such spaces and the underlife of educational environments show practices of resistance whereby children actively negotiate spatial rules and boundaries.

Outside the private sphere, children are peculiarly absent from the public, particularly urban, realm. Despite the increasing surveillance of public spaces, they can be a site of fear for parents where children are subject to the dangers of the adult world, for example increasing traffic levels. In contrast to the anxieties of urban environments, rural landscapes are romanticised. Prevalent images of rurality as symbolising tradition, harmony and safety are constructed as the ideal place for children, masking the social inequalities and issues which prevail in rural areas as they do in urban.

Local spaces have also been considered here, particularly in their relation to the global. Processes of globalisation result in the compression of time, space and individuals and social groups move and communicate across geographical areas in ways previously unprecedented in human history. The concept of diaspora is useful in conceptualising how culture, belonging and identity exist at a transnational level and how children negotiate experiences of movement and migration.

Throughout this chapter, the theme of how socio-spatial norms and discourses impact on children's experiences of place has been considered alongside understandings of children as agentic beings who engage in imaginative use of space. This is concluded in the final discussion exploring children's participation in spatial design and planning. This participation is complex, nuanced and, as with all good research and consultation, should be tailored to the individuals involved. Amidst concerns regarding the tokenism of participation, processes by which children are listened to should be meaningful with participation as an end in itself, rather than a tick box exercise for public planners.

'Children's geographies' is thus a complex discipline which encompasses the investigation of a range of issues within children's experiences of place and how particular spaces are constructed as '(in)appropriate' for children. Children's everyday lives are considered as embedded within particular localities and also part of wider global political, economic and social processes. As a field of enquiry, it attempts to contribute to debates about spatiality within childhood studies, key topics of which have been introduced within this chapter. As Holloway and Valentine (2000: 1–9) state, what is important for children's geographies is recognition of:

the different that place makes, the importance of the different sites of everyday life and the spatial imagery in ideologies of childhood ... a focus on the ways in which children negotiate the childhoods constructed in various times and places.

Evaluate your learning

- How does the concept of spatiality further understanding of how children use (or are unable to access) particular places and environments?
- The home is both a site of domestic life and an abstract concept often signifying rootedness and a key part of individual identity. Why are these concepts destabilised when considering the lives of street children and/or travelling communities?
- Why is it important to consider issues of power and control in the institutional spaces of childhood, i.e. schools?

References

Agnelli, S (1986): *Street Children: A Growing Urban Tragedy.* London: Widenfeld and Nicolson.

Alexandrescu, G (1996): Programme note: street children in Bucharest. *Childhood* **3**(2), 267–70.

Allan, G and Crow, G (eds) (1989): *Home and Family: Creating the Domestic Space.* Basingstoke: Macmillan.

Anderson, B (2010): Preemption, precaution, preparedness: anticipatory action and future geographies. *Progress in Human Geography* **34**(6), 777–98.

Ansell, N (2009): Childhood and the politics of scale: descaling children's geographies? *Progress in Human Geography* **33**(2), 190–209.

Barth, R (1969): *Ethnic Groups and Boundaries: The Social Organisation of Culture Difference.* Oslo: Universitetsforlaget.

Bartlett, S (1999): Children's Experiences of the physical environment in poor urban settlements and the implications for policy, planning and practice. *Environment and Urbanisation* **11**, 63–74.

Bauman, Z (1998): *Globalisation: The Human Consequences.* New York: Columbia University Press.

Beazley, H (2002): Vagrants wearing make up: negotiating spaces on the streets of Yogyakarta. *Urban Studies* **39**(9), 1665–84.

Bhabha, H (1994): *The Location of Culture.* London: Routledge.

Bhatti, G (1999): *Asian Children in Home and at School.* London: Routledge.

Blunt, A and Varley, A (2004): Geographies of home. *Cultural Geographies* **11**(1), 3–6.

Cairns, L (2001) Investing in children: Learning how to promote the rights of all children. *Children and Society* **15**, 347–60.

Christensen, P and James, A (2001): What are schools for? The temporal experience of children's learning in Northern England. In Alanen, L and Mayall, B (eds), *Conceptualising Child-adult Relations.* London: Routledge.

Christensen, P, James, A and Jenks, C (2000): Home and Movement: Children constructing 'family time'. In Holloway, S and Valentine, G (eds), *Children's Geographies: Playing, Living, Learning.* London: Routledge.

Clifford, J (1994): Diasporas. *Cultural Anthropology* **9**(3), 302–38.

Cloke, P (2005): The country. In Cloke, P, Crang, P and Goodwin, M (eds), *Introducing Human Geographies*, 2nd edn. London: Hodder Education.

Cloke, P, Crang, P and Goodwin, M (eds) (2005): *Introducing Human Geographies*, 2nd edn. London: Hodder Education.

Conticini, A and Hulme, D (2007): Escaping violence, seeking freedom: why children in Bangladesh migrate to the street. *Development and Change* **38**(2), 210–27.

Cooke, B and Kothari, U (2001): The case for participation tyranny. In Cooke, B and Kothari, U (eds), *Participation: the New Tyranny*. London: Zed Books, pp. 1–15.

Crang, P (2005): Local-global. In Cloke, P, Crang, P and Goodwin, M (eds), *Introducing Human Geographies*, 2nd edn. London: Hodder Education.

Crawley, H And Lester, T (2005): *No Place for a Child: Children in Immigration Detention*. London: Save the Children.

Daniel, P and Gustafsson, U (2010): School lunches: Children's services or children's spaces? *Children's Geographies* **8**(3), 265–74.

Darlsgaard, A, Franch, M and Parry Scott, R (2008): Dominant ideas, uncertain lives: the meaning of youth in Recife. In Hansen, K (ed), *Youth and the City in the Global South*. Bloomington: Indiana University Press, pp. 49–73.

Department of Health (2004): *Choosing Health: Making Healthy Choices Easier*. London: The Stationery Office.

Douglas, M (1991): The idea of home: a kind of space. *Social Research* **58**(1), 287–307.

Dudek, M (2011): Play in an adult world: designing spaces with children. In Foley, P and Leverett, S (eds), *Children and Young People's Spaces*. Hampshire: Palgrave Macmillan.

Dwyer, C (2005): Diasporas. In Cloke, P, Crang, P and Goodwin, M (eds), *Introducing Human Geographies*, 2nd edn. London: Hodder Education.

Foley, P (2011): Democratic spaces. In Foley, P and Leverett, S (eds), *Children and Young People's Spaces*. Hampshire: Palgrave Macmillan.

Foucault, M (1980): 'On governmentality' in Gordon, C. (ed) *Power/Knowledge*, London: Harvester Press.

Foucault, M (1991): *Discipline and Punish: the Birth of the Prison*. London: Penguin.

Food Standards Association (FSA) (2007): *Shaping the Eating Habits of the Next Generation*. London: FSA.

Gallacher, L (2005) The terrible twos: gaining control in the nursery. *Children's Geographies* **3**(2), 243–64.

Ganetz, H (1995): The shop, the home and femininity as a masquerade. In Fornas, J and Bolin, G (eds), *Youth Culture in Late Modernity*. London: Sage.

Giddens, A (1990): *The Consequences of Modernity*. Cambridge: Polity Press.

Gigengack, R (2000): Critical ommissions: how street children studies can address self destructive agency. In Christensen, P and James, A (eds), *Research with Children: Perspectives and Practices*. London: Routedge.

Glauser, B (1997): Street children: deconstructing a concept. In James, A and Prout, A (eds), *Constructing and Reconstructing Childhood: Contemporary Issues in the Sociological Study of Childhood*, 2nd edn. London: Falmer Press.

Goffman, E (1968): *Asylums*. Harmondsworth: Penguin.

Gough, K (2008): Youth and the home. In Hansen, K (ed), *Youth and the City in the Global South*. Bloomington: Indiana University Press, pp. 127–50.

Harden, J (2012): Good sitting, looking and listening: the regulation of young children's emotions in the classroom. *Children's Geographies* **10**(1), 83–93.

Harvey, D (1989): *The Condition of Postmodernity: An Enquiry Into the Origins of Cultural Change*. Oxford: Blackwell.

Hengst, H (2005): Complex interconnections: the global and the local in children's minds and everyday worlds. In Qvortrup, J (ed), *Studies in Modern Childhood*. Hampshire: Palgrave Macmillan.

Hengst, H (2007): Metamorphoses of the world within reach. In Zeiher, H, Devine, D, Kjorholt, AT and Strandell, H (eds), *Flexible Childhood? Exploring Children's Welfare and Time in Space*. Odense: University Press of Southern Denmark.

Hill, M, Turner, K, Walker, M, Stafford, A and Seaman, P (2006): Children's perspectives on social exclusion and resilience in disadvantaged urban communities. In Tisdall, K, Davis, J and Prout, A (eds), *Children, Young People and Social Exclusion: Participation for What?* Bristol: The Policy Press.

HMIP (Her Majesty's Inspectorate of Prisons) (2008): *Report on an Announced Inspection of Yarl's Wood Immigration Removal Centre*. London: HMIP.

Holloway, S and Valentine, G (eds) (2000): *Children's Geographies: Playing, Living Learning*. London: Routledge.

Hondagneu-Sotelo, P and Avila, E (1997): I'm here but I'm there: the meanings of Latina transnational motherhood. *Gender and Society* **11**(5), 548–71.

Hopkins, P and Hill, M (2008): Pre-flight experiences and migration stories: the accounts of unaccompanied asylum seeking children. *Children's Geographies* **6**(3), 257–68.

Horschelmann, K and van Blerk, L (2012): *Children, Youth and the City*. London: Routledge.

Ingold, T (2000): *The Perception of the Environment*. London: Routledge.

Ingold, T (2008): Bindings against boundaries: entanglements of life in an open world. *Environment and Planning A* **40**, 1796–810.

James, A and Prout, A (eds) (1997): *Constructing and Reconstructing Childhood: Contemporary Issues in the Sociological Study of Childhood*, 2nd edn. London: Falmer Press.

Jones, O (2002). Naturally not! Childhood, the urban and romanticism. *Human Ecology Review* **9**(2), 17–30.

Katz, C (1994): Textures of global change: eroding ecologies of childhood in New York and Sudan. *Childhood* **2**, 103–10.

Knox, P and Pinch, S (2006): *Urban Social Geography: An Introduction*. London: Pearson.

Koser, K (2005): Migrants and refugees. In Cloke, P, Crang, P and Goodwin, M (eds), *Introducing Human Geographies*, 2nd edn. London: Hodder Education.

Law, L (2005): Sensing the city: urban experiences. In Cloke, P, Crang, P and Goodwin, M (eds), *Introducing Human Geographies*, 2nd edn. London: Hodder Education.

Leverett, S (2011): Children's spaces. In Foley, P and Leverett, S (eds), *Children and Young People's Spaces*. Hampshire: Palgrave Macmillan.

Mallett, S (2004): Understanding home: a critical review of the literature. *Sociological Review* **52**(1), 62–89.

Malone, K (2002) Street life: youth, culture, and competing use of public space. *Local Environment* **14**(2), 157–68.

Massey, D. (1994): *A Global Sense of Place: Space, Place and Gender.* Cambridge: Polity Press.

Massey, D and Jess, P (eds) (1995): *A Place in the World?* Oxford: Oxford University Press.

Matthews, H (2003): Children and regeneration: setting an agenda for community participation and integration, *Children and Society* **17**(4), 264–76.

Matthews, Z (2008): *The Health of Gypsies and Travellers in the UK.* London: Race Equality Foundation.

Mayall, B (2002): *Towards a Sociology of Childhood: Thinking From Children's Lives.* Buckingham: Open University Press.

McDowell, L, Ray, K, Perrons, D, Pagan, C and Ward, K (2005): Women's paid work and moral economies of care. *Social and Cultural Geography* **6**, 219–35.

McKendrick, J (2004): Fallacies surrounding the geography of family eating. *Children's Geographies* **2**(2), 293–5.

Mead, M (1973) *Coming of Age in Samoa.* New York: HarperCollins (first published in 1928).

Milbourne, P (ed) (1997): *Revealing Rural Others.* London: Pinter.

Mormont, M (1990): Who is rural? Or how to be rural: towards a sociology of the rural. In Marsden, T, Lowe, P and Whatmore, S (eds), *Rural Restructuring.* London: David Fulton.

Moss, P and Petrie, P (2002): *From Children's Services to Children's Spaces.* London: Routledge.

Pain, R (2006): Paranoid parenting? Rematerialising risk and fear for children. *Social and Cultural Geography* **7**(2), 221–43.

Parnel, R and Patsarika, M (2011): Young people's participation in school design: exploring diversity and power in a UK governmental policy case-study. *Children's Geographies* **9**(3–4), 457–75.

Parry, G, van Cleemput, P, Peters, J, Moore, J, Walters, S, Thomas, K and Cooper, C (2004): *The Health Status of Gypsies and Travellers in England.* (Online). Sheffield, University of Sheffield. Last accessed: 14 August 2012. Available from: http://shef.ac.uk/content/1/c6/02/55/71/GT%20report%20summary.pdf.

Pike, J (2008): Foucault, space and primary school dining rooms. *Children's Geographies* **6**(4), 413–22.

Pink, S (2012): *Situating Everyday Life.* London: Sage.

Prout, A (2003): Participation, policy and the changing conditions of childhood. In Hallert, C and Prout, A (eds), *Hearing the Voices of Children: Social Policy for a New Century.* London: Routledge.

Punch, S (2003): Childhoods in the majority world, miniature adults or tribal children? *Sociology* **37**, 277–95.

Punch, S and Tisdall, K (2012): Exploring children and young people's relationships across majority and minority worlds. *Children's Geographies* **10**(3), 241–8.

Rapport, N and Dawson, A (eds) (1998): *Migrants of Identity.* Oxford: Berg.

Sheller, M and Urry, J (2006): The new mobilities paradigm. *Environment Planning A* **38**, 207–26.

Sibley, D (1995): Family and domestic routines: constructing the boundaries of childhood. In Pile, S and Thrift, N (eds), *Mapping the Subject: Geographies of Cultural Transformation*. London: Routledge.

Skelton, T (2000): Nothing to do nowhere to go? Teenage girls and public space in the Rhondda Valleys, South Wales. In Holloway, S and Valentine, G (eds), *Children's Geographies: Playing, Living Learning*. London: Routledge.

Smith, M (2001): *An Ethics of Place: Radical Ecology, Postmodernity and Social Theory*. New York, State University of New York Press.

Smith, R (2010): *A Universal Child?* Hampshire: Palgrave Macmillan.

Smith, F and Barker, J (2000): Contested Spaces: children's experiences of out of school care in England and Wales. *Childhood* **7**(3), 315–33.

UK Children's Commissioner (2008) *Report to the UN Committee on the Rights of the Child*. (Online). Last accessed: 22 November 2011. Available from: www.sccyp.org.uk/ UK_Childrens_Commissioners_UN_Report.pdf.

United Nations (2002): *Palermo Protocol*. Geneva: United Nations.

Valentine, G (1996): Children should be seen and not heard: the production and transgression of adults public space. *Urban Geography* **17**(3), 205–20.

van Blerk, L (2006): Diversity and difference in the everyday lives of Ugandan street children. *Social Dynamics* **32**(1), 47–74.

Veitch, J, Salmon, J and Ball, K (2007): Children's Perceptions of the use of public open spaces for active free play. *Children's Geographies* **5**(4), 409–22.

Whatmore, S (2005): Culture-nature. In Cloke, P, Crang, P and Goodwin, M (eds), *Introducing Human Geographies*, 2nd edn. London: Hodder Education.

Williams, R (1985): *The Country and the City*. London: Hogarth Press.

Wilson, A (1992): *The Culture of Nature*. London: Routledge.

Young, L (2004): The 'place' of street children in Kampala, Uganda: marginalization, resistance and acceptance in the urban environment. *Environment and Planning D: Society and Space* **21**, 607–27.

Zeiher, H (2003): Shaping daily life in urban environments. In Christensen, P and O'Brien, M (eds), *Children in the City: Home Neighbourhood and Community*. London: Routledge.

Further reading

Cloke, P, Crang, P and Goodwin, M (eds) (2005): *Introducing Human Geographies*, 2nd edn. London: Hodder Education.

Foley, P and Leverett, S (eds) (2011): *Children and Young People's Spaces*. Hampshire: Palgrave Macmillan.

Holloway, S and Valentine, G (eds) (2000): *Children's Geographies: Playing, Living, Learning*. London: Routledge.

Holt, L (ed) (2011): *Geographies of Children, Youth and Families: An International Perspective*. London: Routledge.

Horschelmann, K and van Blerk, L (2012): *Children, Youth and the City*, London: Routledge.

Pink, S (2012): *Situating Everyday Life*. London: Sage.

14 Perspectives on early childhood research

Jayne Taylor

This chapter aims to:
- explore the value of research to the early years professional
- provide an overview of recent advances which emphasise the importance of listening to the voices of children and the participation of children in research
- discuss methodological issues in early years research
- examine ethical considerations involved in undertaking research with children as participants.

Introduction

After a recent visit to a busy children's centre where a small group of us were able to observe 30 little two- and three-year-olds singing and playing, we contemplated how interesting it was that while the majority of children joined in the large group playing 'jumping bunnies' (in which children pretend to be asleep while the adults recite verses; then they wake up and hop around like bunny rabbits), there were a few children who were separate from the group. One child was fascinated by my colleague's shoes, two were playing in the play house and no amount of coaching would persuade them to join the larger group, a couple were clinging to their mums, one was playing with his mother's mobile phone, one only wanted to sit on her grandmother's lap and look at a book. One little boy was screaming at the top of his voice and doing his best to disrupt the game by charging through the group of sleeping bunnies.

Similar scenes are undoubtedly played out in nurseries, playgroups, schools, hospitals and crèches all over the country. The individual differences, as well as the similarities, which exist between children have both puzzled and fascinated professionals, and given them the motivation and material to enable them to delve into the complex world of the child through research. Many answers to countless questions have been discovered through investigation, but many questions remain unanswered, and indeed always will. Children change as society progresses, and they need to develop new behaviours in order to adapt to a complex and demanding world. There will always be questions which can be addressed through research, and as answers to existing questions are found, new and different questions will emerge.

This chapter is included for two main reasons: first, to present a text that will support the training of early years professionals, and research awareness, at the very least, is an expectation of most if not all training programmes; and second, because we are firmly committed to the notion of research as a valuable asset in the advancement of practice. Early years professionals should be able to use other people's research intelligently by developing their own critical reading skills and, where necessary, to undertake research themselves. They should work from an established knowledge base which they understand, and seek to advance knowledge and theory through research.

The chapter begins by exploring the value of research to practice. It then provides an overview of a philosophical shift over recent years to do research *with* children rather than *on* children. The third section examines different approaches and methodologies which have specific relevance to the study of children. There is also a focus on the ethical implications of undertaking research which involves children, with particular reference to early years professionals working within health settings. However, it must be emphasised that all aspects of research methodology cannot be covered within the scope of one chapter. There are many excellent books which do this, and the further reading section at the end of the chapter provides details of some of these.

The value of research in the early years

In the Introduction to this book, we discussed why the study of early childhood is important, with reference to its value as an emerging discipline in its own right. Throughout the other chapters in this volume the work of researchers who have undertaken studies across a range of disciplines relating to aspects of early childhood studies have been referred to. It is because of the contributions of all these researchers and those who went before them that we have the body of knowledge relating to the early years which exists today.

Drawing upon previous research serves a number of purposes. It can, for example, enable the investigation of a particular problem through the study of literature and lead to greater understanding of a certain phenomenon, which can in turn lead to changes in and advancement of practice. It can also predicate further empirical study of an area by informing the future researcher of existing work, tried and tested methodologies and the problems, pitfalls and potential limitations of a specific approach. Existing research can enable researchers to approach topics in a similar or different setting, but it can also inform them so that they do not unnecessarily undertake work which has already been done. Studying previous research is almost always a prerequisite of future research-based activity. This will be explored in more detail.

Using existing knowledge to inform practice

Look again at the vignette presented at the beginning of this chapter. There are so many reasons why a small group of children were 'outside' the main group and as early years professionals it is really important that we try to understand both the resilience of the majority of the children who behave in a similar way, as well as the differences exhibited by the small group of children who do not conform (see Lewis and Kellett, 2005). To help professionals in this complex task of understanding, we can start by looking at the established knowledge of related theory and research. This has been touched on within all of the chapters in this volume. Both theory and research can help to guide our thinking processes and our practices. Take for example the little boy who was creating mayhem in the children's centre. We need to be able to observe his behaviour, describe what he is doing and try to find explanations and solutions. It should be possible through this process to understand his behaviour, predict future behaviours and find ways of managing his behaviour.

Continuing to think about our disruptive little boy, we might try to narrow down the reasons for the differences in his behaviours by studying and understanding previous theory and research. Five classical approaches to the study of early childhood would ask for example:

- Is there a *physiological* reason why the little boy behaves as he does? Might his behaviour be as a result of brain function, or have a biochemical or hereditary cause?
- Is there a *psychodynamic* reason for his behaviour? Are the child's needs for different experiences and stimulation not being adequately met? For example, Romano *et al.* (2006) found that maternal depression and hostile parenting were significant factors in determining persistent aggressive behaviour.
- Is there a *behaviourist* reason for his disruptive conduct? Has he learned to be disruptive through observing, modelling and cognitively processing the behaviour of others, either at home or at the children's centre? For example, the chances of a second child being aggressive are four to five times higher if the first child is aggressive (Baillargeon *et al.*, 2002).
- Is there a *humanistic* reason? Are there fundamental needs within the child that are not being met that might explain his behaviour? Is he hungry, tired or insecure?
- Is there a *cognitive* reason for his behaviour? Are there environmental, social relationship or cultural conventions that can explain his behaviour? (See Reebye (2005) for a full discussion.)

The reality of course is that trying to compartmentalise our little boy's behaviour is unrealistic and his behaviour can most probably not be explained by any single theory – it is likely to be an interaction of some or all five. More recent theory tries to address the links between the child's outer social world and inner psychological world and it is important that when we undertake research with children, that we too consider the whole child and the incredible complexity of children's worlds.

Using research to inform practice is the first (and an essential) step towards making progress, and as professionals we should strive to ensure that each and every part of our practice is informed by research. For the team of early years professionals in our children's centre through thorough and systematic searching of the literature, there are research findings which can inform practice and help them better understand how to manage the little group of different children.

Developing critical reading skills

The use of literature to inform practice is not entirely straightforward. There is a huge range of information available within any given field of study. The amount of research and literature available can be overwhelming and it is really important that you narrow down your field of enquiry so that you are not swamped with too much information. However, it is equally important that you access the literature that will really help you in your study – you do not want to miss important or seminal work in your field. The process of refining a literature search can be difficult and it is usually necessary to undertake some general reading first so that you can identify a series of key words. General reading can be accessed through an academic library (remember that librarians are there to help) or by accessing literature online.

When material has been identified it may, in some fields, reveal conflicting views about certain topics. This is particularly so when the area being researched is new. A classic example was the contrasting information which emerged during the early 1980s about the transmission of human immunodeficiency virus (HIV), which led to a certain amount of panic. It was only as more research was undertaken and reliable data emerged about the virus that some of the previous literature was shown to be incorrect. If you are studying a new or under-developed field where there are contrasting opinions or propositions, then you need to follow the various strands of the emerging theory.

Abstracts at the beginning of published work or in some cases, for example, publications from national bodies and government departments, an executive summary will help you to make an initial assessment of whether the piece of work you have will really help you. The abstract or executive summary should tell you key information about what was done, how it was done, who with and what was found. Using abstracts or summaries should help you to further filter out pieces of work which are not going to be relevant to what you are studying. If your search has led to a large number of pieces of work being located then you may need to be quite brutal in setting aside pieces that are not central to your work. You do need to be able to manage the pieces of work. There is no golden rule about how many pieces of work to look at – clearly if studying for a PhD you will need to look in much more depth than if you are writing a 2000-word essay!

The next stage is to gather your literature, either in a paper-based form or electronically, so that you can begin the process of critical analysis. This may lead to further searching. For example, you may identify key research articles that may make reference to other pieces of work you may also need to look at. If a key article appears in a particular journal and you believe the article will stimulate debate, you should access that particular journal on a regular basis so that you do not miss the developing discussion. In some professional fields, there are specific and pertinent journals in which such debate will occur, while in other professions, there are literally hundreds of journals relating to a particular field. If, however, a discussion and debate article appears in a particular journal, it is normal practice for the debate to continue in the same journal.

When you have accessed your literature, you then need to work through the various pieces of literature that you have. If you only have a few pieces to look at you can usually read these and take some notes about what the researchers did, who they did it with, what they did and what they found. If you have a large number of pieces of work to appraise, then it is helpful to set up a spreadsheet or at least some form of table to help you to summarise the key points. There are many ways of doing this. The example below is just one way and provides the headings you might choose to utilise. Things to include under each heading are:

- **Number** *(No.)*. Number each article and file them in a logical order so that you can easily find each piece.
- **Reference**. Make sure you have the full reference, title, journal, authors, date, etc.
- **Overview**. Scan through the whole article and write down immediate thoughts, for example this was empirical research or a systematic review of the literature; this article

can be used in the methodology section, or in the section of my literature review on ….
If having read through the whole piece you actually find it is not going to help you, then
remove it from your list.

- **Problem studied**. Record here a summary of what the research was investigating and the
  theoretical approach.
- **Sample**. Record here who (or what) was included in the sample. Were there any ethical
  implications you should note?
- **Data collection**. Summarise what methods were used to gather data, for example survey,
  focus group. How reliable were the methods and how were the data-collection
  instruments developed and tested prior to use?
- **Results**. Record briefly how the data gathered were analysed and what the outcomes of
  the work showed.
- **Other**. Record here any other information, such as if the work references a particular
  aspect you need to consider or if the work disagrees or agrees with another piece you have
  looked at.

No.	Reference	Overview/general impression	Problem studied	Sample	Data collection	Results	Other

It is important that early years professionals are able to make informed decisions about
whether research has been carried out in a way which is reliable and valid, so that they do
not make changes to practice on the basis of weak research. Recording different sources in a
systematic way is an incredibly helpful discipline, whether you are using literature to inform
your own research strategies or if you want to make changes on the basis of work which
others have undertaken.

There are clearly a number of ways of learning critical reading skills and there are many
good books which can help (see the further reading section at the end of this chapter).
There are also many professional training programmes which require students to undertake
supervised research themselves and, while the value of this has been questioned by some,
it is a good way of learning to understand the somewhat mystical language of research and
developing skills which will help with critical reading.

Listening to the voices of children

One of the most exciting things to have happened over the last decade or so is the shift
in emphasis from doing research *on* or *about* children to doing research *with* children.
The United Nations Children's Fund (UNICEF, 2002) published guidance about hearing
children's voices in research and evaluation. They cite four articles from the Convention
on the Rights of the Child (Articles 12, 13, 14 and 15) which support the inclusion of
children's voices. These guidelines build on Hart's eight-degree scale of participation
(Hart, 1992) which provides a gradient of participation from 'manipulation' of the child
in research to full participation with the research being child-initiated. Most research will
involve children somewhere in between these two poles. We have included a simplified
scale below:

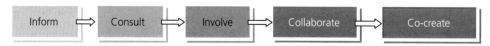

Figure 14.1 Levels of participation

If we are to truly listen to the voices of children, there are three processes that need to take place. First, we need to really listen to what children say, then we need to hear what they say and then we need to act on what they say (Crichton and Barrett, 2007).

Various disciplines working in the field of early childhood studies have embraced children's participation more than others. In medical research, for example, participation is currently most likely to be at the least participative end of the range, whereas in social research the trend has been towards much fuller participation (collaboration and co-creation), so that the voices of children are heard (see Hill, 2005; Balen *et al.*, 2006; Campbell, 2008). The variation between disciplines is due in part to the nature of the research topic, although there should always be a way of helping children to participate in some form. For example, a study of children's accident and emergency attendances provides details of how many children attend, when they attend, how they got there (parental referral, GP referred, ambulance), what happened in terms of treatment when they arrived and what happened to them (admitted, discharged, sent to the GP). The professionals involved in the study were very focused on the need to have a separate waiting area for the children in a minor injuries unit which would involve losing a treatment room, building a separate entrance and knocking down walls, as well as staffing a separate reception. In this study, it was at first a challenge to see how the voices of young children might be heard and also what purpose it would serve. However, gathering together a group of primary school children who had attended the unit highlighted that there were many things that had frightened them such as seeing people on stretchers, not being able to see people coming into treatment rooms, blood and sick because of the position of the treatment trolley and the door, whereas they were perfectly comfortable about sharing waiting space with older people and having to wait for treatment which they said was just like being at their own doctor's surgery.

The debate about the extent to which children should be directly involved in research is one to be highlighted rather than continued. Jones and Welch (2010) provide a more detailed discussion. Suffice it to say that there has been a gradual change over the past decades and the majority view in most circles is that children have a right to participate and to have their voices heard, just as they also have a right to refuse to participate, and that research about children should be with children and not something that is done to children (Balen *et al.*, 2006; Hill, 2006; Campbell, 2008; Coyne *et al.*, 2009; Dockett *et al.*, 2009; Powell and Smith, 2009; Czymoniewicz *et al.*, 2010). Certainly, research is not something that should be done on children without their consent or at least assent.

Undertaking research with children

As stated previously, this chapter is not intended to give a step-by-step guide to undertaking research – that would be neither possible nor appropriate. The main intention is to focus upon aspects of research involving children that are *different* to those which involve adults, so that the early years professional undertaking research may more ably transfer knowledge designed to apply to adult subjects to children in early years settings. Those areas of research methodology where there seem to be a few tangible differences (e.g. identification of problems, question formation) are not discussed. However, a few very broad principles which apply when undertaking research with children are discussed.

Overarching principles

As you have read throughout this book, children are not small adults. They perceive events differently to adults, their understanding of experience is different to that of adults, and the social contexts within which they exist are different to those of adults. Children are very special and deserve special consideration. They are also fascinating because of the way in which they rapidly develop physically, socially, psychologically and emotionally, and because of their ways of knowing and understanding.

The researcher who wishes to study children, particularly during the early years, is faced with a wealth of potential, as well as a few methodological 'headaches'! For example, traditional methods of collecting data may be inappropriate or even impossible because of the child's stage of development. Imagine the stupidity of asking a group of two-year-olds to complete a questionnaire!

The early years researcher must possess those vital qualities which are essential to early years workers in all settings, namely well-developed skills of listening to children (see Chapter 1), knowledge of children's rights, child development, a liking for children, patience and an ability to communicate through a variety of media. In many ways, young children themselves can provide the researcher with an apt role model! From the first days of life, children set out on a voyage of discovery. They explore, investigate, examine, categorise experiences, draw conclusions and seek to extend the boundaries of their knowledge. A very early text (Murray and Brown Smith, 1922) discusses the philosophy of Froebel (see also the Introduction), which summarises this point admirably. He wrote that:

> Like things must be ranged together, unlike things separated. … The child loves all things that enter his small horizon and extend his little world. To him the least thing is a new discovery, but it must not come dead into the little world, nor lie dead therein, lest it obscure the small horizon and crush the little world. Therefore the child would know why he loves this thing, he would know all its properties. For this reason he examines the object on all sides; for this reason he tears and breaks it; for this reason he puts it in his mouth and bites it. We reprove the child for naughtiness and foolishness; and yet he is wiser than we who reprove him.

(Murray and Brown Smith, 1922: 47)

The thorough way in which children investigate new experiences, or seek to find solutions, and the way in which they systematically approach problems and extend the boundaries of their knowledge underpin the principles of undertaking research with young children.

Methodological differences

When engaging upon early years research, the researcher needs to employ all the skills and knowledge referred to above in order to ensure that the research yields results which are both reliable and valid. Three of the main problems, which are inter-related, are sampling, data collection and ethical implications (which will be discussed separately in the next section of this chapter).

Samples are the foundation of research and provide the researcher with the medium to answer research questions through data collection. A sample is anything which is smaller than a full population, and samples are used because it is rarely possible to study an entire population, although this does happen sometimes (e.g. the United Kingdom 10-yearly Population Census, or Graham and Rutter's Isle of Wight study – you will find reviews of this famous study in most British texts on child psychology). The basis of sampling involves two general laws: the first is that a relatively large, randomly selected sample will represent the characteristics of the sample population; the second is that larger groups of data are more highly stable than smaller groups of data.

The importance of sampling during early childhood relates to the homogeneity of groups of children. You will recall the discussions in various chapters in this book about children's development, particularly in terms of their cognition and their social development. It is extremely difficult to identify an homogeneous group of children because age is a relatively poor predictor of cognitive and social development. Therefore, bias in sampling is a problem faced by many early years' researchers. There are ways of overcoming bias, but the researcher must be aware that a group of intellectually intact preschool children (spanning a five-year period from 0 to 5 years) is likely to be a far less homogeneous group than a group of intellectually intact adults (spanning, for example, a five-year period from 34 to 39 years).

However, many early years researchers are not concerned with being able to generalise their results across populations, but *are* concerned with their own practice in their own familiar settings. Samples which are 'convenient' may be biased and non-random and, regardless of the size of the sample, bias will remain in evidence. This presents no difficulty as long as it is recognised and acknowledged that the results cannot be generalised beyond the sample used in the study.

The second main problem relating to undertaking research during the early years concerns *data collection*. We have already mentioned the difficulty of using questionnaires among groups of very young children. Similar difficulties are equally evident when using other self-report methods, such as rating scales. However, as with other data collection methods, modification can enable their use. For example, collecting data about post-operative pain using a numerical rating scale with young children may prove very unsuccessful, but by adapting the scale and using the Faces Pain Scale (see International Association for the Study of Pain, 2001), success can be achieved. Another example is the use of the Cube assessment tool which involves the use of four natural wood cubes in sizes varying from 1 to 5 cm. The smallest cube corresponds to 'no pain' and the largest to 'the most pain'. The Cube assessment was used successfully with children with intellectual disabilities. The child places the appropriate cube onto a body chart so they are able to signify both intensity and site of pain (see Benini *et al.*, 2004). These sorts of tool have been shown to be reliable in measuring pain (Royal College of Nursing, 2009). Similarly, a questionnaire designed to elicit information from hospitalised patients about food was modified by the author for use on the children's wards to include a four-point scale which included the headings 'yuk', 'a bit yuk', 'OK' and 'yummy', instead of the adult version of 'not very good', 'all right', 'good' and 'very good'.

Observation is one of the most important data-collection methods for the early years researcher, and indeed it is one of the most important skills of the early years professional. One particular observation technique derived from ethology, which involves the observation of children in their natural settings, is particularly useful. Observer effects (i.e. changes in behaviour caused by the intrusiveness of the observer within the situation) are problematic, but young children tend to adapt relatively quickly to the presence of, for example, a new adult within their nursery class. Observer effects can be minimised, therefore, by allowing the children being studied to adapt to the presence of the researcher (see, for example, Hawthorn's (1975) classic study of children in hospital), or by the researcher blending into the natural setting of the child (see Greig *et al.*, 2012).

Researchers using observation as a data-collection tool frequently need to adapt their methods to suit the cognitive level of the child. Whereas researchers using adult subjects may be able to ask their subject to use complex skills, early years researchers will use observation of the medium of play and toys in order to collect data (see, for example, Susuki and Kato, 2003; Greig *et al.*, 2012).

Interviews involving young children can also be problematic for the early years researcher, particularly in terms of the reliability of data. We have stressed many times that children and adults perceive experiences in different ways (Bower, 1977), and the reporting of interview data may lead to inaccuracies because of the *interpretation* of a child's language by the researcher. Children may, in fact, use quite complex language, but have limited understanding of the meaning of their words (see Luria and Yudovich (1959) for a fascinating and detailed record of children's conversation), and they may be paraphrasing words that they have heard adults using, or they may understand, but not have the language acquisition to be able to verbalise adequately. Others may pronounce words in strange ways, or use 'pet' words which stand for something completely different! However, it is important to stress that it is valuable to seek information directly from children, rather than relying on data from adults *about* children. Children and adults see the world in very different ways (Nardini *et al.*, 2010). Compas and Phares (1991) explored this issue and suggest that wide variations may exist between the reportings of teachers, parents and the children themselves in relation to specific data, which is something to consider when undertaking research and when reading other people's research. This is perhaps not quite so simple, however, when considering research with children who are, for example, ill. Alderson and Morrow (2011) explore this in some detail in their work on the ethics of undertaking research.

The need for small-scale studies

Well-designed research on a small scale, using small convenient samples and data-collection methods which are appropriate to the child's level of understanding, provides the building blocks of professional knowledge because such research contributes to the generation of theory and, ultimately, to the advancement of practice. Much of the existing knowledge we work with today was originally derived from small beginnings. Axline's (1964) study of Dibs provided the basis for further study in the field of play therapy, and even Piaget himself formulated many of his early working hypotheses through close observation of his own three children! However, whether the research is on a small or large scale, whether it uses observation, questionnaires, interviews or other forms of data collection, it is always necessary to give due consideration to the ethical implications of undertaking research. It is to this important area that we shall now turn.

Ethical implications of research involving children

All researchers have a responsibility to analyse the ethical implications of their work, whether they work in the health services, the educational sector, social services or elsewhere. However, there are clearly some types of research which will carry stronger ethical implications than others and, as a starting point, researchers should always define very clearly what the child will be asked to do in order to participate in the research. If the research is *invasive*, either physiologically, psychologically or socially, then its moral acceptability should be questioned. This applies particularly but not exclusively to healthcare workers, but also to *all* researchers doing research involving child subjects, because of the potential detrimental effects on the child. In addition, as we have discussed in the previous section because children do not perceive events in the same way as adults, seemingly *harmless* experiences can be potentially *harmful* to the child. This poses difficulties for the researcher, parents and others (e.g. members of ethical committees, research supervisors, managers who control access to physical environments) who have to make an informed judgement about the potential effects of involving a child or group of children. This problem has long been recognised, but there is no easy answer, although we shall explore further criteria which can be utilised. However, it is useful to remember the words used in the Platt report:

> It is never safe to assume that a child will be afraid of an experience that an adult regards as frightening, or conversely that an experience which has no terrors for an adult will have none for a child.

(Platt, 1959: 28)

This whole debate makes it so important that as researchers we make sure that we adhere to the various codes of ethics that are in place primarily to protect children, but also to protect the researcher. We need to consider both. There are a number of codes which aim to regulate research within professions, which will be of help to students working in the field of early childhood. For example, the British Psychological Society (2009), the National Children's Bureau (Shaw *et al.*, 2011), the British Sociological Association (2004) and the Medical Research Council (2004) all have clear codes of practice. Students should also look at the comprehensive Framework for Research Ethics produced by The Economic and Social Research Council (2010).

Researchers should also make sure that when undertaking research that they gain permission from relevant ethics committees such as the university committee (for students) and in the UK, in relation to research in the fields of health and social care and under arrangements between the four UK health departments, the National Research Ethics Service (NRES; www.nres.nhs.uk), which sits within the Health Research Authority, is responsible for supporting National Health Service (NHS) Research Ethics Committees in all four countries and, since 2009, the Social Care Research Ethics Committees (SCREC).

The need for strict codes was highlighted after atrocities which took place under the 'guise' of research during the Second World War which are briefly outlined below. Although it is over half a century since the war ended the proceedings of the war crimes trial after the war had, and continue to have, a significant bearing on contemporary ethics.

Post-war codes of ethics

Following the Second World War and the war crimes trial in Nuremberg, and as a direct result of the atrocities which were carried out during the war under the guise of 'research', the Nuremberg code was declared in 1946 as a set of guidelines which should govern the behaviour of those undertaking research on human subjects. This code, and others which have since been developed, have application to working with child subjects, particularly as many of the atrocities which made the design of such codes necessary involved child subjects. Doctor Josef Mengele, chief medical officer of Auschwitz-Birkenau concentration camp, involved many children, usually twins, in inhumane research in an attempt to discover the secret of multiple births so that the Aryan *Ubermensch* (super-race) could be multiplied at a faster rate than normal and world power achieved (Vigorito, 1992). Segal (1992) documents that this research included cruel, scientifically senseless and sometimes lethal methods carried out in atrocious conditions, resulting in needless suffering and the early death of innocent children.

The war crimes trial, and particularly what became known as the 'medical case', brought to light many issues surrounding experimentation on human subjects, and the need to ensure that the 'safety rails' such as the Hippocratic Oath, which should protect human subjects, cannot be removed again (Neuhaus, 1992). The Nuremberg code (Nuremberg Military Tribunals, 1949), the Universal Declaration of Human Rights (United Nations, 1948), the Declaration of Helsinki (World Medical Association (1964), amended in 1975, 1983, 1989, 1996, 2000, 2002, 2004, 2008), the European Commission Directive 91/507/EEC (European Commission, 1991) and other profession-specific codes such as those mentioned in the section above. Derived from, and incorporated within, the various codes mentioned above are the basic ethical principles upon which all research should be based (after Beauchamp and Childress, 2008):

- respect for persons and their autonomy
- justice and fair treatment
- beneficence
- non-maleficence.

While it is not possible to explore these principles further, there are many excellent texts which do so and which are cited in the further reading section at the end of this chapter.

Consent issues

Informed assent and consent should be sought from children involved in research (if they are able to give such consent or assent) and the consent of those with parental responsibility should also be sought prior to their involvement in the research. The child, as well as the parent, must be aware of the implications of the research. The key intention is to make sure that children know:

- they have a choice as to whether to participate in the research – in other words, that they are true volunteers
- they have the right to withdraw from the research at any time if they so wish without detriment to their care
- exactly what their role in the research is
- what will happen to the data that are generated from the research.

Where a child does not reside with their parent, Shaw *et al.* (2011) suggest gaining permission from resident parents and informing non-resident parents who have substantial contact with their children.

Learning activity

Find a research article that has directly used children as research subjects (it can be about anything and can be a classic article or one from a recent journal).
- Read the article carefully.
- Identify any possible ethical implications, particularly any risks or harm to the child. What steps (if any) did the researchers take to ensure that their research met ethical standards?

Conclusion

This chapter has focused on three main areas. First, it is important to emphasise that research is of great value to all of us who work with children. It is research which has enabled us to develop those theories which underpin our practice, and it is important that we are able both to access previous research and to develop skills so that we may critically read and intelligently use previous research. It also enables us to undertake further research and to build upon the existing body of knowledge so that the boundaries of practice can be extended.

There has been a significant impetus over the last few years to undertake research with children rather than on children and we have looked at the scope of participation with the clear aim of shifting towards working with children as partners in research.

It is important to recognise that undertaking early years research is not straightforward, and we may need to adapt and modify methodologies so that the design of the research is appropriate to the age and cognitive and social development of the child. Undertaking research with child subjects also involves additional ethical considerations which were discussed in the last section of this chapter.

Research involving children can be problematic, but the rewards of systematic study in the complex world of the child make the efforts of the researcher very worthwhile.

Evaluate your learning

Identify three research papers relevant to your field and:
(a) Look at the levels of child participation and identify from figure 14.1 what level of participation the study achieved.
(b) Did researchers use measurement scales, and if so, how reliable were these?
(c) How did the researchers address gaining permission and informed consent? Were these adequate?

References

Alderson P and Morrow V (2011): *The Ethics of Research with Children and Young People*. London: Sage.

Axline, V (1964): *Dibs in Search of Self*. Harmondsworth: Penguin.

Baillargeon, R, Tremblay, R and Willms, JD (2002): Physical aggression among toddlers: does it run in families? In Willms, JD (ed), *Vulnerable Children: Findings from Canada's Longitudinal Study of Children and Youth*. Edmonton: University of Alberta Press.

Balen, R, Blyth, E, Calabretto, H, Fraser, C, Horrocks, C and Manby, M (2006) 'Involving children in health and social research: 'human becomings' or 'active beings'? *Childhood* **13**(1), 29–48.

Beauchamp, TL and Childress, JF (2008): *Principles of Biomedical Ethics*, 6th edn. New York: Oxford University Press.

Benini, F, Trapanotto, M, Daniela Gobber, D, Agosto, C, Carli, G, Drigo, P, Eland, J and Zacchello, Z (2004): Evaluating pain induced by venipuncture in pediatric patients with developmental delay. *Clinical Journal of Pain* 20(3), 156–63.

British Psychological Society (2009): *Code of Ethics and Conduct*. Leicester: BPS.

British Sociological Association (2004): *Statement of Ethical Practice*. Durham: BSA.

Bower, T (1977): *The Perceptual World of the Child*. London: Fontana/Open Books.

Campbell, A (2008): For their own good: recruiting children for research. *Childhood* **15**(1), 30–49.

Compas, BE and Phares, V (1991): Stress during childhood and adolescence: sources of risk and vulnerability. In Cummings, EM, Greene, AL and Karraker, KH (eds), *Life-Span Developmental Psychology: Perspectives on Stress and Coping*. Hillsdale, NJ: Lawrence Erlbaum Associates, pp. 111–30.

Coyne, I, Hayes, E and Gallagher P (2009): Research with hospitalized children: ethical, methodological and organizational challenges. *Childhood* **16**(3), 413–29.

Crichton R and Barrett W (2007): The contribution of psychological/sociological perspectives to an understanding of effective participation, in 'Seeking and Taking Account of the views of children and young people: a psychological perspective'. Available from: www.itscotland.com/pdp/. pp. 12–24.

Czymoniewicz-Klippel, MT, Brijnath, B and Crockett, B (2010): Ethics and the promotion of inclusiveness within qualitative research: case examples from Asia and the Pacific, *Qualitative Inquiry* **16**(5), 332–41.

Dockett, S, Perry, B and Einarsdottir, J (2009): Researching with children: ethical tensions. *Journal of Early Childhood Research* **7**(3), 283–98.

Economic and Social Research Council (2010): *Framework for Research Ethics*. (Online). Available from: www.esrc.ac.uk/about-esrc/information/research-ethics.aspx.

European Commission (1991): *European Commission Directive 91/507/EEC*. Brussels: European Commission.

Greig A, Taylor J, and Mackay T (2012): *Doing Research with Children*, 3rd edn. London: Sage.

Hart, RA (1992): 'Children's Participation: From Tokenism To Citizenship', Innocenti Essays No.4 Series. Florence: UNICEF International Children Development Centre.

Hawthorn, P (1975): *Nurse, I Want My Mummy!* London: Royal College of Nursing.

Hill, M (2005): Ethical considerations in researching children's experiences. In Greene, S and Hogan, D (eds), *Researching Children's Experience: Methods and Approaches.* London: Sage, pp. 61–86.

Hill, M (2006): Children's voices on ways of having a voice: children's and young people's perspectives on methods used in research and consultation. *Childhood* **13**(1), 69–89.

International Association for the Study of Pain International Association for the Study of Pain (2001): (Online). Available from: http://www.iasp-pain.org/Content/ NavigationMenu/GeneralResourceLinks/FacesPainScaleRevised/default.htm.

Jones P and Welch S (2010): *Rethinking Children's Rights: Attitudes in Contemporary Society.* New York: Continuum International Publishing Group.

Lewis V and Kellet M (2005): Disability. In Fraser S, Lewis V, Ding S, Kellet M and Robinson C (eds), *Doing Research with Children and Young People.* Philadelphia: Open University Press.

Luria, AR and Yudovich, F (1959): *Speech and the Development of Mental Processes in the Child.* Harmondsworth: Penguin.

Medical Research Council (2004): Medical Research Involving Children. London: MRC. (Online). Available from: www.mrc.ac.uk/Utilities/Documentrecord/index. htm?d=MRC002430.

Murray, ER and Brown Smith, H (1922): *The Child Under Eight.* London: Edward Arnold.

Nardini, M, Bedford, R and Mareschal, D (2010): Fusion of visual cues is not mandatory in children. *Proceedings of the National Academy of Sciences* **107**(39), 17041–46.

Neuhaus, RJ (1992): The way they were, the way we are. In Caplan, AL (ed), *When Medicine went Mad: Bioethics and the Holocaust.* Totowa, NJ: Humana Press, pp. 211–32.

Nuremberg Military Tribunals (1949): *Nuremberg Code.* Washington, DC: US Government Printing Office.

Platt, H (1959): The Welfare of Children in Hospital: Report of the Committee on Child Health Services. London: HMSO.

Powell, MA and Smith, AB (2009): Children's participation rights in research. *Childhood* **16**(1), 124–42.

Reebye P (2005): Aggression during early years. *Infancy and Preschool Journal of the Candian Academy of Child and Adolescent Psychiatry* **14**(1), 16–20.

Romano E, Tremblay RE, Farhat A and Côté S (2006): Development and prediction of hyperactive symptoms from 2 to 7 years in a population-based sample. *Pediatrics* **117**(6), 2101–10.

Royal College of Nursing (2009): *The Recognition and Assessment of Acute Pain in Children.* London. RCN.

Segal, NL (1992): Twin research at Auschwitz-Birkenau: implications for the use of Nazi data today. In Caplan, AL (ed), *When Medicine went Mad: Bioethics and the Holocaust.* Totowa, NJ: Humana Press, pp. 281–300.

Shaw, C, Brady, L-M and Davey, C (2011): *Guidelines for Research with Children and Young People.* London: National Children's Bureau.

Susuki, LK and Kato, PM (2003): Psychosocial support for patients in pediatric oncology: the influences of parents, school, peers and technology. *Journal of Pediatric Oncology and Nursing* **20**(4), 159–74.

United Nations (1948): *Universal Declaration of Human Rights*. New York: United Nations.

UNICEF (2002): Evaluation Technical Notes. Children Participating in Research, Monitoring and Evaluation (M&E) – Ethics and Your Responsibility as a Manager. (Online). Last accessed: 7 March 2012. Available from: www.unicef.org/evaluation/files/TechNote1_Ethics.pdf.

Vigorito, SS (1992): A profile of Nazi medicine: the Nazi doctor – his methods and goals. In Caplan, AL (ed), *When Medicine went Mad: Bioethics and the Holocaust*. Totowa, NJ: Humana Press, pp. 9–14.

World Medical Association (1964) (and subsequent amendments): *Declaration of Helsinki*. World Medical Assembly, Helsinki: World Medical Association.

Further reading

Beauchamp, TL and Childress, JF (2008): *Principles of Biomedical Ethics*, 6th edn. New York: Oxford University Press.

Cohen, L, Manion, L and Morrison K (2012): *Research Methods in Education*, 7th edn. London: Routledge.

Greig, A, Taylor, J, and Mackay T (2012): *Doing Research with Children*, 3rd edn. London: Sage.

15 Leading and managing child-centred services

Jayne Taylor

This chapter aims to:
- explore the core principles of leading and managing child-centred services
- examine leadership and management principles and how these apply specifically to working with children.

Introduction

There are a growing number of early years professionals who become managers of services and a growing importance is placed on developing leadership skills among front-line leaders and managers. Effective and competent leaders and managers are needed to drive forward the agenda to improve the range of children's services which we have referred to throughout this book. Driving forward improvements to services means putting into practice theory and policy (Department for Children, Schools and Families, 2008), and this requires a core repertoire of skills, knowledge and behaviours. The chapter will explore management and leadership principles as they apply to working with children, giving examples of how these differ from those qualities required by adult-centred workers.

In order to structure this chapter, we have drawn on the framework developed by the Department for Children, Schools and Families in their 2008 publication *Leading and Managing Children's Services in England: A National Professional Development Framework*, which in turn builds on *Championing Children: A Shared Set of Skills, Knowledge and Behaviours for Those Leading and Managing Integrated Children's Services* (Children's Workforce Development Council, 2007).

The National Professional Development Framework

The *National Professional Development Framework* identifies 20 competencies for leaders of children's services. Through the discussions in this chapter we will work through the 20 competencies and explore in more depth how the competencies can be translated into practice, giving examples from early years settings. The 20 competencies are:

1. Understand how strategic, commissioning and policy development roles are undertaken.
2. Translate strategic vision into local plans in collaboration with professionals, partners and users.
3. Use the collective knowledge base to challenge the status quo and to do things differently to meet the needs of children and families more effectively.
4. Influence the governance of children's services locally.
5. Build a shared value base and common purpose.
6. Display leadership across the whole system through behaviours such as listening, building alliances and challenging others.
7. Promote the development of leadership attributes at all levels by supporting others to talk knowledgeably about issues in their area of professional expertise and produce innovations in those areas.
8. Make sure that staff understand how their role contributes to the *Every Child Matters* (ECM) agenda and that they are clear about how their performance and development is measured.
9. Make clear how improved service performance and end user satisfaction can be achieved through a responsive and flexible service that reflects the needs of children, young people and families and delivers across the five ECM outcomes.
10. Continually develop the quality of all services offered, ensuring the clear focus is on improving outcomes for children, young people and families.
11. Work for equality, both within the service and around it, and be a credible and compelling advocate for equality.
12. Develop a culture of, and systems to support, a high level of responsiveness within the service.
13. Influence the environment and local strategy by taking opportunities to share ideas and enthusiasm about children's services and what can be achieved.
14. Know the legislative frameworks for all services to children and young people, and where to go for detailed information and interpretation, if required.
15. Develop a culture of, and systems to support, effective use of data in order to inform strategic planning.
16. Empower the end user.
17. Seek out and promote evidence-based practice.
18. Understand and demonstrate how effective resource and finance management can lead to improved outcomes for children, young people and families.
19. Ensure that everyone working with and for children has a high level of awareness of a child's need and right to be safe, and a clear understanding of how their professional practice contributes to the safeguarding of children.
20. Ensure that all children, young people and families are involved in ongoing dialogue about their needs and aspirations and their ideas for service improvement, seeking out, in particular, the views of looked-after children.

Understand how strategic, commissioning and policy development roles are undertaken

The vision for leaders defined in the National Professional Development Framework (Department for Children, Schools and Families, 2008) is to have 'resilient, well-informed, creative and innovative leaders with the requisite skills, knowledge and experience to ensure the effective delivery of integrated provision for children, young people and families at the local level' (p. 10).

At an organisation or service level, good leaders and managers can only effectively deliver their part of the service if they understand their own roles and those of others who work in leadership and management roles in their own service and in other services with which they come into contact (Management Standards Centre, 2008). For example, a team leader working in a health visiting service should understand the role of his or her manager, what roles the directors undertake, how the service is commissioned by the Clinical Commissioning Group and which individuals within that organisation undertake which roles and functions. Without this understanding it is difficult, if not impossible, to work with other people in an effective way. According to the NHS Institute for Innovation and Improvement (NHSI, 2011), good leaders will build relationships with those other people with whom they come into contact, they will develop networks, they will encourage the contributions of others within and outside of their own service to bring about quality improvements and they will work within teams where they have understanding of their own role and the roles of others. The Management Standards Centre (2008) confirms the view of the importance of understanding roles and responsibilities of others and the 'interests and concerns of colleagues and stakeholders and working with and supporting them in various ways. The need to monitor and review the effectiveness of working relationships with colleagues and stakeholders is also a key requirement.'

There are practical things that leaders and managers can do to help with their understanding of the roles of others such as developing a relationship map. A simple one is shown in Figure 15.1. You can design a number of these for different processes within your organisation or service using a similar format. Relationship maps can be used to define people's roles and the roles and relationships between various groups and committees.

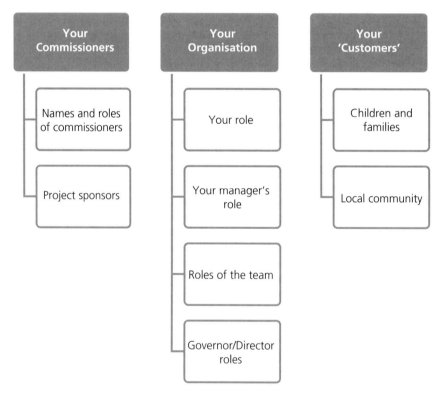

Figure 15.1 Relationship map

Early Childhood Studies: A Multidisciplinary and Holistic Introduction

Translate strategic vision into local plans in collaboration with professionals, partners and users

Leaders and managers working within early years services will most usually be required to work within a strategic framework set by another body – for example, children's health care workers may be employed by an organisation which is part of the National Health Services or a local authority. These large organisations may set strategic vision for a country or county service. Leaders and managers will need to make sure that their local service plans align to the higher strategic vision. An excellent paper produced by a task force working for the Scottish Government, the NHS in Scotland and the Convention of Scottish Local Authorities (COSLA) (COSLA, NHS Scotland and the Scottish Government, 2012) shows how a country-wide strategic vision and shared priorities aims to improve the life chances of children across Scotland. Leaders and managers working in early years settings in Scotland have a clear framework to guide their own local plans and they can develop change programmes for their own services which in turn will support the delivery of the strategic vision.

In practical terms, leaders and managers should know and understand what their strategic vision is and they should make sure that the 'golden threads' of the vision are explicit in their own plans. This can be best achieved by mapping local plans against the strategic vision and identifying where plans support the vision as well as any contradictions or gaps (Management Standards Centre, 2008).

Use the collective knowledge base to challenge the status quo and to do things differently to meet the needs of children and families more effectively

Leaders and managers must be able to innovate which means they need to try different ways of undertaking processes if they are to continuously improve services to meet the needs of children and families. Innovation begins with creative ideas, and while this is a necessary starting point for innovation, it is not enough. Creative ideas (invention) need thorough testing and piloting followed by successful implementation and widespread diffusion. The three component parts of the innovation pathway are shown in Figure 15.2.

Figure 15.2 Three component parts of the innovation pathway

Innovation, according to the NHS Institute for Innovation and Improvement (2011) requires leaders to:

- question the status quo
- act as a positive role model for innovation
- encourage dialogue and debate with a wide range of people which should include staff and end users
- develop creative solutions to transform services and care.

There are a number of practical things that managers and leaders working in early years settings can do to innovate:

- Deliberate and systematic broad scanning of other service providers to generate new ideas which have the potential to make someone or something better. For example, setting up a system for looking in key journals in the field of provision where research is published.
- Establishing an *e-Innovation Forum*: a high profile forum on the organisation's website where staff, children and families can post innovative ideas. It is advisable to include an option for anonymous posting so that people are free to propose even radical ideas without fear that they will be criticised.
- Setting up a process of systematic and regular analysis of ideas with a robust feedback loop to identify those:
  - ➤ which will be accepted
  - ➤ which require more working through or thought
  - ➤ which will not be taken through at this time with reasons provided.
- Testing and evaluation of ideas which is critical to learning. Through this, it is possible to identify ideas that do not work as anticipated. Failure is an integral part of the innovation process. Failing successfully means that a leader can collect data and evidence about the changes tried, and they can reflect on the learning that can be drawn.
- Adoption and diffusion. Adoption is the process where ideas implemented in one area are applied in another area. Diffusion of ideas can occur through a managed process where information is stored and shared through informal networks and relationships. In many cases during this process, the ideas are adapted to suit the context of the local service. Adoption and diffusion should be considered as equally important as invention and innovation.

Influence the governance of children's services locally

Leaders and managers have a responsibility to ensure that the way in which services are provided adhere to a defined set of rules. UNESCO (2007: 1) identifies that good governance 'can ensure that services attain quality standards, are affordable, meet local demand, promote cost-effectiveness and achieve equity goals'.

Governance refers to the way in which an organisation or service governs itself. It defines the processes by which decisions are made and which people or bodies are accountable for the outcomes of the decisions that are made. Good governance means that leaders and managers are clear about lines of accountability and responsibility, how conflicts of interest are managed, and will usually require a set of policies and procedures to make sure that the organisation or service runs smoothly.

One type of governance that will be familiar to most is school governance, which is actually set down in an Act of Parliament (The School Governance (Procedures) (England) Regulations 2003). Schools will have a governing body as well as various committees which will carry out functions on behalf of the governing body. The National College for School Leadership (2012) defines four key themes for good governance: right information, right incentives, right interventions and right innovations.

The importance of having clear and well-defined governance arrangements cannot be underestimated. A good tip is to work with your team and explore a number of common scenarios such as if a child has a minor accident while in the care of a particular service. Work through the scenario and ask:

- Do you have clear protocols and policies which tell you what immediate, short-, medium- and long-term actions you need to take?
- If the accident was due to faulty equipment, what actions must you take to protect other children?
- Is everyone in the team clear about their own roles in this scenario?
- Do you know where and how to report the accident?
- What records do you need to keep about the accident?
- How long do you need to keep records?
- Where do you store records?

Working through scenarios will soon tell you if there are any anomalies in your governance arrangements and if all members of staff understand what to do in common and less common situations.

Learning activity

Here are a few more suggested scenarios to work through:
- It has snowed heavily overnight and the heating system in your nursery is broken.
- A member of staff working in a children's ward has reported that she has chicken pox.
- At the end of the school day a child has not been collected and you are not able to make contact with the parents.

Build a shared value base and common purpose

Leaders and managers of services need to be aware that a successful service or organisation is one that knows what it is aiming to achieve (its common purpose) and how it wishes to get there (its value base). Everyone within the service needs to be 'signed up' to the common purpose and values, and once defined they need to ensure that they model the values and they can articulate them to the end service user in ways that they understand. In early years settings, this means helping children and families to understand what the service or organisation aims to do and the way in which it does it.

The common purpose and values is something that might be influenced by a set of higher rules and principles. For example, health services for children must adhere to the principles outlined in the NHS constitution (Department of Health, 2012a), schools and other early years provision must comply with the framework for the regulation of provision on the Early Years Register (Ofsted, 2012). However, within the higher framework, each service or organisation can and should define how it will play its part.

So what are values? According to Blake *et al.* (2006), values are what inspire us; they determine what we do and how we do it; and they are what we are trying to achieve. We have included two value statements below, both from different spheres of early years, but both of which have common elements:

Our values guide everything we do. They apply to everyone in Ofsted and all those who work on our behalf.

Putting children and learners first

We act in the interests of individual children, young people and learners of all ages, whatever their background.

Achieving excellence

We focus on how standards can be raised and outcomes improved. We always try to 'do good as we go' and have high expectations of ourselves, and of those who provide the services we inspect and regulate.

Behaving with integrity

We work without fear or favour and report on the basis of inspection and regulation evidence. We listen and respond to what people tell us about the services we inspect and regulate, and about the way we work.

Valuing people's differences

We promote equal opportunities and take action to help ensure that improvement is made where it is most needed.

Figure 15.3 Ofsted values from the 2011–2015 Strategic Plan (Ofsted, 2011). Contains public sector information licensed under the Open Government Licence v1.0.

Our second example is from Acorns Children's Hospice Trust, which is an organisation providing palliative care for children and their families. Its values are:

Acorns, a responsive and innovative organisation that puts children and young people and their families first in all of its services, whilst embracing the diversity of its regional communities and demonstrating integrity and quality in everything it does.

Developing a set of values can best be achieved by encouraging those working within the organisation to explore what they believe the values of the service are and to work through any inconsistencies. If everyone in the team is to live the values of the service, they must know and understand what they are. They need to recognise that they must work by these values even if they may differ slightly from their own values. Values statements should be short, understandable to the end user, realistic and achievable.

Developing a common sense of purpose and a shared value base requires leaders and managers to:

● define them
● teach them
● live them
● measure them
● reward them.

We have discussed values, but how does this differ from a common purpose? Kurtzman (2010: xii) states 'it is that rare, almost palpable experience that happens when a leader coalesces a group, team or community into a creative, dynamic, brave and nearly invincible "we"'.

In order to have a common purpose there must clearly first be an agreed set of values. Leaders and managers cannot change the common purpose or values of a service or organisation without knowing where the organisation wants to be or what elements of the current service or organisation need to change. The people who deliver the service must also know and understand the values and purpose.

Display leadership across the whole system through behaviours such as listening, building alliances and challenging others

Leaders and managers have a responsibility to be good role models. The Management Standards Centre (2008) has set out a range of occupational standards which can support managers and leaders to meet this competence.

Listening is a vital attribute for any leader or manager – listening to children, families, staff, commissioners, other providers and other stakeholders. The National Children's Bureau (2010) has produced a helpful fact sheet about listening to children which identifies that there are many valuable reasons to listen to what children and parents say, which can tell leaders and managers what end users think about services and to help them plan improvements. Listening involves observing non-verbal cues (body language), as well as what is being said and noticing inconsistencies between verbal and non-verbal messages.

The 'Skills you need' website provides a useful list of ten tips for good listening:

1. Stop talking
2. Prepare yourself to listen
3. Put the speaker at ease
4. Remove distractions
5. Empathise
6. Be patient
7. Avoid personal prejudice
8. Listen to the tone
9. Listen for ideas – not just words
10. Wait and watch for non-verbal communication

(See www.skillsyouneed.co.uk/IPS/Listening_Skills.html)

Listening is one attribute that leaders and managers need in order to be able to build alliances and challenge others. The Management Standards Centre (2008) defines occupational standards including 'developing working relationships with colleagues, within your own organisation and within other organisations that are productive in terms of supporting and delivering your work and that of the overall organisation'. Developing productive relationships is the foundation of building alliances both within and outwith the service or organisation and to being able to challenge others when there is dissonance around a particular issue.

Promote the development of leadership attributes at all levels by supporting others to talk knowledgeably about issues in their area of professional expertise and produce innovations in those areas

This competence requires leaders and managers to ensure that there are ways within the service or organisation to enable those with expertise in a particular area to share their expertise and to support action planning to bring about service improvements. No leader or manager can be an expert in everything and good leaders and managers delegate to others where this is appropriate.

The Management Standards Centre (2008) identifies the need to 'motivate all the people working in your area to identify ideas for new products and/or services and improvements and other potential sources of ideas and encourage the sharing of this information'. This can only happen if leaders and managers put in place forums where ideas and expertise can be shared.

An example of this would be to make sure in Clinical Commissioning Groups that children's clinical leads are appointed and empowered on behalf of the group to broad scan areas of best practice, to develop proposals for change and to be able to share these more widely.

Make sure that staff understand how their role contributes to the Every Child Matters agenda and that they are clear about how their performance and development is measured

Managing and leading staff is an important competence for leaders and managers. Teams working in early years settings must understand their individual roles and how they contribute to the wider objectives of the service or organisations. Daly *et al.* (2008) have produced an excellent text which includes a section on managing staff and how to facilitate the team to meet the requirements of *Every Child Matters* (ECM).

Helping teams to be clear about their own development needs and to understand how their performance is managed and measured is a core occupational standard defined by the Management Standards Centre (2008). The standard states that leaders and managers should be 'monitoring the progress and quality of the work of individuals and/or teams to ensure that the required level or standard of performance is being met and reviewing and updating plans of work in the light of developments'. This is done through a robust appraisal system and on a practical level making sure that job descriptions are regularly reviewed and updated.

Make clear how improved service performance and end user satisfaction can be achieved through a responsive and flexible service that reflects the needs of children, young people and families and delivers across the five ECM outcomes

Leaders and managers have a responsibility to continually review and improve services in response to feedback from end users about the current service provided (Management Standards Centre, 2008). Responsiveness and flexibility are two of the key requirements for delivering a world class service. Hanna (2011) identifies five attributes of a world class, customer-focused service which leaders and managers can develop within their teams:

1. Know your business and what it is that every part of your business provides.
2. Listen to what your end users say about your services.
3. Respect your end users. Whatever the area of early years provision, whether a hospital, a nursery, a school, etc., it needs people to use the service otherwise the service will fail. Bad publicity from end users, particularly in this era of easy access to information, has the potential to severely damage a service.
4. Communicate when things go wrong. Hanna identifies that end users 'do forgive when organisations take extra efforts to correct problems'.
5. Ownership. It is important that if end users provide feedback of any sort that employees are responsive and do not make end users wait for a response.

There are some practical things that leaders and managers can do to assess how responsive and flexible their service or organisation is and these can be linked to the five outcomes of *Every Child Matters*. Using Hanna's five attributes, leaders and managers can, for example, make sure that:

- all members of the team know the services provided and how each of these contributes to the five outcomes
- the team is aware of all formal and informal processes available to listen to service users and members of the team know what to do with that feedback so that it is considered appropriately
- members of the team embrace a culture of respect for all service users, including those who may be challenging or sometimes difficult. An example of doing this might be to bring service user stories or recent incidents to team meetings or one-to-one meetings
- there are known and understood channels of communication within the organisation and between the organisation or service and individual service users
- every member of the team knows their responsibility to manage feedback and the escalation process if they cannot manage the feedback themselves.

Continually develop the quality of all services offered, ensuring the clear focus is on improving outcomes for children, young people and families

Effective leadership requires individuals to make a real difference by delivering high quality services and by developing improvements to services. The NHS Leadership Framework (NHS Institute for Innovation and Improvement, 2011) identifies that competent leaders will do this through:

- obtaining and acting on end user feedback and experiences
- assessing and analysing current processes within the service using up-to-date improvement methodologies
- identifying improvements and creating solutions through collaborative working
- appraising options and planning and take action to implement and evaluate improvements.

What this means in practice is that leaders and managers working within early years settings will need to identify a range of methods for identifying how children and their families experience the services they use. Action for Sick Children and the NHS Centre for Involvement (2009) developed a guide which, although written for the health sector, can be used across any service based on a cycle of obtaining and using feedback.

Figure 15.4 Cycle of obtaining and using feedback

The key to obtaining good feedback is to break services down into processes and to design a range of ways of obtaining feedback which is appropriate to the processes being evaluated. A simple matrix can help managers and leaders to think about this:

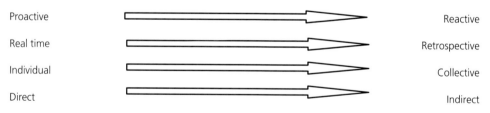

Proactive	Reactive
Real time	Retrospective
Individual	Collective
Direct	Indirect

Figure 15.5 Matrix demonstrating the cycle of obtaining good feedback

● An example of *proactive* feedback would be to talk to children every day for a week about what they think about the quality of food and snacks. This might involve a member of staff asking children, using a smiley faces scale, to rate each meal and to record if children eat the food or leave some or all of it. You might undertake this sort of work to make sure that you are meeting the needs of children in terms of eliminating food waste and making sure that children like the food that is being offered.

- A *reactive* example would be to respond to a complaint about food from a group of parents.
- An example of *real time* feedback is the patient experience trackers commonly used in the NHS. Machines can be placed in a children's outpatient setting and prior to leaving the department children and parents are asked to rate their experiences at the time.
- A *retrospective* example is the annual hospital surveys which are undertaken looking back on people's experiences some months after the actual hospital stay.
- An example of *individual* feedback might be to interview individual children and parents about their experiences of the first week of starting a new nursery, whereas an example of *collective* feedback would involve getting all the children and parents to complete a small questionnaire at the end of the first week.
- An example of *direct* feedback would involve asking questions of children about their experiences of using a children's play area in a local superstore.
- An example of *indirect* feedback would involve asking play workers about their views of how children experience the facility.

After you have obtained feedback, the next step is to analyse the data you have obtained and make plans to instigate appropriate changes. It is important that when analysing feedback you make sure that you are not making drastic change on the basis of one or two non-representative views. A really good example of this would be that you change the morning snack menu because one child does not like apple slices and the result is you have 19 other unhappy children who no longer get the apples that they liked!

Once you have decided that end user feedback indicates that a process needs to be changed, you can start to plan the change. If the change is to provide a new induction programme for children and parents starting at nursery you should undertake some work to see what others in similar services are doing and why they do things differently to you.

A simple improvement methodology that is used to carry out the change is the PDSA cycle: plan, do, study, act. The PDSA cycle tests an idea by temporarily trialling a change and assessing its impact.

The four stages of the PDSA cycle are:

Plan the change to be tested or implemented
Do carry out the test or change
Study data before and after the change and reflect on what was learned
Act plan the next change cycle or full implementation.

Using PDSA can help you to come up with a range of options to test out and after testing to come up with a range of options which includes articulating the strengths and weaknesses of each approach.

Improving services is an aspiration for all managers and leaders, but improvements should be based on sound evidence and collaboration with end users.

Work for equality, both within the service and around it, and be a credible and compelling advocate for equality

Services for children and their families must be built on the principles of fairness, dignity and respect. Statutory services have a duty to promote equality of opportunity, foster good relations and eliminate discrimination. The Equality Act (2010) replaces previous anti-discrimination legislation and has simplified the law, removed inconsistencies and made it easier for people to understand and comply with. It has also strengthened the law, helping to tackle discrimination and inequality.

The Equality Act (2010) protects people from unfavourable treatment because of the following ('protected') characteristics, some of which apply to everyone while others apply to groups of people:

- Age
- Disability
- Gender re-assignment
- Marriage and civil partnership
- Pregnancy and maternity
- Race, including national identity and ethnicity
- Religion or belief
- Sex (that is, male or female)
- Sexual orientation.

As leaders and managers working in early years settings, it is essential that services are compliant with the Equality Act (2010). Although some of the protected characteristics may not apply directly to children they all apply to the families that come into contact with the service.

There are a number of practical actions that leaders and managers can take to ensure that the equality legislation is adhered to. These might include the following:

- Collecting data across the protected characteristic groups and ensuring that information is reviewed, analysed and used to inform the development of services that meet the needs of those using the services where gaps are identified.
- Assessing all policies, procedures and protocols to determine whether they have a disparate impact on any of the protected groups (an Equality Impact Assessment template can be found on the Equality and Human Rights Commission website, see www.equalityhumanrights.com).
- Making sure that any service change meaningfully engages with all end users to ensure changes meet the needs of all protected characteristics.
- Developing staff training programmes to make sure that all of those people who come into contact with children and families are aware of their responsibilities to support the equality and diversity agenda.
- Advancing the equality agenda within the service to ensure equality and diversity is mainstreamed and embedded across the organisation.

Develop a culture of, and systems to support, a high level of responsiveness within the service

According to the Health and Safety Executive, culture can best be understood as 'the way we do things around here'. Culture is not something that can be instantly achieved – it takes time and good leadership and management to build and promote it. According to the Chartered Institute of Personnel Development (CIPD, online):

Organisational culture is a system of shared values and beliefs about what is important, what behaviours are appropriate and about feelings and relationships internally and externally. Values and cultures need to be unique to the organisation, widely shared and reflected in daily practice and relevant to the company purpose and strategy. But there is no single best culture.

The Institute of Customer Service (2011) has developed a helpful evidence-based model which can assist leaders and managers to consider how to ensure that service performance is high and end user satisfaction is achieved. The model is built around three broad organisational aspects: strategy and culture, people, and processes.

The part of the model around culture stresses that, 'Promises are kept, service is delivered at times that suit customers and superb service recovery systems are in place'. In other words, the organisation or service does what it says it will do, in a way that service users want, and when things fail the service or organisation responds quickly to put things right. Everyone reading this text will be able to identify organisations, for example shops and businesses that have a strong customer-focused culture where you know that if you have cause to complain you will be met with courtesy, respect and a solution. You will all be able to identify other organisations that you find an enormous challenge to deal with and consequently will not use again.

Leaders and managers can, at a practical level, take steps to assess the culture of their service or organisation by, for example:

● seeking feedback from end users about their views of how responsive their service is
● following up every complaint or concern raised to ascertain if the views expressed were dealt with appropriately
● using the 'family and friends' test – asking service users if they would recommend the service to others.

Influence the environment and local strategy by taking opportunities to share ideas and enthusiasm about children's services and what can be achieved

The early years environment is very important to supporting and extending children's development and learning. The first impressions that children and their families get of the physical environment when they visit a nursery, a hospital, a school or any premises will influence how they feel about the service or organisation. First impressions stay with us and shape what follows – they really do matter. The Early Years Matters website (http://earlyyearsmatters.co.uk) includes useful information which describes:

● the emotional environment
● the outdoor environment
● the indoor environment.

The key aim is to design the environment so that children feel safe, relaxed and at home. Leaders and managers should be aware of the importance of the environment when they are working in early years settings (Ashman and Green, 2005).

Access the Enabling Environments sheet from the Early Years Matters site (http://earlyyearsmatters.co.uk) and assess the environment of your service or organisation. For example:

Criteria	Assessment	Action required
The indoor environment		
The indoor environment contains resources which are appropriate, well maintained and accessible for all children		
Indoor spaces are planned so that they can be used flexibly and an appropriate range of activities is provided		
The outdoor environment		
Outdoor space gives children first-hand contact with weather, seasons and the natural world		
Outdoor environments offer children freedom to explore, use their senses, and be physically active and exuberant		
The emotional environment		
The people in the environment are warm and accepting of everyone		
Children know that their feelings are accepted and they learn to express them, confident that adults will help them with how they are feeling		
Adults empathise with children and support their emotions		

Developing an action plan from the simple assessment above can be achieved through a series of linked activities such as:

- getting feedback from end users about how they see the environment – including potential end users who then decide to go elsewhere, for example, parents who visit a school but then choose to place their child elsewhere
- visiting other similar organisations that are known to be successful and offer a good environment
- regularly asking members of the team for their ideas
- asking external visitors routinely for their objective and critical feedback on the environment.

Leaders and managers who work within services which are part of a larger organisation, such as a hospital which provides a number of environments for children, should also ensure that children and families are able to easily navigate their way through the various services they might need to access. Taking time to regularly 'walk the pathway' from outpatients, to radiology, to pathology, to the children's ward, can highlight many gaps – we often are aware of our part of the service, but not the connecting corridors, the lifts and so on.

Know the legislative frameworks for all services to children and young people, and where to go for detailed information and interpretation if required

Leaders and managers must keep up to date with current legislation. The Management Standards Centre (2008) identifies the need for services to have knowledge of and obey the law in key areas, such as health and safety, employment, finance and company law.

On a practical level, this means that there must be a robust way for leaders and managers to keep themselves up to date with changes in legislation. This means having a regime to make sure that there is a structured way for finding out about changes and for acting on those changes when they occur. There are several ways of achieving this such as reviewing regular bulletins about early years services, broad scanning relevant websites and journals, ensuring that there are discussion forums in place to review current issues and having mechanisms in place for sharing changes with staff.

Develop a culture of, and systems to support, effective use of data in order to inform strategic planning

Using data effectively and intelligently is another vital competence for managers and leaders. Leaders and managers must have a good understanding of how their service or organisation is performing, how productive it is, how much their service costs and how well the service does in comparison to similar services. Good data can help leaders and managers to understand areas for improvement which can then be translated into robust planning. Bhatia (2005) sums up the need for data:

- If you can't measure something, you really don't know much about it.
- If you don't know much about it, you can't control it.
- If you can't control it, you are at the mercy of chance.

Data can be very complex and in some organisations the amounts of data collected can be overwhelming. Bhatia's article (2005) is entitled 'Data rich, information poor? Focus on right metrics' – beautifully illustrating the problem that many leaders and managers experience in a world of full of rich and readily available information. The NHS produces masses of data (Department of Health, 2012b), as does the education system (Amli *et al.*, 2011) and almost every sector that you are likely to work in. Leaders and managers need to be able to extract the information they need from the data to inform their work and their plans.

An example of the use of data in strategic planning is the exploration of children's unscheduled attendances within health services. Accident and Emergency data are available on the ages of children, the time of day and the day of the week they attend, whether they were brought into the department by ambulance, referred by their GP or if they were brought in by their family, what happened to them in the department and where they went after their attendance, for example, discharged home, admitted, transferred to another facility. The information is able to inform those commissioning and providing services to understand trends in attendances and can help those managing a children's Accident and Emergency Department to calculate when they need additional staffing capacity, for instance at weekends, in the early evening, when they need to have particular staff on duty, for example, to care for small babies.

Empower the end user

Empowering the end user means that children and their families understand the service and have the information in an appropriate form about the service so that they can influence what goes on within that service in an informed way. There is a superb manual that leaders and managers can access (Gibbs *et al.*, 2002) about empowering children and, although some of the examples and games are designed for older children, there are many activities which can readily be adapted for younger children too. The model used by Gibbs *et al.* is based on:

- drawing out children's experiences and looking for shared patterns of experience and knowledge
- exploring new ideas and information
- supporting children to practise various life skills
- planning for, and taking action
- reflecting on what has been learned and how things have changed as a result of their work.

Hart (2005: 207) also provides a helpful discussion on empowerment through consultation which she states gives practitioners, 'A fantastic way to evaluate your setting from the child's perspective'. She reports on a project which used a range of tools to engage with young children across various ages concluding that children, even at a very young age, have subtle ways of communicating, if we take the time to really listen (Hart, 2005: 212).

Learning activity

Try out different approaches yourself. A good place to start is to adapt one or more of the games in the manual produced by Gibbs *et al.* (2002) to explore a specific aspect of your service with children.

Seek out and promote evidence-based practice

Evidence-based practice is a way of working that makes sure that decision-making processes are based on the best available scientific research evidence (Buysse and Wesley, 2006). Leaders and managers need to be competent to:

- identify evidence
- assess evidence
- use evidence
- evaluate the use of evidence.

In Chapter 14, the first two competences are explored in more detail:

- Accessing evidence and particularly being able to 'pin down' key words to help you to search for evidence.
- Developing critical reading skills to help you assess evidence (the guidance mentioned below on looked-after children published by NICE and SCIE in 2010 provides an excellent example of how different forms of evidence can be assessed and used).

After the process of sourcing and assessing evidence has been undertaken, the next stage is to use evidence in practice. The Centre for the Use of Research and Evidence in Education

(2007) has produced a useful publication, *Harnessing Knowledge to Practice: Accessing and Using Evidence from Research*, which discusses how to do this in education. In particular, they identify barriers to the implementation of evidence and urge those generating evidence to help practitioners by making clear the implications of the evidence and exemplars of how to implement evidence in practice.

In our experience across early years settings, decisions about how to use evidence are best made with discussion and input from whole teams. Leaders and managers can facilitate these discussions through:

- making evidence clear and digestible to the team
- identifying the easiest parts of evidence to implement initially and then exploring larger-scale decisions
- setting out from the beginning how evidence-based decisions will be measured and monitored
- discussing how to involve end users in decisions
- identifying who will be responsible for which parts of implementation, measuring and monitoring.

The final stage of the process is to undertake evaluation of evidence implementation and this should be done in a structured way, involving the team and end users.

Understand and demonstrate how effective resource and finance management can lead to improved outcomes for children, young people and families

Effective resources usage and management is a vital competence for leaders and managers. No organisation or service has infinite resources and even if leaders and managers are not budget holders, they still need to understand how their organisation is funded and what it spends its resources on.

Leaders and managers must be able to understand their own responsibility for resource allocation and monitor the effective use of resources (Management Standards Centre, 2008). They need to be able to quickly identify when and why variances within budgets exist, so that they correct deficits. Ashman and Green (2005) have written an entire book on managing the environment and resources in early years settings which covers budget setting, resource management planning and monitoring.

Practically, leaders and managers should at any point in time be able to articulate what their budget is, the pressure points within the budget, for example which areas are under- or overspent, and the forecast for the end of the year, i.e. will the service be delivered on budget and the nature of any variance.

Ensure that everyone working with and for children has a high level of awareness of a child's need and right to be safe, and a clear understanding of how their professional practice contributes to the safeguarding of children

In Chapter 10, the legislative framework for safeguarding young children was discussed, as well as responsibilities within services for safeguarding.

Leaders and managers have a specific responsibility to ensure that children are safe within the services they provide. When children are placed within an early years setting, for example in a nursery or a school or when they are in hospital, there is an absolute expectation that they will be safe while they are there and this requires a clear understanding and awareness of the systems and processes that are in place to make sure that this happens.

According to the Health and Safety Executive, there are ten questions that leaders and managers should ask themselves about their service or organisation:

1. How do you demonstrate the board's commitment to health and safety?
2. What do you do to ensure appropriate board-level review of health and safety?
3. What have you done to ensure your organisation, at all levels including the board, receives competent health and safety advice?
4. How are you ensuring all staff – including the board – are sufficiently trained and competent in their health and safety responsibilities?
5. How confident are you that your workforce, particularly safety representatives, are consulted properly on health and safety matters, and that their concerns are reaching the appropriate level including, as necessary, the board?
6. What systems are in place to ensure your organisation's risks are assessed and that sensible control measures are established and maintained?
7. How well do you know what is happening on the ground, and what audits or assessments are undertaken to inform you about what your organisation and contractors actually do?
8. What information does the board receive regularly about health and safety, for example performance data and reports on injuries and work-related ill health?
9. What targets have you set to improve health and safety and do you benchmark your performance against others in your sector or beyond?
10. Where changes in working arrangements have significant implications for health and safety, how are these brought to the attention of the board?

Leaders and managers can work through the questions themselves and with their teams, and any questions that cannot be answered sufficiently should be addressed through a structured programme of development.

Ensure that all children, young people and families are involved in ongoing dialogue about their needs and aspirations and their ideas for service improvement, seeking out, in particular, the views of looked-after children

Involving children and families in continuous discussions about how services can meet their needs and seeking out their views about how services can be improved is a competence that all leaders and managers should have and has been covered in earlier sections of this chapter. This is important for all service provision, but is even more important when services are being delivered to vulnerable children, such as children being looked after away from home. As the end users of services, these children are best placed to inform service changes.

The National Institute for Health and Clinical Excellence (NICE) and the Social Care Institute for Excellent (SCIE) (2010: 11) have produced comprehensive guidance about looked-after children and one of their core principles is to 'put the voices of children, young people and their families at the heart of service design and delivery'.

Recommendation 24 of the guidance is to 'Meet the individual needs and preferences of looked-after children and young people' and outlines a number of practical steps that can be taken to make sure that looked-after children have a voice. These include assertiveness training and including children in the development of policies that affect them.

Conclusion

This chapter has explored the principles of management and leadership in early years settings. The need to listen to end users has been emphasised as a core and underpinning competence for leaders and managers. User feedback is crucial to being able to develop and improve services.

Evaluate your learning

- What can leaders and managers do to ensure that the service or organisation provides a good environment for children?
- How can leaders and managers promote innovation in their service or organisation?
- Why is it important for leaders and managers to invite feedback from children and families using the service?

References

Acorns Children's Hospice Trust *Vision, Mission and Values.* (Online). Available from: www.acorns.org.uk/vision-mission-values.

Action for Sick and the NHS Centre for Involvement (2009): *Involving Children and Young People in Healthcare – A Planning Tool.* (Online). Available from: www.actionforsickchildren.org.

Amli M, Baharum A and Ahmad BE (2011): Information management issues of data rich, information poor in higher education institution: a study of contributing factors. *European Journal of Social Sciences* **21**(2), 260–4.

Ashman, C and Green, S (2005): *Manage Environment and Resources.* London: David Fulton Publishers.

Bhatia, A (2005): *Data Rich, Information Poor? Focus On Right Metrics.* (Online). Available from: www.tdan.com/view-articles/5115.

Blake G, Robinson, D and Smerdon, M (2006): *Living Values. Links UK in Partnership with the Governance Hub.* (Online). Available from: www.community-links.org/uploads/documents/livingvaluespocketguidefortrustees.pdf.

Buysse, V and Wesley, P (2006): *Evidence-Based Practice in the Early Childhood Field Zero to Three.* Washington: National Center for Infants, Toddlers and Families.

Centre for the Use of Research and Evidence in Education (CUREE) (2007): *Harnessing Knowledge to Practice: Accessing and Using Evidence from Research*. Coventry: CUREE.

Children's Workforce Development Council (2007): *Championing Children*. Leeds: CWDC. (Online). Available from: www.everychildmatters.gov.uk/deliveringservices/championingchildren.

CIPD Vision and Values: Organisational Culture and Values as a Source of Competitive Advantage. (Online). Available from: www.cipd.co.uk/research/_visionandvalues.htm.

COSLA, NHS Scotland and the Scottish Government (2012): *The Early Years Taskforce Shared Vision and Priorities*. (Online). Available from: //www.scotland .gov.uk/Topics/People/Young-People/Early-Years-and-Family/earlyyearstaskforce/visionandprioritiespaper

Daly M, Byers E and Taylor W (2008): *Early Years Management in Practice*, 2nd edn. Harlow: Heinemann.

Department for Children, Schools and Families (DCSF) (2008): *Leading and Managing Children's Services in England: A National Professional Development Framework*. Nottingham: DCSF Publications.

Department of Health (2012a): *The NHS Constitution for England*. London: Department of Health.

Department of Health (2012b): *The Power of Information*. London: Department of Health.

Early Years Matters *Enabling Environments*. (Online). Available from: http://earlyyearsmatters.co.uk/index.php/enabling-environments/.

Equality Act 2010 (2010): (Online). Available from: http://www.legislation.gov.uk/ukpga/2010/15/contents.

Gibbs S, Mann G and Mathers N (2002): *Child-to-child: A Practical Guide, Empowering Children as Active Citizens*. London: Child-to-Child Trust. (Online). Available from: www.child-to-child.org/guide/guide.pdf.

Hanna, D (2011): *To Deliver World-Class Customer Service, Use a Customer-Centric Strategy*. (Online). Available from: http://socialmediatoday.com/douglashanna/551157/deliver-world-class-customer-service-use-customer-centric-strategy.

Hart, M (2005): Listening and learning: empowering children in early childhood services. In Schonfeld H, O'Brien, S and Walsh, T (eds), *Questions of Quality*. Dublin: The Centre for Early Childhood Development and Education, pp. 205–13.

Health and Safety Executive *Health and Safety Leadership Checklist*. (Online). Available from: www.hse.gov.uk/leadership/checklist.htm.

Institute of Customer Service (2011): *Model for World Class Service*. (Online). Available from: www.instituteofcustomerservice.com/1848-6942/Model-for-World-Class-Service.html.

Kurtzman, J (2010): *Common Purpose How Great Leaders Get Organizations to Achieve the Extraordinary*. San Francisco: Jossey-Bass.

Management Standards Centre (2008): *National Occupational Standards (NOS) for Management and Leadership*. (Online). Available from: www.management-standards.org.

National Children's Bureau (2010): *Let's Listen*. London: NCB. (Online). Available from: www.ncb.org.uk/media/71974/let_slisten.pdf.

National College for School Leadership (2012): *Good Governance*. (Online). Available from: www.thegovernor.org.uk/freedownloads/recentreportsongovernance/good-governance-2012_1.pdf.

NHS Institute for Innovation and Improvement (2011): *The NHS Leadership Framework*. (Online). Available from: http://www.leadershipacademy.nhs.uk/develop-your-leadership-skills/leadership-framework/the-framework-overview.

NICE and SCIE (2010): *Promoting the Quality of life of Looked-after Children and Young People*. (Online). Available from: http://www.nice.org.uk/PH28.

Ofsted (2011): *Raising Standards, Improving Lives: The Office for Standards in Education, Children's Services and Skills Strategic Plan 2011–2015*. (Online). Available from: http://www.ofsted.gov.uk/resources/raising-standards-improving-lives-office-for-standards-education-childrens-services-and-skills-strat-0.

Ofsted (2012): *Framework for the Regulation of Provision on the Early Years Register Manchester: Ofsted. The School Governance (Procedures)(England) Regulations 2003*. (Online). Available from: www.legislation.gov.uk/uksi/2003/1377/contents/made.

UNESCO (2007): Good governance of early childhood care and education: lessons from the 2007 EFA Global Monitoring Report. *UNESCO Policy Briefs on Early Childhood*, no. 40.

Further reading

Lindon J and Lindon L (2011): *Leadership and Early Years Professionalism*. London: Hodder Education.

16 Understanding children's rights: examining the rhetoric with reality

Emma Bond and Stuart Agnew

This final chapter examines some of the key themes and debates that have been considered by the authors who contributed chapters to this edition through a discussion of children's rights. Understanding the impact of the United Nations Conventions on the Rights of the Child (UNCRC) on how we view and understand young children's lives and how we treat young children is an essential underpinning principle of early childhood studies (ECS) and one which permeates every aspect of early childhood.

> *Human rights are general rights, rights that arise from no special undertaking beyond membership of the human race. To have human rights one does not have to be anything other than a human being. Neither does one have to do anything other than be born as a human, a human being.*

(Donnelly, 2003: 10)

The recognition of children's rights was a 20th century awakening that is exemplified by the children's charter outlined by Jebb in 1923 (cited in Rutgers, 2011: 1), that children must be given the formal resources for normal development, both materially and spiritually; the hungry child must be fed, the sick child helped, the delinquent child reclaimed and the orphan child sheltered; children must be the first to receive relief in times of stress; children must be able to earn a living and be protected from exploitation and that children must be brought up in the 'consciousness that their talents must be devoted to the service of humankind'. According to the Children's Rights Alliance for England (CRAE, online) the UNCRC, agreed by the United Nations in 1989, gives children and young people all over the world over 40 major rights and in 1991, the British Government agreed to follow the UNCRC and, therefore, reports to the UN Committee on the Rights of the Child every five years.

Only the US and Somalia have not ratified what is otherwise a globalised framework that provides obligations upon nation states and Kofi Annan, while UN Secretary-General argued that:

> *The idea of children's rights, then, may be a beacon guiding the way to the future – but it is also illuminating how many adults neglect their responsibilities towards children and how children are too often the victims of the ugliest and most shameful human activities.*

(Kofi Annan cited in Alderson, 2008: 13)

As a result of the UNCRC, 'the concept of children took a radical turn: girls and boys ceased to be regarded as objects of protection and became recognised as subjects of rights' (Maurás, 2011: 52). In Chapter 1, *Early childhood studies: first principles*, Emma Bond highlights the historical debate surrounding the development of a rights-based approach from the dominant ideology of welfarism, however, it should also be acknowledged that these arguments are not as dichotomous as is normally suggested. There is no doubt that the adoption of the UNCRC by the British Government on 16 December 1991 could be seen as a triumph of the rights-based approach supporters over those whose ideals suggested that children were vulnerable and required protection. However, that is a far too simplistic an argument to make, and Article 3, for example, clearly acknowledges that the best interest of the child must be seen as a primary consideration in all actions concerning children. This demonstrates that even a rights-based approach recognises that the outcome of welfarism, and that the best interest of the child, is of fundamental importance.

The issues that encapsulate the debate surrounding children's rights are complex and have implications far beyond national borders, yet for informed critical discussions to be had, children and their lived realities needed to be seen as a valuable subject matter to explore within an academic framework. Chapter 1 provides an insight into the developments of ECS as an academic programme, highlighting many of the challenges faced when investigating the lives of children from historical periods and identifies key concepts and debates that will inform your studies. A key concept that all ECS students must embrace is that relating to the social construction of childhood. Bond frames the notion of historical understandings and growing enlightenment within academia regarding the historical social changes that impacted upon societal views of children.

The introduction of the UNCRC presents an international benchmark for valuing children, setting out the needs and obligations on nation states regarding respecting children and their childhoods. A major aspect of this is to listen to children, enshrined in Article 12, that acknowledges children have the right to form their own views and to express them. This facilitates the meaningful participation of children in the decisions that impact upon their lives, although one must accept that the power relations that exist in society are constructed in such a way that children continue to be marginalised (James and James, 2004). This provides the backdrop for all ECS research and teaching, understanding the cultural, social and structural limitations placed upon children and how the UNCRC should be seen as an emancipatory approach that informs what you as an ECS student should consider when studying and working with children, together with the key principles outlined in Chapter 1.

In Chapter 2, *New beginnings: factors affecting health and well-being in the neonate*, Heather Passmore and Samantha Chennery-Morris outline the factors that can affect the health and well-being of babies. For students of ECS this knowledge and understanding is of paramount importance as these factors can have a significant impact on the healthy development of children during not only the early years of their lives, but through childhood and into adulthood also. This is a theme also discussed in the chapters on development and Sue Hollinrake's consideration of children with disabilities in Chapter 12 and, therefore, our understanding of issues during (even prior to) pregnancy and immediately after birth can inform how we advise women and the development of early screening to identify problems and to support mothers and families in promoting the optimum environment for the developing child.

Article 6 of the UNCRC sets out 'States parties recognize that every child has the inherent right to life. A. States parties shall ensure to the maximum extent possible the survival and development of the child'. In Chapter 2, readers were presented with a detailed account of fetal development and how socio-economic and lifestyle factors can impact on healthy development. However, as Montgomery (2009) argues, there are blurred boundaries between understandings of the terms child, foetus and embryo and different social, cultural and legal constructs. How these terms are understood can have a significant impact on how children's rights are understood. The contested nature of the unborn child is extremely apparent in the current abortion debate in the United States, for example (Montgomery, 2009), and more recently in the UK. These debates and the changing constructions around these terms influence both legislation and healthcare policy.

Article 24 of the UNCRC states that states parties must 'ensure appropriate pre-natal and post-natal health care for mothers'. Currently in the UK there is a comprehensive programme of antenatal care and dedicated health professionals who work together to offer information and health promotion advice, screening and health-related services to families. As noted by Passmore and Chennery-Morris, these developments are a result of increasing understanding about prenatal development and the knowledge that optimising maternal health maximises the neonate's well-being. However, not all women take advantage of the services provided, many pregnancies are unplanned and some women continue with lifestyle behaviours which may have adverse effects on their child's health. Smoking is well known to have a negative impact on fetal development and, according to the NHS (online), babies from deprived backgrounds are more likely to be born to mothers who smoke and to have much greater exposure to second-hand smoke in childhood. From the figures available (at the time of writing) 26 per cent of mothers in England smoked at some point in the 12 months immediately before or during their pregnancy, but of mothers who smoked before or during their pregnancy just over half (55 per cent) gave up at some point before the birth (NHS online). In the UK, emphasis is on encouraging women to embark on a programme of pre-conceptual care, giving up smoking and alcohol, for example, and increasing their intake of folic acid before they get pregnant and ensuring that mothers-to-be are offered screening and healthcare advice and regular health check-ups during their pregnancy. This development, together with improved standards of living and safe birthing procedures, has had significant impact on infant mortality rates which have fallen from 23 per 1000 live births in 1960 to 4 in 2011 (UNICEF, online). However, from an international perspective, we can see that antenatal policies are often absent and many countries lack such programmes of healthcare and according to UNICEF (online) in Sierra Leone, for example, 220 babies died per 1000 live births in 2011, in Afghanistan the figure was 73 and in India 47. In our consideration of the health and well-being of the neonate and thinking about new beginning, we should be mindful of the fact that many thousands of babies are in fact denied the 'inherent right to life' that the UNCRC sets out as states parties are failing to ensure the health and development of children from the very beginning.

In *Embodied childhoods*, which is the focus of Chapter 3, Jessica Clark follows the trajectory of the health of the very young baby through early childhood to outline young children's physical growth and development, and takes the reader from the very early days of life to critically evaluate the dominance of developmental and biological models in understanding children's bodies. This is an important aspect of ECS – one which has frequently been overlooked – and there has been, perhaps for too long, an uncritical acceptance of these models in understanding young children's health. The emphasis on health screening during pregnancy in the UK continues during the first years of a child's life. This surveillance arguably is underpinned by the 'right of the child to the enjoyment of the highest attainable standard of health' (see Article 24 UNCRC) but, as Clark suggests, it is not unproblematic. 'The moulding of the category of the normal child owes much to both new techniques of observation and the rapid increase or research and knowledge in such fields as hygiene, paediatrics and psychology' (as outlined by Graff (1995) and Rollet (1990) in Turmel (2008: 61)). Scholars of early childhood studies need to remember the notion of 'becoming' as a dominant concept in relation to early childhood development and to consider how these practices have come about. It is, as Clark argues, highly questionable whether they are culturally specific and appropriate for all children.

Current concerns in relation to young children's bodies centre around whether developmental milestones are being met on time, polarised anxieties on body size and image with an epidemic of childhood obesity (see Le Billon, 2012) and increasing numbers of young children dieting and being treated for anorexia (Hill, 2007). The lack of opportunity for outside physical play and an increase in digital technologies combined with a junk/processed food diet dominate the debate in western societies, while for young children in the Majority South, it is malnutrition, lack of access to safe water and sanitation facilities and dying from preventable diseases which dominate. Although Article 24(e) sets out that 'to combat disease and malnutrition, including the framework of primary health care, through inter alia, the application of readily available technology and through the provision of adequate nutritious foods and clean drinking water, taking into consideration the dangers and risks of environmental pollution' and some progress has been made, with the total estimated number of under-five deaths falling from nearly 12 million in 1990 to 6.9 million in 2011, 19 000 children under the age of five died every day in 2011 (UNICEF, online).

Anne Greig in Chapter 4 highlights growing concern regarding the personal, social and emotional (PSE) development of young children and she presents evidence to suggest that not engaging with this aspect of child development may have negative connotations for them later in life. Therefore, to see that children have a wide variety of opportunities afforded to them, we must initially ensure that children grow up in a way that provides them with the PSE skills that will empower them to actively engage in society. As such, by engendering an environment where children can explore their emotional literacy appears to produce positive outcomes in terms of social skills and academic ability. There are clear links with this perspective and with the provisions covered by Articles 28 and 29 with regards to the right to education for children. Not only must education be provided by governments (Article 28), but the education must facilitate the development of the child's personality, mental and physical abilities in addition to preparing them for a responsible life in a free society (Article 29). Therefore, we must explore to what extent this function is adopted throughout all nations that have adopted the UNCRC. Certainly within the United Kingdom, there is a focus within the educational setting identifying the importance of PSE development and that current practice in both early years settings and primary schools focus on this aspect of child development.

It could be argued that many of the debates above regarding the development of PSE competence do not necessarily have to occur in formal settings, such as a school or preschool environment. In Chapter 5, *Children's relationships*, David Rutherford explores how different relationships that children have impact upon their lived realities and highlights the importance placed upon familial relationships, not forgetting the complexity that the label 'family' has in late modernity. Many of the competencies discussed in Chapter 4 can be directly related to the experiences children have within their family network and as such the importance that the UNCRC places upon the family as the natural environment for the development and well-being of children can be seen within, for example, Article 5, that respects the rights and duties of parents, Article 7, that states that children should be cared for by their own parents, Article 8, relating to the preservations of family relations and Article 9, relating to the separation of children from the parents and being able to maintain contact with their parents as long as it is in their best interest.

It can be seen from the evidence provided that both academic research and the principles that underpin many of the Articles within the UNCRC that the well-being of children is paramount and that a significant contributor to this is the relationship children have with their family. There is much to be said regarding the pro-social role modelling that can occur within familial relationships, but one must also accept that families can also have devastating effects on children through neglect and abuse, emotional, psychological, physical and sexual, as Rutherford here and Chapter 10 discuss. As such, although the Articles above appear to protect the sanctity of family life, there is always a caveat that family relationships can only be maintained where it is in the best interest of the child. The relationship a child has with his or her parent(s) is fundamental to the development of PSE competencies and as a result the parental approaches identified by Baumrind (1991) indicate that different parenting techniques will result in different levels of PSE competence.

ECS students are expected to consider this emphasis upon positive familial relationships with a critical eye. You are expected to think beyond the traditional and dominant ideologies to consider what happens when the familial relationship is not positive. In what ways do the UNCRC Articles protect children and what obligations are placed upon nation states? If negative familial relationships hamper children's development and well-being what actions are to be taken by the state to ensure that children are in a positive environment? Article 9 provides guidance regarding when it is appropriate for a child to be removed from their family, however, we must question to what extent this will provide children with improved opportunities to develop. In relation to the UK, according to Barnardo's (online), 'it is well established that these children are more likely to have poor educational experiences, leave school with fewer qualifications, are at higher risk of offending, becoming a teenage parent and being not in education, employment or training.' We must evaluate the extent that children are being protected by the state and provided with opportunities to develop and to be an active participating citizen within the 21st century. One must also consider to what extent care settings are offered in an international context, the quality of provision, the emotional and psychological support provided to children and possible isolation and stigmatisation that may be experienced by children who live away from their families. There is no doubt that what is seen in the child's best interest may differ depending upon the cultural expectations of the local environment and that by developing social capital within communities, within the confines of cultural relativism, children's lived experiences should be improved.

The adoption of the UNCRC by nation states can be seen as formal acceptance of children as human beings that should have rights and entitlements afforded to them, not just because of their status as human beings but also because of their position within society. Communities, parents and governments all expect the future generations to advance and contribute to society. The emphasis that these expectations place upon children also justifies in some ways, the growing number of theoretical positions, research and debates surrounding children as autonomous actors (see also Chapter 8, *Understanding childhood in late modernity*). However, when considering the debates surrounding children in late modernity, we can see that children are not always portrayed in the best possible light. In fact, at times it would be reasonable to doubt the impact of the UNCRC when considering some of the views and beliefs expressed regarding children and that they are unable to participate fully or have their voice heard.

The importance placed upon the family may be a valid construction, but to what extent this focus is based around 'what is best' for the child or the anxieties of late modernity are challenging discussions that ECS students must have. Our responsibility is to ensure that we carefully consider the actions of everyone: parents, wider networks, communities and the state, so that they can be held accountable to the various Articles espoused in the UNCRC. The controls that are placed upon children in late modernity call into question the realistic opportunities that all children have in being able to fully participate within society and also to have their voice heard (Burr and Montgomery, 2003; see also Chapter 1). This is further complicated when considering the diverse lived realities facing children and young people, in terms of socio-economic position in society, discrimination and geo-political instability. As such, the marginalisation faced by children highlights the inadequacies of many governments regarding the introduction of policies and practices that will enable children to be recognised as active social agents, who are able to provide an insight into their own self-determination. As Boylan and Dalrymple (2009: 61) succinctly state, 'if children and young people had the right to self-determination, the right to participation would not be necessary, as is the case for many adults.'

Chapter 6, *Play, language and learning*, by Anne Grieg highlights the importance of play, language and learning relating to the development of children (also see Wyness (2012), Corsaro (1997) and James *et al.* (2010) for an extensive discussion) and there are a number of Articles that would specifically apply when considering the provision of services that will help promote the child's well-being. Much has been written previously on the beneficial aspect of play and how it helps facilitate the development of a multitude of skills, such as communication and peer relationships. There are many aspects of the UNCRC that are relevant to the debate presented here – Article 3 'what is in the best interest for the child'; Article 13 that highlights freedom of expression; Article 15 that highlights freedom of association; Article 17 that highlights the role of the mass media especially in terms of linguistic development of children; Article 27 that highlights 'the right of every child to a standard of living adequate for the child's physical, mental, spiritual, moral and social development'; Articles 28 and 29 that highlight the right to education and its focus; and finally Article 31 that explicitly highlights the right of leisure and play, are all applicable.

Clear links are made with various theoretical positions about child development and learning and it can be seen how important this is as it is specifically identified by Article 31, where not only should children have the right to play, but also participate in 'cultural, artistic, recreational and leisure activit(ies)' that are open to all and provided exempt of discrimination. James *et al.* (2010: 83) highlight how through 'the particular temporal, social positioning of children who, individually and collectively, are learning to "do" culture.' This, then, embeds an obligation on the state to encourage play and learning as it provides essential developmental opportunities, let alone fun! However, the extent that this can be facilitated throughout the world is open to debate and we must accept that there will be occasions when this is not seen as a priority for national governments. Living in late modernity within a capitalist society, it is easy to see how the busy lives of families, together with harsh economic conditions that result in pay freezes, massive public expenditure cuts and high levels of unemployment, may impact upon the opportunities to play and access leisure activities. That is not to suggest that all leisure activities have a financial cost and that children are unable to 'use their imagination', but it does highlight that in some societies, children may have to participate in the workplace and contribute to the familial income.

Discussions surrounding play must also be considered within the context of Chapter 13, *Children's geographies*, where Jessica Clark highlights the challenges children face in terms of using public and private space. Play and leisure activities can be seen as an ideal opportunity for children to 'constitute themselves as competent social actors' (Wyness, 2012: 179) rather than the traditional perspective of a regulating space and time that are constructed by and for the benefit of adults. Therefore, having a rights framework should facilitate this change of focus to enhance the well-being of the child rather than the management of the child and the child's education. Corsaro's (1997) discussion regarding the role of the family (parents) in deciding when it is appropriate to introduce children into peer groups highlights the influential role of adults in children's play. It is understandable that parents may wish to conduct a pseudo-vetting procedure prior to their child 'mixing' with others, but this does call into question the amount of agency afforded to children. However, while we must not be too critical of parents wishing to protect their children, we must acknowledge that this restriction does occur.

UNICEF (2011: 13) emphasises the importance of early learning and entering primary school at the correct age as 'some of the most critical ingredients for completion, especially for disadvantaged children. Quality education, attained through well-trained teachers and the use of appropriate learning materials, is another important element'. In Chapter 7, *Early childhood education and care*, Beverly Nightingale and Sally Payne discuss the underpinning principles and philosophies of early childhood education and care which they contextualise within an historical, legal and social-cultural framework. They draw on the UNCRC Articles 3 and 28 which affirm children's fundamental rights to education and care and consider the importance of adopting a holistic philosophy and a commitment to inclusion and equality of opportunity. The prominence of early years education and care (ECEC) in current policy both nationally and internationally is well documented and Nightingale and Payne highlight the roles and responsibilities in ECEC settings through partnership approaches and inter-agency working. Their chapter emphasises how important it is for ECS scholars to understand children's needs and development, as well as socio-cultural contexts, and how early years professionals must work collaboratively, respectfully and effectively together in the best interests of children's welfare and education.

While this can be challenging, the knowledge, understanding, skills and attitudes of educators are key to providing excellent care and high quality education for young children and to developing integrated working and genuine cooperation. 'The long-term efficacy of ECEC seems to be best ensured by an approach that involves child, family, school and high school – a continued "nurture" that broadens the scope of the intervention to include the family context and extends the approach far into elementary school' (EACEA, 2009: 12). Good outcomes for children, Chapter 7 argues, are related to educators having a sound knowledge of child development, clear policies, working with parents in a supportive, stimulating environment and planning and providing age-appropriate educational learning opportunities. There are, however, variations across the UK in ECEC governance and regulation and in curriculum frameworks and approaches, while the language of children's rights is underpinned by an equality of opportunity. Recent European research published by the EACEA (2009) suggests that models and systems of early childhood education and care differ vastly in terms of coverage, intensity, quality and probably impact. In their chapter, Nightingale and Payne draw on the inspiration of Reggio Emilia (in northern Italy) which adopts a socio-constructivist perspective and which views children as 'active, rich and competent co-constructors in their own development'. Furthermore, the key principles of empowerment, holistic development, family and community and relationships from the New Zealand Early Childhood Framework offer fundamental tenets for early years practice. It is, as also argued in Chapter 1, therefore, vital for ECS students and EY professionals to critically consider both their own values and those which underpin EY settings and reflect on how other wider perspectives, both nationally and internationally, may inform and improve ECEC practices. Emerging influences on ECEC highlight how early childhood remains a sphere of development, no longer conceptualised in Piagetian child development terms, but in continually striving to improve and to advance both our academic knowledge, and also in working together to improve in practice how we educate and care for young children wherever they may be.

Bond and Agnew critically explore in Chapter 8, *Understanding childhood in late modernity*, the arguments of self-determination for children in late modernity, enhancing our understanding of key themes within the debate and highlighting the impact of a universal set of rights specifically for children with global implications. Here we see the discussion surrounding aspects of agency for children, the limitations placed upon them by parents and wider society. Power relations are explored and debates around the control of children linked to restrictions in children's access to public space and also wider theoretical constructions of 'risk'. The idealisation of the private sphere as the most suitable arena for children to develop is critiqued, questioning the extent to which children are able to exercise their rights under the UNCRC. Additionally, familial relationships and structure have changed in late modernity to those that were experienced historically, together with wider social changes, and have clearly impacted upon children and their experiences. Paranoia surrounding 'stranger danger' or 'kids out of control' demonstrate the dichotomous debate surrounding where children are placed within late modernity by society.

Restrictions placed on children through notions of 'risk', where children are seen either as 'potential victims or dangerous demons', are investigated, questioning the emphasis that is placed upon the concept of risk that clearly impacts upon children's opportunities to participate fully in society. Whether or not children are seen as potential victims in need of protection, the fundamental issue relates to the power relationship between children, parents, families, communities and the state. It could be argued that the risk-based approach identified within late modernity, that takes an adult-centric perspective, increases anxieties surrounding the activities of children and as such, restricts their opportunities, demonstrating the lack of agency that the UNCRC hoped to alleviate. ECS students must also critically engage with the debates regarding 'risk', as Beck (1992) highlights the globalised nature of 'risk' and ECS investigates, in part, the globalised nature of childhood and the impact of the UNCRC on children's lives. This presents an excellent framework to conceptualise the UNCRC, especially when considering the variety of Articles that specifically deal with international 'risks'.

Bond and Agnew's discussion surrounding the tensions between self-realisation and control (Giddens, 1990, 1991) and the pattern of public institutions that are aimed at controlling children provide a useful insight into late modernity and the governance of children. Although the private sphere is seen as the arena where children are able to explore and develop as individuals, negotiating complex boundaries with parents regarding their access to the public sphere, these discussions are undoubtedly skewed regarding the power dynamics of the relationship. That is not to suggest that children lack any power and that they are unable to negotiate favourable terms regarding exercising their right to participation, it is just that as an ECS student, you must acknowledge that these tensions exist and may impact on outcomes. If, as a society, we fully adopt the principles of the UNCRC, then we must also accept that children have the right to disagree and to challenge the boundaries that have been constructed around them. We must accept that children understand their lives, in many ways better than adults do. There may be elements of 'bounded rationality' – not seeing the bigger picture due to limited experience, but that should not automatically negate their voice.

Although technological advancements within the sphere of new media have provided many children with the means to access information and to form their own opinions (Articles 13 and 14), the anxieties placed upon the lack of control over the content viewed are primarily adult-focused and do not acknowledge the risk management skills that children develop as individuals and as members of a cultural group (Green, 1997).

A major development within late modernity is the increase in nations that are considering alternative mechanisms to measure poverty rather than traditional annualised incomes or which welfare benefits someone qualifies for. By accepting that participating within late modern society requires children and their families to engage in activities and practices that go beyond 'your parents annual income' (Davis *et al.*, 2012), nation states can be seen to be embracing the wider aspects of participation. This highlights that as societal change occurs, what is necessary to be included within society also changes, in terms of the skills required and physical possessions, such as a mobile phone or computer that has internet access. As can be seen, the challenges facing a student of ECS within late modernity requires them to look beyond the obvious and seek out how wider social changes impact upon children, always considering the influence of the UNCRC.

This textbook adopts a multidisciplinary approach and the complex inter-connectivity of the various chapters must by now be evident to you as a student of ECS, no topic stands alone, no theory exists in isolation and most importantly no policy can be discussed without recourse to those that developed it and those that are influenced by it. Although the discussion within Chapter 9, *Children and social policy: an introduction,* is focused upon social policies within the UK, it should be noted that the experiences of children around the world are impacted upon by the various social policies initiated within their own nation states. Article 3 clearly states the expectations placed upon the state in ensuring that children receive the protection and care they require for their well-being, and it must be accepted by ECS students that they have an obligation to understand this in an international context. However, the specific measures of support and protections that nation states provided are not dictated and this permits debate over the appropriateness of a number of policies based around political ideology.

As discussed previously, children are in a unique position as they are expected to meet the future needs of society and as such by providing social policies that enhance children's well-being, increases their participation in society and provides them with a mechanism to be seen as agents capable of their own self-realisation certainly benefits society and demonstrates a willingness to embrace the fundamentals of the UNCRC. This argument is skilfully explored by Sarah Richards in Chapter 9 and requires ECS students to use their sociological imagination (Mills, 2000) to identify the further implications for policies that have been developed under the guise of children's well-being. Often, complex arguments are over-simplified, providing a misrepresentation of the actuality of any given situation; this is also evident in discussions surrounding the provision of welfare, the underlying ideologies that inform them and also debates surrounding whose perspective rights should be based on. As the UNCRC does not infer upon governments any particular political standpoint, this, it could be argued, presents a multitude of challenges for those that advocate children's rights and hold governments accountable to their obligations. As demonstrated in Chapter 9, political change and economic conditions impact profusely upon social policies that will help nations meet the requirements of children, with the guidance from Article 3(3):

States parties shall ensure that the institutions, services and facilities responsible for the care or protection of children shall conform with the standards established by competent authorities, particularly in the areas of safety, health, in the number and suitability of their staff, as well as competent supervision.

We must accept, for national governments, there are a large number of priorities that draw against public funding and even though we have highlighted the unique role and responsibility that is placed upon children, they are just one of a number of areas that need government support. Therefore during harsh economic times, irrespective of which country you live in, it should not be surprising that those who have the quietest voice, those who have yet to gain recognition and are disempowered, are among the first to lose state support. Reductions in funding of children and youth services by many local authorities in the UK and changes to the welfare system that will disproportionately impact upon families must be seen in this context and also within the realm that the UNCRC permits national governments to decide for themselves what are appropriate standards.

In Chapter 10, *The multi-disciplinary child protection system: current policy and practice*, Jackie Plenty explores the legal and policy framework underpinning the child protection system in England and Wales and critically analyses inter-agency collaboration and partnership working. Article 19 of the UNCRC states:

1. Parties shall take all appropriate legislative, administrative, social and educational measures to protect the child from all forms of physical or mental violence, injury or abuse, neglect or negligent treatment, maltreatment or exploitation, including sexual abuse, while in the care of parent(s), legal guardian(s) or any other person who has the care of the child.
2. Such protective measures should, as appropriate, include effective procedures for the establishment of social programmes to provide necessary support for the child and for those who have the care of the child, as well as for other forms of prevention and for identification, reporting, referral, investigation, treatment and follow up of instances of child maltreatment described heretofore, and, as appropriate, for judicial involvement.

While the UNCRC provides a global framework for child protection, national legal and policy frameworks are also based on a rights-based approach. Jackie Plenty offers readers a comprehensive overview of the historical development of legal and policy frameworks in England and Wales and documents key inquiries resulting from child abuse cases. Understanding child abuse is a complex and difficult aspect of childhood studies and of working with young children and their families. However, while this topic is difficult and often very complicated it is one that cannot be ignored nor trivialised. Article 34 of the UNCRC sets out that 'States parties undertake to protect the child from all forms of sexual exploitation and sexual abuse.' The sexual abuse of children is a subject of considerable controversy and debate and emotions often run high when child abuse cases are discussed or come to light. Many recent child protection inquiries have highlighted how we continually fail to listen to children and to take their views and experiences seriously.

EY professionals and all those working with children must have a good knowledge of the signs and symptoms of child abuse, understand the child protection policies and procedures and know how to recognise abuse and respond appropriately. As Plenty points out, the prevalence of child abuse only reflects the numbers of children that are known to local authorities and many cases of child abuse remain undetected and unreported and many children are not protected from abuse. Inter-agency collaboration and working in partnership is again fundamental to effective child protection procedures and reflect the most recent recommendations set out in Munro's (2011) review to work directly with and promote better engagement and stronger partnerships with children and their families. Working within a rights-based approach enables professionals not only to strive for effective child protection mechanisms as outlined in Article 19 and also Articles 12 and 13 which form the basis for the right to participation, but as Boylan and Dalrymple (2009: 39) observe, 'the relationship between the capacity to participate and opportunities to participate is very relevant here'. It is argued that capacity can be enabled, even for very young children, if the appropriate opportunities are provided and the right information and support is given and that we need to develop a culture and a discourse of children's advocacy 'as a way of resisting the oppression of children and young people and enabling them to come to voice' (Boylan and Dalrymple, 2009: 4).

Effectively safeguarding young children includes online environments and organisations like the Child Online Protection Centre (CEOP), the NSPCC, Childnet International and Beatbullying continue to raise awareness of the risks to young children of the virtual world, but also of children's rights. It is important, therefore, for ECS scholars to conceptualise children's rights as extending to the new media and the online world also. Livingstone (2009), for example, examines the key debates in relation to children and their use of new media, drawing on empirical evidence from the realities of their everyday lives to argue against some of the rhetoric and moral panics commonly associated with children and the internet. Livingstone (2009) considers children's rights as set out in the UNCRC and proposes a Children's Internet Charter based on sound rights-based principles. Her recommendations are well considered, they clearly highlight some of the practical challenges to improving provision and rightly argue that the responsibilities for maximising opportunities and minimising risks in relation to young children and the internet lie within the wider social structure. Thus, Chapter 10 provides readers with essential knowledge and understanding of child protection through not only historical developments, but also the key contemporary debates in effective partnership working to safeguard young children. Within these debates children's rights to participate must be upheld and respected within their right to be protected and this balance is not always a straightforward one to achieve in practice.

Article 24 of the UNCRC sets out 'the right of the child to the highest attainable standard of health and to facilities for the treatment of illness and rehabilitation of health. States parties shall strive to ensure that no child is deprived of his or her right of access to such healthcare services.' In Chapter 11, *Child health*, Jayne Taylor and Helen Donovan explore the origins of child health practice from a historical perceptive and examine contemporary issues through a discussion of the changes to the commissioning of children's healthcare and the public health system. They encourage readers to consider the key issues in working with ill children and, as in the previous chapter on child protection, the emphasis on effective partnership working is highlighted. Taylor and Donovan aptly bring to readers' attention that no matter what discipline or professional background, illness in early childhood is part of the young children's everyday experiences and one which anyone working with or for children needs to understand. As highlighted earlier in this concluding chapter, the health needs of young children vary according to time and space and as such there are different priorities in relation to child health according to the shifting patterns of healthcare needs and priorities. After the Second World War, for example, Taylor and Donovan discuss how, with the decline in infectious diseases and nutritional problems, public attention turned to chronic illness and disability, but children's rights to basic healthcare needs in many countries of the world are still not being met and the focus on malnutrition and ameliorating the devastation of infectious diseases remains. Nationally, in the UK, the prevalence of child ill health also demonstrates many inequalities and according to geographic location and social class (even during pregnancy as discussed in Chapter 2) and according to Barnado's (online) three-year-olds living in households with incomes below about £10 000 are two and a half times more likely to suffer chronic illness than children in households with incomes above £52 000. Recent policy developments to tackle inequalities in the early years include the 2011 Health Visitor Implementation plan *A Call for Action* (Department of Health, 2011), but also highlight not just the role of health workers but children's centres, educators, parents and children and the wider community in addressing inequality. Chapter 11 thus provides an overview of the need to improve healthcare services for children and the need for adequate training in child healthcare issues, as the UK remains far behind other European Countries in the outcomes for children when the indicators for children's health are compared. Children's health is closely intertwined with poverty and the right to provision to healthcare as set out by the UNCRC is not one that is equally met for all children. These inequalities need to be addressed, but as Anderson (2008) also points out, young children's rights in relation to their health are not simply one of provision, they are also about participation. She argues that children, including very young children, should have the right to be listened to and consulted in matters affecting their health and that, with the right information, young children can actively and meaningfully participate in healthcare decisions. Illness in early childhood poses both unique and highly complex challenges to early years professionals and, in our attempts to gain knowledge and understanding of early childhood, these experiences cannot be ignored.

In Chapter 12, *Young children with disabilities*, Sue Hollinrake points out that young children with disabilities, while having additional specialist needs resulting from specific impairments, otherwise have the same needs as all children – a need for food and warmth, for love and affection, praise and recognition, stability and stimulating activities and new experiences through play. The guiding principles of the UNCRC exemplified in Chapter 1 highlight the impact that the convention may have on the policies of national governments regarding specific marginalised groups. For example, the principle of non-discrimination and rights apply to all children (Article 2), all actions that relate to the child should be in the child's best interest (Article 3), the right to life and development (Article 6) and finally listening to the voice of children, allowing them to express their opinion freely (Article 12). Here it can be seen that children with disabilities are being recognised internationally as a group that can no longer be separated from the rest of society. The UNCRC in conjunction with wider social attitudinal change and campaigns by specialist interest groups have all had a major impact upon the lived reality of children with disabilities.

Recent policy developments can be seen to link closely with the Articles identified above in terms of accessibility to education and support services, certainly in England, where disabled children have been able to access education within mainstream school settings where possible, although there are some specialist providers outside traditional schools. This level of inclusivity clearly supports the principle of participation, lack of discrimination and also for children with disabilities to develop within society. However, this has to be seen within the debates surrounding inclusion or segregation within schools as, although there may be a guiding principle regarding the lack of discrimination against children with disabilities, there is still a clear divide between those who seek to include all children within mainstream education and those who feel the adaptations that would need to be made to facilitate this, could be detrimental to other children within the school. This would especially be an issue when a child's behaviour could be linked to a disability and that this may disrupt classes.

Hollinrake highlights aspects of cultural relativism within the debate as although within fairly stable societies disabled children may have access to high levels of support to facilitate their participation within society, in other countries, especially those that may be in conflict, the rights of all children are not always protected (Jones, 2001). This calls into question the universality of the UNCRC as it appears to be more relevant to established first world nations than developing states.

Working with children with disabilities and their families requires exceptional self-reflection skills as it is fundamentally important that you understand your own values and beliefs surrounding disabilities and ensure that these do not negatively impinge upon your personal practice. Ensuring that you value the child and respect their parents (Scope, 1994) should provide you with the foundations of creating a positive and productive professional relationship. This is a practical application of many principles of the UNCRC and by acknowledging that at times the relationship with both children, and/or those that care for them, may become emotionally charged, this should provide a useful resource for understanding the issues and potential responses to them (see Sen and Yurtserver (2007) for a contemporary discussion). This is fundamental to minimising many of the barriers that families with disabled children face which can range from accessing schools that can support their child to finding appropriate venues and opportunities for their child to play with children without disabilities, providing them with an opportunity to develop many communication and language skills.

The discussion provided by Jessica Clark in Chapter 13 relating to *Children's geographies* highlights the importance of place, space and time within children's lives. A key theme that emerges when investigating children and the spaces that they traditionally inhabit is the importance of the child's voice, the structural limitations placed upon their agency in determining how that space is used and who has access to it. Therefore, the participation of children within any examination of domestic space is fundamental for ECS students (Gallacher, 2005). It should also be noted that Article 13 provides children with the right to freedom of expression, however it must be questioned to what extent living in a family home provides that opportunity. Parents and guardians are recognised within the UNCRC as having a right to influence and provide appropriate guidance and direction to children (Article 5). However, what is deemed appropriate within the sphere of a familial home is unclear, especially when considering the impact that the home has regarding identity formation in early childhood (Christensen *et al.*, 2000).

There is a potential danger when considering early childhood of making the assumption that children are one homogenous group, and as these chapters have conserved, they are not! We must acknowledge that different children have different experiences and those with diverse cultural differences from what is often assumed the 'norm' not only have different lived realities, but their experience of space will be different also. If mainstream society bases its support services surrounding traditional norms, how do children who live within families that are seen to be 'different', 'hard to reach' or 'troublesome' access the services that they not only need but have a right to? Furthermore, for those children who are homeless or labelled as a street child (Agnelli, 1986), it could be argued that the state is failing in its duty of care regarding protection of the child (Article 19) and it needs to ensure adequate accommodation is in place for children who are deprived of their own family environment (Article 20).

The agency of children is fundamental when discussing space, how it is used, who constructs and controls it, whether or not boundaries can be negotiated or even whether the space itself is contested as a viable place for children to be, both online and offline. Fear and a focus on risk aversion may be a factor in the decision-making process for adults in late modernity regarding the amount of agency children are permitted to have, however, this again as Clark suggests, provides evidence of an adult-centric perspective regarding space and its use. We must consider these fears regarding space and children within the wider context of societal views of children and how as children grow older, they may be viewed as more of a threat to younger children and adults rather than as a potential victim. Therefore by restricting access to a variety of spaces for what can be seen on many occasions as being based on ill-conceived assumptions, arguably contemporary society is restricting children from fully developing the necessary skills that will enable them to become productive citizens. Furthermore, as scholars of ECS you should critically examine the idealised spaces that are regularly presented as being more ideally suitable, such as the idyllic, romanticised notions of the countryside which lack detailed analysis of the opportunities that these spaces may provide, especially, for example, regarding limitations relating to children's services.

In Chapter 14, *Perspectives on early childhood research*, Jayne Taylor explores the value of undertaking research for early years professionals and considers the philosophical developments in doing research *with* children, rather than *on* them. This development reflects the shift in the broader trajectory of childhood studies as discussed in Chapter 1 and of viewing children as *beings* rather than as *becomings*. Clearly from reading Chapter 14, scholars of ECS will have an idea about the importance that research plays in studying childhood and how we gain knowledge and understanding from the research of others and the theoretical developments that are bought about as a result of research. Research also underpins policy developments and, for early years professionals, research plays a significant role in managing and leading children's services (see Chapter 15). The main conceptual shift in relation to early childhood research is undoubtedly based around the change of listening to children rather than observing them and this emphasis mirrors the ever-increasing importance of Articles 12 and 13 of the UNCRC. Taylor considers in her chapter how the UNCRC also informs the UNICEF guidance on hearing the voices of children in research and evaluation for developing meaningful participation. Hart's (1992) ladder depicts the different levels of participation and it is essential that we critically consider what level of participation is actually afforded to children in research. If we are to genuinely seek to 'assure to the child who is capable of forming his or her own views the right to express those views freely in all matters affecting the child' (Article 12) and their right to freedom of expression 'either orally, in writing or in print, in the form of art, or through any other media of the child's choice', then researchers of early childhood should be competent and confident in employing a wide range of child-centred research methods which meaningfully foster young children's participation. Children's drawings, child conferencing, guided walks, self-directed photography, self-directed video, story-telling, role play activities and puppets are just a few of the broad range of child-centred research methods employed (see Clark and Moss (2001) and Lancaster and Kirby (2010)). Thus, the contemporary research endeavour is informed by children's rights to participation in research and, by drawing on interpretative methodologies and children's narratives, we can understand their views and experiences in late modern society. Methods used by qualitative researchers exemplify a common belief that they can provide a deeper understanding of the social phenomena than would be obtained from purely quantitative data and the rich detail they provide assumes an interpretativistic approach. The theoretical literature on undertaking research with children and young people is examined in Chapter 14 and it highlights recent developments in the knowledge and understanding of this subject, drawn from the new social studies of childhood, children's rights and gives consideration to the appropriateness of child-centred methods in research. Furthermore, the importance of ethical considerations is discussed and important procedures to this end are outlined to expand readers' knowledge and understanding of ethical considerations in early childhood research. Methodology refers to philosophies, ideologies, principles and values that inform the research process (Roberts-Holmes, 2005) and for ECS scholars the importance of a child-centred methodology cannot be over-emphasised. Resonating with the principles of 'emancipatory' science outlined by Benton and Craib (2001: 8) and of 'feminist epistemology developed from Marxism, that suggest that an oppressed group has access to knowledge in a way that other groups do not', there is increasing recognition that it is children themselves who are expert in their own lives and not the adults who have previously dominated the role of the expert. The concept of competence in children's participation in research that has previously been so dominant has recently been challenged through new research methods and early childhood research, previously dominated by developmental perspectives, emphasises the child-centred participatory approaches that are becoming increasingly recognised and used in contemporary research. As Lundy and McEvoy (2012: 142) argue, 'a children's rights based approach asks adult researchers to empower children through the provision of information, support and guidance in the research process'. Therefore, in exploring the methodologies that draw on children's strengths rather than focusing on what they are unable to do, issues of power and social exclusion can be addressed and facilitate children's active participation in research and allow their voices to be heard.

Finally, in Chapter 15, *Leading and managing child-centred services*, Jayne Taylor discusses the leading and managing of child-centred services and throughout this volume the emphasis has been on promoting and developing a child-centred approach. We need to work together to effectively challenge how we meet the needs of children and their families and a key component of changing children's lives for the better is through innovative leadership and management. If we are to put children first, a rights-based agenda is essential in striving to continually develop the quality of all services offered and in improving outcomes for children and their families, and in Chapter 15 the importance of acting as an advocate of equality is set out. Boylan and Dalrymple (2009: 32) chart the development of advocacy for children and suggest that, 'the advocacy role of professionals can be constrained both by policy imperatives and by the concept of "best interests" ... Governments in the UK also recognise the need for children and young people to have a voice and the development of a range of advocacy services is testament to that fact'. Understanding the implications of the UNCRC Articles 12 and 13 should underpin how we can effectively foster meaningful participation for young children. In Article 12, the cornerstone of the UNCRC (McLeod, 2008), the statement that children who are capable of forming his or her own views must be given the right to express those views freely and that they are given due weight in accordance with the age and maturity of the child is one which is often overlooked in relation to very young children. Alderson (2009: 10), however, argues that 'from babyhood, children are significant actors and potentially powerful partners in shaping relationships and societies in which they live'. Leaders and managers of early years settings need to develop a culture of and systems to support a high level of responsiveness and this can only be achieved through effective mechanisms for listening and through empowering children and their families by providing information so that they can influence how services are provided. McLeod (2008: 198) observes that 'effective listening to a young person is more likely to be achieved in the context of an ongoing relationship in which trust and support can be achieved rather than a brief encounter'. This is, therefore, an important consideration for the managers and leaders of early childhood settings and services especially as evidence-based practice ensures that decisions are based upon research (Buysse and Wesley, 2006). To this end, leaders and managers of early childhood settings and services must be competent to identify the evidence and be able to use and assess it. These skills are discussed in more detail in Chapter 14 on researching early childhood, but deserve additional consideration in relation to leading and managing children's services. If we are to take children's views seriously then we need to ensure that we take steps to allow their voices to be heard and supporting children's involvement in decision making has to be resourced (McLeod, 2008) as well as considering how we must ensure that children and their families are involved in ongoing dialogue about their needs and aspirations for service improvement.

Conclusion

The articulation of the universal rights and needs of children reflects the growing importance of international organisations and legalisation throughout the 21st century (Fass, 2011), but as Alderson (2008: 215) powerfully argues:

The concerns of children in Britain seem slight in comparison to the rest of the world, but my aim is to illustrate how the UNCRC and respect for the youngest children's rights can benefit all children – and adults. The hope for peace, justice and prosperity in the global village involves a massive transfer of power and resources from white to black and Asian peoples, from men to women, and from aging minority societies to the much younger majority world. This will happen when rich adults trust poor young people. Prejudices are too deeply entrenched for adults, from individual parents to world leaders, to change their attitudes to young people unaided. A crucial task for all societies in the 21st century is therefore, to rethink traditions in order that adults can learn from and with children how to create a better future.

In this volume, we hope that we have introduced readers to early childhood through an holistic and multidisciplinary perspective. In setting out some of the key debates and issues currently at the forefront of ECS, it was also our intention to begin to challenge some of the unhelpful ways in which children have been viewed not least by ECS as a discipline itself. In outlining the shift in emphasis from observing to listening and respecting young children's views and experiences we hope that readers of this edition will also have begun to question the way that they themselves and others view early childhood. The key arguments set out in this edition are ones which currently concern and contest contemporary childhoods – local and global – and they are also ones that can be better understood through a children's rights perspective. If we are to make the world a better place for children – for *all* children – then we must begin to take children and young children seriously and work with them in a respectful way for them. 'Similarly, children and child advocates are themselves part of the process of globalisation and may make critical and powerful use of international legal arrangements designed to promote the rights and interests of children' (Kaufman and Rizzini, 2011: 433). Early childhood studies has come a long way since its introduction as a field of academic study a couple of decades ago and we have witnessed a burgeoning interest in the study of early childhood evidenced by the increasing number of textbooks, research and theorising in relation to early childhood. As an early childhood scholar, we hope that you will be inspired to read on further than this volume and to take some of the key arguments and debates set out here and to investigate them further through some of the key readings and the references that we have drawn on throughout this edition. Early childhood is, as Margaret Woods stated in the previous edition, a fascinating field of academic study and we hope that from reading this third edition readers will be challenged but also inspired to further advance their scholarship and to learn more about early childhood as, as our title suggests, this book is an introduction – an holistic and multidisciplinary one – but an introduction nevertheless.

References

Agnelli, S (1986): *Street Children: A Growing Urban Tragedy.* London: Widenfeld and Nicolson.

Anderson, P (2008): *Young Children's Rights Exploring Beliefs, Principles and Practice*, 2nd edn. London: Jessica Kingsley.

Alderson, P (2009): Younger children's individual participation in matters that affect them. In Percy-Smith, B and Thomas, N (eds) *Handbook of Children's Participation.* London: Routledge, pp. 88–96.

Barnardo's (2012): *Children in Care.* (Online). Last accessed: October 2012. Available from: http://www.barnardos.org.uk/what_we_do/campaigns/campaigns_children_in_care.htm.

Baumrind, D (1991): The influence of parenting style on adolescent competence and substance use. *Journal of Early Adolescence* **11**(1), 56–95.

Beck, U (1992): *Risk Society: Towards a New Modernity.* London: Sage.

Benton, T and Craib, I (2001): *Philosophy of Social Science.* Basingstoke: Palgrave.

Boylan, J and Dalrymple, J (2009): *Understanding Advocacy for Children and Young People.* Berkshire: Open University Press.

Buysse V and Wesley P (2006): *Evidence-Based Practice in the Early Childhood Field Zero to Three.* Washington: National Center for Infants, Toddlers and Families.

Christensen, P, James, A and Jenks, C (2000): Home and movement: children constructing 'family time'. In Holloway, S and Valentine, G (eds), *Children's Geographies: Playing, Living Learning.* London: Routledge.

Clark, A and Moss, P (2001): *Listening to Young Children: the Mosaic Approach.* London: National Children's Bureau for the Joseph Rowntree Foundation.

Corsaro, W (1997): *The Sociology of Childhood.* London, Pine Forge.

CRAE (Online). Children's Rights Alliance for England. Available from: www.crae.org.uk/.

Davis, A, Hirsch, D, Smith, N, Beckhelling, J and Padley, M (2012): *A Minimum Income Standard for the UK in 2012: Keeping up in Hard Times.* (Online). Available from: www.jrf.org.uk/sites/files/jrf/minimum-income-standards-2012-full.pdf.

Department of Health (2011): *Health Visitor Implementation Plan 2011–15: A Call To Action.* (Online). Available from: www.dh.gov.uk/en/Publicationsandstatistics/Publications/PublicationsPolicyAndGuidance/DH_124202.

Donnelly, J (2003): *Universal Human Rights in Practice.* Ithaca: New York: Cornell University Press.

EACEA (2009): *Tackling Social and Cultural Inequalities through Early Childhood Education and Care in Europe.* (Online). Available from: http://eacea.ec.europa.eu/about/eurydice/documents/098EN.pdf.

Fass, PS (2011): A historical context for the United Nations convention on the rights of the child. *The Annals of the American Academy of Political and Social Science* **688**, 17–29.

Gallacher, L (2005): The terrible twos: gaining control in the nursery. *Children's Geographies* **3**(2), 243–64.

Giddens, A (1990): *The Consequences of Modernity.* Cambridge: Polity Press.

Giddens, A (1991): *Modernity and Self-Identity Self and Society in the Late Modern Age.* Cambridge: Polity Press.

Green, J (1997): Risk and the construction of social identity: children's talk about accidents. *Sociology of Health and Illness* **19**, 457–79.

Hart, RA (1992): Children's participation from Tokenism to Citizenship. Florence: UNICEF ICDC.

Hill, A (2007): Miranda almost died from anorexia. She is eight years old. *The Observer* Sunday 18 November 2007.

James, A and James, A (2004): *Constructing Childhood.* Basingstoke: Palgrave.

James, A, Jenks, C and Prout, A (2010): *Theorizing Childhood.* Cambridge, Polity Press.

Jones, H (2001): *Disabled Children's Rights: A Practical Guide.* Sweden: International Save the Children Alliance.

Katz, C (2008): Childhood as spectacle: relays of anxiety and the reconfiguration of the child. *Cultural Geographie* **15**, 5–17.

Kaufmann, NH and Rizzini, I (2011): Closing the gap between rights and the realities of children's lives. In Qvortrup, J, Corsaro, WA and Honig, MS (eds), *The Palgrave Handbook of Childhood Studies.* Basingstoke: Palgrave.

Lancaster, YP and Kirby, P (2010): *Listening to Young Children,* 2nd edn. Maidenhead: Open University Press.

Le Billon, K (2012): *Parents Can't End Britain's Child Obesity Epidemic Alone. The Guardian,* Friday 17 August 2012. (Online). Available from: http://www.guardian.co.uk/profile/karen-le-billon.

Livingstone, S (2009): *Children and The Internet. Great Expectations, Challenging Realities.* Polity Press, Cambridge.

Lundy, L and McEvoy, l (2012): Children's rights and research process: Assisting children to (in)formed views. *Childhood* **19**(1), 129–44.

Maurás, M (2011): Public policies and child rights: entering the third decade of the convention of the rights of the child. *The Annals of the American Academy of Political and Social Science,* **633**, 52–65.

McLeod, A (2008): *Listening to Children A Practitioner's Guide.* London: Jessica Kingsley.

Mills, CW (2000): *The Sociological Imagination.* Oxford: Oxford University Press.

Montgomery, H (2009): *An Introduction to Childhood Anthropological perspectives on Children's Lives.* Oxford: John Wiley.

Munro, E (2011): *The Munro Review of Child Protection: Final Report A Child-centred System.* (Online). Available from: www.education.gov.uk/munroreview/downloads/8875_DfE_Munro_Report_TAGGED.pdf.

NHS (2012): *Statistics on Women's Smoking Status at Time of Delivery: England, October to December 2011 (Q3 – Quarterly report).* (Online). Available from: http://www.ic.nhs.uk/webfiles/publications/003_Health_Lifestyles/Womens_Smoking_Status_1112q3/Smoking_1112Q3_NHS_Key_Facts_v2.pdf.

Roberts-Holmes, G (2005): *Doing Your Early Years Research Projec./* London: Paul Chapman Publishing.

Rutgers, C (ed.) (2011) *Introduction in Creating a World Fit for Children Understanding the UN Convention on the Rights of the Child.* New York: International Debate Association.

Scope (1994): *Right from the Start.* London: Scope.

Sen, E and Yurtsever, S (2007): Difficulties experienced by families with disabled children. *Journal for Specialists in Pediatric Nursing* **12**(4); 238–52.

Turmel, A (2008): *A Historical Sociology of Childhood.* Cambridge: Cambridge University Press.

UNICEF (Online). Available from: www.unicef.org.uk

Further reading

Anderson, P (2008): *Young Children's Rights Exploring Beliefs, Principles and Practice,* 2nd edn. London: Jessica Kingsley.

Boylan, J and Dalrymple, J (2009): *Understanding Advocacy for Children and Young People.* Berkshire: Open University Press.

Kaufmann, NH and Rizzini, I (2011): Closing the gap between rights and the realities of children's lives. In Qvortrup, J, Corsaro, WA and Honig, MS (eds), *The Palgrave Handbook of Childhood Studies.* Basingstoke: Palgrave.

Lancaster, YP and Kirby, P (2010): *Listening to Young Children,* 2nd edn. Maidenhead: Open University Press.

Index

emotional intelligence 65, 67–8

emotional literacy 67

empathy 74

England, curriculum framework 146–7, 150–1

environments
  for education 276–8
  for learning 139
  see also geographical studies

equality 135, 173

Erickson, M. 57

ethics 302–4

ethnicity 94

Every Child Matters 52, 140, 142, 189, 194–5, 210, 252

experiential education 152

exploitation 4
  see also child protection; safeguarding

expression, right of 4

false-belief task 73

families
  of disabled children 262–4
  and 'late modernity' 165–6
  relationships in 90–6
  and social policy 193–5

father-child relationship 101–13

fertilisation 28–9

fetal development *see* embryo development

Field, F. 200

Flouri, E. 102

folic acid 31, 34

forest schools 139

Foucault, M. 55–6, 164

'fragile families' 97–8

Franklin, B. 4

Friedman, R. 17

friendly societies 184

friendships 74, 107–9
  see also relationships

Froebel, F. 135

Furedi, F. 92–3, 163, 166

Gardner, H. 67

Garvey, C. 113

gay and lesbian parents 94–5

gender 59–60
  and play 78
  and toy preferences 76

geographical studies 272–88
  domestic setting 274–5
  educational places 276–8
  inner cities 279–82

migration 282–5

public spaces 279

rural spaces 280–2

street children 275

Giddens, A. 165, 169–71

Goddard Blythe, S. 52

Goffman, E. 57

Goldschmeid, E. 51

Good Childhood Report (2012) 91

Goodyer, I.M. 66, 73

grandparents 105–6

Grant Consortium project 69

Green, J. 169

Greene, S. 16

Greig, A. 66

Grosz, E. 59, 60

Handy, C. 264

Hart, H. 3

Hayes, D. 141

health 6, 11–12
  of children 39, 228–42
  definition of 27
  family-centred care 239–41
  maternal 27, 30–5
  public health approach 234–7
  and social policy 195–7

Hendrick, H. 10, 11, 191

Hendrick, S.H. 164

hierarchy of needs 71

historical perspectives 9

Hobson, P. 74

Hogan, D. 16

Holland, P. 12

Holloway, S.L. 163, 175

home setting 136–7, 163, 274–5

homeless children 275

Hood, S. 166

Howes, C. 107

Howlin, P. 72

Hughes, C. 104

Human Genome Project 28

human rights 3–6

humanism 71

hypoglycaemia 37

ICT (information and communications technology) 171–6

immunisation 6

inactivity 52

inclusion 135, 249, 259

independence 167, 190